Urban Life
in the Renaissance

THE CENTER FOR RENAISSANCE AND BAROQUE STUDIES

The Center for Renaissance and Baroque Studies at the University of Maryland, College Park, sponsors programs in all disciplines of the arts and humanities as well as in such allied fields as the history and philosophy of science. Designed primarily for faculty and graduate students, the Center's scholarly programs include an annual Scholar-in-Residence program, conferences and colloquia, lectures, an annual interdisciplinary symposium, and a series of summer institutes for secondary school teachers. Programs in the arts include concerts, lecture-demonstrations, exhibitions, and the annual Maryland Handel Festival. The Center is administered by its executive director and its director in conjunction with an advisory board of outside consultants and a faculty advisory committee.

Urban Life
in the Renaissance

EDITED BY
Susan Zimmerman
and
Ronald F. E. Weissman

DELAWARE

Newark: University of Delaware Press
London and Toronto: Associated University Presses

Associated University Presses
440 Forsgate Drive
Cranbury, NJ 08512

Associated University Presses
25 Sicilian Avenue
London WC1A 2QH, England

Associated University Presses
P.O. Box 488, Port Credit
Mississauga, Ontario
Canada L5G 4M2

The paper used in this publication meets the requirements of the American National Standard for Permanence of Paper for Printed Library Materials Z39.48-1984.

Library of Congress Cataloging-in-Publication Data

Urban life in the Renaissance.

Selected papers delivered at two symposia sponsored by the Center for Renaissance and Baroque Studies, University of Maryland, College Park: Urban life in the Renaissance (3–4 March, 1983) and Forms of play in the early modern period (22–23 March, 1984).
  Includes bibliographies and index.
  Contents: Social stratification in Renaissance urban planning / James S. Ackerman and Myra Nan Rosenfeld—The construction of Pienza (1459–1464) and the consequences of Renovatio / Nicholas Adams — Houses divided / Barbara Diefendorf — [etc.]
  1. Cities and towns, Renaissance—Congresses. 2. City and town life—Europe—History—Congresses. I. Zimmerman, Susan, 1939– . II. Weissman, Ronald F. E. III. University of Maryland, College Park. Center for Renaissance and Baroque Studies.
HT131.U695   1989   307.7'6'094   86-40595
ISBN 0-87413-323-8 (alk. paper)

Printed in the United States of America

Contents

Director's Preface
  S. SCHOENBAUM   7

Introduction
  SUSAN ZIMMERMAN and RONALD F. E. WEISSMAN   9

PART I. *The Renaissance City: Theory and Practice*

1 Social Stratification in Renaissance Urban Planning
  JAMES S. ACKERMAN and MYRA NAN ROSENFELD   21
2 The Construction of Pienza (1459–1464) and the
  Consequences of *Renovatio*
  NICHOLAS ADAMS   50
3 Houses Divided: Religious Schism in Sixteenth-
  Century Parisian Families
  BARBARA DIEFENDORF   80

PART II. *Renaissance Culture: Courtly and Urban*

4 Leisure and Sociability: Reading Aloud in Early
  Modern Europe
  ROGER CHARTIER   103
5 Trickery, Gender, and Power: The *Discorsi* of Annibale
  Romei
  WERNER L. GUNDERSHEIMER   121
6 Minstrels and Their Repertory in Fifteenth-Century
  France: Music in an Urban Environment
  HOWARD MAYER BROWN   142
7 History, Politics, and the Portrait of a City: Vermeer's
  View of Delft
  ARTHUR K. WHEELOCK, JR.   165

PART III. *Authority and Order in the Renaissance Town: The Politics of Ritual*

8 Celebrating Authority in Bristol, 1475–1640
DAVID HARRIS SACKS   187

9 The Palio of Siena: Game, Ritual, or Politics?
SYDEL SILVERMAN   224

10 "Thou Idol Ceremony": Elizabeth I, *The Henriad,* and the Rites of the English Monarchy
RICHARD C. McCOY   240

PART IV. *Renaissance Urban Identity: The Uses of Ambiguity and Parody*

11 The Importance of Being Ambiguous: Social Relations, Individualism, and Identity in Renaissance Florence
RONALD F. E. WEISSMAN   269

12 Ceremonial Play and Parody in the Renaissance
THOMAS M. GREENE   281

List of Contributors   294
Index   296

Director's Preface

Established in 1981 through the vision of Dr. Shirley S. Kenny, provost of arts and humanities at the University of Maryland, and the beneficence of the Maryland legislature during an all-too-familiar period of retrenchment in high education, the Center for Renaissance and Baroque Studies held its Inaugural Conference on 11 and 12 March 1982. From the outset the university has envisaged the center as multidisciplinary. Music and the visual arts, literature in several modern European languages, philosophy, and history—indeed all the appropriate disciplines in the humanistic pantheon—come within our sphere. Each autumn we have a Handel festival—performed music, panels, and papers; in the spring, a symposium. Throughout the academic year the center reminds staff and students of its presence with a continuing program of scholars-in-residence, public lectures, and musical recitals.

This volume brings together selected papers delivered at two symposia sponsored by the Center: Urban Life in the Renaissance (3–4 March 1983) and Forms of Play in the Early Modern Period (22–23 March 1984). Both conferences were in keeping with the Center's multidisciplinary commitment.

As the program for the urban life symposium noted in its prologue, the development of Renaissance cities gave rise to new social, economic, and religious structures, and to new urban art forms. The meetings examined these transformations in European and American cities. The meetings produced a wide-ranging set of contributions on the urban habitat, the arts in the city, urban family life and social relations, and ritual in the urban milieu. Papers took up (among other topics) the transformation of the cities in the Renaissance, social structure in the ideal city of the Renaissance theorists, rituals of the Renaissance Popes, and social relations in Renaissance Florence. Presentations also included contributions toward a theory of everyday play, discussions of ceremonial plays and parody in Renaissance literature, games in Dutch art, and dance and society in Renaissance Italy.

Indeed, the symposium on play took play seriously, albeit (it is hoped) not solemnly.

S. Schoenbaum

Introduction

Susan Zimmerman
and
Ronald F. E. Weissman

What could be more synonymous with the *Renaissance* than urban life?
Merchant guilds, city states, civic humanism, architecture and the arts,
town planning, civic pageantry, and royal ceremonial are all so closely
connected with what scholars mean by "Renaissance culture" that the
concept of "Renaissance urban life" seems almost redundant. Any study
of the Renaissance is, at least by implication, a study of its emerging urban
character.

There is, however, a strong awareness among contemporary scholars of
how difficult the definition of "Renaissance urban life" is, of how complicated are the factors that make up this definition. Scholars no longer share
the axiomatic certainty of their predecessors concerning, for example,
rigid contrasts between city and country, between "intimate" medieval
towns and "modern" and impersonal Renaissance cities, or between
feudal and bourgeois cultures. Not all scholars still view Renaissance
cities as precociously modern.

This volume of essays explores our current sense of the complexity of
urban existence and seeks to locate Renaissance urban life in the Renaissance, rather than in modern-day expectations of what the term *urban*
must necessarily imply. The canvas for this set of studies is cross-national;
the volume includes essays on Italy, France, England, Holland, and (secondarily) Spain, ranging from the fifteenth through the seventeenth centuries. Although each essay analyzes an urban phenomenon within a
particular geographical and chronological framework, collectively the essays explore several overlapping themes concerning the problematics of
Renaissance urban culture and urban identity.

The first of these themes is the relationship between urban habitat and
the character of Renaissance social groups. The Renaissance town was the
locus of new social groups and new forms of social relations, such as
guilds, coexisting with older social forms transplanted into the urban
milieu. How did the architectural shape and physical plan of the town
correlate with the reconfiguration of social groups? How did family units

cope with the religious tensions of a larger and more complex environment? What new claims to leadership and legitimacy arose as a result of shifting social hierarchies? And how, finally, did towns, as aggregates of smaller social groups, relate to larger regional or national structures?

If the urban habitat affected social structure, so did it affect cultural life. The distinctions between popular and courtly forms of art, between public and private intellectual pursuits, were shifting in response to social change, and new cultural forms were developing to meet the needs of emerging social groups. In what ways were older forms of art and culture integrated into, or rejected by, the new urban environment? How did painting and architecture represent cities and urban space? What were the connections between iconography and city politics? The nature of urban tastes and the development of a new, city-oriented culture are the second major thematic concern of this volume.

Closely connected with this latter set of themes is another—the place of ritual in the definition of self and society, and the development of secular ritual and ritualized politics in the Renaissance city. Medieval townsmen had defined themselves through their ceremonies, religious rituals, and feasts, but many of these activities were no longer options for the sixteenth-century city-dweller, or they were available in radically altered forms. Transformations of social and religious rituals, or what some scholars see as the deritualization of Renaissance urban life, reflected shifts in political realities and in Renaissance concepts of authority. What took the place of traditional ritual in the Renaissance townsman's search for meaning, for personal and social identity? What were the new ceremonial mechanisms for expressing urban authority?

These then are the recurring areas of inquiry in this volume. All deal with what might be termed the emergence of Renaissance urban self-consciousness, the slow evolution of an unabashedly urban identity. The essays of this volume, divided into social, cultural, and political categories for the sake of convenience, reflect this transformation and collectively demonstrate its complexity.

The Renaissance City: Theory and Practice

The first two essays in the collection examine the connections between Renaissance social philosophy and the actual practices of urban development. Acording to James Ackerman and Myra Rosenfeld, Italian architectural theorists argued for a hierarchical social order, a stratification of dwellings based on class and income, in effect, a system of segregation. This concept, derived partly from classical antecedents, was fundamentally humanist. In practice, however, particularly in Renaissance Rome and

Paris, the views of these theorists proved largely ineffective in influencing the behavior of city planners, whose objectives were primarily practical and profit-oriented. Although some aims of the theorists were incidentally realized in these cities, their social philosophy was virtually ignored.

Nicholas Adams's detailed analysis of the transformation of medieval Corsignano into Renaissance Pienza examines an exception to this rule. Pienza, often cited as one of the most brilliant cases of Renaissance urban planning, was transformed from a medieval village into a Renaissance exemplar of urban design under the patronage and autocratic direction of Pope Pius II Piccolomini. Combining his personal vision with those of several architectural theorists, Pius developed and imposed a hierarchical city model, but at great social cost to many of the town's inhabitants. Ultimately, his gentrification led to the dismembering of a traditional agricultural community, as well as to the imposition of foreign values on the remnants of that community. Adams's essay forcefully reminds us that Renaissance city development required strong political pressure and often caused significant social dislocation among those not materially able to celebrate the glories of the new city.

A different kind of social disruption can be seen in the urban response to religious dissension, in particular, the threat of the Reformation to divide Renaissance families. Examining sixteenth-century Parisian families who found themselves on opposite sides of the Reformation, Barbara Diefendorf analyzes the effects of religious conflict on individual family members and on the larger network of social relations underlying French urban society. In the end, familial obligations often survived the divisions created by religious dissent, despite the sometimes radical opposition between these obligations and those of individual faith.

Renaissance Culture, Courtly and Urban

A central and pervasive theme in this collection of essays is the definition of Renaissance urban culture and the identification of the audiences for this culture. The "learned" environment of cities was clearly not limited to intellectual elites alone. A relatively high rate of literacy has often been cited as one of the key cultural characteristics separating the Renaissance town from its countryside, and indeed, this new literacy can be said to have provided the audience for the Renaissance itself. But few have examined the nature or psychology of literacy. It has generally been assumed that reading was one more characteristic of the supposedly intimate, privatized culture of the emerging urban bourgeoisie.

In Roger Chartier's analysis, however, the practice of reading emerges as a highly public, social act, reinforcing rather than negating social ties.

Shared among family and friends, the practice of reading aloud was, according to Chartier, one of the quintessentially urban forms of behavior, one that supports the interpretation of the town as a social rather than an impersonal or anonymous place, and which establishes its culture as interpersonal rather than simply interior.

Renaissance culture is frequently understood as being synonymous with such urban values as learning, civility, and intellectual prowess. If these values characterized Renaissance towns, did they also characterize late Renaissance courts? Werner Gundersheimer's assessment of cultural style in the Duchy of Ferrara under Alfonso II (1559–1597), describes the uneasy interplay between the two cultures of the Renaissance court, one masculine, aristocratic, and physical, the other feminine, bourgeois, and cerebral; the former chivalric, the latter intellectual. His essay serves as a useful reminder that feudal values were very much alive at court, even if they were at odds with self-styled modes of urbanity, and that despite the familiar association of the Italian Renaissance with towns and civic worlds such as Florence, complex cultural struggles were taking place elsewhere as well.

Architecture and literature do not, of course, exhaust the repertoire of Renaissance cultural forms. Music and art were equally urban forms of cultural expression native to the Renaissance. Indeed, the French minstrels examined by Howard Brown were, in his view, "quintessentially urban," and they were organized into that most Renaissance of urban institutions, the guild. Apart from the church choir, the minstrel was the most characteristic urban musical phenomenon in France. Closely connected through the guild structure to royal minstrels, the minstrel served as a bridge between what heretofore have been considered separate urban and courtly musical cultures. Like Gundersheimer's analysis of Ferrara, Brown's discussion of French minstrels cautions us against too rigid a notion of what, exactly we expect from "urban" or from "courtly" environments, given the persistent survival of chivalric and courtly motifs in the Renaissance urban world.

Perhaps the most striking urban art form, apart from urban planning itself, was urban iconography, the practice of celebrating the city through its painted image. Arthur Wheelock's essay examines one series of iconographic images, those of Delft. These representations, culminating in Vermeer's *View of Delft*, reflect a seventeenth-century long dialogue within the community about the proper political and social role of Delft and her sister cities within Holland, debates particularly about the extent to which the cities should embody Dutch unity under the House of Orange, or should fight to preserve equally strong traditions of local autonomy. According to Wheelock, the ambiguity of Vermeer's painting underlies the fact that Delft never conclusively opted for a single political vision and indeed achieved only an uneasy reconciliation of conflicting ideologies.

The themes discussed by Wheelock, local autonomy versus national identity, and the conflict between old and new ideologies of authority and orders, recur in many of these essays. If the city of Delft struggled to resolve such conflict with only partial success, so too did many urban communities in the Renaissance.

Authority and Order in the Renaissance Town: The Politics of Ritual

The Renaissance city, characterized as it was by older as well as emergent social groups, by tradition as well as innovation, was not a place in which legitimacy or authority was necessarily stable or abiding or viewed without question as part of the natural order of things. Order and legitimacy—both structuring relations within the community and between the community and larger political entities (as between Delft and Holland)—had to be created and recreated.

For David Sacks's Bristol, authority always had to demonstrate its legitimacy. Examining the structures of ritual exchange and deference that demarcated Bristol's politics between the Renaissance and the Reformation, he finds a transformation from authority based on community and expressed through communal rituals to authority based on hierarchy, expressed, in large part, through devotion to images of monarchy. Authority, once understood as an outgrowth of civic medieval brotherhood, had become, by the Renaissance, majestic sovereignty, descending from God and monarch. Gone were many of the collective political celebrations accompanying holy day festivities, which had been among the great moments of civic pageantry in late medieval Bristol.

Coincident with the Reformation was Bristol's transformation from a self-contained corporate community to a major center of economic power. Bristol's replacement of celebrations of community by celebrations of hierarchy reveals both the deritualizing sensitivities of Reformation England, and the integration of Bristol into the emerging nation state.

In sixteenth-century Siena, described by Sydel Silverman, similar processes of political integration were accompanied by a very different ritual process. In Siena, the loss of local political independence to the Medici-ruled Tuscan Grand Duchy led the Sienese to focus their ceremonial life increasingly inward. The Palio of Siena, the horse race that was to become the town's leading commentary on its identity and its most celebrated form of public play, took shape during these years.

Bristol's growth in importance within a national state system was characterized by an emphasis on ceremonial links to national styles of pageantry. Within the framework of regional powers and rivalries, Siena's absorption by the Medici Dukes was reflected in her serious political decline; after the fall, Siena's ritual life focused on just those sorts of local ties, in this case, local territorial divisions, which Bristol had outgrown. To emphasize regional ties would have reminded the Sienese of their political weakness. And so the Sienese retreated within their own walls to celebrate the myth of Siena, in her former, Republican glory.

Bristol's new-found ceremonies of sovereignty were based, ultimately, upon the rituals of royalty celebrating Elizabeth and the monarchy. As Richard McCoy demonstrates in his comparison of the theatrics of royal ceremony, particularly those associated with the cult of Elizabeth, and the theatric depiction of royalty on the English stage, the deritualizing tendencies of the sixteenth century could have consequences for secular political ceremonial as well as for sacred ritual. Ceremonial, in its very essence, has a "made-up" quality, a sense of its own arbitrariness. In explicitly calling attention to this quality of ritual, including royal ritual, Elizabethan theater reflected the growing disbelief, even among Elizabeth's own circle, in the power of secular ritual to safeguard the political order and the monarchy. How was identity projected and maintained in this deritualized world?

Renaissance Urban Identity: The Uses of Ambiguity and Parody

Through ritual and ceremony, through the word and through pictoral representation, through symbolic play and state politics, the Renaissance town tried to come to grips with its own legitimacy, its own order, rules, and values. But how could order, legitimacy, or meaning inhere in a world in which the sources of order—the relations among social groups, the nature of religious truth, belief in the efficacy of ritual, the permanence of institutions—were themselves fragile and subject to substantial change or even disbelief?

In this vein, a final theme running through these essays is the extent to which the Renaissance town was a place of social creativity where meanings were often unclear, a place where—in the absence of unquestioned traditions, sacred or secular—ambiguity and give-and-take dominated. In Ronald Weissman's interpretation, Florentines were bound to each other through kinship and friendship, through neighborhood and politics, in many complementary and yet antagonistic ways. This social complexity fostered a sense of the theatrics of everyday life, in which the adoption of artful ambiguity, of trickster behavior, allowed the townsman to negotiate the heavy demands of sociability without losing honor or friends. Projecting ambiguity, rather than clarity, became a highly prized mechanism for preserving the self.

In Thomas Greene's view, ceremony as a public, repetitive, symbolic act had been used in the Middle Ages to define identity; its breakdown can be seen in the rise of literary parody, particularly parody of the culture of ceremony, which is a recurring theme in European Renaissance literature. The distinction of Renaissance parody is that it makes space for improvisation and ambiguity, for freedom, creativity, and play. It reflects the unravelling of the traditional ceremonial fabric even as it points the way to a new symbolism, more experimental and open-ended. In the Renaissance, then, both literary patterns and social patterns depended not on the structured conventions of the past but on ambiguities and makeshift solutions—hallmarks of the new urban environment, and symptoms of a fundamental cultural change.

Taken separately, these essays offer suggestive insights into the fundamental questions of Renaissance urban studies from a number of disciplinary perspectives, including those of the anthropologist, social scientist, literary critic, social historian, music historian, and art historian. The methodologies are similarly wideranging, although most combine theoretical insights with a foundation based on local context and sources.

But the essays make a collective point as well. Taken together, they reflect what might be viewed as an emerging synthesis of opinion about the Renaissance city, one that gives full weight to the complicated texture of urban experience. Contemporary scholarship can no longer rely on formulas that view urban life in the Renaissance through simple dichotomies, or through a myopically modern lens. This volume persuasively demonstrates that whatever the attendant difficulties for researchers, study of the Renaissance city must be firmly situated in the complexities and ambiguities of its own time.

Urban Life
in the Renaissance

PART I

The Renaissance City: Theory and Practice

Social Stratification in Renaissance Urban Planning

James S. Ackerman
and
Myra Nan Rosenfeld

Sebastiano Serlio prepared the sixth book of his treatise on architecture, devoted to domestic architecture in the country and in the city, while he was employed at the French court in the later 1540s. Unlike the other books in the treatise, it was never published, although two autograph copies have been preserved and are available in facsimile editions with extensive scholarly commentary.[1] Of all Renaissance treatments of housing, Serlio's is the most highly articulated.[2] Not only does he propose plans and elevations for the residences of every class of society, but every stratum is subdivided according to income, from hovels for poor artisans to a project thought to be an early scheme for the Louvre of Francis I.

The lowest stratum (fig. 1), provides essentially two groundfloor rooms and an overhead loft, probably for storage. Serlio writes of these proposals:

> First of all, habitations of the poorest men are in the *borghi* a little outside town near the gates, and these are artisans of various low arts and the habitations so far as I have seen them in various countries are on narrow but deep lots. For this reason, I shall start by designing the hut for the poorest artisan within the city, which can serve also for the *borghi*. It shall not be less than ten feet wide, having on the front only a little door and a window and the first room shall be the bedroom, fourteen feet long with a fire in the center. The room, however, will actually be twenty feet long, but a space for the bed shall be divided off by a wall. There is a little court with a toilet at its head, and wall of the street to be shared by neighbors.[3]

Like all earlier theorists, Serlio here divides his house-types not only by dimensions and design, but also by placement within the city, locating his

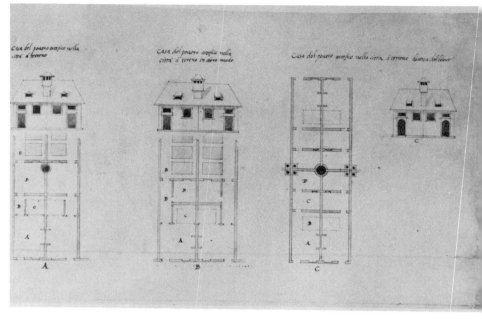

Figure 1. Sebastiano Serlio, *Houses for the Poorest Artisans,* Book VI, folio 48, projects A–C, ink on paper, 1541–46. *(Courtesy of The Avery Architectural Library, Columbia University, New York.)*

lowest level of society outside the walls, in the *borghi* or suburbs. However, he adds, deferring to the interest of his potential clients:

> Sometimes there will be a site nearer the center of town, where property is dearer, where a rich man will seek income rather from small houses than from a large house in which he can live himself. . . .[4]

The second group of drawings shows projects for the dwellings of artisans of more substantial means. The houses are wider, and two have two stories (fig. 2). The elevation at the far right of figure 2 shows a house in the French style. French alternatives are proposed for those social levels for which it is inappropriate to consider the use of classical orders and ornament (which would have been reserved for the privileged classes). Above that level, it is no longer considered appropriate to recognize national traditions.[5]

At the level immediately preceding the introduction of the smaller palace in the classical mode, Serlio proposed houses for merchants or citizens (by which he means professionals such as lawyers, physicians, notaries and the like) (fig. 3). The Italian model on the left of figure 3 has a portico, which Serlio believes to be healthier than closed-wall construction, because walls hold moisture. He also points to the advantages of protection from sun and rain. For this level and the next above, Serlio observes:

> I do not want to dedicate a house specifically to a merchant rather than to a citizen or rich gentleman because minds are not always at the level of rank. Sometimes a very rich citizen will have a spirit so low and vile that, overcome by avarice, he will live in an old, smoky, even ruinous house.[6]

Conversely, a person may sell everything he has to build a beautiful house. For Serlio, not to dwell as elegantly as one could afford to was an index of moral decay. The observation might be related to the fact that in the course of nearly a decade only one French patron showed sufficient passion for architecture to commission a residence from Serlio.

The stratification of the dwellings in Serlio's book six is based partly on the hierarchical structure of French society imposed by the monarchy and partly on the antecedents established by earlier Renaissance architectural theorists. Serlio, in fact, adapted a basically Italian social structure to France. He included in his urban housing types dwellings for the com-

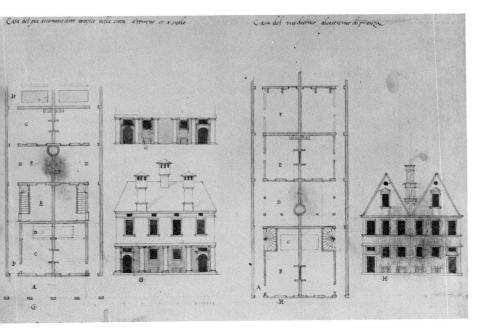

Figure 2. Sebastiano Serlio, *Houses for an Artisan of More Substantial Means*, Book VI, folio 49, projects G–H, ink on paper, 1541–46. *(Courtesy of The Avery Architectural Library, Columbia University, New York.)*

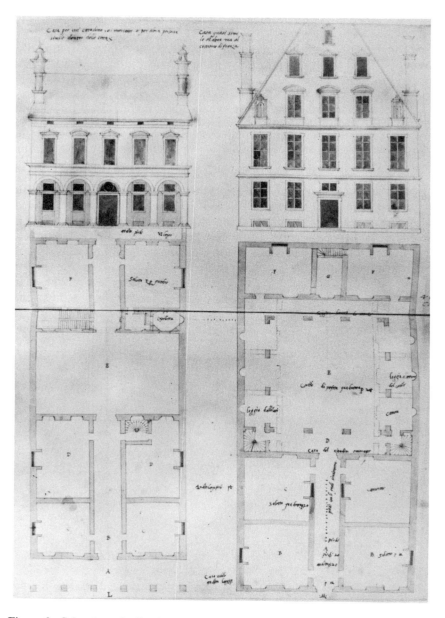

Figure 3. Sebastiano Serlio, *Houses for a Merchant or Citizen*, **Book VI, folio 50, ink on paper, 1541–46.** *(Courtesy of The Avery Architectural Library, Columbia University, New York.)*

mander of the militia *(capitano),* the mayor *(podestà),* and the governor *(governatore).* Whereas the commander of the militia was a post found in the cities of the *terraferma* (mainland) controlled by Venice, such as Vicenza and Padua,[7] the dual posts of governor and mayor reflect the governmental structure of Paris. The king appointed the governor, a post created by Louis XI, while the representatives of the merchants *(echevins)* appointed the *prévot* or mayor, a position equivalent to that of the *podestà* in Italian cities.[8]

When Serlio arrived in France, Francis I (1515–1547) was following the lead of Louis XI (1461–1483) in gradually dismantling the feudal system in order to establish a strong monarchy. One of the ways both monarchs consolidated their power was to encourage the merchant class or bourgeoisie. The merchant class had gained in power and had grown larger during the reigns of Francis I and Louis XI. Not only did both kings elevate members of the bourgeoisie to the nobility, but they also permitted nobles to engage in commerce.[9] These practices may account for the fact that Serlio proposes more types of urban dwellings in book six for members of the bourgeoisie than for members of the two other estates that were represented in French government, the nobles and the clergy. Serlio, in fact, did not include in book six a separate category of urban dwellings for the clergy.[10] In adopting a secular social structure for book six based on a monarchical system of government with an affluent and large bourgeoisie, Serlio was influenced by Claude Seyssel's important treatise, *La grant monarchie de France,* which had been published in Paris in 1519. Seyssel had advocated a strong bourgeoisie loyal to the king as essential to the development of a modern monarchy. Serlio was guided by Seyssel in his combination of the characteristics of the cities of the Venetian *terraferma* with those in France, since Seyssel had compared the systems of government of Venice and France.[11]

Serlio's illustrated manuscript of the Roman writer Polybius' *Sixth Book on Roman History* is important as a background for book six. The illustration of the ideal fortified city (fig. 4) gives us an idea of how Serlio may have organized the different urban dwellings in book six. In his ideal fortified city, the houses are also arranged according to a secular, social hierarchy—that of army ranks. The dwelling of the soldiers (D–E, F–G, K–N), similar to those for artisans and merchants in book six, are placed along streets in a grid pattern. The most important house in the center, that of the general (A) is located at the apex of a pyramid, at the top of the main street, surrounded by the house of the magistrate to the left (B) and the forum to the right (C).[12] If one transfers Serlio's conception of the fortified camp to book six, one can imagine his domestic buildings ordered in a similar way, with the king's palace taking the place of the general's house,

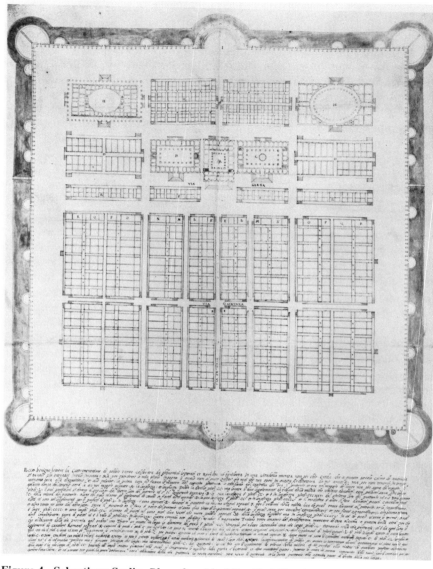

Figure 4. Sebastiano Serlio, *Plan of an Ideal Fortified City*, from *Polybius. On Roman Fortifications*, Codex Icon. 190, folio, 1r, ink on parchment, 1537. *(Courtesy of Der Bayerische Staatsbibliothek, Munich.)*

and the houses of the artisans, merchants, and gentlemen replacing those of the various ranks of soldiers (D–G, K–L, L–R).[13]

The ultimate source of the Renaissance tradition that was reflected in Serlio's work was Leon Battista Alberti. Alberti's treatise, completed in about 1450, proposes that the ideal city be planned with two concentric circular rings of walls. He places the more prosperous citizens in the outer rings, while the prince is yet farther removed to lessen the annoyance of petitioners. Alberti assigns the center to butchers, factories, and produce-vendors, who must be close to what he calls the forum. He says:

> The wealthier citizens, desiring more space, will readily assent to live outside the first circle of walls, leaving the center with the slaughterhouse, the artisans' shops and stores to the salesmen of produce around the forum; and the city will be more secure and less disrupted if those in power are separated from the feckless mob of poultry salesmen, butchers, cooks and the like.[14]

In another part of the treatise, Alberti locates bankers, decorators, and goldsmiths near the forum and, "a little way off," spice merchants, tailors, and respectable crafts.[15] Dirty and smelly activities are put on the periphery, to the north so as not to be windward. As to whether the most frequented services should be distributed equally in each of the quarters, and whether palaces should be surrounded by shops, Alberti is undecided. There are obvious inconsistencies in his provisions that reflect the fact that he was writing with no traditon to guide him and that his book was a long time in the making.

In the treatise of Antonio Averlino, called Filarete, completed some fifteen years later, the class divisions are somewhat more clearly drawn. He suggests five classes: the poor, whose houses would be ten to twelve *braccia* wide (between sixteen and twenty feet); the artisan, with houses of thirty by fifty *braccia;* the merchant (the class he calls *popolari*), the gentlemen, and the prince.[16] The house of the merchant (fig. 5) is characteristically overblown in elegance and seems to be of palatial grandeur, and that of the gentleman is also sumptuous beyond the normal practice of the time.

Filarete does not illustrate the house of the poor man, saying that it is built any way the owner can manage in order to have shelter, and that the plan is arranged according to his choice.[17] On the cathedral piazza Filarete places the palaces of the nobility and of the gentlemen, official buildings, and private houses. The main piazza is highly articulated, with buildings for each branch of government, a prison, a guildhouse, and two churches (fig. 6).

Some services in the city are dispersed in several neighborhoods, like barbers and pharmacists, while the guilds are concentrated in areas spec-

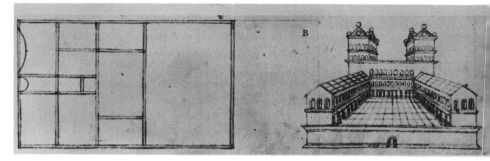

Figure 5. Il Filarete, *House for a Merchant*, from Filarete's *Treatise on Architecture*, *ed. cit.*, (note 16), fol. 73r. *(Courtesy of Yale University Press.)*

ified for them: wool merchants, weavers, and dyers are together in one place.[18] Outside the walls Filarette places coopers, shipwrights, wheelwrights, and ropemakers. Blacksmiths are at the gates.

Francesco di Giorgio's treatise in its second version, revised just before 1492, offers a similar heirarchy of classes and dwellings, with six levels of domestic dwellings.[19] Unlike Filarete, Francesco designs for his countrymen of the lowest class, saying that they should have farmhouses adapted to city use. His middle class has two divisions: merchants and *"studianti."* The latter includes notaries, administrators, lawyers, physicians, and men of learning. The house of the artisan, next to the lowest (fig. 7), has accommodations for a *bottega,* an office, and family rooms. Like Filarete, Francesco accords considerably more elegance to each level than the existing economy would have supported.

The merchants' houses are almost as lavish as those of Filarete (fig. 8) and they include storage areas and segregated rooms for guests. The palaces of princes are distinguished by being raised freestanding.[20] The city hall is placed in the main piazza, with the houses of the officers of prisons and of customs. Banks and warehouses are also there. Nearby, but hidden from sight, are *tavole calde* (cafeterias) and the gallows.

Francesco puts the silk guild in the most frequented street, but removes the woolmakers from the center because of the noise and their need to be where there is water. Dyers, leathermakers, and armorers are also at the periphery, while spice merchants and tailors are assigned to the main streets.[21]

Finally, Serlio was probably influenced by the ideal fortified city plan published by Albrecht Dürer in Nuremberg in 1527, in *Etliche Unterricht zu Befestigung der Stett, Schloss und Flecken* (fig. 9). Dürer integrated houses of artisans and merchants into an ordered city place based on a monarchical type of government. He placed a square in the center of his town with the king's house in the middle. The dwelling of the prince was

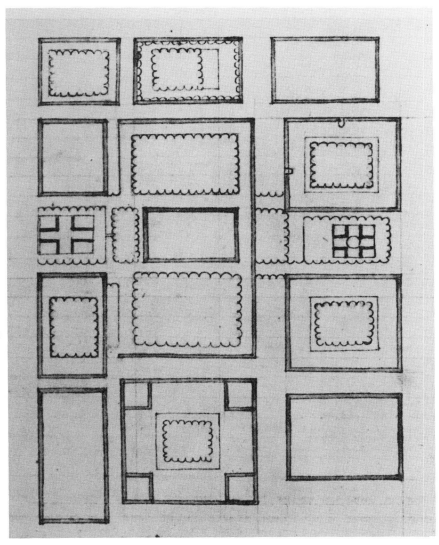

Figure 6. Il Filarete, *Civic Piazza*, from Filarete's *Treatise*, fol. 86r. *(Courtesy of Yale University Press.)*

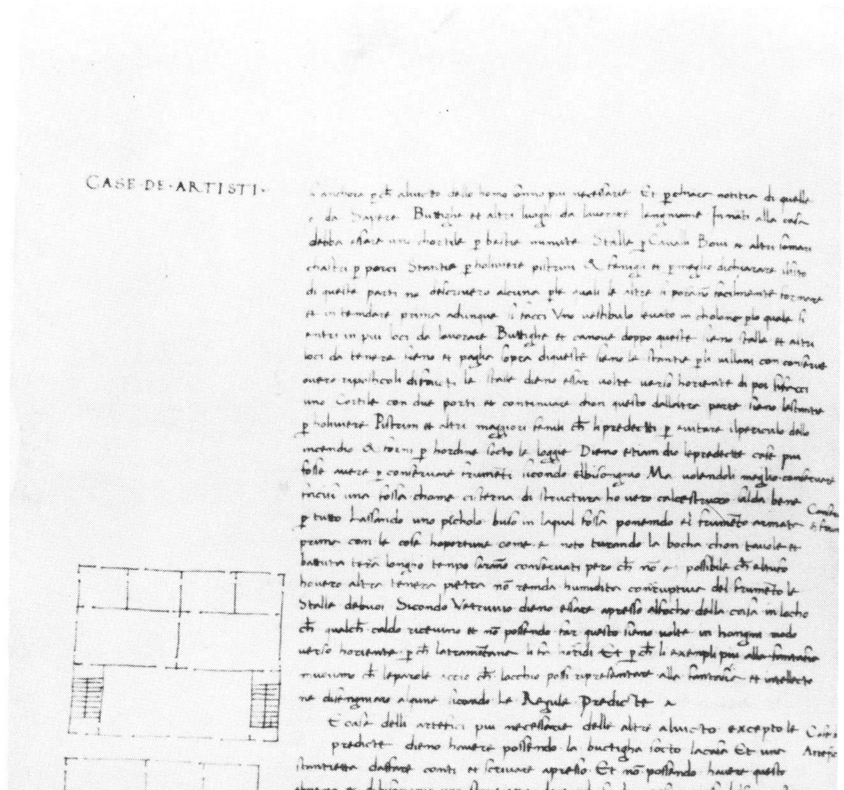

Figure 7. Francesco di Giorgio Martini, *Houses for an Artisan*, from *Trattati di architettura ingegneria e arte militare*, fol. 16v, pl. 192, *ed. cit.* (note 19). (*Courtesy of Edizioni Il Polifilo, Milan.*)

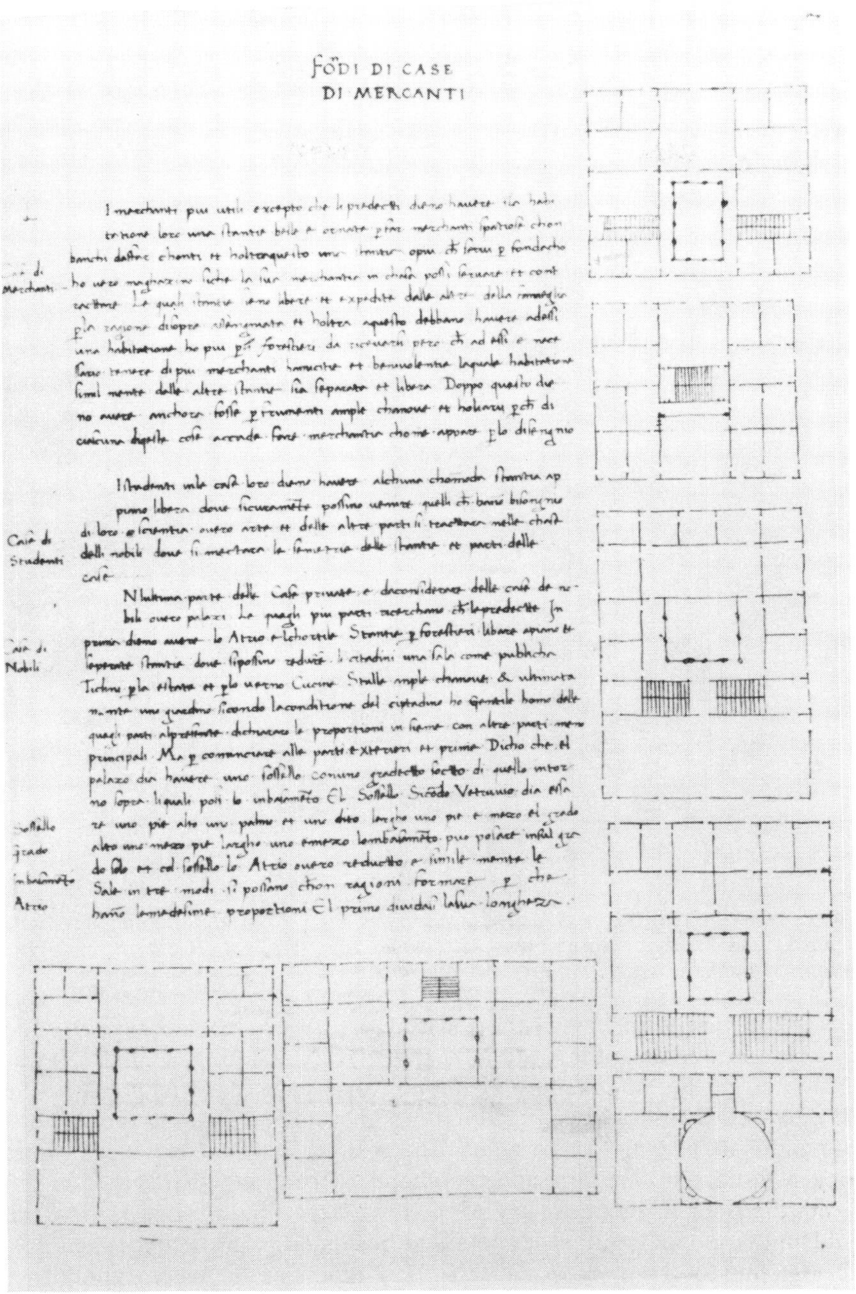

Figure 8. Francesco di Giorgio Martini, *Houses for a Merchant*, from *Trattati*, fol. 17, pl. 193, *ed. cit. (Courtesy of Edizioni Il Polifilo, Milan.)*

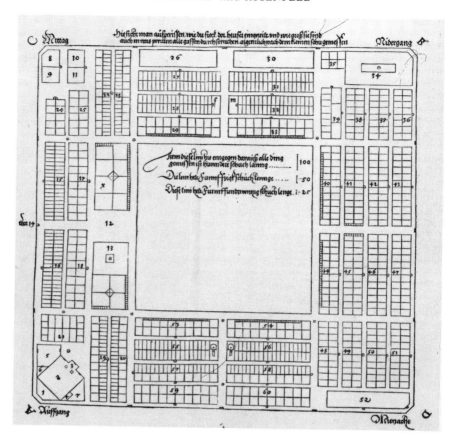

Figure 9. Albrecht Dürer, *Plan of a Fortified City,* **from** *Befestigung der Stett, Schloss, und Flecken,* **Nuremberg, 1527, folio Eiv, Woodcut.** *(Courtesy of Metropolitan Museum of Art, gift of Felix M. Warburg.)*

located at the periphery of the town at the lower right corner (D). The church was located at the lower left corner (A,2), and the town hall (X) was to the left of the main square facing the royal palace and adjacent to the (12) market. Dürer enlarged the quarters Filarete had given to the artisans and guilds in his plan for Sforzinda. The artisans lived in the houses where they worked. The artisans and merchants were grouped together in different districts at the periphery of the town according to their trades: the goldsmiths, coppersmiths, tanners and blacksmiths in the upper left corner (C), and food purveyors near the food depots at the lower right corner (D). The arsenals, granaries, timber warehouses, and baths were located in the upper right corner of the town (B), while the soldiers' barracks were placed along the sides of the city.[22] Although Dürer did not include any illustrations of actual dwellings for his ideal fortified city, these houses may have resembled his drawings of a Venetian artisan's house now in the British Museum (fig. 10).[23]

Although the early theorists operated at a level of abstraction removed from the actualities of building, the individual projects of Serlio were rooted in his experience, as the French elevations and the porticoes from his native Bologna indicate. This combination of factors raises the question of whether there is a relationship between theory and practice in Renaissance housing policy.

There are several surviving examples of mass-housing projects from the period preceding these theoretical writings. The one that must have been best known to Serlio was a group of three blocks built for old and disabled sailors by the Republic of Venice in 1395.[24] The project, called the *Marinarezza,* appears in the bird's-eye view of Venice designed by Jacopo de' Barbari in 1500, at the lower right of figure 11. Another such block, separated from the street by walls at either end, appears at the top center. Serlio lived in Venice prior to his employment at the French court, and his dwellings for the lower classes must have been influenced by the Venetian experiment.[25] Only five years later, a quite similar block was constructed by the lord of Ferrara for aged widows; it is called the *Casa delle Vedove.*[26] And in 1516, the Fuggers, a private family who were the great banking clan of the Holy Roman Empire, built a large complex modeled on the *Marinarezza* in Augsburg for indigent and pious Catholics.[27]

As Eugenio Garin suggested years ago before most of the Renaissance texts on the ideal city had been adequately published, the attitude toward class distinctions manifest in the theoretical literature grew out of ancient writing on politics and government.[28] The most widely read of these were Aristotle's *Politics* and Plato's *Laws* and his *Republic*. These works do not provide identical divisions of society, but they are similar in establishing four or more clearly defined levels, constituting a hierarchy, with laborers at the base and rulers at the summit. Aristotle, for example, attempted to coordinate the ranks of society with communal needs. The basic need being food, the base, or lowest class, would be farmers; the need for arts and crafts would be fulfilled by artisans, one level up, and so on, arms and defense would be provided by soldiers, control of property by the propertied classes, the service of God by priests, and leadership and justice by the governing class.[29] In the *Laws,* Plato pragmatically associated class strata with income and permitted the connection to be flexible.

> there must be graded property classes to ensure that the offices and taxes and grants may be arranged on the basis of what a man is worth. In short, the citizens must be esteemed and given offices as far as possible

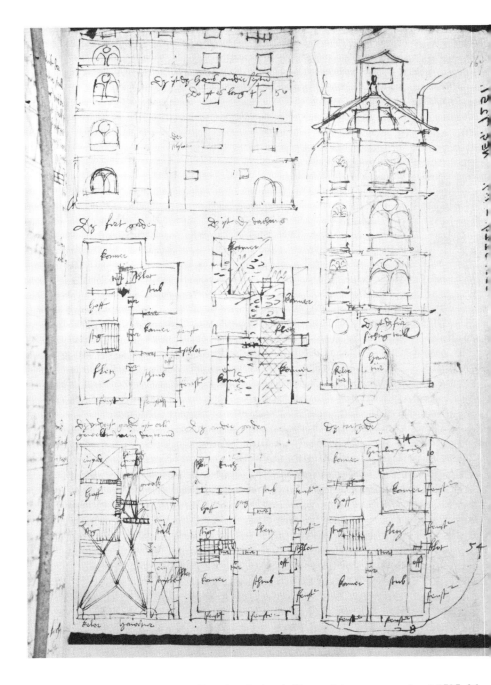

Figure 10. Albrecht Dürer, *Venetian Artisan's House*, ink on paper, about 1505–06, British Museum, Manuscript Department, Add. 5229, folio 167. *(Courtesy of British Museum, London.)*

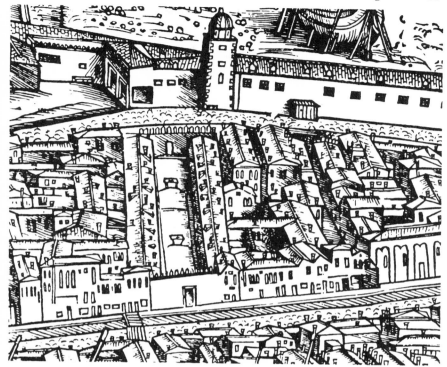

Figure 11. Jacopo de' Barbari, *Plan of Venice,* **1500, detail showing the "Marinarezza" housing.**

on exactly equal terms of "proportional inequality," so as to avoid ill feeling. For these reasons, four permanent property classes must be established, graded according to wealth: a man will either keep his original classification, or, when he has grown richer or poorer than he was before, transfer to the appropriate class. The legislator will use the land holding as his unit of measure and allow a man to possess twice, three times and up to four times its value. If anyone acquires more than this, he should hand over the surplus.[30]

Vitruvius offered a watered-down version of what the philosopher had said on the subject in a brief treatment in book six of his treatise on architecture (written in the first century B.C.), in which he recounts the particular program requirements of bankers and revenue farmers and of lawyers.[31] But his overall view of the subject is limited to a sententious homily to the effect that one would not be criticized for saying that a dwelling should be accommodated to the class of the owner. It is clear that this is an area in which Renaissance theorists could not get help from their most admired ancient mentor.

Political writings of the early Renaissance did not stray far from the material culled by their authors from ancient texts. The *De Republica* of Lauro Quirini (1449–50), for example, frequently quotes Aristotle, Plato, Cicero, Seneca, Plutarch, and others.[32] His class divisions derive in the main from Aristotle and add nothing of note. The political theories of Machiavelli and Guicciardini are another matter. Their more pragmatic and fluid view of human affairs was incompatible with the fixed strata preserved by the architectural theorists. Machiavelli undoubtedly helped to preserve the pragmatic approach to urban building described below, if not the theory.

The church hierarchy may have provided a subliminal model for the theorists, who could see that the structure of the church was considerably more stable than that of the state. Clear-cut lines or divisions segregated the priest from the canon, the bishop and archbishop from the cardinal and pope, and certain architectural types were firmly linked to some of these strata, such as the parish church, the monastic church, and the cathedral. Moreover, it was possible for the churchmen, like Plato's land-holders, to rise not only from one stratum to the next, but also through the entire hierarchy to the top. Nonetheless, on the conscious level, the theorists remained typically humanist in their attempts to structure the environment on a classical model.

The kind of initiative represented by these housing blocks appears to be more characteristic of the late medieval period than of the Renaissance. But the study of the subject is still in its early stages and it is hard to say whether there was a consistent policy of urban investment in the later fifteenth and sixteenth centuries. We do, however, know enough about Rome and Paris to get an image of Renaissance housing practices that contrasts sharply with the principles of the theorists.

After the return of the papacy from Avignon early in the fifteenth century, Rome had developed an increasingly powerful urban planning agency, headed by two men, usually selected from the old patriciate, called *magistri stratarum*. In charge of streets, squares, and water access, these officers had a determining role in the actual shaping of the city.[33] Although they could condemn private property to create a public space, to widen or straighten a street, or to upgrade an area by discouraging inelegant structures, they could not impose on the owners of private property a scheme for its development, and this restriction made it difficult to put the idea of theorists or of popes into practice.

The development of new areas of Rome during the sixteenth century was unmatched anywhere in the world, because the city expanded from a miserable settlement of seventeen thousand in the early 1400s to over one hundred thousand two centuries later.[34] Great tracts of land were in the possession of monasteries, hospitals, and confraternities, which shifted

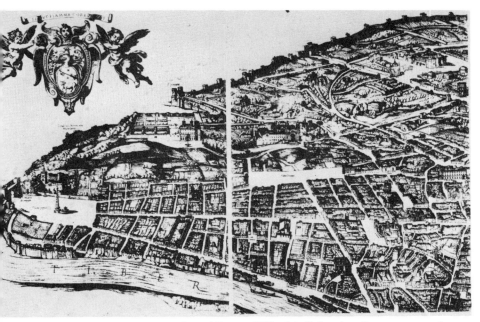

Figure 12. Antonio Tempesta, *Plan of Roma,* **1593, detail showing the area around Piazza del Popolo and the Church of San Giacomo degli Incurabili.**

their use as soon as demand warranted from agriculture to housing. The entire area of the Campomarzio, for example, from the Piazza del Popolo at the northern entrance to the city to the base of an almost equilateral triangle shown at the bottom of the map in figure 12, an area of vineyards with scattered huts in 1500, was intensely developed from 1510 to 1585.[35] The largest landholder, the Hospital of San Giacomo degli Incurabili, roughly in the center of the tract, was the earliest developer. The hospital block is the rectangle appearing in the lower right of the late sixteenth-century map (fig. 12).

The initial enterprise was a stretch of modest housing along the river with frontages on the street. It was laid out in 1519 by the planners of Leo X, Medici, probably after designs by Raphael. The Via Leonina, later called Ripetta and Scrofa, ran straight from the major gate of the city to the Medici Palace. The hospital and similar institutions appear to have undertaken their development directly rather than through contractros, as is made evident by planbooks prepared by their administrators and represented by sheets such as that in figure 13. The books were kept as guides for the rent collectors, enabling them to identify the properties held and to provide a basis for setting rents in relation to the dimensions of each structure.

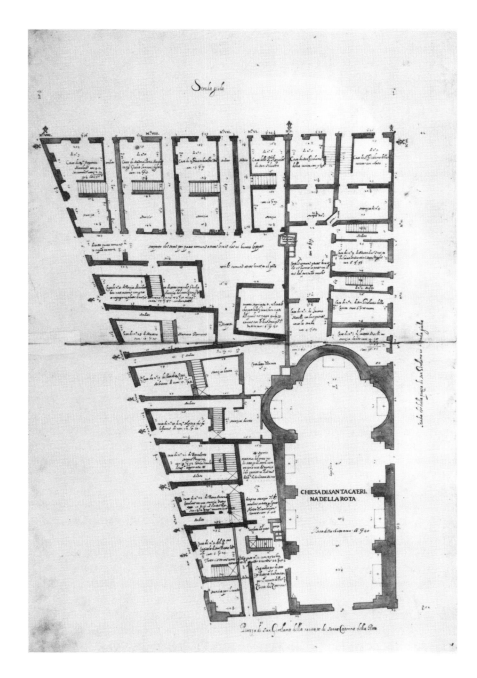

Figure 13. *Roman property record*, seventeenth century, from *Archivio del Capitolo di S. Pietro, Catasti e Piante*, **21**, fol. 6v-7. *(Courtesy of Archivio fotografico, Biblioteca Apostolica Vaticana.)*

While the developers were seeking income to improve and to expand public welfare services (in the case of the Hospital of San Giacomo, primarily the care of lepers and syphillitics), their approach to housing was strictly that of hardheaded capitalists, exploiting the market for what it would bear. In the plan of the hospital holdings (fig. 14), prepared by Roberto Fregna from the record albums, we see the hospital and its oval church at the top, and the lot divisions of the earliest period starting in 1509 in the narrow strip between the river and the Via Leonina. The date of the subdivision is indicated on each lot. Later campaigns are indicated on the second plan (fig. 15). The developers also added a short north-south street, Via Lombarda, in 1520. The minimal lots in this program remind us of those proposed by Serlio, and they must reflect a practice reaching back centuries.

However, by contrast to the dicta of the theorists and the projects in Venice and Augsburg, there is no sign of any segregation of living quarters either by class or by trade. In fact, the very opposite consideration seems to have dominated housing practices—a commitment to what today we call mixed use. This may have reflected a conscious effort to maintain a social mix and to assure the viability of a variety of goods and services on every street. More likely it was simply the survival of customs characteristic of the medieval city with roots in ancient Roman practice. In any case, mixed use was the rule both in the oldest quarters of Rome and in those newly developed. The situation is vividly illustrated by a sixteenth-century drawing of a block of the Via dell Pellegrino in the heart of the Renaissance quarter (fig. 16). A wide variety of commercial activities are accommodated, and the dwellings range from minimal to modest; most of the structures survive today unchanged.

To get an impression of the extraordinary mix of Roman neighborhoods, one has only to examine the documents prepared by the *magistri stratarum* on the occasions when they ordered the widening, paving, or repair of a street and recorded the assessments levied on the abutting tenants according to the value of their property. One document shows the high-and-mighty settled alongside the modest artisan and laborer (the levies are clearly above the means of the very poor). The volume entitled *Presidenza delle strade* no. 445 in the Roman Archivio di Stato records a levy made by the Maestri di strada Latino Giovenale di Manetti and Hieronimo Maffeo to widen the street leading to Via Giulia from the enclave of the Incoronati family on 6 May 1542.

The houses of master Valerio Dolce overlooking the Ambassador, 6 ducats
House of Madonna Caterina baker, 6 ducats
House of Choniasso Severo, 1 ducat. . . .
House of the heirs of Master Johanne Canbellocco, 15 ducats

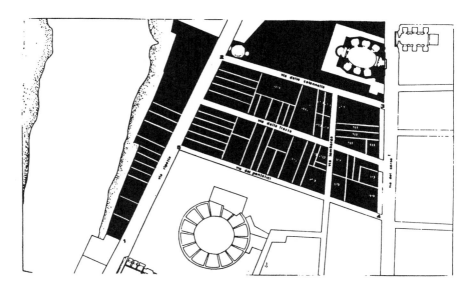

Figure 14. Early development of property in the area of the Church of San Giacomo degli Incurabili, Rome (numbers on the houses indicate years in the sixteenth century). After Fregna and Politi, (note "Primi dati" 35), 5. *(Courtesy of Controspazio.)*

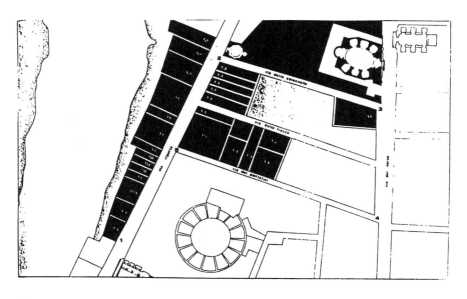

Figure 15. Later development of property shown in fig. 14. Fregna and Politi, "Primi dati". *(Courtesy of Controspazio.)*

The church of St. John, 100 ducats

The house of Master Bernardino Incoronato with the palace and other houses of his, 200 ducats

The houses of Master Francesco perfumer, 100 ducats

The houses of Master Adriano Tetellino, 2 ducats

House of Master Diego the Spaniard with the stable opposite, 10 ducats

The two houses of the anglesi or of the Bishop of Vasona, 15 ducats

The house of the same bishop in which his son lives, 40 ducats

Alongside the nuns of Sto Sisto lives Madonna Cucia, 20 ducats

The Palace of the Archbishop of Nicosia, 100 ducats

The two houses of the heirs of Maestro Viver the German in which there are two carpenters, 20 ducats

The house of Maestro Simone the shoemaker, 6 ducats[36]

The assessments are quite steep by modern standards: many amount to or surpass the annual salary of an artisan, and one assumes that none of the individuals mentioned was poor.

These few examples of Roman practice indicate a trend confirmed by the published and unpublished material now available. A tradition of mixed use was confirmed by developers concerned primarily with profits

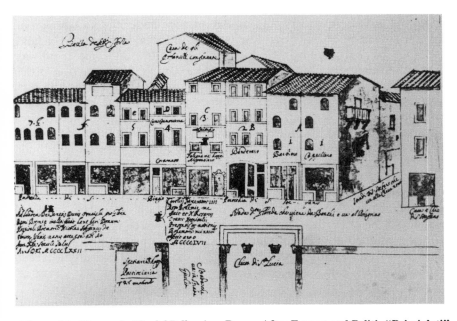

Figure 16. *Houses in Via del Pellegrino,* Rome. After Fregna and Politi, "Primi dati" 19. *(Courtesy of Controspazio.)*

on the open market. They exploited the available land to the maximum, providing only as many amenities at each income level as the pool of prospective tenants and buyers demanded. At the same time, a degree of social responsibility must have been a factor in building, because new minimal housing accommodations were made available to the poor, if not to the very poor, along with those of comfortable and affluent means.

Paris, like Rome, witnessed a boom in the building industry during the second half of the fifteenth and first half of the sixteenth centuries. The population of Paris had declined from a high of two hundred thousand in 1328 to a low of about one hundred thousand in 1400 at the height of the Hundred Years' War. When the war ended and Paris became the capital of France again in 1437, there was a new influx of residents; by the end of the sixteenth century, the population had reached one hundred and fifty thousand.[37] This influx produced a surge of building activity in response to the destruction caused by the war. Investment in property also developed as a revenue-producing activity. Many members of the noble and bourgeois classes built dwellings for artisans and members of the lower classes near their own more sumptuous homes and rented them out for income.[38]

Paris in the fifteenth and sixteenth centuries had much in common with Rome. Large tracts of land were owned by the king and members of the nobility, the upper bourgeoisie, religious institutions, the university, and the municipality of Paris. Although the applications of building regulations, the upkeep of streets, and sanitation were under the jurisdiction of the Parliament of Paris,[39] the development of individual parcels of land could not be controlled by a central authority. Thus as in Rome, there was a mix of different social strata throughout the city. A reconstruction of the central section of the right bank or Paris around Les Halles through fifteenth- and sixteenth-century documents (fig. 17) has revealed that residences of the aristocrats and members of the upper bourgeoisie, shown in black, were located side by side with smaller houses of artisans and merchants.[40] Although the houses of the nobles were initially built near the fortified wall, they immediately attracted conglomerations of smaller, more modest houses.

Individual developers in Renaissance Paris were not at all concerned with the segregation of housing for different strata of society, as were Serlio and the other theoreticians. The mode by which individual parcels of land were built with this mixture of social strata can be illustrated by an analysis of the development between 1334 and 1489 of the urban fabric around the Hôtel de Cluny, the residence of the abbot of the Order of Cluny.

The Hôtel de Cluny is located in the left bank of Paris in the center of the Latin Quarter, as can be seen in a detail from the Map of Paris published by Olivier Truschet and Germain Hoyau around 1550 (fig. 18).

Figure 17. *Aristocratic Dwellings in the Area of Les Halles, Paris, at the End of the Fifteenth Century*, drawing by Jean Blécon, from F. Boudon, A. Chastel, H. Couzy, F. Hamon, *Système de l'Architecture Urbaine, le Quartier des Halles à Paris, 1977, plate 26.* (*Courtesy of Le centre national de la recherche scientifique, Paris.*)

The order had a school nearby in the vicinity of the Sorbonne. The Hôtel de Cluny was built over the Roman Baths of Paris between the Rue de la Harpe, the Rue du Foin, and the Rue des Mathurins (formerly known as the Rue du Palais des Thermes). It was adjacent to the convent of the Mathurins and was surrounded on three other sides by smaller houses for artisans as well as by the large palace of the archbishop of Bourges.[41]

The Order of Cluny had bought several houses in 1334 located over the Roman Baths of Paris. The land itself was apparently owned by the Parliament of Paris.[42] According to land rents paid to the Parliament of Paris between 1424 and 1489, the order destroyed the original houses on the lot and constructed sometime after 1334 a new series of houses around

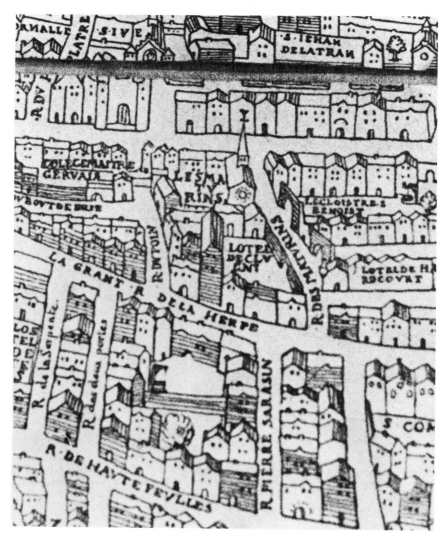

Figure 18. *Site of the Hôtel de Cluny,* detail from *Map of Paris* by Olivier Truschet and Germain Hoyau, Woodcut, about 1550, Basle, Offentliche Kunstsammlungen. *(Courtesy of Bibliothèque Nationale, Paris; photo by Myra Nan Rosenfeld.)*

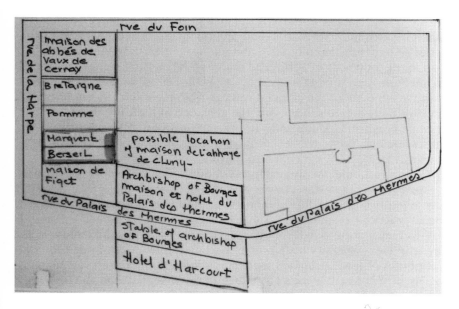

Figure 19. *Reconstruction of the Site of the Hôtel de Cluny, Paris,* **1424–28.** *(Drawing by Myra Nan Rosenfeld; photo courtesy of The National Gallery of Art, Washington, D.C.)*

their own property, which they rented for profit to artisans.[43] If we examine a drawing of the site as it can be reconstructed from land rents paid between 1424 and 1428 (fig. 19), we see that the Order of Cluny owned four houses along the Rue de la Harpe, *Les maisons à L'enseigne de Bretagne, Marguerite, Pomme, et Berseil,* which were probably artisans' houses with shops on the street. These were adjacent to two other houses owned by members of the clergy, *The maison des Abbés de Vaux de Cernay,* and the *Maison et Hôtel du Palais des Thermes* belonging to the archbishop of Bourges. Other classes of society are represented by the palace of the Comte d'Harcourt, a member of the nobility, and the *Maison de Figet,* which was probably owned by a professional rather than an artisan since it had no shop sign.[44] This practice of the mixed use of urban residential areas was continued in Paris during the sixteenth century, as can be seen in the development of the land occupied by the former royal Hôtels de Bourgogne, d'Artois, de Flandres, d'Estampes and Saint Pol from 1543 to 1556, and of the tract known as the Culture Sainte-Catherine after 1545. In the latter case, the land was developed by the Crown; in the former case, it was developed by the prior of the Church of Sainte-Catherine.[45]

The accommodations produced by this free-market economy turned out to be remarkably like those of Serlio, the most practical of the theorists, for the poorest classes. Those for clients at higher economic levels—the wealthier artisans, merchants, and professionals, to accept Serlio's categories—were substantially less commodious in actual building practice than in the proposals of Serlio and other theorists—that is in the nature of architectural and urban theory. But one could still deduce the social level of the inhabitants of the actual dwellings from their size, the number and kinds of their public spaces, and the elegance of their ornaments. Social practice conformed sufficiently to the classical philosophical position to cause housing types to be stratified much the way they were in the humanist treatises.

By contrast, the theoretical prescription encouraging architects and builders to segregate the classes into distinct urban quarters appears to have been rejected by Roman and Parisian investors. The economic and social practices of the Renaissance preserved the traditional mixing of classes that had survived from the formation of cities in the middle ages. Powerful landowners, whose property tended to be concentrated in integral blocks of land, benefited from providing housing for all segments of society. It was to everyone's advantage to avoid segregation and, as far as possible, to provide services, jobs, and the goods needed for everyday use in every neighborhood.

Notes

1. Munich, Bayerische Staatsbibliothek, Col. Icon., 189, commentary by Marco Rosci, *Il trattato di architettura di Sebastiano Serlio,* 2 vols. (Milan, [1967]); New York, Columbia University, Avery Library, commentary by Myra Nan Rosenfeld, *Sebastiano Serlio on Domestic Architecture* (New York; Cambridge, Mass., 1978). The MSS were first extensively studied by William Bell Dinsmoor, "The Literary Remains of Sebastiano Serlio," *The Art Bulletin* 24 (1942): pt. 1, 55–91; pt. 2, 113–54. Citations below will be made from the Avery Library MS, unless otherwise noted.

2. Among the few studies touching on Renaissance housing theory and practice are K. Forster, "Sozialer Wohnbau, Geschichte und Gengenwart," *Archithese* 8 (1973): 2–5; P. Portoghesi "Casa, palazzo e città nel Rinascimento," *Marcatrè* 2 (1964): 23ff.; H. Rosenau, "Zum Socialproblem in der Architekturtheorie des 15. bis 19. Jahrhunderts," *Festschrift für Martin Wackernagel* (Cologne, 1958), 188ff.; T. Zarebeska, "Technical Aspects of Italian Townplanning Theory in the Fifteenth and Sixteenth Century," *Actes du XIème Congrès International d'histoire des sciences,* 6 vols. (Warsaw-Crakow, 1965; Warsaw, 1968), 6:130ff.

3. Book 6, fol. 48 (text), ills., A–C.

4. Book 6, fol. 48 (text).

5. Book 6, fol. 49, ill., G–H.

6. Text, Book 6, Munich MS., fol. 49v (cf. M. Rosci, *Il trattato*) ill., Avery MS., folio L.

7. Avery MS, Projects R(fols. 60–61), S(fols. 62–64), T(fols. 65–66); see Rosen-

feld, 42, and Brian Pullan, *Rich and Poor in Renaissance Venice* (Cambridge, 1971), 25–26.

8. Rosenfeld, *Sebastiano Serlio*, 47–49; see also Gaston Zeller, "Royal Administration before the Intendants: Parliaments and Governors," in *Government in Reformation Europe*, ed. Henry S. Cohen (New York, 1972), 225–36.

9. J. H. M. Salmon, *Society in Crisis, France in the Sixteenth Century* (London, 1975), 25, 47–52, 54–55, 62–72, 92–95.

10. Rosenfeld, *Sebastiano Serlio*, 44–45, 49. Serlio included houses for clergymen in the category for gentlemen's houses in the section on country dwellings. See Book 6, fol. 13, the house of the Cardinal of Ferrera.

11. Rosenfeld, *Sebastiano Serlio*, 48; see also J. H. Hexter, *The Vision of Politics on the Eve of the Reformation, Moore, Machiavelli, Seyssel* (New York, 1973), 204–30.

12. This manuscript of thirty-six folios, mainly on parchment, is in the Munich Staatsbibliothek, Codex Icon 190. It is believed to have been composed by Serlio in Venice before he came to France. See Paolo Marconi, "Un Projetto di città militare," *Constrospazio* vol. 1, pt. 1, 1 (June 1969): 51–59; pt. 2, 3 (September–October 1969): 53–59; and Rosenfeld, 37 (fig. 17), 36, (figs. 33–35), 46–47. Behind the house of the general are located the baths and amphitheater (H).

13. Rosenfeld, *Sebastiano Serlio*, 47.

14. Leon Battista Alberti, *L'architettura (De Re Aedificatoria)*, ed. G. Orlandi and P. Portoghesi, 1 (Milan, 1966), Chapter 5, i, 335. Other passages relating to stratification in urban planning appear in Chapter 5, xiv, 399 ff; xviii, 435 ff.

15. Ibid., Ch. 7, i; 2:537.

16. *Filarete's Treatise on Architecture*, translated with an introduction and notes by John R. Spencer, 2 vols. (New Haven, 1965): 1, the translation, 2, the facsimile, chap. 12: 86, 86v; vol. 2 is taken from the major MS. of this treatise, Florence, Biblioteca Naziomole, Magliabecchianus 2, 4: 140. See also Luigi Firpo, "La città ideale del Filarete," *Studi in memoria di Gioele Solari* (Turin, 1954): 43ff.

17. Filarete, *Treatise*, 2:86, 86v.

18. Ibid., 20: 163v.; 21: 171 r, v.

19. Francesco di Giorgio Martini, *Trattati di architettura ingegneria e arte militare*, ed. C. Maltese, 2 vols. (Milan, 1967), 2: 342ff. The dating is discussed in the introduction. See R. J. Betts, *The Architectural Theories of Francesco di Giorgio* (Ph.D. diss., Princeton University, 1971), 74ff.

20. Martini, *Trattati*, 2:364ff.

21. Ibid.

22. Rosenfeld, *Sebastiano Serlio*, 36–37, figure 16, 35, 47. See also Alexander von Reitzenstein, "Die Befestigungslehre, Das Fechtbuch," in *Albrecht Dürer, 1471–1971* (Munich, 1971), 355–62; Martin Biddle, Introduction to the facsimile edition of Dürer, *Etliche Unterricht zu Befestigung der Stett, Schloss, und Flecken* (Zurich, 1971), 77–139; Hans Rupprich, *Dürer, Schriftliche Nachlass* (Berlin, 1969), 3:369–425; and Teresa Zarebska, "Théories militaires et habitations collectives," *Archithèse* 8 (1973): 9–14.

23. Rosenfeld, *Sebastiano Serlio*, 47, figure 36, 48. British Museum, Manuscript Department, Codex Additional 5229, folio 167. Dürer's drawing is similar to a house in the Calle dei Furlani in Venice of the fifteenth century. See E. Trincanato, *Venezia minore*, (Milan, 1948), 184–85, ills.

24. See E. Trincanato, "Residence collettive a Venezia," *Urbanistica* 42–43 (1965): 7–14; and Rosenfeld, *Sebastiano Serlio*, 44, fig. 31, 43.

25. Rosenfeld, *Sebastiano Serlio*, fig. 32, 44, and H. Günther, "Studien zum

venezianischen Aufenthalt des Sebastiano Serlio," *Münchner Jahrbuch der bildende Kunst,* 32 (1981): 42–94.

26. Bruno Zevi, *Biagio Rosetti architetto ferrarese* (Turin, 1960), 46, figs. 85–86.

27. Norbert Lieb, *Die Fugger und die Kunst* (Munich, 1952–58), 1: 250–58, 2: 282–86.

28. E. Garin, "La città ideale," *Scienza e vita civile nel rinascimento italiano* (Bari, 1965), 33–56.

29. Aristotle, *Politics,* trans. and ed. E. Barker (Oxford, 1946), bk. 7, viii, 6ff.

30. Plato, *The Laws,* trans. Trevor Saunders, (Harmondsworth, 1970), 5: 744.

31. Vitruvius, *De Architectura,* bk 6, v, 2–3 (Loeb ed.) 36 ff.

32. Suggested by Felix Gilbert. "Il *De Republica* di Lorenzo Quirini," in *Lauro Quirini umanista, (Civilta veneziana: Saggi,* ed. Carlo Seno and Giorgio Revegnani (Venice, 1977), bk 2: 149ff.

33. E. Re, "Maestri di strada," *Arch. Società romana di storia patria* 43 (1920): 5–101; C. Scaccia Scarafoni, "L'antico statuto di 'Magistri stratarum' e altri documenti relativi a quella magistratura," *Arch. Società romana di storia patria* (1927): 237–308.

34. The major recent contributions to the study of Renaissance urban planning in Rome have been by P. Portoghesi, *Roma nel rinascimento,* 2 vols. (Rome, 1971); Christoph Frommel, *Der Römische Palastbau der Hochrenaissance,* 3 vols. (Tübingen, 1973), 1:11–23; Luigi Salerno, Luigi Spezzaferro, Manfredo Tafuri, *Via Guilia, una utopia urbanistica del '500* (Rome, 1973); R. Fregna, "Edilizia di Roma tra il XVI e il XVII secolo," *Controspazio* 5 (1973): 48–61; L. Spezzaferro and R. Tuttle, "Place Farnèse, urbanisme et politique," in *Le Palais Farnèse,* ed. André Chastel and Georges Vallet, 3 vols. (Rome, 1981), 1:85–123; I. Insolera, *Roma, immagini e realtà dal X al XX secolo,* (Bari, 1980); J. Ackerman, "The Planning of Renaissance Rome," in *Rome in the Renaissance. The City and the Myth,* ed. P. A. Ramsey (Binghampton, 1982), 3–17; see also the studies cited in note 33.

35. R. Fregna and S. Polito, "Fonti di archivio per una storia edilizia di Roma, 1: I libri delle case dal '500 al '700: forma e esperienza della città," *Controspazio* 3 (September 1971): 2–20; "Fonti di archivio per una storia edilizia di Roma, 2: Primi dati sull' urbanizzazione nell'area del Tridente," *Controspazio* 4 (July 1972); 2–18; F. Bilancia and S. Polito, "Fonti di archivio per una storia ediliza di Roma, 3: Via Ripetta," *Controspazio* 5 (November 1973): 18–47; R. Fregna, "Edilizia a Roma tra XVI e XVII secolo," *Contraspazio* 5 (November 1973): 48–92.

36. Rome, Archivio di Stato, *Presidenza delle strade,* no. 445, fol. 199r. The entries appear under the heading. "In nomine domini amen. Questo e un getito [demolition] novamente fatto ordinato per li magnifici signori maistri de strada cio Mx Latino Juvenale di Manetti et mx hieronimo Maffeo per allargare la strada transversale delli Incoronati alla via Julia consulta la camera apostolica fatto lanno 1542 adi 6 di magio.

Case che hanno a fare restoro per dicto Iectito."

37. Jean Favier, *Paris au XVe siècle,* (Paris, 1974), 54–62, 241; and Bernard Chevalier, *Les bonnes villes de France du XIVe au XVIe Siècle,* (Paris, 1982), 29, 36–38. Both authors agree on general trends, but not on actual numbers of the population. I have used the accounting of Chevalier.

38. Chevalier, *Les bonnes villes,* 149, 162, 189–90.

39. Zeller, "Royal Administration," 238–39.

40. See Françoise Boudon, André Chastel, Hélène Couzy, Françoise Hamon, *Système de l'architecture urbaine, le Quartier des Halles à Paris* (Paris: Centre national de la recherche scientifique, 1977), vol. 1 text, and album, pl. 26, drawn by Jean Blécon.

41. The map is in the Offentliche Kunstsammlung, Basle; see H. Legrand, *Atlas des anciens plans de Paris* (Paris, 1880), vol. 1, pl. 10.

42. See Rosenfeld, "The Hôtel de Cluny and the Sources of the French Renaissance Palace, 1350–1500." (Ph. D. diss., Harvard University, 1972), 298. For the act of Parliament, see Leroux de Lincy, *Recherches sur les propriétaires et les habitants du Palais des thermes et de l'Hôtel de Cluny* (Paris, 1848), 3: 21–22, formerly Paris, Bibliothèque Royale, Chartes.

43. Rosenfeld, 299; Jacques Monnicat, *Archives Nationales, Registres des comptes de Parlement du Paris* (Paris, 1958), 402–13. Seventeenth-century copies, comptes de Jehan Lhuillier.

44. Rosenfeld, "The Hôtel de Cluny," diagram M5; Paris, *Archives Nationales, Comptles du Parlement de Paris* 402–03, folios 55v–56r.

45. See note 38 above; David Thomson, *Renaissance Paris* (London, 1984), 30–37; see also *La Maison de ville à la Renaissance* (Tours: Université François Rabelais, Centre d'Etudes Supérieurs de la Renaissance, Colloquim, 10–15 June 1983, forthcoming). Seventeenth-century initiatives in urbanism in Paris are discussed by Hillary Ballon in The Places Royales of Henry IV and the Urban Development of Paris, 1600–1615, (Ph. D. diss. Massachusetts Institute of Technology, 1985), summarized in *National Gallery of Art, Center 4, Center for Advanced Studies in Visual Arts, Reports and Record of Activities* (Washington, 1984), 33–34. See p. 28a for author's comment.

2

The Construction of Pienza (1459–1464) and the Consequences of *Renovatio*

Nicholas Adams

The village of Pienza is some thirty miles southeast of the central Italian town of Siena on a ridge that slopes gently up from two directions to form an escarpment overlooking the wide valley of the River Orcia (fig. 1).[1] Here, on the eastern fringe of the Sienese republic, Pope Pius II (Enea Silvio Piccolomini) undertook one of the most celebrated urban transformations of the Renaissance. Inspired by the ancient example of Septimius Severus at Leptis Magna and helped by the Florentine architect Bernardo Rossellino (1409–63), Pius turned his native village into a personal and family memorial. In broad outline, what Rossellino did was to realign and rebuild the Church of Santa Maria, build a family palace for the Piccolomini, and direct the renovation of the bishop's palace, the construction of the town hall, and possibly other structures (figs. 2 and 3).[2] The village was made a bishopric in August 1462 and the pope's familiars and cardinals were encouraged to buy, renovate, or build houses. The village's name was then changed from Corsignano to Pienza, in honor of its patron and most distinguished citizen.

The organization of the buildings around the central piazza, it is often remarked, is one of the masterpieces of Renaissance urban planning (fig. 4). Ludwig Heydenreich, in particular, noted the importance of Renaissance perspective theory in the layout of the main piazza and the corresponding relation of the buildings to Pius's beloved *paesaggio di patria* of Mont' Amiata; from the loggia at the rear of the family palace Pius could gain inspiration for his intellectual and political labors (fig. 5).[3]

Pienza is interpreted most frequently as a great work of humanistic scholarship. It unites an attentive reading of Vitruvius (possibly provided by Alberti), architectural elements gathered by Pius from his trips to Germany, and loving attention to nature. In *Architecture in Italy 1400–1600,* Heydenreich wrote, "Pienza was the first ideal city of the Renaissance to take on visible form."[4] In *The Architecture of the Renaissance,* the Italian architectural historian Leonardo Benevolo wrote:

Figure 1. Map of Central Italy to Show Location of Pienza. *(Courtesy of Fritz Lab Graphics, Lehigh University.)*

Here one may recognise the mark of the personality of Pius II, and the city can really be said, without any rhetorical approximation, to be the concrete image of his cultural ideal; love of form and human participation come together in a mood of literary serenity, as in the prose of the *Commentari,* and produce a balance to some degree detached from time and strangely untouched by the struggles of the century.[5]

Those who have walked through Pienza's narrow streets on a spring or summer morning, tempted on by the illuminated brilliance coming from the central piazza or detained by the chalky smell of *pecorino fresco*

Figure 2. Bernardo Rossellino, Palazzo Piccolomini, Pienza, 1460–62. *(Courtesy of Nicholas Adams.)*

coming from the doorways of the *alimentari* will have had a contemporary sense of the great beauty of Pius's achievement.

Despite the grace of today's Pienza, Pius's transformation of Corsignano was not achieved effortlessly. The burden of conception fell first on the shoulders of the pope and his architects and the task of construction fell to the masons and laborers, many of whom had to be imported from outside the area. Moreover, Corsignano was not a *tabula rasa,* an empty slate on which Pius and his architect could sketch in the *città d'autore,* as the yellow signposts leading to Pienza used to say before they were replaced by more prosaic markers. Rather, it was a village with a certain form, certain traditions, and a culture of its own; theirs were values that were poorly related to Pius's ambitions and ideals. In order to realize his humanistically inspired vision, Pius was obliged to establish political, economic, and cultural control over the village. Far from being unaffected by the struggles of the century, Corsignano was touced by elements of the kind of refeudalization found in other parts of Italy during the early Renaissance.[6] From being a tiny, agriculturally based village dominated by a small number of relatively prominent families (some of whom were probably absent much of the year), Pienza became a cult center for the pope and a dynastic home for the Piccolomini. In addition, a new aristoc-

Figure 3. Bernardo Rossellino, Cathedral, Pienza, 1460–62. *(Photo: author.)*

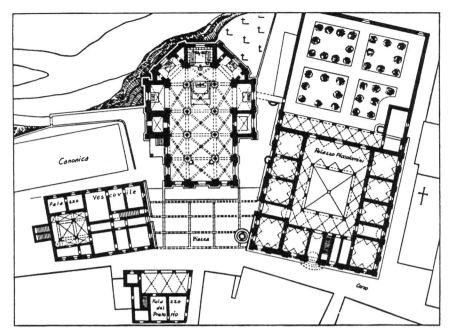

Figure 4. Plan of the Piazza Pio II. The eastern extent of the Palazzo Vescovile is somewhat exaggerated in this plan. *(Courtesy of Enzo Carli, Pienza: la Città di Pio II.)*

Figure 5. View of Mont 'Amiata from Pienza. *(Photo: author.)*

racy of Italian and foreign cardinals, papal dignitaries, and their servants moved into the village with powers that swept the traditional inhabitants of Corsignano to the side.

In the past, Pienza has been studied largely through the methods of Warburgian architectural and intellectual analysis, of which the best representative was Ludwig Heydenreich. Now, using techniques drawn from social and economic history, we may enlarge our sense of the purposes and effects of urban planning during the Renaissance. Rather than appreciating the village for its great beauty or admiring the pope for his visionary design, we shall examine what the pope's architectural ambitions did to Corsignano's native population. Through an analysis of Pius's urban plans as they affected the lowest members of society in Pienza, by seeing the effects from the ground up, so to speak, we can define in new ways the character and quality of the first example of town planning in the Renaissance style to have survived more or less intact.

It is unclear precisely when Pius was moved to reconstruct the village of Corsignano. In the *Commentaries,* his third-person autobiography, the moment of decision seems suspended between his sense of disappointment at the wretched state of Corsignano's inhabitants and his own desire for immortality prompted by his first visit to Corsignano as pope.

> Returning to it at this time he hoped to have some pleasure in talking with those with whom he had grown up and to feel delight in seeing again his native soil; but he was disappointed, for most of those who were left kept to their house, bowed down with old age and illness, or, if they showed themselves, were feeble and crippled and like harbingers of death. At every step the Pope met with proofs of his own age and could not fail to realise that he was an old man who would soon drop. Pius stayed at Corsignano for the feast of Saint Peter's Chair and said mass. He decided to build there a new church and a palace and he hired architects and workmen at no small expense that he might leave as lasting as possible a memorial of his birth.[7]

In this description of his visit of February 1459, his first in many years, Pius's memory of the past jostled with present reality. He saw his own decrepitude taken one stage further in the faces and bodies of his old neighbors. He felt a kind of romantic disillusion when he looked at the state of the comrades of his youth and was moved to sense his own mortality; as a result he claimed to seek renovation of the village as a monument to himself.

Yet the decision to renovate Corsignano was not motivated entirely by the need for personal aggrandizement of so permanent a kind. The Piccolomini family, led by the newly elected Piccolomini pope, sought to use the occasion of the ascension of one of their own to the throne of Saint

Peter to advance their interests. Of the total of 820 appointments made by Pope Pius II and recorded in the Vatican archives, Richard Hilary has noted that, broadly defined, 23.5 percent were nepotistic in nature.[8] In Siena, most notably, the Piccolomini expanded their interests. Property purchases totalling many more thousand of lire than those made in Corsignano were made by the Piccolomini in Siena: palaces (Piccolomini, della Papesse), logge (del Papa) and piazze (Piccolomini) were built (figs. 6,7,8). A major addition was made to the walls of the city of Siena in order to include the Church of San Francesco, the site of the Piccolomini family tombs within the circuit (fig. 9).[9] From the beginning, therefore, the reconstruction of Corsignano was part of an important dynastic plan by the Piccolomini as well as a memorial to the pope. Indeed, as Pius moved speedily and violently to remake Corsignano, we can see that the process of reconstruction was tightly tied to political favor and family advancement.

In late 1458, Pius II let it be known that he would bestow no pontifical favors on the Sienese unless they agreed to allow the return of the Piccolomini and the *monte* to which they belonged from political exile. Moreover, he announced that unless his demands were met, he would not even set foot in Sienese territory.[10] The rulers of Siena, from the *monte* of the *popolari,* reluctantly notified Pius, then in Perugia, that they would discuss his terms. In mid-February 1459, Pius crossed into Sienese territory for the first time as pope.[11] On 19 February 1459, he entered Corsignano. Initially, Pius sought only to improve the financial position of the village, as a set of provisions presented to the Sienese government in April 1459 make clear;[12] the decision to rebuild may have been taken over the summer, because work began only at the end of the year.[13]

The pope's involvement in Corsignano was clearly favored by the Sienese and favorable to their interests. Apart from the minimal advantages in jobs that accrued to Siena as a result of papal investments, there were important military advantages. During the same years, the Sienese had colonized Saturnia, slightly to the southwest, which served as a look-out toward the Maremma.[14] With the Florentine salient of Montepulciano to the east of Corsignano, the development of this zone to provide a regional counterbalance represented a practical defense strategy. In Sienese terms, therefore, one of the first of the pope's favors was the strengthening of one of the bordering towns.[15] In October 1459, as if affirming Sienese support for the project, new artillery was supplied to Corsignano.[16]

Pius's acquisition of Pienza came in three phases. In 1459–60 he, his Sienese family, and his Roman intimates purchased land and houses. This phase culminated with the completion of the Duomo and the Palazzo Piccolomini, inspected by the pope in August 1462. The second phase, 1462–63, included purchases by the cardinals and the pope's political allies

Figure 6. Pietro Paolo Porrina, possibly on the design of Bernardo Rossellino, Palazzo Piccolomini, Siena, begun 1462. *(Photo: author.)*

Figure 7. Bernardo Rossellino, Palazzo delle Papesse, Siena, 1460–95. *(Photo: author.)*

Figure 8. Antonio Federighi, Logge del Papa, Siena, 1462. The area between the *logge* **and the Piccolomini Palace was known as the Piazza Piccolomini** *(Photo: author.)*

and creatures, and involved the construction of the bishop's palace, the Town Hall, and renovations by the cardinals. Finally, in 1463–64, the pope continued to acquire property for himself for the newly founded diocese. The purpose of these final purchases is not entirely clear, but by this time the pope and his associates owned about 12 percent of the property in Corsignano.[17]

While new building construction must have provided jobs and money to local builders and suppliers, this period of development also must have been awkward. Awkward physically, to be sure, because the streets and the new piazza would have been so littered with materials belonging to buildings under construction and destruction that movement through the village must have been troublesome. In addition, there were new immigrants, building crews, and a papal entourage that needed to be fed, housed, and cared for.[18] To understand the difficulties created by the pope's intervention as fully as possible, we must try to imagine Corsignano before the pope's arrival. It is a difficult task, for we have no description of the village, no inventory, and not even a population count from the 1400s, when so much counting of hearths and heads was done elsewhere in Tuscany. Our best source, possibly the only one that can be quantified

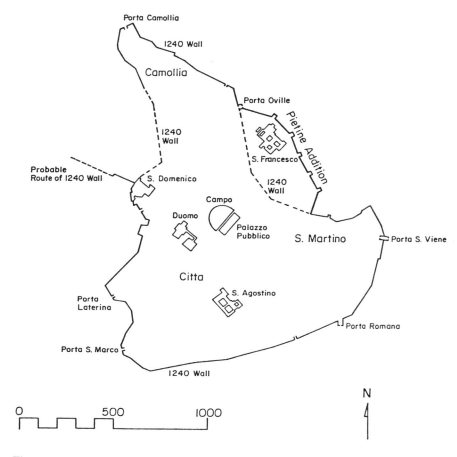

Figure 9. Plan of the City of Siena with the Pietine Addition to the Walls near San Francesco marked in double thickness. *(Courtesy of Fritz Lab Graphics, Lehigh University.)*

effectively, is an eight-hundred-folio estimo for the village of Corsignano compiled by the Sienese government circa 1320 (now in the Archivio di Stato, Siena, appropriately enough, the Palazzao Piccolomini).

Estimo 41, as it is catalogued, provides an alphabetical listing of all residents in Corsignano who own property within the walls (in *castro*) or in the surrounding region (in *curia*). Each record describes the approximate site of the property, its use, its buildings, and its adjacent properties (by owner), and ends with a valuation *(stima)*. Unfortunately, the volume is incomplete; the "A," "B," and part of the "C" entries are missing. Since many of the property-owners resided outside of Corsignano, and thus were not listed, we must rely on the adjacency listings. Nevertheless, the 342 property-owners and their properties listed in Estimo 41 form the best source we have for the construction of an economic, social, and architectural picture of pre-Pietine Corsignano. On the basis of Estimo 41 we can judge the nature of the pope's intervention and evaluate the effects of his renovation more effectively.[19]

Estimo 41 records a total of 286 houses and huts in the village; tracking missing references through the adjacencies we arrive at an approximate total of 350 houses and huts. Using the rough figure of 4.5 people per hearth, we arrive at an approximate population in Corsignano of 1,575.[20] Compared with Repetti's population figure of 1,222 for Pienza in 1833, this suggests the typical high population count of Tuscany before the Black Death.[21]

The economy of Corsignano in 1320 was based on agriculture. Those who held property in the village of Corsignano (in *castro*) held an average of 8.5 pieces of land in the countryside (in *curia*) for every piece in *castro*.[22] For every lira of assessed value in *castro,* property-holders owned an average of 8.5 lire in *curia*.[23] There was also a sizable population that owned no land whatsoever in *castro,* and there is no record of housing on their land in the country. On the average, they owned about three (2.8) country properties.[24]

Of the 342 property-holders listed in the estimo, some 144 fell into this category. Where did they live? Some, certainly, lived in the countryside. There were four farms exceeding seventy *staiori* listed in the estimo that may have been populated by sharecroppers or property-owning peasants, but there were relatively few smaller properties with a house in *curia*.[25] Thus, while some Corsignano residents lived and worked in *curia,* there must have been at least two kinds of residents in *castro* forming the bulk of the population:[26] (1) a *castro* resident with a house in *castro* who worked a number of fields on his own or with the help of others; (2) a *castro* inhabitant who owned no property in *castro,* but who had a number of smaller properties in *curia* and who had probably spent much time in the service of others. Such inhabitants may have had a part-time artigianal occupation as well.

The comparative strength and importance of agriculture can be suggested by the absence of any industrial property from the estimo and the silence of the estimo about workshops or *botteghe*. Indeed, the artisan population as a whole appears to have been relatively weak. Only four people were listed as *fabri* and though there may have been others, they either owned no property or they owned sufficient property so as not to depend wholly on their labor.[27] Of the four known *fabri,* none owned property in *castro*.

The distribution of property in Corsignano across the population reveals

Table 1

DISTRIBUTION OF PROPERTY WEALTH FROM ASS *ESTIMO* 41

% Population	% Wealth[a]	% Wealth[b]
10	0.2	0.4
20	0.87	1.2
30	1.8	2.6
40	3.4	4.8
50	5.8	8.2
60	9.3	13.4
70	14.8	20.1
80	21.3	31.0
90	37.8	49.0
100	100.	100.

[a] Based on all property-holders
[b] Based on those owning property in *castro* only

an inequality typical of this period (table 1). In relation to villages such as Piuvica near Pistoia (1243) or Impruneta near Florence (1330), both studied by David Herlihy, Corsignano's profile appears even flatter. This may not mean that the residents of Corsignano were severely impoverished; it may only mean that a great many people had a lot less than the wealthiest few. Given the nature of the estimo, it is difficult to know precisely where the propertied resided. Owners whose main residences were elsewhere were not, of course, recorded, and they were probably among the wealthiest members of the community. The largest holdings for one family were those of the Uguccione.[28] Prominent Sienese families were also recorded in the estimo and a number had considerable holdings: Buonsignori, Piccolomini, Benincasa, Orlandi, Petrucci.[29] But while the distribution of the wealth curve in *castro* reveals a high concentration of wealth in the hands of the very few as measured in property, by number no one held more than 2 percent of *castro* properties, and by value, no more than 3 percent. In short, even among the wealthy, village property was a relatively insignificant part of their total wealth.[30]

Estimo 41 does not tell us a great deal about the urban habitat of Corsignano in 1320, but it does tell us something. The scribe or notary who compiled the estimo informs us that there were some 223 houses owned individually; twenty-three sets owned as pairs; there were two groups of three and one group of four. The range of value was not great; a minimum of two lire and a maximum of two hundred lire (table 2).[31] Of course, many factors determined value: the location within Corsignano, the material, size, and state of repair. Just being in Corsignano was a mighty depressant on value. A comparison with Siena during the same period reveals values as high as three thousand lire and as low as two lire, clearly a minimum valuation.[32] Nonetheless, in Corsignano the average house valuation was thirty-three lire, with the majority of single houses falling between eleven and forty lire. With only six houses valued between ninety-one and one hundred lire and only four over one-hundred-and-one lire, we can see that there was only a relatively small group of houses that stood out because of prime size, quality, or location. Yet just as there were relatively few prominent houses, so too there were relatively few of true insignificance; *casalini* that stood on their own lots number only four, and their median value was five lire. There were only twelve houses valued at ten lire or less.

More interestingly, there was evidently relatively little open space in the

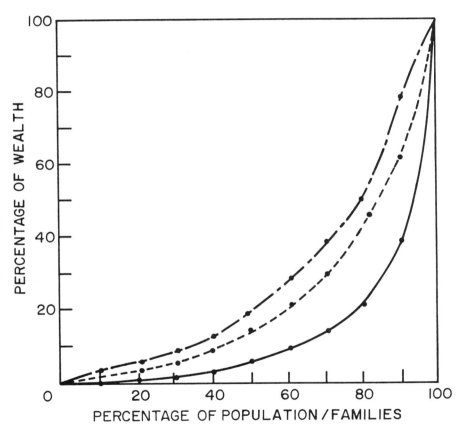

.—.—.—.—. Distribution of Taxable Wealth at Impruneta (1330) adapted from Herlihy.

------------ Distribution of Wealth in the Commune of Piuvica (1243) adapted from Herlihy.

_____ Distribution of Wealth Based on Assessed Land Values at Corsignano (1320) based on ASS *Estimo* 41.

Table 2

DISTRIBUTION OF HOUSE VALUATIONS FROM ASS *ESTIMO* 41

Lire	Number	Percentage
0–10	16	5.5
11–20	84	29.5
21–30	73	25.3
31–40	61	21.3
41–50	20	6.9
51–60	10	3.4
61–70	6	2.1
71–80	8	2.6
81–90	0	0
91–100	6	2.0
101 and over	4	1.2

Corsignano of 1320. The only piazza referred to that bounds a piece of property is the *piazza del comune* (probably, but not necessarily, the present-day Piazza del Duomo) and there were only a handful of small gardens in *castro* not attached to a house. Finally, *piazze (platée)* without houses were extremely rare; there were nine in all. Seven of these were valued at two lire each and were probably *banchi*, though two more prominent areas, possibly associated with larger market or trade areas, were valued at twenty lire each.[33]

In conclusion, everything we know about Corsignano from the estimo and from on-site observation would encourage us to assume that it had a relatively homogeneous architectural character in materials and quality. Few houses standing in Pienza today speak convincingly of pre-Pietine Corsignano (fig. 10). Overall, then, Corsignano appears to have been relatively densely built, with multihouse ownership by row or island not uncommon (table 3). Moreover, it was inhabited by a relatively poor, agriculturally based population; workers travelled daily from the village to their workplace in the fields. Like many small Tuscan towns, that migration provided the essential motif of daily life in medieval Corsignano.[34]

From 1459 to 1464, Pius and his agents and associates (including some reluctant cardinals) purchased what the Sienese tax records defined as one palace, thirty-nine houses (some with cloisters or huts), and three basements, or approximately 12 percent of Pienza's housing stock.[35] In the countryside around Pienza, Pius and his agents were also active. Purchases by Jacomo di Mino Battista Piccolomini included a *podere,* partly in Pienza and partly in Montechiello, "di qua e di la della Tressa" as the document says, for eight hundred florins (on 7 February 1459) and a number of smaller purchases by family members elsewhere totalling 350

Figure 10. House on the Via Elisa, Pienza. This seems to be one of the few houses that remain on site that may go back to pre-Pietine Corsignano. *(Photo: author.)*

Table 3
HOUSES OWNED BY NUMBER OF HOUSES BASED ON ASS *ESTIMO* 41

Single	223
Double	23
Triple	2
Quadruple	1
Casalinum	4
Palatium	1

NOTE: There is no assurance that houses listed by group were necessarily not broken by an alley or a small street. Estimo Forty-one is not unfailingly accurate with adjacencies. Nonetheless there is reasonable certainty, given the present state of Pienza, with its islands of houses and the general diffusion of single houses, that a listing of a pair or more signifies that the houses share a wall.

lire.[36] Pius's intention was to provide his memorial with a property income to maintain it.[37]

The acquisition methods employed by the pope were particularly blunt. Money was the first advantage the Piccolomini had over the local inhabitants of Corsignano; although the pope did not spend a great deal, he owned much more than anyone else. Purchases listed under his name alone amount to around thirteen thousand lire; and with the addition of purchases by his aides and retinue we arrive at over thirty thousand lire spent in the village alone.[38] Moreover, he was willing to spend what was needed and then some. In their tax denunciation of 1465, Andrea and Jacomo Piccolomini note that a number of properties were purchased at a high price by the pope so that he would not have to bargain with those poorer than himself. The property at Porrona, for example,

> was bought most dearly. And because it was owned by monks and many other people it was extremely difficult to buy at that price. Because Pope Pius wanted to leave everything in order he did not consider the cost and, moreover, since it belonged to monks and poor people he didn't want to seem to be cheap.[39]

If we look more closely at the price paid for city property in the period 1450–58 prior to the pope's intervention in Corsignano, we find prices averaging 105 lire, ranging from a high of 560 lire to a low of 4 lire (table 4). During the years of the pope's intervention, we find higher prices. Except during a lull in 1461, purchases averaged 554 lire, with a high of 2400 lire and a low of 20 lire (table 5).

The pope and his friends had not only the money to buy what they wanted but also the backing of local authorities. On 4 October 1460 the Sienese Concistoro voted in favor of the proposition that any courtier of His Holiness Pope Pius II of Siena who wishes to build a house or piazza on the main street of the *castro* of Corsignano may do so; those who own said houses or piazze must and shall sell to his courtier for an agreed price declared by two referees chosen one for each party; and if they cannot agree, the podestà of Corsignano at that time will declare said price.[40]

Even with this provision, which allowed for forced sales, the clear inference from the price paid by the pope and the testimony of his heirs suggests that prices well over market value were being paid. Given the obvious generosity of the pope, we may wonder why he faced protests.

The major trouble seems to have occurred in 1462 when the cardinals came to Corsignano to select their houses. Bartolommeo Marasca, the Mantuan ambassador, wrote to Barbara of Brandenburg that the pope spent the entire day of 12 September 1462 telling young Francesco Gonzaga that if he didn't buy a house in Pienza he would regret it. Later that day, Marasca reports that Gonzaga had bought an *isola* of four houses. But, notes Marasca, there is "great trouble and noise from the wretched men who do not wish to sell their dwellings."[41] The dense urban character of the village would not have allowed the opening of new areas, and it is unlikely, given the low level of housing turnover in the years prior to Pius's elevation, that there was a great deal available for those who were

Table 4

PROPERTY PRICES IN *CASTRO* BASED ON ASS *GABELLA DEI CONTRATTI* PRIOR TO POPE PIUS'S INTERVENTION

	Sales	High	Low	Median
1450	4	400	30	165.5
1451	1	224	224	224
1452	5	84	24	61
1453	1	40	40	40
1454	1	140[a]	140	140
1455	7[b]	150	29	87
1456	4	108	33	72
1457	8	560[c]	4	112
1458	4	440[d]	16[e]	127
Total	35			105

[a] Ass *Gabella dei Contratti* 227, fol. 27 includes two pieces of vineyard, a piece of land and a garden totalling 5⅓rd *staiori*.

[b] Includes the sale of one piazza sold on its own.

[c] ASS *Gabella dei Contratti* 233, fol. 62v sale of the house which includes piazza, cistern and oven.

[d] ASS *Gabella dei Contratti* 236, fol. 25 sale of the house includes dovecote.

[e] ASS *Gabella dei Contratti* 237, fol. 2 is sale of ¼ house "pro industria."

Table 5

PROPERTY PRICES IN *CASTRO* BASED ON ASS *GABELLA DEI CONTRATTI*
DURING POPE PIUS'S INTERVENTION

	Sales	High	Low	Median	Total
1459	10	1000	40	423	4232
1460	16	2000	6	327	5233
1461[a]	8	160	8	65	522
1462	30	6795	10	598	17926
1463	16	2110	10	399	6387
1464	6	8500	27	1702	10217
	86			518	44517

[a]None of the purchases during this year were by the pope or his followers.

bought out by the pope. Very few among this group returned to the
housing market.[42] Even with the pope's inflated prices, with the backing of
the Sienese government two hundred lire might buy a house for a cardinal,
but that same two hundred lire might not be converted into a residence for
the peasant and his family. Moreover, for renters (or nonowners) who lived
in *castro* the situation would have been doubly difficult, for they would
have received no compensation and would have been forced to find new
accommodations as well! The house in *castro,* after all, served not only as
a residence for the owner but as a base for labor operations; from the
house the peasant went out to his fields in the morning and to that house
he returned at night. The destruction of that base eliminated part of the
natural economic ecology of Corsignano. Thus Corsignano residents
might well have been extremely angry.

Other problems were created by the pope's new interests in Corsignano.
Housing for the courtiers was difficult to find and agents were dispatched
to study the problem.[43] On the occasion of the pope's first visit to Corsignano, his courtiers were sent off to Cuna, a *grancia* owned by the Hospital
of Santa Maria della Scala, because there was nowhere to stay. More
troublesome was the fact that there never seemed to be enough food for
the pope and his entourage and food had to be sent from Siena.[44] The
pope's activities must have brought a new kind of person into Corsignano;
although the social and property patterns were unique, the situation recalls
those of many towns and villages whose populations had been disturbed
by the arrival of new aristocracies "on vacation."[45] On the one side was a
highly regimented working-class culture; on the other, a new class of
service workers and their leisured employers. The baptismal records of
1466–75 reflect the new situation.[46] One can well imagine the anger of the
residents of Corsignano at the callous righteousness of wealthy Sienese,
Mantuans, and Romans walking the muddy streets of Corsignano looking
for a house to buy.

The pope certainly became aware of some of the problems created by his development of the town. Two practical responses were made to the gentrification of Corsignano. In 1463 a group of twelve houses, the so-called *case nuove,* were built by Pietro Paolo Porrina, a Sienese mason and assistant to Bernardo Rossellino (fig. 11). They were rented either singly or were divided among families; it is probable that others were intended for some of the "wretched men" dispossessed by the pope and his entourage; the income went to the new chapter.[47] The pope also left money in his will for the construction of something of lasting value for the village, a mill.[48] The pope's concern was registered first in August 1462, after the cardinals had made their purchases, when Niccolò Severini noted the pope's pleasure at the new constructions, the Duomo and the Palazzo Piccolomini, "worthy things . . . appropriate and well disposed." But the pope also "wants to build there something that will be worthy, glorious and useful for the wretched men who have given their own works and useful to those who will be in charge."[49] Whether it was the houses or the mill that was on the pope's mind we do not know; both produced income. What is clear is that the pope saw the consequences of some of his actions and sought, in some way, to mitigate their effect.

Pope Pius forced foreign values on Corsignano. Two of the pope's key gifts suggest how he wanted the new village/city to conceive of itself. One

Figure 11. Pietro Paolo Porrina, The *Case Nuove,* Pienza, 1462–65. *(Photo: author.)*

was a *mappamondo*, which the Pope had painted in Rome by a certain Venetian, Girolamo Bellavista, and sent up to Pienza.[50] With this addition Pienza became an identifiable place; it could define itself in cosmological and geographic space. Pius's second gift was a clock, to enable the village to partake of the modern conception of chronology;[51] time measurement "gave the employer bounds to fill and the worker bounds to work"[52] It certainly must have opened up changes in the way work was defined, changes that may not always have been welcome.[53] And the old residents must have been startled by many of the new customs of the visitors: a shipment of oranges and pomegranates would have been cause for wonder.[54]

In the construction of the new central core and in the embellishment of the main street, Pope Pius also forced foreign values on Corsignano. The palaces and the church that he caused to be built represented not only a new scale of building but a new style. This does not mean simply that their formal character was of the Renaissance, but rather something larger. These buildings bypassed principles of traditional village function as conceived in medieval society to make a larger symbolic, dynastic, and political statement. The cardinals, too, contributed to this change. Cardinal Jean Jouffroy, for example, brought a new scale of construction to the main street.[55] The imposition of this proprietary domination by the Piccolomini through the new abstract ideology of space and time, through city planning and architectural form, may strike us as bold, possibly even brave, but certainly as self-centered and insensitive. Even the Piccolomini who inherited the great family palace were mystified when they thought of its practical purpose. In their tax declarations they stated that it was without value whatsoever "except for its fame," which "daily brings a fair number of foreigners from far away who add to our expenses."[56] Indeed, in later years the arrival of foreigners to use Pienza was the source of great difficulty; now "on the map," she could be found by those who might have just passed her by in the past.

In 1502 Cesare Borgia chose Pienza as the site for an encampment in his campaign against Siena.[57] In 1525 Don Lope Soria used Pienza as the site for negotiations between the Sienese government and an exiled political faction.[58] In both cases, armed forces moving into Pienza suffered the typical troubles associated with visiting troops. But the most interesting of the ripples that derived from Pius's aggrandizement of Corsignano occurred during Sienna's mid-sixteenth-century wars. In 1552 Paul de la Barthe, sieur de Thermes, the commander of the French troops in Siena, ordered the defense of sixteen towns in the Sienese *contado* in readiness for Spanish attack. In the original lists, Pienza was not included; smaller towns like nearby Montechiello were to be carefully defended, but the two gently sloping access routes (from San Quirico and Montepuliciano) must have persuaded the French captains that no useful defense could be made at Pienza. The Piccolomini protested the omission of Pienza, their private fiefdom, so strongly that government policy was changed and a *commissario,* Conte Achille d'Elci, was sent to Pienza to build a pair of bastions on the road from San Quirico and a ditch toward Montepulciano.[59] It was clearly an absurdly conceived assignment, and despite the provision of a thousand *guastatori,* badly needed elsewhere, the Sienese representative wrote the government of the impossibility of a successful defense. Indeed, when the Spaniards chose to present themselves at Pienza on 26 February 1553, the Sienese defenders simply walked away leaving Pius's town to the enemy.[60] During the ensuing years, Pienza was more than once sacked and the only serious engagment fought there, in June 1557, was a fine escalade planned and led by the crafty French soldier Blaise de Monluc.[61]

We have seen a new Pienza, one that united some of the new formal abstractions of Renaissance urbanism with the kind of control that had characterized feudalism. Renaissance "feudalism" looks different from medieval feudalism—it defines time and space in new ways. The pope's sense of responsibility toward the village emerged after he began construction of his memorial and after the people of Corsignano had protested. For them there was no new order, merely the imposition of an old order with troublesome consequences for their livelihoods and their way of life. Fame and glory accrued to Pius, Piccolomini, and Pienza, but for its inhabitants there was only unwelcome notoriety. This image of Pienza leads us to a new reading of Italian urbanism in this period. While it is true that intellectual theories required new kinds of architecture and new kinds of space, they also required traditional forms of political power and pressure of the kinds that did not go out of style in the fifteenth and sixteenth centuries. Indeed, the demands for grander, wider, and finer open spaces within the city may well have created for rulers a need to reassert ever more forcefully political and economic prerogatives, prerogatives that continue to characterize early modern Europe.

Appendix

Pope Pius II proposes tax relief and financial aid for the village of Corsignano to the Sienese government. ASS *Consiglio Generale* 228, fols. 105–105 v. 28 April 1459.

Magnifici et potenti Signori .S. priori Governatori del Comune et Capitnao di populo instantia. La Santità di Nostro Signore papa pio più et più volte ha adomandato ala nostra comunita di fare qualche gratia ad la terra et huomini di Corsignano. Et veduto ne dí passati le provisioni ordinate essarsi perdute in simile conseglio L'è paruto ad contemplatione dela Sua Beatitudine compilare le infrascritte provisioni et dinanzi ale Vostre Spectabilita proponare.

In prima che la conmunita e huomini di Corsignano predetta dal dì della approbatione della presente provisioni in la per lo advenire in perpetuo non sieno tenuti ad pagare al Magnifico Comune di Siena o ad altri per lui alcuna tassa ò gabella excepto quelle che per infino a questo di fussero state concedute in detta a Castellani ò altri. Ma esse sintendino relassate in modo non sieno per detta cagione più molestati. Et sieno tenuti li executori di Gabella fare adaptare le scripture in termini valida et habbisi in tutte le cose come se pagassero dette taxe et taxioni o gabelle.

Item che el Comune et huomini dessa terra et terrieri dessa habitanti in essa terra et altri conferenti inveritate con loro habitanti in essa terra ò corte dessa non sieno tenuti ne obligati per lo advenire di pagare alcuna gabella di mosto si ricogliesse per loro nella corte dessa terra, ma si essa gabella alloro imperpetuo rilassate. Con questo che per detto rilasso paghino ogni anno al Comune di Siena et per esso ali Castellani a quali erano deputati le loro tasse lire cinquanta. Et con questa limitatione che se alcuno de detti terrieri et conseventi conmettesse alcuna fraude per volere sotto questo rilasso fare che di altro vino non si pagasse la cabella ordinata sintenda per ciascuno grosso pagarne tredici. Et per obviare quanto si puo che fraude non si conmetta sintenda inviolabilmente proveduto che non possino comprare vino da alcun altra persona obligata ad pagare detta Gabella in qualunque luogo si fusse ne imbottare se prima non se scripto el vino in detti luoghi ad quelli debbano pagare dali scriptori o altri ad ciò ordinati pena ad qualunque contrafacesse cosi venditore come compratore lire cinquanta per ciascuna persona et per ciascuno et ciascuna volta da pagarsi dette penna di facto al monte. Et possino di ciò essere cogvitori et executori tutti li offitiali del Comune di Siena et nominatem li executori et sei de .xxiv. et lo notaio di Gabella et abbi di quarto lo offitiale el quarto lo accusatore et laltra metà si del monte.

Item ad contemplactione del prefato Sanctissimo Papa Pio secondo che qualunque persona del contado et Iurisdicione di Siena fusse absentia dela Città contado et Iurisdictione di Siena ad un anno addrieto per debito civile havesse con alcuna persona particulare possi liberamente et securamente ad dare ad habitare in essa terra et sua corte et sia securo in avere et in persona per tempo di anni dieci e quali finiti sieno tenuti et obligati tali debitori a pagare a loro creditori ogni anno soldi due per lire de tuto quello avessero ad pagare et ad pui non possino essere gravati.

Item atteso che esso comun ogni sei mesi pagha al podestà di Sancto Quirico lire novantatre denari dieci che di calende febraio proximo ad venire in la non sieno tenuti pagare ad detto podesta detta lire .lxxxxiii. denari .x. ma al tucto al pagamento di quelle sieno // liberi et exempti. Et intendasi proveduto che alloro vicaro che a Gennaio proximo incominciara el suo offitio et successive alli altri paghino oltra le sexanta pagano al presente lire quaranta in tutto lire cento per ciascuno sei mesi et tenghi uno fameglio El quale si eleghi in questo modo che el detto Comune et huomini eleghino tre per monte come toccha si che di mano in mano ogni monte abbi el suo de quali uno che sara approvato per li Magnifici Signori e Gonfaloniere sintenda essere loro vicaro con le vacationi ordinate Et fa febraio proximo in la El podesta di Sancto Quirico non vi abbi alcuna auctorita nelle civile.

Item che al detto Comune et huomini sia lecito in perpetuo fare le fiere et mercato generale in detta terra et loro corte del mese di maggio da incominciarsi adi tre del detto mese immediate doppo vespero cioe finita la indulgentia di plenaria rimessione la quale comincia adi due del detto mese ad vesparo Et dura per infino ad vesparo del di seguente. Et duri el detto mercato sei dì Al quale durante detto tempo sia lecito securamente ad ciascuno andare stare et prenoctare et per allora con sue bestie et cose come lo parra non obstanti qualunque debiti publici o private Excepti li condennati per malefitio salvo sempre che nissuna cosa possa trarve fuore di quello di Siena senza pagamento dela della gabella ordinata. Et che si lecita a ogni persona della Citta et contado si Siena portare al detto mercato ogni qualità di vino pane et carne et pescie crudo et cotto et vendare ad minuto pagando prima la debita cabella ala detta Communita di Corsignano.

Et in tutte le altre cose esso comune et huomini sia tenuto et obligato al Magnifico Comune di Siena comme è al presente. Et più altesi li predetti rilassi sieno obligati ad mantenere et rifare sempre le loro mura quando et quante volte bisognasse ad tutte loro spese siché el comune per lo advenire non v'è abbi ad mettare denaio.

Item se avessero aver dal Comune di Siena alcuna quantità di denari o altra cosa non possino domandare alcuna cosa si che in tutto el Comune di Siena da esso debito sia libero.

Et le predette gratie et rilassi giudicono di benignitade doversi fare ala detta Communità per contemplatione dela Santita pel prefato Sommo Pontefice papa pio el quale con instantia della communita ha raccomandata da la cui Santita la vostra comunita infiniti benefitii ha ricevuti et sperarsi riceverare come da pastore benignissimo el clementissimo et affectionatissimo ala sua dolce patria.

Notes

1. My research on Pienza has been aided by grants from the National Endowment for the Humanities (summer stipend), the Mellon Committee on Faculty Development at Lehigh University, the Università degli Studi, Aquila/Department

of Italian Studies at the University of Pennsylvania, and the North Atlantic Treaty Organization (Research Grant #RGOO180: Study of a Historical Town by Sampling). I have also been aided by the advice and comments of Samuel K. Cohn, Henry A. Millon, Michael Baylor, Richard A. Goldthwaite, and the late Judith Hook. As always, the staff of the Archivio di Stato, Siena, Sonia Fineschi and Nello Barbieri in particular, were of great help. Don Aldo Franci kindly let me spend time in the Archivio Vescovile, Pienza.

2. The major general work on Pienza is by Enzo Carli, *Pienza: la città di Pio II* (Rome, 1967). See also Giancarlo Cataldi, Fausto Formichi et al., *Rilievi di Pienza* (Florence, 1977), Luciana Finelli and Sara Rossi, *Pienza, tra ideologia e realtà* (Beri, 1979), C. R. Mack, *Studies in the Architectural Career of Bernardo di Matteo Ghamberti called Rossellino* (Ph.D. Dissertation, University of North Carolina, Chapel Hill, 1972), and Armando Schiavo, *Monumenti di Pienza* (Milan, 1942). See, most recently, C. R. Mack, *Pienza: The Creation of a Renaissance City* (Ithaca, N.Y., 1987).

3. L. H. Heydenreich, "Pius II als Bauherr von Pienza," *Zeitschrift für Kunstgeschicte* 6 (1937): 105–46. This important article has now been translated by Eric Garberson and will appear in *Studi e Documenti* 13 (1988).

4. L. H. Heydenreich and Wolfgang Lotz, *Architecture in Italy 1400–1600* (Baltimore, 1974), 43.

5. Leonardo Benevolo, *The Architecture of the Renaissance,* 2 vols. (Boulder, Colo., 1978) 1:163.

6. See Ruggiero Romano, "Agricoltura e contadini nell'Italia del XV e del XVI secolo," *Tra due crisi: L'Italia del Rinascimento* (Turin, 1971), 59–68. In Lombardy refeudalization took on a more legalistic cast; see Giorgio Chittolini, "Infeudazioni e Politica Feudale nel Ducato Visconteo-Sforzesco," *Quaderni Storici* 19 (1972): 57–130. In Tuscany, see the instances cited by Judith Brown *In the Shadow of Florence: Provincial Society in Renaissance Pescia* (New York, 1982). John Muendel has also spoken to me about cases of refeudalization in the Casentino where the Hospital of Santa Maria Nuova moved onto large tracts of land as a corporate landowner. I am grateful to Ronald Weissman who provided me with much of this bibliography and who suggested that I test it against the Pienza material.

7. A. S. Piccolomini, *Memoirs of a Renaissance Pope: The Commentaries of Pius II,* transl. Florence A. Gragg (New York, 1959), 102. A new Latin edition edited by Adriano van Heck has been issued in the series *Studi e Testi* (312 and 313): Pii II, *Commentarii Rerum Memorabilium Que Temporibus Suis Contigerunt* (Vatican City, 1984).

8. Richard B. Hilary, "The Nepotism of Pope Pius II 1458–1464," *Catholic Historical Review* 64 (1978): 33–35.

9. The records of the *Gabelle dei Contratti* in the Archivio di Stato, Siena (hereafter ASS) reveals the extraordinary investment in Siena made by the Piccolomini. This investment is currently being investigated by Irene Fosi Polverini.

10. Ludwig Pastor, *History of the Popes,* 24 vols. (London, 1949) 3:51; Piccolomini, *Memoirs,* 98–99. See also ASS *Consiglio Generale* 228, fols. 96–97 (15 April 1459).

11. Pastor, *History,* 3:51–52; Piccolomini, *Memoirs,* 101.

12. ASS *Consiglio Generale* 228, fols, 105–105 v (28 April 1459). This document, unpublished so far as I know, provides an interesting demonstration of the development of Pius's thinking about Corsignano. I have transcribed this deliberation in Appendix 1.

13. The decision to start work on Pienza was taken during the spring or summer, in all probability, but the first acquisitions were not made until the fall. See Adams, "The Acquisition of Pienza 1459–1464," *Journal of the Society of Architectural Historians* 44 (1985): 97–108.

14. Giovanni Cecchini, "Saturnia, l'opera di colonizzazione senese nel secolo XV," in *Studi in onore di Amintore Fanfani,* 3 vols. (Milan, 1962) 2 : 301–65.

15. Montepulciano had been part of Florentine territory since the 1390s and the border was often troubled. Andrea and Jacomo Piccolomini in their tax declaration of 1465 (ASS *Lira* 160, unpaginated) note that their holdings on the border with Montepulciano "in times of war your honors know how they are treated." In 1496 the Sienese again took control of Montepulciano. The first task was to refortify the town in the direction of Florence; see S. Borghesi and L. Banchi, *Nouvi Documenti per la Storia dell 'Arte Senese* (Siena, 1898) 355–57.

16. ASS *Concistoro* 558, fol. 24 (1 October 1459).

17. Adams, in "Acquisition," documents this process more completely. From "Acquisition," I was able to make a rough map of Pienza and show the sequence of purchases by area. The figures will be analyzed later in the text of this paper.

18. The feeding and housing of the entourage was of great concern to the Sienese. In January 1459 Antonio di Giovanni was ordered to make "all those necessary and appropriate provisions which are expedient in order to receive the most Holy Shepherd. . . . Providing rooms and all needed and necessary things, abundant provisions such that it will satisfy the comfort of all those who follow his Holiness the Pope." (ASS *Concistoro* 1677, fol. 11 v. 29 January 1459). In a letter to the ambassador with the pope (11 February 1459), orders were given to forward those who could not be accommodated in Corsignano on to Cuna (ASS *Concistoro* 1677, fols. 16 v–17). There were also appeals to local communities "to make furnaces and cut wood and other necessary things" (ASS *Concistoro* 1677, fol. 65, 22 May 1459). Issues were also raised regarding the storage of building materials (ASS *Concistoro* 1678, fol. 68, 23 May 1460).

19. ASS *Estimo* 41 is not an easy document to read. There is no title page or introductory matter. The modern numbering runs from fol. 1 to fol. 846 with the original numbering beginning at fol. 175 and running up to fol. 1046. The first reference is to the property of Coluccio Berti (original pagination fol. 175). The references are organized by landholder with the name of the landholder, his or her place of origin, and a description of the property. This is followed by an estimated value in lire. Below the valuations are often found dated sales and transfers made after the valuation; these sometimes cancel ownership of one property and add it to another list. The first of these additional notes is dated 1321, which gives us a date around 1320 for the preparation of the estimo. Since the volume is alphabetical, I have referred to property references by owner rather than by giving folio numbers. *Estimo* 41 is divided into two parts; the original valuation of circa 1320 (fols. 1–625) and records of later sales and transaction (fols. 626–846). The first section is written entirely in one hand. The scribe appears to be relatively consistent, and terms like *domum, casalinum* and *palatium* seem reasonably related to price valuations. Ideally the study of *Estimo* 41 should be carried on in conjunction with archaeological study in Pienza.

20. It is an approximate total because in a few instances the scribe refers to *domibus* without number. I have counted these references as two houses although it is possible that there were more. For the determination of population I have used relatively low multipliers. Note that they varied from a high of six at San Gimignano (Enrico Fiumi, *Storia economica e sociale di San Gimignano* [Florence,

1961] 159), to four at Prato and 4.65 at Pistoia (David Herlihy, *Medieval and Renaissance Pistoia: The Social History of an Italian Town* [New Haven], 61.)

21. Emanuele Repetti, *Dizionario Geografico Fisico Storico della Toscana* 5 vols. (Florence, 1841) 4:196. This phenomenon is discussed extensively by Herlihy, *Pistoia*, 102–20.

22. $1676 \div 198 = 8.4646$.

23. 90,240 lire $\div$ 10634 lire $= 8.4859$ lire.

24. Those who were taxed for land and property in Corsignano probably did not have a house elsewhere; in all probability a resident of Corsignano used his house as his major base.

25. The four farms were owned by the heirs of Pietro Accursi (70 *staiori*, 911 lire, 13 soldi, 4 denari); Paruta Uguccione (122 *staiori*, 1294 lire, 13 soldi), which is noted "cum palatio et domum"; Rosso Bandi (107 *staiori*, 963 lire); Sozzo Uguccione (92 *staiori*, 944 lire), which is noted with "palatium, domum" and land dedicated to vineyard and forest. Of smaller properties with houses in the countryside, I note only one belonging to the heirs of Venturelli Folceri that had only eight *staiori* and is valued at 34 lire and 13 soldi.

26. Characteristics of the relation between city and country workers have been explored by Enrico Fiumi, "Sui rapporti economici tra città e contado nell 'età communale," *Archivio Storico Italiano* 114 (1956): 18–68. See also David Herlihy, *Pistoia*, 121–47 and Brown, *Pescia*, 94–95.

27. Carlo di Jacopo *faber* owned four pieces of property with a total valuation of 140 lire 6 soldi. Gratianellus *faber* had one piece of land valued at 52 lire and 4 soldi. Maestro Albertoccio, a Lombard *muratore*, owned a small garden valued at 2 lire 13 soldi.

28. I have summarized the holdings for each individual: Peruzzo Uguccione, 1 property, 23 lire, 7 soldi; Petruccio Uguccione, 13 properties, 784 lire, 5 soldi; Paruta Uguccione, 28 properties, 4645 lire; Sozzo Uguccione, 19 properties, 3931 lire, 8 soldi.

29. Casella Benincasa, 20 lire, heirs of Nino Buonsignori, 2351 lire, 19 soldi; magister Domenico Orlandi, 753 lire, 9 soldi; Nino Chigi, 169 lire, 4 soldi; Tessa Petrucci, 92 lire, 17 soldi. The heirs of Corrado Piccolomini are cited in the adjacencies (see Coluccio di Betto). Although relatives of prominent Sienese families, they were not particularly well off.

30. The largest single landholder listed with property in *castro* was Ser Meo Benedicti, who owned at least six properties (*domibus*, again) worth a total of 344 lire.

31. In other instances, as in the case of Ser Meo (see fn. 30) an owner was referred to as owning "houses" (*domos* or *domibus*). There is no way that I know of determining the number of houses owned. I have counted these references as two houses, although it might easily have been as many as four.

32. The house valued at 200 lire was owned by Ser Meo and bounded the hospital (or land owned by it), property of Meo di Giovanni, two streets. The most likely location would have been the site of the present-day Palazzo Vescovile or a fraction of it. We do not know which other palaces faced the main piazza. The communal palace, listed under the holdings of the commune of Corsignano, is flanked by a street and property owned by the Hospital of Santa Maria della Scala. Duccio Balestracci and Gabriella Piccini, *Siena nel Trecento: Assetto Urbano e strutture edilizie* (Florence, 1977), 113–30. Unfortunately, Piccini and Balestracci do not provide regression analyses, thus effective comparisons cannot easily be made. On the whole their figures are rather difficult to read.

33. The *piazze* valued at two lire were owned by Duccio Bartalini, Grillo Grilli, Meo di Giovanni, Nutio Renaldi (2), Tessa Bindinelli (2). Those valued at twenty lire were owned by Guidoccio Ranucci and Nino Giovanni Boria. The house on the "platea comunis" was owned by Ser Meo Benedicti and was valued at two hundred lire.

34. I take this image from the description of Brown, *Pescia*, 61–74. See also Emilio Sereni, *Storia del Paessaggio Agrario Italiano* (Bari, 1961), and Maria Serena Mazzi and Sergio Raveggi, *Gli Uomini e le cose nelle Campagne Fiorentine del Quattrocento* (Florence, 1983). Contemporary descriptions of peasant life in Europe are evocative. See, for example, John Berger, *Pig Earth,* (New York, 1981) or Carlo Levi, *Cristo si è fermato a Eboli* (Turin, 1945). See also the classic sociological study of peasant life in France, Laurence Wylie, *Village in the Vaucluse* (Cambridge, 1957).

35. See Adams, "Acquisition," 104–05.

36. Jacomo Piccolomini's purchase was from Bartolommeo Petroni (ASS *Gabella dei Contratti* 237, fol. 20).

37. In relation to a property near Montichiello, for example, the tax denunciations read, "It was bought for a lot of money, because Pope Pius has built the palace in Pienza and wanted to leave it a dowry in order to maintain it; thus, he did not count every penny" (ASS *Lira* 161, unpaginated). Extensive references to Pienza are found in *Lira* 161 recording the holdings of the entire Piccolomini family at the death of Pius. Enea and Carlo Piccolomini note, for example, "that during the time of Pope Pius even though we were Piccolomini we were not papal in our earnings."

38. These figures are inherently untrustworthy. It is difficult to know exactly what Pius himself bought and what was for his courtiers. Moreover, the Roman documents published by Mack in *Rossellino* must be included and it is hard to know where they overlap with the Siena documents. The more significant point surely is that the pope had a sackful of money to spend in relation to the locals.

39. (ASS *Lira* 160, unpaginated). "Fu tenuta carissima. Et perchè era in mano di frati & di più altre persone pure grande fadiga fu haverla per lo detto pregio et perche papa Pio ebbe desiderio di lassarci uno bello capo strigato non volse guardare a denari & anco essendo cosa di frati & povare persone non volse guardare al sottile." The tax declarations of Jacomo and Andrea Piccolomini are the most interesting: "Item in nela città di Pientia uno palazo con sue appartenentie el quale come ciascuno puo sapere ci da spesa gradissima senza alcuna utilita che per la fama sua" and as a result they give no valuation. They also own "nela corte di Pientia due poderi uno chiamato Palazuolo & l'altro Casale," but these are given a valuation along with other properties at Bibbiano, Petroio and Montechiello.

40. ASS *Concistoro* 564, fols, 18 v–19. "Quod si aliquis ex cortisianis D(omini) N(ostri) pape Pii II Senensis vellet emere aliquam domum et platean pro edificando iunxta stratem principalem castri Corsignani. Illi qui habet ibi domos ut plateas debeant et teneant illas vendere dictis cortigianis pro convenienti pretio declarando pro duos arbitros eligandos unam pro quolibet parte et si non essent in concordia potestas Corsignani que pro temporem fuerit sit tum vis et declarandum dicti pretia. . . ."

41. D. S. Chambers, "The Housing Problems of Cardinal Francesco Gonzaga," *Journal of the Warburg and Courtauld Institutes* 39 (1976), 41 (document 12).

42. Francesco Antoncello Turini, for example, sold a house for 200 lire (ASS *Gabella dei Contratti* 238, fol. 32 v, 12 September 1459). He later purchased a

house for 84 lire from the Commune (ASS *Gabella dei Contratti* 243, fol. 9, 2 December 1461). He was also active elsewhere in the land market. Niccolò Diedi sold a house on 2 September 1462 (ASS *Gabella dei Contratti* 245, fol. 29) for 320 lire. He later bought a house for the same price (ASS *Gabella dei Contratti* 245, fol. 35 v, 6 October 1462).

43. ASS *Concistoro* 2004, no. 13 (19 July 1462). A letter from the *podestà* notes "Ieri fu chivi Misser gilioforte (Giliforte di Buonconto, papal treasurer) trexauriere di nostra S(antita) et Misser Nicholo picholuomini che intendare chome queste stanze sono inpunto et ciarcharo molte chase per disfare et rifare et tutte misuraro et portaro iniscrittis perche io fui molto chonesso loro intesi che nuovamente cisidia fare cinchue chase per chortigiani. . . ."

44. The problems emerge early on, see ASS *Concistoro* 1677, fol. 11 (29 January 1459); *Concistoro* 1677, fols. 17 v–18 (12 February 1459). Cuna wasn't even large enough, see *Concistoro* 1993, no. 70 (21 February 1459). The accommodations for the pope's entourage was even a problem in Siena, see *Concistoro* 1682, fols. 20 v–21 (2 February 1464).

45. This relation has not been studied historically, so far as I know. I have drawn my image of life in Pienza from such sociological studies as Ulla Wagner, "Out of Time and Place—Mass Tourism and Charter Trips," *Ethnos* 42 (1977) : 38–52, and Valene Smith, *Hosts and Guests: The Anthropology of Tourism* (Philadephia, 1977). The number of foreigners brought into the village is not easily determined. *Estimo* 41 includes so-called "Lombards," e.g., Domenico Lombardo and Maestro Albertoccio Lombardo, and prior to the intervention of the pope there were records of Lombards there in the fifteenth century, e.g., a certain Giovanni di Jacopo Guglielmi de Lucani Lombardi (ASS *Gabella dei Contratti* 234, fol. 41, 11 November 1457).

46. The record of baptisms in the Archivio Vescovile, Pienza, *Battesimi* 1466–1567, is rich in interest. A rough count of baptisms in the first years of the volume shows the following: 1466, 29 (May-December); 1467, 42; 1468, 52; 1469, 43; 1470, 46. During 1466–67 the parents and testators are largely local with a mixture of foreign-born carpenters and masons (e.g., fol. 3, Tomme Giovanni di maestro Giovanni da Bogna maestro di Pietra, baptized 21 December 1466; fol. 5 v Francesca Alexandra di maestro Pietro Pauolo maestro di legname di Domenico di Pietro da Pientia, 17 April 1466). Later (1468–71) the children of the inhabitants of the great palace are brought to the font by visitors and friends of the Piccolomini e.g., fol. 7 Ser Giovanni di Crivelli da Malano *(sic?)* "prete in peregrinaggio" acts as a testator 25 January 1468; fol. 8 v, Misser Nicholao di Jacomo da Pacini da Ferrara "servitore familiare del Reverendissimo Cardinale di Pavia" acts as a testator 27 July 1468; fol. 11 v, Gironimo di Andrea da Castel Sancto Giovanni di qua di Firenza habitante in Pientia & factore di Messer Nanni Picholhoumini acts as a testator, 30 July 1469; fol. 11 v, Matteo di Geri da Fiesole gharsone & lavoratore del sopra decto Misser Nanni Picholomini acts as a testator, 20 July 1469. Other examples, see fols. 11 v. 18 August and 23 September 1469, 13 v 3 April 1469, fol. 14 25 July 1469, 14 v 11 November 1470, fol. 15 6 January 1471. The origins of the testators and infants brought to baptism will form part of a future study. For now, note the following baptism (20 August 1469): "Matteo di Martino di Michele delle parti di Egipto di battizò adi 20 di decto. Levollò dal sacro fonte Monsignore Domenico di Piero da Sarteano canonico pientino" ("Matteo di Martino di Michele from the parts of Egypt baptized on the 20th of said month. Lifted from the sacred well by Monsignore Domenico di Piero da Sarteano, canon of Pienza").

47. Fausto Formichi, "Le Dodici Case Nuove di Pienza," *Studi e Documenti di Artchitettura* 7 (1978): 119–28. Also the talk by Henry A. Millon, "Housing Types and Possible Sources: Housing in Pius II's Pienza" (with Nicholas Adams), College Art Association Annual Meeting, San Francisco, 1980. On the rental of the *case nuove,* see Archivio Vescovile, Pienza (hereafter AVP) *Libro di Pigione* (1531–43). The houses were numbered up to twelve. There are records of gifts to the poor of Pienza, such as a payment recorded in the Archivio di Stato, Roma (hereafter ASR) *Camerale I* (Tesoreria Segreta) 1288, fol. 77, 8 April 1462 "a uno povaro homo da corsigniano" and fol. 119 v 18 September 1462 "a Monna Lisabetta da pientia vecchia con parecchie nipoti piccoli." There is also a payment to "quindici povari homeni" on 26 September 1462, but a location is not specified (*Camerale I* 1288, fol. 121 v). In 1463–64 the pope's activity seems to have been concentrated on providing an income for the new chapter.

48. "Esponsi per li vostri servitori comunita & homini dela citta vostra di Pienza. Come havendo la sancta memoria di papa Pio lassato ala loro comunita ducati trecento di camera per farne qualche capitale, decti vostri servitori hanno principato uno mulino con gualchiere. . . ." ASS *Concistoro* 2133, fol. 20, 16 June 1466.

49. ". . . et pargli avere fatto cose degne si come sonno/et ogni spesa e benfatta/ avuto respetto agli hedifitii in se/perche sono molto apti et bene composti/piacia a dio/fargli avere vogla di hedificare costa che selofa fara cosa molto degna et gloriosa/et utile per gli povari huomini che prestaranno lopare loro/et utile a chi ne rimarra padrone. . . ." ASS *Concistoro* 2004, no. 30, 11 August 1462.

50. ASR *Camerale I* (Tesoreria Segreta) 1288, fols, 94v, 96v, 100, 101, Spring 1462. The *mappamondo* is sent to Pienza, see ASR *Camerale I* 1289, fol. 101, 19 October 1463.

51. ASR *Camerale I* (Tesoreria Segreta) 1289, fols. 121v, 122v. See also the provision of a bell for the campanile in 1465 in AVP *Massa* 1 (Camerariatus Capituli Pientini).

52. David S. Landes, *Revolution in Time: Clocks and the Making of the Modern World* (Cambridge, 1983), 74.

53. The kinds of protest registered by E. P. Thompson, "Time, Work-Discipline and Industrial Capitalism," *Past and Present* 38 (1967): 59–97 are not unlike those of the Florentine Wool workers in the fourteenth century. There is no evidence of this kind of protest among Pienza's inhabitants.

54. ASR *Camerale I* (Tesoreria Segreta) 1289, fol. 65v.

55. I have analyzed the Jouffroy palace in conjunction with Fausto Formichi, "The Identification of the Palazzo Jouffroy, Pienza," *Studi e Documenti di Architettura* (in press).

56. ASS *Libra* 160 "without any utility save for its fame among foreigners who every day come there causing us much expense."

57. Arnaldo Verdiani-Bandi, *I Castelli della Val d'Orcia e la Repubblica di Siena* (Siena, 1926), 115. See also Orlando Malavolti, *Dell 'Historia di Siena* (Venice, 1599), pt. 3: bk. 6:110.

58. Verdiani-Bandi, *Castelli,* 119.

59. Verdiani-Bandi, *Castelli,* 157–58; Malavolti, *Siena,* pt. 3, bk. 10: 156 v–157.

60. The case for Pienza is discussed by Judith Hook, "Fortifications and the End of the Sienese State," *History* 62 (1977): 372–87.

61. Blaise de Monluc *Commentaires 1521–1576,* ed. J. Giono and P. Courteault (Paris, 1964), 397–405. Monluc has little to say about the urban fabric of Pienza.

3

Houses Divided: Religious Schism in Sixteenth-Century Parisian Families

Barbara Diefendorf

> I come not to send peace, but a sword.
> For I am come to set a man at variance against his father,
> and the daughter against her mother,
> and the daughter-in-law against her mother-in-law.
> And a man's foes shall be they of his own household.
>
> Matthew 10:34–36

These verses have a special importance for those who lived through the era of the Reformation. Catholic and Protestant preachers alike urged their listeners to heed the words of the evangelist that "He that loveth father or mother better than me is not worthy of me," and both sides taught that spiritual kinship was to be valued over carnal kinship. In principle, both Catholics and Protestants placed their religious faith and spiritual obligations above their personal and familial loyalties. In practice, the situation was less simple. It is the situation in practice that interests me here.

Most work on the history of the family in early modern times has emphasized the themes of paternal authority, the dominance of husband over wife, and the solidarity of the larger family unit. My intention is to examine the effects of religious schism on these patterns of authority and solidarity.

The city of Paris is a particularly good setting for a study of the effects of religious discord because it stood at the very center of the political and religious turmoil that reduced France to anarchy in the second half of the sixteenth century. A bustling mercantile and administrative capital, Paris was the nerve center of the monarchy. Courtiers seeking favor, officers of justice and finance, and tradesmen catering to the varied needs of the city's growing population crowded into the still-walled urban center. Transients and natives, students, clerics, day laborers, and an inevitable contingent of homeless beggars swelled the city's numbers to two hundred thousand or more by mid-century, making it the largest city in northern Europe.[1]

Always a volatile city, Paris had long been accustomed to feeling the weight of the king's authority. Far more than most other French cities, municipal liberties had been curbed in favor of the exercise of royal power and control. Officers of the city shared with officers of the crown the responsibility for keeping peace in Paris, although it might be argued that neither agency performed this function very effectively.[2] Unrest in the city had a disproportionate effect on royal policy, which is why many of the most dramatic events of the era of civil and religious wars were played out on Parisian soil.

Paris abounded with the sort of individuals who proved elsewhere in France to be among the most enthusiastic converts to the new religion: educated urbanites with some exposure to humanistic learning, merchants of middling stature, and skilled craftsmen such as goldsmiths and printers.[3] The leaders of the Reformed church attached a special importance to establishing a strong following among such Parisians. Hoping to demonstrate that the new sect had a hardy base among "the people of the better sort," Reformed church ministers in 1562 encouraged their Parisian followers to turn out in large numbers and in their finest clothing to sing psalms and hear sermons in the fields outside the city gates.[4] Parisian Protestants were urged to show the strength of their convictions as well as their numbers—to become martyrs, if necessary, to the cause. When a large number of Protestants were arrested in 1557 for attending covert services in a house on the Rue Saint-Jacques, they were visited in their cells of the Conciergerie by Reformed church ministers, who brought them letters from Calvin himself, exhorting them to stand firm in their faith in the face of the pleas of their relatives and the threats of their judges.[5] "The ashes of pious men are fertile," the prisoners were told, and the women were reminded that God often chooses the weak to strike down the strong.[6] By overcoming the weakness ordinarily associated with their sex, they might be potent examples of the true faith.

The attempts of the reformers to secure a large following in Paris were thwarted, however, by more powerful forces already present in the city. Catholic churchmen, the judges of Parlement, and royal and municipal officers worked in combination to try to keep the capital free of heresy and firm in its traditional religious allegiance. Parish clergy and mendicant preachers were notorious for inflaming the local populace with their incendiary sermons, and even before the famous St. Bartholomew's Day massacre of 1572, incidents of religiously motivated violence were common.[7]

There was an inevitable ebb and flow of Protestant sentiment in the city, as the force of persecution alternately intensified and relented. It is generally agreed that the high point of popular Protestantism occurred in 1561 and early 1562, when Catherine de Medici assumed the regency for the young Charles IX and sought the means of compromise by which to preserve the state from war. After March 1562, when François, duc de Guise, marched triumphantly into Paris after the massacre of Huguenots gathered for worship at Vassy, religious rioting in the capital reached a fever pitch, and many Protestant sympathizers found it prudent to return to the Mass. Others joined the growing stream of emigrants to safer climes. A sharp drop in Huguenot numbers thus occurred under the pressures of the first civil war; a second sharp drop occurred six years later, during the second war; and in 1572 the violence of St. Bartholomew's Day frightened many of the remaining Huguenots in the city back into the Catholic fold.[8]

It is in this troubled and tumultuous setting that I wish to examine the problem of religious discord. The scale that I have chosen is not that of the city but rather that of the family, because this was the fundamental social unit on which traditional society was built.[9] A complex web of kinship bound up Protestants and Catholics in the city of Paris. Historians have generally ignored this question of religious divisions within the family, and yet there is much we can learn from it about the role of religion and the nature of the family in early modern society.[10]

A major obstacle to approaching this subject is that it is impossible to know just how often families divided along religious lines. By simple reasoning, I would say that the nature of the conversion process and the semiclandestine way the Reformation spread in northern France meant that few families were ever converted in their entirety. There were probably few French Protestants who did not have a sibling, a parent, or even perhaps a spouse who remained Catholic. But Protestantism was the religion of only a small minority. A more important question, then, might be how many Catholics had families touched by schism. Here I can offer only one bit of quantitative evidence. While researching the Paris city councillors, I found that nineteen of the ninety city councillors I was studying had close kin (by which I mean parents, children, siblings, or the spouses of these relatives) who became Protestants.[11] I have since found eleven more of these families to have been divided, which is to say that fully one-third of the ninety city councillors included in my study had one or more close relatives who stood on the other side in the religious disputes.

Although they concern only a small group, these numbers are suggestive. The city councillors were the nucleus of a civic elite that was known for its staunch Catholicism. Professionally, they were above the level at which French Protestantism has been shown to have had its greatest appeal. If the civic elite was this riven with heresy, I think it probable that religious division was also common in the families of merchants, petty officials, and prosperous artisans—the middling groups whose members' names appear most commonly on lists of known Protestants. Divided families were probably less common among the Parisian populace, for the simple reason that the new religion found fewer recruits there.

The analysis that follows has three parts. I will take up in turn the consequences of religious divisions between husbands and wives, between parents and children, and within the larger kinship network. Although some statistical evidence exists, the best way to demonstrate the tensions that arose out of these religious disputes and the ways in which families dealt with them is to discuss concrete examples; I will consequently be relying more on descriptive than on quantitative techniques.

Husbands and Wives

The dominant role of the husband in sixteenth-century marriage was clearly established in law and practice. The customary laws of the Paris region, like those of most other areas at the time, explicitly stated the legal incapacity of married women. Women's upbringing and education, moreover, tended to reinforce lessons of submissiveness and obedience to husbandly authority. The fact that sixteenth-century Parisian brides, at least among the wealthier classes, tended to marry men eight or more years their senior must also have strengthened the husbands' position as the head of the household.[12]

Given these traditions of marital authority, it is perhaps surprising to find that women might dissent from their husbands' views on so important an issue as religion. There is, however, evidence that women did make independent judgments about the matters of religious practice and faith. An anonymous police report from late 1562 or early 1563 lists more than sixty officers of the king who were suspected of having Protestant sympathies in Paris. In nine cases, the fact that the officer's wife was known to have attended Huguenot preaching is cited among the principal reasons for suspecting the officer of heretical views; in four cases, it is the only reason for the suspicion. The authors of the report show a certain sympathy with several of the suspects.

> Monsieur Faye is reputed to be a good man; but his wife has been regularly attending [Huguenot] services, . . . it is a great shame to have such a wife. . . . Maître Jacques Viole, a counselor in Parlement, has a wife who has been seen at [Huguenot] preaching, and it is said that it is too bad he has to put up with her.[13]

The records of the Paris city government and of the Parlement of Paris contain a number of cases of women who claimed to have remained good Catholics, even though their husbands were Huguenots. These women, usually women whose husbands had fled because of the wars, were often trying to avoid arrest or the confiscation of property, so one may reasonably be a bit suspicious about the sincerity of their claims. Still, the women who made them had to provide documentry evidence from their parish priests and their neighbors, attesting to their observance of Catholic rites and their good conduct, so we can be sure that they were living as Catholics, whatever their private sympathies.[14]

The same records show that many women became Protestants, even though their husbands remained at least outwardly faithful Catholics. It was quite common for a woman arrested for violation of the laws against Huguenots to be released to the custody of her husband, which would not have been done if the husband was believed to share her religious sympathies.[15]

It is very difficult to quantify this sort of information—to answer with any precision the question of just how often did husbands and wives differ in their religious affiliations. Some insight, however, may be provided by a non-Parisian source, a set of lists that were drawn up in 1588 or 1589 in Coutances, in Normandy, to identify the responses of local Huguenots to the Treaty of Nemours in 1585 and the Edit de l'Union in 1588, both of which placed heavy pressure on Protestants to abjure. If we compare the list of abjurors with the lists that identified those who fled, those who took up arms against the crown, and those who refused to abjure, it appears that a very high proportion of women remained Protestants, even though their husbands returned to the Catholic church. At a minimum, fifty-seven of the ninety women on the list were married. Of these, nineteen (or one in three) had husbands whose names appeared on the list of abjurors.[16] The explanation for this phenomenon may be that men were in greater personal and legal jeopardy than women if they remained Protestant, since they were more likely to have borne arms against the crown or to have been assumed to have done so, but whatever the explanation, a significant number of wives differed from their husbands' confessional choice, and the choice they made, to remain Protestant in the face of intense pressure to convert, was one that required great courage.

How did husbands react to wives who dissented from their religious views? This question can best be answered by examining several examples. On the one hand, we have Jacques de Mornay, who was tolerant of his wife's Protestant leanings. He encouraged her to be cautious, "warning her not to bring him into trouble, seeing how cruel the times were," but he did not try to change her beliefs.[17] On the other hand, we have the husband of Mme de Rantigny, one of the prominent noblewomen arrested in the affair of the Rue Saint-Jacques, who did everything possible to make her give up her faith. When she refused to attend Mass, he kept her a virtual prisoner in his house. At one point he even had her forcibly carried to church, though she apparently succeeded in her refusal to attend the services.[18]

Catholics blamed the reformers for the quarrels that destroyed traditional family allegiances.[19] In 1558, for instance, several counselors of the Parlement of Paris spoke out in favor of taking harsher measures against the Calvinists on the ground that they were "taking women from their husbands."[20] But what was the attitude of the reformers toward the family schisms the new doctrines provoked?

Calvin's opinion on this matter is clearly expressed in his letters. He counseled the wives of Catholic husbands to stay with them and to attempt to win them to the true faith. Even if she failed in this, however, a woman was not justified in leaving her husband. This, according to Calvin, was justified only when her life was in danger. "We mean by this," he explained, "not when the husband uses rough measures or threats, not even when he beats her, but when there is imminent peril of death."[21] For Calvin, then, a woman's obligation to submit to her husband's authority ended at precisely that point at which her life—or her salvation—was imperiled. In this way, he was able to reconcile the conflicting demands of religious faith and marital authority.

Because marriage in early modern times was first and foremost a social and economic alliance and only secondarily a personal union, even families torn by confessional conflicts could remain united in their pursuit of common economic benefits. Thus, for example, while Guy d'Arbaleste took refuge in the Huguenot-held city of Orleans during the first religious war, his Catholic wife remained in Paris and attempted to protect the family's properties there.[22] When Arbaleste died in 1570, he left his wife with the full responsibility for seeing to the division of the family estates.[23] Michel de L'Hospital and Jacques de Mornay, both Catholics with Protestant wives, did the same. According to Mornay's daughter-in-law, "he made no will, telling his wife that he left his children and his house in her care in full confidence."[24]

The laws of the Paris area placed strict limits on the rights of married persons to the properties of their partners.[25] This tendency to keep separate the properties of husband and wife could have important consequences for married couples professing different religions. At various times in the religious conflicts, the properties of accused Huguenots were subjected to special taxes, even to confiscations; they were also vulnerable to vandalism and pillage.[26] We cannot expect that angry crowds respected legal niceties and spared the belongings of the Catholic spouses of the Huguenots they persecuted, but the king and the courts usually did make an effort to distinguish between the properties of accused Huguenots and those of innocent family members. The records of the

Parlement of Paris provide a number of examples of women who went to court to secure the return of properties that they claimed had been confiscated as a result of the erroneous supposition that they belonged to the Protestant husband and not the Catholic wife or children. In each case in which the wife was able to demonstrate a legitimate claim to the confiscated property, the court ordered the property returned.[27]

In a similar fashion, Claude Le Mercier, whose parents were brutally murdered in the St. Bartholomew's Day massacre, presented himself before the city council just a week after those events to show his certificates of Catholic practice and to request the return of properties that had been taken in the course of the massacres.[28] This Catholic son of parents who died for their Calvinist faith exemplifies the common problem of religious divisions between parents and their children.

Parents and Children

In the opinion of Paris Catholics, the religious divisions of the Reformation posed the same threat to paternal authority as they posed to marital authority. In 1563, for example, Parlement was asked to create a special commission to look into the problem of "children of good family" being seduced away from their old faith against the wishes of their parents.[29] The outcry against children who abandoned the faith of their fathers has a parallel in the contemporaneous outcry raised against children who married or took religious professions without the permission of their parents. Although Catholic theologians defended marriage and ordination as sacraments requiring only the consent of the individuals taking the vows, there was in the sixteenth century a concerted effort on the part of laymen to strengthen the authority of parents by requiring their consent to the nuptial and religious vows of their children.[30] This effort bore fruit in 1556 in a royal edict against clandestine marriage, which allowed parents to disinherit children who married without their permission. In subsequent years, several further measures on the part of the kings and Parlement made it increasingly difficult for children to marry without the knowledge or consent of their parents.[31]

Protestants shared the desire to strengthen parental authority. One of the most strongly worded arguments against marriage without parental consent came from the pen of the Huguenot jurist Jean de Coras.[32] Protestant theologians were careful, however, to place in all things the obligation to earthly fathers second to the obligation to "the heavenly father." Only in this way was Theodore Beza able to justify the rebellion that led him to refuse the career for which his father intended him, to marry without his father's consent, and ultimately to abandon the Catholic faith.[33]

Beza's break with his father was a painful one. It is significant, however, that the estrangement between the two men was neither total nor permanent. Beza continued to try to justify himself to his father; he wrote his "Confession of Faith" for this very purpose.[34] For his part, the elder Beza was not entirely closedminded. He continued to try to persuade his son to return to France and to the Catholic church, but he was willing to engage in a dialogue that included a serious consideration of the younger man's theological principles. His response to Beza's "Confession of Faith," for instance, appeals to the Biblical notion of apostleship to defend the Catholic institution of the priesthood, as opposed to Beza's understanding of the ministry.[35] Equally important, paternal love, and not paternal authority, sounds the dominant note in his letters to his son.[36] When Theodore Beza came to France in 1561 for the Colloquy of Poissy, his ailing father wanted to see him and to meet his wife—whom he greeted as "my daughter," despite the fact that Beza had married without his consent.[37] A final meeting between Beza and his father was never to take place; political troubles and illness on Beza's part prevented it. It is clear from the final letters that passed between the two men, however, that the bonds of affection and family feeling had surmounted the religious rupture.

Beza's father did not attempt to disinherit him, in spite of his disobedience, his illicit marriage, and his abandonment of the Catholic faith.[38] Other parents did, however, disinherit children who abandoned their faith, and documents concerning the transmission of family properties offer important information about relations between parents and children who differed in religion. For one thing, these documents can disabuse us of the simplistic notion sometimes advanced that the Reformation was a revolt of sons against their fathers.[39] People were attracted to the teachings of the reformers at all ages and stages of life; sometimes it was the parent who adopted the new beliefs and the child who clung to the old.

Consider, for example, the last will and testament of Ysabeau Menon, the widow of a Parisian magistrate, who moved to Geneva in 1549. Leaving all the properties she had in Geneva to her daughter, who had followed her to that city, she gave her son back in Paris only the token sum of ten pounds, cutting him off from any other claims to her estate on the grounds that he had been "disobedient and ungrateful," and because he had tried with all his might to prevent her from going to Geneva. He had accused her of bringing shame and dishonor on the family and had even had all of the personal properties that she had arranged to have sent to Geneva seized, so that none of them ever reached her there.[40]

Ysabeau was very clear about the fact that she did not want what property she had in Geneva to fall into the hands of the "papists." In fact, she later revised her will to make it even more explicit on this point. A grandson brought up in Geneva had returned to France and to "idolatries, superstitions, and papistic abominations," and she consequenty cut him off from any claim to her estate, adding that if any of her other heirs were similarly to "retire from the truth," they were likewise to be excluded from her inheritance.[41]

Clauses restricting inheritance to those who followed the Calvinist faith are relatively common in the wills of French refugees to Geneva. Among the papers of the Genevan notary, Jehan Ragueau, himself a French refugee, are the wills of 160 French refugees. Twenty-seven of these wills (17 percent)) contained clauses that explicitly made an inheritance or testamentary bequest conditional upon religious affiliation. (The percentage would have been much higher had I been able to eliminate those cases in which there were no prospective heirs who might have differed from the testator in religious faith, but there was no way I could do this with any confidence of consistency.)

Many of these wills disqualified heirs who remained in France or who returned to that country from receiving any properties that had been brought to Geneva or acquired there. Others offered an inheritance almost as a bribe to induce conversion. Guyonne de Cuchermoys, for example, gave a *préciput,* or bonus, of fifteen hundred pounds to the two children who had accompanied her to Geneva and offered the same bonus to any other of her eleven children who would come to Geneva within three months of the time that they were notified of her death with the intention of living according to the Reformed church. The money was not to be paid immediately; they had first to live in Geneva more than a year, and they had to convince the executers of Guyonne's estate (who included Jean Calvin!) of the sincerity of their beliefs.[42]

If Genevan law and practice permitted the tying of inheritance to religious faith, the situation in France was more complex. Children were legally entitled to a share of the parental estate, and parents who wished to exclude a child from their inheritance had to establish that that child had proved unworthy of sharing in the patrimony.[43] Religious dissidence was not, however, necessarily sufficient grounds for disinheritance. By the Edict of Beaulieu, which settled the fifth of the religious wars in May 1576, previous acts of disinheritance motivated by "religious hatred" were declared null and void and in the future such acts were forbidden.[44] These provisions were repeated in 1577 in the Peace of Bergerac and in 1598 in the Edict of Nantes.[45] The situation prior to 1576 is more ambiguous, but it would seem that by ordering the cessation of all religious quarrels and guaranteeing certain rights to Huguenots, even the earlier peace settlements gave good grounds for challenging acts of disinheritance motivated solely by religious differences.[46]

The records of Genevan notaries show that French refugees spent a great deal of time, energy, and money pursuing claims to properties back in France. They clearly felt entitled not only to properties left behind at the time of emigration, but also to inheritances that were anticipated but not yet claimed.[47] Pursuing such claims could be dangerous business, and more than one French émigré lost his life when he went back into France to assert his right to properties there.[48]

It is interesting, though perhaps not suprising, that many French refugees to Geneva saw no inconsistency or contradition between their determination to disinherit relatives who failed to adhere to their Calvinist faith and their pursuit of claims to properties held by Catholic relatives back in France. Theodore Beza was an exception here. He abandoned his French estates to his co-heirs there, even though he felt they had treated him unfairly in refusing to give him his share of these properties.[49] He did, however, tie the inheritance of his Genevan properties to continued loyalty to the Calvinist church. By contrast, the Huguenot polemicist François Hotman fought for years for the inheritance to which he considered himself entitled as the eldest son of a prominent Parisian magistrate. Hotman refused to give up these claims, even after years of frustration. In his will, written in 1590, he left to his son Jean the patrimony he had never been able to possess. At the same time, he disinherited his second son, Daniel, for returning to the Catholic faith.

(I have found, by the way, that it is almost impossible to determine whether or not the suits of Protestants to regain the estates they had been denied by French relatives were successful. Each case must be followed up on an individual basis through what seem to be interminable legal proceedings. Jean Hotman eventually did bear the title of the patrimonial lands that his father tried to leave him, but I have not been able to determine whether he attained the lands through successful lawsuits, through purchase, or through the gift of Henri IV, whom he served.)[50]

The fathers most strongly motivated to disinherit children who differed from their religious views were those who took an active part in the political struggles of the period. François Hotman's disinheritance of his son Daniel serves as a good example here. Daniel had not only returned to the Catholic faith in spite of his father's best efforts to persuade him otherwise, but he had also become involved in the arch-Catholic political cause that Hotman had spent his life fighting. "My one-time son Daniel is doing the work of the Guises," wrote Hotman in 1587.[51] Daniel had not only apostatized, he had become a political enemy.

Economic motives as well as personal and political ones could be manifested in the act of disinheritance. We can see this quite clearly in the will of the Parisian refugee to Geneva, Robert Estienne, who disinherited two sons who had returned to Paris and sharply limited the portions going to three other children in order to leave his printing firm intact to his eldest son. This inheritance was tied to the son's willingness to continue in both the "true faith" and the printing trade; otherwise it was to revert to the youngest son, providing of course that he remained true to the faith and the trade.[52]

Although French law forbade disinheritance for purely religious reasons, there were always ways to conceal the true motive of an act of disinheritance. Thus, for example, André Guillart disinherited his son Louis on account of "his debauchery and the corruption of his morals," but it is clear from the context of this act and from other documents relating to the Guillart family that Louis's "debauchery" consisted of nothing more than his profession of the Calvinist faith.[53] The edict of 1556, which permitted the disinheritance of children who married without parental permission, could also be used to give legal substance to an act of disinheritance motivated primarily by religious differences.

Disinheritance was a means of exerting parental authority. As such, it was an act of symbolic importance as well as of financial consequences. Disinheritance must not, however, be seen as an isolated act of personal vindictiveness. It must rather be viewed within the larger context of a family's strategy for economic survival and continuity. This larger question of the survival and continuity of families divided by religion is my next and final subject.

Siblings and the Larger Kinship Network

Just as close ties of mutual support and dependency went beyond the nuclear family unit in the early modern period, so did the personal and political repercussions of religious dissent. Many persons were accused of being Huguenots because members of their close families were dissenters. In October 1562, for instance, a city officer and notable merchant by the name of Pierre Croquet was arrested and had his horse and arms taken because his brother Nicolas and his daughter Nicole were notorious Huguenots. Nicolas and Nicole Croquet and their respective spouses had been among a group of Parisians seen in the city of Meaux at a time when iconoclastic riots broke out there. For their presumed part in these riots, their property was confiscated and they were sentenced to be hanged in effigy in the city of Paris. Pierre's arrest occurred at about the same time as the mock execution, and it was clearly motivated by the assumption that he shared the religious sentiments of his kin. Protesting his innocence,

Pierre swore before the Parlement of Paris that he had always lived as a true Catholic and good citizen and that these facts were well known to the governor of the city, who had not included him on the list of Huguenots ordered out of Paris but had allowed him to remain in his home. Pierre was released, but only after he presented evidence that he had regularly attended Mass, went to confession at Easter, and demonstrated other signs of faithful Catholic practice.[54]

Pierre remained active in city politics despite the prominence of his relatives in the Huguenot cause. There is no record of his reaction to the scandal that was created in 1564 when the burial of his Protestant sister-in-law in the Cemetery of the Innocents nearly set off a riot in the city.[55] Nor do we know his reaction to the arrest of his brother Nicolas in January 1569 for participation in illicit religious services. When, however, Nicolas was condemned to death and executed later that year, after a lengthy and much publicized trial, Pierre stepped forward to assume the guardianship of his orphaned nieces and to administer what properties remained to them. He appears, in fact, to have managed to protect some properties that should have been included in the court-ordered forfeiture, such as the house Nicolas owned on the Rue Saint-Denis.[56]

It was not unusual for Paris Catholics to be given custody of Protestant relatives. The children of arrested Huguenots were often placed with Catholic relations, and even adult Huguenots might be turned over to their Catholic kin.[57] In 1569 and 1570, laws against religious dissidents placed Parisian Huguenots under virtual house arrest. Violators of these laws were sometimes released only on the condition that they take up residence with a Catholic relative who would promise to guarantee their good behavior.[58] Marie Passart spent more than a month in prison and nearly two months in the custody of her brother-in-law before she was allowed to return home to her seven small children.[59] Marie Creichant was released from the Conciergerie only when she was about to give birth, and even then her release was conditional upon the promise of the relatives who took her in to have the child baptized in the Catholic church.[60]

Catholics also assumed important roles in the protection of the properties of their Protestant kin, petitioning authorities for the return of confiscated properties and even, on occasion, making secret agreements to represent the Protestants' properties as their own and thereby avoid confiscation. How well families cooperated in such affairs depended, of course, on the personalities of the individuals involved. I have found no way to research this question except to follow individual cases, of which two constrasting examples will be discussed.

In the case of the famous printing family, the Estiennes, we have a pattern of consistent and apparently successful cooperation. When Robert Estienne left Paris for Geneva in 1550, he left his two younger daughters behind with his Catholic brother Charles. Charles subsequently engaged in an important legal action on behalf of his brother's children, and he welcomed back into his house three of Robert's sons, who returned to Paris because they could not get along with their stepmother in Geneva. Two of the three sons eventually returned to Geneva. The third, Robert Estienne the younger, readopted the Catholic faith and remained in Paris, where he carried on the pattern of cooperation established by his father and uncle. He engaged in several lawsuits on behalf of his Genevan siblings; he also published several books by his Genevan brother Henri. To all appearances, he dealt amicably with his Genevan brothers-in-law when they came to Paris on family business in 1564, and we find his youngest brother, François, another of the Protestant Estiennes, among the participants at the family councils that met in Paris in 1575 to name guardians for Robert's children and those of his uncle Charles.[61]

By contrast, in the Spifame family, we have evidence of chicanery on all sides. A member of a prominent Parisian family, Jacques Spifame was the bishop of Nevers until he ran away to Geneva in 1559 with the woman he called his wife and their two children. Spifame was rumored to have made secret arrangements with his nephews, to whom he turned over his offices and properties, in order to retain a handsome income during his exile in Geneva, and, indeed, according to a will Spifame made in 1560, such agreements did exist. Claiming that he had given his houses and seigneuries to his nephews solely to avoid their confiscation, Jacques asked in his will that the nephews turn the properties over to their rightful heirs, his son and daughter. The nephews not only refused to do so, they had the Genevan claimants turned off the lands as trespassers and filed legal charges against them. Arguing that Spifame's marriage was illegal and his children illegitimate, the nephews set in motion a legal battle that was to last at least twenty years.[62]

Obviously, the stress of religious division could aggravate other family quarrels, and under certain circumstances religious differences could become an excuse for betraying one's kin. We should be wary, however, of assuming that religious differences were themselves the fundamental cause of such conflicts. The two incidents I have discovered of family quarrels so violent that they resulted in murder were both in their essence quarrels over property and not over religion. Both incidents involved Protestants who had returned from exile during the wars only to discover that the properties they had confided to the care of Catholic relatives had been dissipated or pillaged during their absences.[63] In both cases it was the anger over this outrage and not the religious issue that provoked the murder. A similar incident concerns the printer Oudin Petit, who is said to have been killed on St. Bartholomew's Day on the orders of his stepfather because of a disagreement over an inheritance.[64] It is possible, of course, that some persons did die at the hands of their relatives for reasons of faith alone. How can one know the truth behind such vague references as that of Agrippa d'Aubigné to "an uncle [who] killed two little nieces who had hidden themselves under the bed, thinking that they were about to be beaten?"[65] Better documented, however, are cases like that of Charlotte d'Arbaleste, who found refuge and not death in the houses of her Catholic kin.

A known Huguenot, Charlotte was in Paris in August of 1572 to settle the estates of her father and her first husband.[66] She could not go to her Catholic mother's house when the massacres erupted because guards had been sent there to arrest her, so she took refuge with a more distant kinsman. During the week that followed, Charlotte was sheltered successively by a blacksmith (the husband of one of her mother's servants), by a prominent parisienne (her mother's godmother), and by a grainseller (a servant of the godmother). Finally, eleven days after the massacres began, arrangements were made for her to leave the city by boat. Even here the dangers did not end, and more Catholic kinsmen and their servants were involved in the various stages of this escape.[67]

Throughout these perilous adventures, Charlotte was pressured to abjure her faith and to return to the Mass. Her mother, she tells us in her memoirs, had saved her brothers by inducing them to go to Mass, and she tried to save Charlotte by the same means. Even the blacksmith tried to convince her to go to Mass. At one point after her escape from Paris, she asked Michel de L'Hospital to shelter her at his estate at Vallegrand. De L'Hospital replied that she was welcome, but she would have to go to Mass, as his own wife had been forced to do.[68] The attempts to secure an abjuration were well-intentioned, however, and those who sought to make Charlotte abjure did not withdraw their support when she refused but rather assisted her in her escape. In the course of this flight, a good many Catholics of both high and low station put their own lives at risk.

Can we synthesize from these varied examples a coherent view of family relationships in sixteenth-century Paris? In one sense, we cannot. The varieties of individual experience depicted here do not lend themselves to simple modelling or patterns. And yet there is a consistent theme in the demonstration that the traditional ties of family loyalty and mutual obligation remained a firm basis for social relations in sixteenth-century Paris.

It is true that religious differences placed a heavy psychological burden on the family. Patterns of belief and behavior that had been little questioned were brought to consciousness and articulated. Believers of both faiths were asked to weigh the bonds of spiritual and earthly kinship. Which is closer to you, asked the parish priest, your spiritual brother in the Catholic and Christian faith or your carnal brother the Huguenot?[69] Would it not be better to die a hundred times, asked Calvin, than to break your sacred and perpetual tie to Christ in favor of your earthly and perishable marriage?[70]

It would seem, however, that these questions were primarily rhetorical. For the most part, Catholics and Protestants alike viewed the obligation all men owed their spiritual father and family as complementary to, not as conflicting with, their obligations to their earthly fathers and families. Both Catholics and Protestants reaffirmed traditional family relationships and patterns of authority.

This family unity could break down when persecution became too intense and personal danger too great. It could also be ignobly ruptured if one family member chose to place personal gain ahead of mutual obligation, and it could, on occasion, prove too weak to surmount the obstacles of misunderstanding. With all the good will in the world, Charlotte d'Arbaleste's Catholic mother could not understand why her daughter refused to save herself by going to Mass. She saw this as stubborn willfullness and could not understand Charlotte's conviction that this bending of the knee was a submission to idolatry that would cost her immortal soul.

It was on this level of life and death that the real family dramas of the Reformation were played out, which brings me to my second major conclusion. The study of religious conflicts in Parisian families has reinforced my conviction that—at least in northern France, where Protestantism had no real territorial base—the crucial determinants of confessional choice were individual conscience and will. Parental and husbandly authority could be exerted to enforce an outward show of religious practice, but they could not force the faith itself. Many Parisian families divided not over their initial attraction to the Reformed church message, but over the willingness of individual members to endure the pressures of persecution and the threat—all too often realized—of exile, pillage, and imprisonment. Over the course of the wars, a great many Parisian Protestants abjured. They either lost their faith or chose to deny it. Under the circumstances, family solidarity was important, but, ultimately, courage was an individual matter.

Notes

1. Population figures for sixteenth-century Paris are very unreliable, but all place Paris at two hundred thousand or more at midcentury. See Pierre Chaunu, *La Mort à Paris* (Paris, 1978), 198; Pierre Lavedan, *Histoire de Paris* (Paris, 1967), 32. London, on the other hand, had less than one hundred thousand at midcentury, growing to perhaps one hundred fifty thousand by 1600, Fernand Braudel, "Premodern Towns," in *The Early Modern Town: A Reader,* ed. Peter Clark (London, 1976), 83.

2. On the relations between the municipality and the monarchy in sixteenth-century Paris, see my *Paris City Councillors in the Sixteenth Century: The Politics of Patrimony* (Princeton, 1983), 3–33.

3. Phillip Benedict, *Rouen during the Wars of Religion* (Cambridge, 1981), 71–81; Joan Davis, "Persecution and Protestantism: Toulouse, 1562–1575," *Historical Journal* 22 (1979): 31–51; Natalie Zemon Davis, "The Sacred and the Body Social in Sixteenth-Century Lyon," *Past and Present,* no. 90 (1981): 50–51; Janine Garrisson-Estèbe, *Protestants du Midi: 1559–1598* (Toulouse, 1980), 22–56; J. H. M. Salmon, *Society in Crisis: France in the Sixteenth Century* (New York, 1975), 133–38.

4. Denis François Sécousse, ed. *Mémoires de Condé, servant d'éclaircissement et de preuves à l'Histoire de M. de Thou* (London, 1743), 1:72: "Journal de Bruslart."

5. Letter from Macard to Calvin, 22 May 1558, published in Athanase Coquerel, *Précis de l'histoire de l'Eglise réformée de Paris* (Paris and Strasbourg, 1862), 40–41.

6. *Johannis Calvini Opera quae supersunt omnia,* 59 vols., ed. W. Baum, E. Cunitz, E. Reuss, vol. 16 (Braunschweig, 1872–79), cols. 629–34: Les Ministères de Genève à l'Eglise de Paris (16 September 1557), Calvin aux Prisonnières de Paris (n.d.).

7. One can see the developing religious tensions in the records of the Hôtel de Ville for the two years prior to the outbreak of religious war: Alexandre Tuétey, ed., *Registres des délibérations du Bureau de la Ville de Paris* (Paris, 1892), 5:47–48, 52–53, 87, 90–91, 103, 108–09, 111–12, 116–63. See also, Claude Haton, *Mémoires contenant le récit des événements accomplis de 1553 à 1582,* ed. Félix Bourquelot (Paris, 1857), 179–86 and 208–21; the documents in *Archives curieuses de l'histoire de France,* 15 vols., ed., L. Cimber and F. Danjou (Paris and Beauvais, 1834–1840), 4:51–103; the *Histoire ecclésiastique des églises réformées au royaume de France,* 3 vols., ed. G. Baum and E. Cunitz (Nieuwkoop, 1974; reprint of Paris, 1883–89 edition), 1:192–94, 284, 740–51; and the "Journal de ce qui s'est passé en France durant l'année 1562, principalement dans Paris et à la Cour," *Revue Rétrospective,* series 1, 5 (1834): 81–111, on Catholic preaching, incidents of violence, and the growing religious tensions in late 1561 and early 1562.

8. Denis Richet, "Aspects socio-culturels des conflits religieux à Paris dans la seconde moitié du xvie siècle," *Annales, Economies, sociétés, civilisations* 32 (1977): 766–67; more generally: Benedict, *Rouen,* 234–42.

9. On the role of the family in the spread of the Reformation in southern France, see Garrisson-Estèbe, *Protestants du Midi,* 56.

10. Erik Erikson's *Young Man Luther* (New York, 1958) is a brilliant speculation on the influence of Luther's family relationships on the formation of his religious thought and his break with the Catholic church, but it has little to say about the effect of Luther's break with the church on his relationships with his parents. Donald Kelley takes up this theme at intervals in his *François Hotman: A Revolutionary's Ordeal* (Princeton, 1973), and in *The Beginning of Ideology: Consciousness and Society in the French Reformation* (Cambridge and New York, 1981), 51–87; and Steven Ozment touches upon it at several points in *When Fathers Ruled: Family Life in Reformation Europe* (Cambridge, Mass., 1983).

11. Diefendorf, *Paris City Councillors,* 73–80.

12. On the legal status of married women see Paris Coutume de 1580, articles 223 and 224. François Olivier-Martin, *Histoire de la coutume de la prévôté et vicomté de Paris,* 2 vols. (Paris, 1922–26), 2:237–41; Jacques Bréjon, *André Tira-*

queau, 1488–1588 (Paris, 1937), 110–37. On the Renaissance ideal of womanhood, see Ruth Kelso, *Doctrine for the Lady of the Renaissance* (Urbana, 1960). On marriage patterns in the families of the Parisian elite, see Diefendorf, *Paris City Councillors,* 179–84.

13. Bibliothèque Nationale [hereafter BN], Ms. fr. 4047, fols. 8r–10r, included as an appendix and analyzed in chapter six of the unpublished dissertation of Linda Taber on "Heresy in the Parlement of Paris in the 1560s" (Stanford University, 1982). Linda Taber identifies the authors of the report as the *capitaines* of the Paris *dizaines,* who were commissioned by Parlement in November 1562 to supply them with a list of officers of the sovereign courts who were known or suspected Huguenots. Richet suggests, on the other hand, that parish priests were probably responsible for the anonymous document (Richet, "Conflits religieux," 768).

14. Archives Nationales [hereafter AN], X^{2B} 57 (27/9/69): Catherine Le Jeune, wife of Philippes Le Gendre; X^{2B} 57 (15/9/69): Claude du Vivier, wife of Oudin Petit; X^{2B} 58 (7/10/69): Marguerite Merlin, wife of Girard Vaupolly, suspected on account of her first husband; X^{2B} 58 (19/11/69): Marguerite de Luxembourg, wife of Philibert de Cuvillier; X^{2B} 60 (22/4/70): Catherine Joanne, wife of Jacques Chabouille; X^{2B} 62 (7/9/70): Magdaleine Chevalier, wife of Guy d'Arbaleste; X^{2B} 73 (15/10/72) and X^{2B} 75 (8/4/73): Jehanne de Rosmadecq, wife of Jehan de la Pommeraye; Y 105 (3/5/64): Jehanne Chartillière, wife of François Falot; Z^{1H} 71 (30/9/72): Magdaleine Guerard, wife of Alexandre Patras; Z^{1H} 71 (30/9/72): Marie Harelle, wife or widow of Guillaume Faulchet.

15. See, for example, AN, X^{2B} 56 (22/5/69): Genevieve Gosseau, wife of Philibert Motteau; X^{2B} 56 (26/5/69): Catherine Erondelle, wife of Charles Lespine; X^{2B} 57 (6/6/69): Anne Seguier, wife of Jehan Payot; Z^{1H} 59B (24/10/62): Ysabeau Le Riche, wife of Jehan Boullenger.

16. "Etat nominatif des Protestants de la Vicomté de Coutances," *Bulletin de la Société de l'histoire du Protestantisme français* 36 (1887): 246–58.

17. Charlotte Arbaleste de la Borde de Feuguères, *Mémoires de Madame de Mornay,* ed. Henriette de Witt, 2 vols. (Paris, 1868), 1:10–12. An English translation of those portions of the memoirs dealing with family affairs was published by Lucy Crump under the title of *A Huguenot Family in the Sixteenth Century: The Memoirs of Philippe de Mornay, Sieur du Plessis Marly, Written by his Wife* (London, n.d.).

18. Letters from Macard to Calvin dated 7 February, 6 March, 12 April, 22 May, 11 July, and 26 August 1558, in Coquerel *Précis,* xxvii, xli, xlviii, liii–liv, lxiv, lxix.

19. *Remonstrances faictes au roy* [1562].

20. Coquerel, *Précis,* p. 40: letter of Macard to Calvin, 22 May 1558.

21. *Calvini Opera,* vol. 17, cols. 131–32: letter of Calvin to Mme de Rantigny, 10 April 1558, and col. 539: letter of Calvin to an unnamed lady, 4 June 1559. These and other letters of Calvin to women are analyzed in Charmarie Jenkins Blaisdell's "Calvin's Letters to Women: The Courting of Ladies in High Places," *Sixteenth Century Journal* 13 (1982):67–84.

22. Arbaleste, *Mémoires,* 56. Maintaining the family's economic unity through the strain of religious schism and civil war was not easy. In the summer of 1563, quarrels between Arbaleste and his wife over the amount of money that should be given to their daughters resulted in a lawsuit before the Parlement of Paris. It is worth noting, however, that Parlement's response to the dispute was to turn it back to the family. A family council, consisting of up to ten relatives from each side of the family, was summoned to meet before two officers of the court. The members

of this council were instructed to mediate the quarrel and to try to reconcile the two parties. The fact that Arbaleste left his wife in charge of his estate when he died suggests that the attempted reconciliation was successful. AN, X^{1a} 1606, fols. 49 (23 July 1563) and 162v (21 August 1563).

23. Arbaleste, *Mémoires*, 50 and 58.

24. Ibid., 11, as translated by Crump, *Huguenot Family*, 82. A similar statement appears in the will of Michel de L'Hospital, who made his wife the administrator of all of his possessions, even though his only child was a married woman in her thirties. L'Hospital stated that he was confident that his wife's management would be to the profit of his heirs, and he forbade them to ask for an account of her stewardship. Michel de L'Hospital, *Oeuvres complètes*, 5 vols., ed. P. J. S. Duféy (Geneva, 1968; reprint of Paris, 1824–1826 edition), 2:425–26.

25. Paris Coutume de 1580, articles 223–26.

26. Edicts ordering the confiscation of Huguenot property are identified by Nicola M. Sutherland in *The Huguenot Struggle for Recognition* (New Haven and London, 1980), 333–72.

27. See, for example, AN, X^{2B} 57 (15/9/69): Claude de Vivier, wife of Oudin Petit; X^{2B} 58 (19/11/69): Marguerite de Luxembourg, wife of Philibert de Cuvillier; X^{2B} 60 (22/4/70): Catherine Joanne, wife of Jacques Chabouille.

28. AN, Z^{1H} 71 (3/9/72).

29. AN, X^{2A} 131, fol. 280r–v (13 July 1563).

30. See, for example, Etienne Pasquier's letter to Pierre Airault, *lieutenant criminel* of Angers (book 11, letter 9) in his *Lettres familières*, ed. Dorothy Thickett (Paris, 1974), 193–99. See also Diefendorf, *Paris City Councillors*, 156–70; and Ozment, *When Fathers Ruled*, 25–49, on the larger problem of parental consent to marriage.

31. François André Isambert, et al., *Recueil général des anciennes lois françaises*, 29 vols. (Paris, 1822–33), 13:469: "Edit contre les mariages clandestins" (Paris, February 1556; registered March 1556); also 14:392: "Ordonnance de Blois."

32. Jean de Coras, *Paraphrase sur l'edict des mariages clandestinement contractez par les enfans de famille, contre le gré et consentement de leurs pères et mères* (Paris, 1572).

33. Théodore de Bèze, *Correspondance*, 12 vols. to date, ed. H. Aubert, F. Aubert, H. Meylan, A. Dufour, A. de Hensler (Geneva, 1960–), 3:43–52; letter from Beza to Melchior Volmar, Geneva, 12 March 1560.

34. Ibid., 3:360 from the preface to the French Confession of Faith.

35. Ibid., 4:47–48 letter from Pierre de Bèze to Théodore de Bèze, 16 February 1562.

36. Ibid., also 15–16, letter of 2 January 1562.

37. Ibid., 15–16.

38. Ibid., 5:178–79, *lettres patentes* of Charles IX in favor of Théodore de Bèze, Roussillon, 1 August 1564.

39. For example, Kelley, *Beginning of Ideology*, 78.

40. Archives d'Etat de Genève [hereafter AEG], Ragueau 5:588, 30/1/63.

41. AEG, Ragueau 8:641, 26/11/66.

42. AEG, Ragueau 4:547, 17/8/60.

43. Gabriel Lepointe, *Droit romain et ancien droit français: Régimes matrimoniaux, liberalités, successions* (Paris, 1958), 450.

44. Edit de Beaulieu (6 May 1576), art. 31. The text of the edict is given in André

Stegmann, ed., *Edits des Guerres de Religion* (Paris, 1979), 97–120.

45. Ibid., 14, Paix de Bergerac, September 1577, and 237, Edit de Nantes, April 1598.

46. Ibid., 32–36, Edit d'Amboise, 19 March 1563; 53–58, Paix de Longjumeau, 23 March 1568; 69–82, Paix de St. Germain, August 1570; 86–93, Edit de Boulogne, July 1573.

47. The records of the notary Ragueau, for example, contain many procurations by French refugees to give authority to relatives or other persons travelling back into France to claim the inheritances due them. To cite just one example, in 1566 François Budé named his brother Jean his *procureur* with regards to his claims to share in the estate of his niece Marguerite Budé (Ragueau 8:122–25 [21/2/66]). One also finds reference in Genevan testaments to properties claimed but not recovered back in France, and sometimes one finds testaments written by persons who were setting off for France to pursue claims to properties there where it was feared they might never return.

48. Jehanne Abeline added a codicil to her testament in 1565 because her husband, Pierre Le Brun, who had gone to France to try to claim his properties there, had been gone three years, and she did not know if he was alive or dead (AEG, Ragueau 7:173 [7/2/65]). Loys Enoch was so afraid of the dangers of the trip that, though he ordered his wife in his testament to pursue his property claims back in France, he forbade her to go herself or to send their son, for fear they would not survive the trip (AEG, Ragueau 9:76 [11/2/67]).

49. AEG, Ragueau 8:502 (1/10/66).

50. Kelley, *François Hotman,* 46, 273, and 325.

51. Ibid., 310. Disinheriting Daniel was, however, largely a symbolic act, since Hotman had pitifully little property at the time of his death.

52. AEG, Ragueau 3:185–91; published in Antoine-Augustin Renouard, *Annales de l'Imprimerie Estienne, ou, Histoire de la famille Estienne et de ses éditions* (Paris, 1843), 579–82.

53. AN, Y120, fols. 273r–274v (20/11/78). André Guillart did not cut off Louis without a sou, but rather he gave over to him the landed property of Saint-Govert, near Meaux, so that he would have a source of income and might enter into royal service. He also hoped, by ending Louis's financial dependence on his Huguenot mother, to draw him away from her influence. He did not succeed in doing so. The year following his disinheritance, Louis made a prestigious alliance with the daughter of an important Huguenot nobleman. Guillart was present for the signing of the marriage contract, as were some of the family's other prominent Catholic members, though he did not contribute financially to the match. His role was limited to the formal consent that was required in order for his wife to give Louis a share of her properties. (AN, Y121, fols. 53r–55v [31/8/79]).

54. AN, X2B 34 (29/10/62). On Pierre Croquet's Huguenot relatives, see Paul Guérin, "Délibérations politiques du Parlement et arrêts criminels du milieu de la première guerre de religion (1562)," *Mémoires de la Société de l'histoire de Paris* 40 (1913): 70–74.

55. Jean de la Fosse, *Journal d'un curé ligueur de Paris,* ed. E. Barthélemy (Paris, 1866), 68.

56. On the arrest and trial of Nicolas Croquet, see [Nathanaël Weiss], "Poursuites et condamnations à Paris pour hérésie de 1564 à 1572, d'après les registres d'écrou de la Conciergerie du Palais," *Bulletin de la Société de l'histoire du Protestantisme français* 50 (1901): 640; La Fosse, *Journal d'un curé ligueur,* 102; AN, U* 815, fols. 12r–14v, and X2B 56 (30/6/69). On Pierre Croquet's guardianship

of his nieces, see BN, Pièces originales 944 Croquet, 1570 receipt; and on their property, see BN, ms. fr. 11692, fol 57v.

57. For example, AN, X^{2B} 58 (14/10/69): Jean Ricart was ordered to have his children brought back to Paris to be raised as Catholics; X^{2B} 60 (8/3/70): Anne and Louis Erondel were released to custody of uncles Philippes Henault and Thibault Pasquier; X^{2B} 73 (15/10/72): the daughter of Jehan de la Pommeraye was ordered turned over to a Catholic relative.

58. For example, AN, X^{2B} 58 (6/10/69): Marie Mynier, wife of Pierre Berthrand, released to custody of her brother-in-law Jean Berthrand; released from his custody after proof of Catholic practice (X^{2B} 59 [16/1/70]; X^{2B} 60 (17/3/70): Jeanne de Moussy, wife of Jean Gobelin, was released to the custody of Genevieve de Moussy, her daughter Claude Gobelin was released to custody of her uncle, Leonard de Varengene.

59. AN, X^{2B} 57 (9/7/69), (5/8/69), and (28/9/69): Marie Passart, wife of Pierre Feret.

60. AN, X^{2B} 60 (10/3/70): Marie Creichant, wife of Loys Brecheux. Katherine Musnier was also released from prison only on condition of having her child baptized as a Catholic (X^{2B} 56 [6/5/69]).

61. See Renouard, *Annales des Estienne,* 319–23 n; Henri Stein, "Nouveau Documents sur les Estienne, imprimeurs parisiens (1517–1665)," *Mémoires de la Société de l'histoire de Paris et de l'Ile de France* 22 (1895):275–76; AEG, Ragueau 5:1067 (17/7/63): AN, Y 105, fols. 82v–83v (5/2 and 19/4/64); and Philippe Renouard, *Documents sur les imprimeurs . . . ayant exercé à Paris de 1450 à 1600* (Paris, 1901), 95 (documents dated 12/7/75 and 2/8/75).

62. AEG, Ragueau 3:405–15 (11/3/60) and 4:480 (28/10/61); and Crespin 1:13v (5/84). AN, X^{2B} 40 (26/9/65), X^{2B} 43 (17/8/66), and X^{2B} 44 (18/9/66). See also André Delmas, "Le procès et la mort de Jacques Spifame," *Bibliothèque d'humanisme et Renaissance* 5 (1944): 105–37; and Haton, *Mémoires,* 84–85.

63. AN, X^{2B} 52 (12/7/68): Anthoine Colin; X^{2B} 1095 (20/6/73): Jehanne de Salmon. Neither incident took place in the city of Paris.

64. Most accounts probably derive from Jean Crespin's *Histoire des Martyrs persecutez et mis à mort pour la verité de l'évangile,* new ed., 3 vols., ed. Daniel Benoît and Mathieu Lelièvre (Toulouse, 1885–89), 3:675. Though I have found a number of notarial contracts concerning Petit and his family and have consequently been able to confirm that he did indeed die in the troubles of August 1572, I have found no indications that members of his family were involved in the crime. Weiss, "Poursuites," 594n is incorrect in saying that Petit was already dead in July 1572. The date on the document in question is September and not July (AN, Y 114, fols. 286r–287v [4/9/73], referring to the contract of 21/9/72, found in Y 113, fol. 231).

65. Théodore Agrippa d'Aubigné, *Histoire universelle,* 10 vols., ed. Alphonse du Ruble (Paris, 1886–1907), 3:336.

66. Arbaleste, *Mémoires,* 58.

67. Ibid., 62–71.

68. Ibid., 64, 63, and 68.

69. Haton, *Mémoires,* 213n.

70. *Calvini Opera,* vol. 17, col. 132, letter from Calvin to Mme de Rantigny, 10 April 1558.

PART II

Renaissance Culture: Courtly and Urban

Leisure and Sociability: Reading Aloud in Early Modern Europe

Roger Chartier
Translated by Carol Mossman

In the course of the sixteenth and seventeenth centuries in Western Europe, reading, for the literate elite, became the act par excellence of intimate, private, and secret leisure. Witnesses aplenty describe the pleasure to be taken in the retreat from society, a withdrawal from the affairs of the city to the sheltering silence of solitude. This is how one imagines Montaigne, in the refuge of his library, secluded from his civic concerns and the demands of familial sociability: "J'essaie à m'en rendre la domination pure, et à soustraire ce seul coin à la communauté et conjugale, et filiale, et civile." ("I try to make my authority over it absolute, and to withdraw this one corner from all society, conjugal, filial, and civic.")[1] Thus also do we see Prospero, preferring the privacy of his study to the glories of government: "Me, poor man, my library / Was dukedom large enough".[2] And thus Tristan L'Hermite's Seneca, imploring his emperor to let him go to his books:

> Permets qu'ayant servi sous un si digne maître,
> J'aille me délasser en un séjour champêtre,
> Où bien loin du murmure et de l'empressement,
> Je puisse entretenir mes livres doucement.
> (Allow me who have served under so worthy a master
> To take relaxation in some rustic abode
> Where far away from noise and social pressures
> I can indulge in the sweet pleasures of my books.)[3]

In these texts, as in many others, dealings with books produce the same effect on readers: they distance them from the city, from those in power, from the multitude ("l'empressement," the social pressures says Seneca, "la presse," the matters of urgency writes Montaigne). In social practices as well as in the way they are depicted, the act of reading defines a new consciousness that is constructed outside the sphere of public authority and political power, and outside the network of interrelationships that make up social and domestic life.

Yet reading in the sixteenth and seventeenth centuries was not always, nor everywhere, a gesture of reclusive intimacy. Reading can itself create a social bond, unite people around a book, foster convivial social relations, on the condition that it be neither solitary nor silent. At a time when the ability to read silently (at least for the upper classes) had become sufficiently common that understanding a text no longer depended on its being "vocalized,"[4] reading aloud was no longer a necessity for the reader, but rather an exercise in sociability practiced on any number of occasions and to diverse ends. The present essay seeks to identify these conditions on the basis of a preliminary collection of documents.

Certain works of fiction depict reading aloud, as performed by a reader vocalizing a text for an assembly of listeners grouped about him, to be a common method of circulating the work. The tragicomedy, *La Celestina,* completed by Fernando de Rojas, was published for the first time in Burgos in 1499. In the Toledo edition dated 1500, the "corrector de la impresión" (the proof-reader) added a six-stanza poem at the end. The fourth stanza indicated in the following terms how the text is to be read under the title: "Dice el modo que se ha de tener leyendo esta tragicomedia" ("Where it is indicated the way in which this tragicomedy is to be read"). The reader being addressed here is supposed to read out loud, delivering the asides in a low voice ("cumple que sepas hablar entre dientes" ["one has to know how to talk between one's teeth"]), vary his pitch (he should read "a veces con gozo, esperanza y pasión / a veces airado, con gran turbación" ["sometimes with gaiety, hope, and passion / sometimes angry, in despair"]), impersonate each character in turn ("pregunta y responde por boca de todos / llorando y riendo en tiempo y sazón" ["he questions and replies for all / cries and laughs at the right time"]). By thus summoning up "mil artes y modos" ("a thousand ways and manners"), his reading will enthrall those who are listening—"los oyentes."[5]

Like the Latin humanist comedies, the *Celestina* was written for a vocalized and dramatized reading, but nonetheless a reading for a solo voice intended for a small and select audience. The size and character of the latter was sketched out in a prologue that appeared in the 1507 Saragoza edition (and perhaps five years earlier in a Seville edition, now lost). Alluding to the contradictory judgments passed on the work ("unos decían que era prolija, otros breve, otros agradable, otros oscura" ["some have said it was diffuse, others too short, some agreeable, others unclear"]), the author justified this diversity of opinion by relating it to the very circumstances surrounding its reading:

Así que cuando diez personas se juntaren a oír esta comedia, en quien quepa esta diferencia de condiciones, como suele acaecer, ¿quién negara que haya contienda en cosa que de tantas maneras se entienda?

(So then, when ten persons congregate to hear this play there will naturally be a variety of reactions among them. Who will deny that there will arise dissension about something which may be understood in so many different ways?)[6]

Ten listeners assembled voluntarily about a reader: here the book is placed at the center of a literate social gathering, one that is friendly, worldly, and cultivated, and in which the unicity of the relation to the text—heard by the audience—in no way precludes the plurality of its potential interpretations.

In *Quixote*, Cervantes plays in a variety of ways with the motif of reading aloud and its corollary, an audience listening to the text being read. First, after the manner of the *Celestina*, he takes it for granted that his book can indeed be the object of such a reading. This assumption finds its illustration in the title of chapter 66, part two: "Que trata de la que verá el que lo leyere, o lo oirá y que lo escuchare leer" ("Which treats of what the reader shall see or the listener hear"). To read it oneself in direct contact with the text, or else to listen to it being read, benefitting from the intermediary of the spoken word: these are the two explicit readings postulated by Cervantes for his novel.

The second alternative is staged several times in the text itself. In part one, chapter 32, two readings conducted aloud are depicted. The first is a reading of the books of chivalry performed by a harvester for his assembled companions and the family of the innkeeper, Juan Palomeque:

Porque cuando es tiempo de la siega, se recogen aquí, las fiestas, muchos segadores, y siempre hay algunos que saben leer, el cual coge uno destos libros en las manos, y rodeámonos dél más de treinta, y estámosle escuchando con tanto gusto, que nos quita mil canas.

(For at harvest time a lot of the reapers come in here in the mid-day heat. There's always one of them who can read, and he takes up one of those books. Then as many as thirty of us sit around him, and we enjoy listening so much that it saves us countless grey hairs.)[7]

Gathered around *Don Cirongilio de Tracia* or *Felixmarte de Hircania* or the *Historia del Gran Capitán Gonzalo Hérnandez de Córdoba,* the innkeeper, his daughter, Maritornes, and the peasants at rest all listen to the reading, never tiring of it, each absorbed in his own thoughts. "Querría estar oyéndoles noches y días" ("And I could go on listening night and day"), declares the innkeeper.

Further on in the chapter, another reader proposes a reading. Urged on by Cardenio and Dorotea, the barber and Sancho, the priest agrees to read *La novela del curioso impertinente (The Tale of Foolish Curiosity),* a text "de ocho pliegos escritos de mano" ("eight sheets of manuscript") that had been found among the books and manuscripts preciously guarded by the inn's host and kept in an old trunk. The priest declares: "Pues así es, esténme todos atentos; que la novela comienza desta manera" ("Well, well! Listen to me, all of you, for this is how the tale begins"). It is as if the reader of the novel were being invited to join the little group listening to the adventure of the "curioso impertinente" and to "listen" in his silent reading to the word being read aloud.[8] In making use of this technique, which, granted, is not exclusively his, Cervantes recreates in the domain of fiction and for the solitary reader the circumstances of a totally different relationship to the text, as if readings conducted in the privacy of one's self should not be permitted to erase the custom of the text shared in common.

Whether reading aloud (and being read to) is actually depicted as a fact by certain literary texts or merely postulated as an implicit approach to them, it is a common practice in older societies. This practice nurtures the bonds of leisure and friendship. The memoirs of a Norman nobleman, Henri de Campion, a military man by profession, first an *enseigne* and later a *lieutenant* in the Normandy regiment, furnish ample evidence of this sort of kinship. Between 1635 and 1642 he was in the military and often in the field. Although books occupied his leisure hours, reading them was most often not a solitary activity:

> Pendant ce repos, j'avais mes livres, qui faisaient une partie de la charge de ma charrette, auxquels je m'occupais assez souvent, tantôt seul, et la plupart du temps avec trois de mes amis du régiment, gens spirituels et fort studieux.

> (During these respites, I had my books which made up a good part of my cart's load. They were my frequent occupation, I sometimes being alone, but most of the time with three of my friends, who were most studious and witty people.)[9]

These friends were the Chevalier de Sévigné, "un homme d'esprit studieux, qui avait beaucoup de lecture" ("a man of studious temperament, who was an extensive reader"); Le Breuil-Marcillac, "qui avait étudié jusqu'à vingt-huit ans, ses parents l'ayant destiné pour l'église" ("who had studied until he was twenty-eight, his parents having destined him for the priesthood"); and d'Almivar "mon intime ami" ("my intimate friend"). Among this foursome, the book that is read, listened to, and discussed weaves a strong and lasting social bond:

C'étaient-là les trois hommes avec lesquels je passais mes heures de loisir. Après avoir raisonné ensemble sur les sujets qui se présentaient, sans dispute aigre ni envie de paraître aux dépens les uns des autres, l'un de nous lisait haut quelque bon livre, dont nous examinions les plus beaux passages, pour apprendre à bien vivre et à bien mourir, selon la morale, qui était notre principale étude. Beaucoup prenaient plaisir à entendre nos conférences, qui, je crois, leur étaient utiles, puisqu'il ne s'y disait rien qui ne portât à la vertu. Je n'ai point trouvé depuis de société si commode et si raisonnable: elle dura les sept années que je servis dans le régiment de Normandie.

(Those were the three men with whom I spent my leisure hours. Together having pondered the subjects which came up, with no bitter arguments nor desire on the part of one to show up the others, one of us would read some good book aloud. We would examine its most beautiful passages with the intent of learning how to live well and likewise to die in accordance with moral science, which was the chief object of our study. Many people took pleasure in listening to our discussions, which, I do believe, were useful to them since nothing was ever said therein which did not have a bearing upon virtue. I have not since found so accommodating and reasonable a company: it remained together the seven years I served in the Normandy regiment.)[10]

Thus military leisure time encompassed a variety of modes of readings and relating to books, modes that define closely linked practices and interlocking structures of socializing. Individual readings nourished study and personal meditation. Conducted aloud, readings elicited commentary, criticism, debate, and the frequent but informal discussions among friends could attract others—silent auditors—instructed through listening to the texts being read or the exchange of arguments. Judging from Henri de Campion, books, along with gambling, were the customary pastimes of officers on duty, and, like gambling, they promised pleasures taken neither in solitude nor with the multitude. Read aloud, books both signified and reinforced the commitment of friendship.

Other "accommodating" and "reasonable" small societies, such as the one described by Henri de Campion, also existed in the city. Between the sixteenth and the eighteenth centuries, it was around a text being read aloud, a book leafed through and then discussed that the various forms of intellectual sociability were constructed: the sociability of the *salon,* the more regulated form typical of the academy, the casual sociability of the unannounced visit.

France in the seventeenth century witnessed a proliferation of these literate *compagnies,* which clustered around the word being read. These readings could be learned ones, offering as part of the listening program either the *mémoires* proposed by each respective member of the erudite coterie (such was the practice in Paris, even before the founding of the Académie Française in 1635, in the circles assembled around Father Mersenne, Habert de Montmort, or Valentin Conrart), or they could be lectures intended for a wider public, composed of listeners who were not all potential authors (as in the case of the Bureau d'Adresse instituted by Théophraste Renaudot). True to the practices of the late sixteenth-century academies (for instance, Baïf and Courville's Academy of Poetry and Music and the Académie du Palais), these readings were conducted before a select audience most often brought together in friendly and erudite complicity. They were to become the standard format observed by the Parisian academies and later by those of the provinces when requiring contributions from their individual members.[11] Listening to a reading was the essential activity of these learned assemblies, where no debate might take place until a speech had first been heard.

Of course, there was a considerable gap between the officially recognized academies with their restrictive statutes, and the smaller and freer societies (the self-attributed titles of "académie" notwithstanding) which had preceded them. For an example of the latter, one can look to a painting by Le Nain (in the Musée du Louvre) in which seven connoisseurs are gathered around some books and a lute, around music and knowledge, or to that Lyon society that the lawyer Brossette described in a letter written in 1700 to his friend Boileau:

> L'endroit où nous les tenons [i.e., les assemblées] est le cabinet de l'un de nos académiciens, nous y sommes au milieu de cinq à six mille volumes qui composent une bibliothèque aussi choisie qu'elle est nombreuse. Voilà déjà un secours bien prompt et bien agréable pour des conférences savantes.
>
> (The place where they [the assemblies] are held is the study of one of our academicians. There we are in the midst of the five to six thousand volumes which compose a library whose quality is as select as its quantity considerable. There one has at one's disposal a succor most convenient and pleasant for learned conferences.)[12]

But whatever the form taken, the practice remained identical, perhaps defining the academy in all its variations: readings conducted aloud and heard in audience.

These are also the staple of salon life, as can be seen in the two following illustrations. The first is a literary parody, consisting of the three initial scenes of the act III of the *Femmes Savantes (The Learned Ladies)* by Molière; the second, a painting. In the comedy, it is reading aloud that defines literate sociability (comically, in this case). The assembly is first and foremost an audience ("Donnons vite audience" ["Let's listen, with concentration"]), declares Philaminte, impatient to hear and critique the sonnet, and then the epigram by Trissotin, and then ready to listen to the "petits vers" by Vadius. The matrix of the scene consists of two practices that revolve around reading aloud. In the first case, these readings are performed by the authors themselves, criticized by Vadius, who is blind to his own ridiculousness:

> Le défaut des auteurs, dans leurs productions,
> C'est d'en tyranniser les conversations,
> D'être au Palais, aux Cours, aux ruelles, aux tables,
> De leurs vers fatigants lecteurs infatigables.

> (The fault of authors is their inclination,
> To dwell upon their works in conversations
> And whether in parks, or parlours, or at table,
> To spout their poems as often they're able.)[13]

Second, there are the salon readings—like the one during which Vadius had heard Trissotin's sonnet:

> Avez-vous vu un certain petit sonnet
> Sur la fièvre qui tient la Princesse Uranie?
> Oui, hier il me fut lu dans une compagnie.

> (Have you seen a certain sonnet
> About the fever of Princess Uranie?
> Yes, it was read to me yesterday at tea.)[14]

Our second example of just such a gathering was depicted by Jean-François de Troy in a serious, pictorial representation fifty years later (in the Marchioness of Cholmondeley collection). In a rococo salon, at three-thirty in the afternoon, according to the clock, comfortably installed in low bergère-style armchairs, five women and two men listen to a reading being conducted by one of them, an unbound book in hand. This company was separated from society by a closed door and a screen, forming a circle around the word being read. The title of the painting indicates the identity of the author, who has captured the attention of each person, feeding his or her thoughts in this instant in which the act of reading is surprised and interrupted: it is Molière.

On certain occasions, reading aloud for one's hosts could be a sort of gift offered by the visitor. This is borne out in the correspondence of Laurent Dugas, a Lyon notable, counsellor at the city's Cour des Monnaies. In 1733 M. de la Font, gentleman to the queen, received an autographed copy of a new book by Voltaire. He hastened to his friends, the Dugas:

M. de la Font arriva et me dit qu'il avait cru que je serais bien aise
d'entendre la lecture d'un ouvrage nouveau de M. de Voltaire intitulé *Le
Temple du Goût;* mais que si je le trouvais bon, nous attendrions mon
fils qui était allé le matin à Brignais pour revenir le soir. Il arriva une
demi-heure après et il fut le lecteur; la lecture dura une bonne heure et
demie, ma femme qui vint sur les sept heures en entendit les trois
quarts.

(M. de la Font arrived and told me that he had thought that I would
enjoy hearing the reading of a new work by M. de Voltaire entitled *Le
Temple du Goût,* but that if I found it to my liking, we would wait for my
son who had gone that morning to Brignais, to return that evening. He
arrived a half hour later, and he was the reader; the reading lasted a
good hour and a half. My wife who arrived home around seven o'clock,
heard three-quarters of it.)[15]

Laurent Dugas heard a second reading of the text several days later at the
academy:

J'ai entendu une seconde fois la lecture de cet ouvrage à l'académie et je
l'ai écoutée avec plaisir [. . .] M. l'abbé Tricaut qui devait parler n'a pas
été long et on a eu le temps de lire *Le Temple du Goût* mais on n'a pas lu
les notes que l'auteur a mis au bas des page et dont quelques-unes sont
très curieuses.

(I heard for the second time the reading of this work at the academy and
I listened to it with pleasure [. . .] Abbé Tricaut who was to speak, did
not take long, and we had the time to read *Le Temple du Goût,* but the
notes that the author put at the foot of the pages were not read, and
some of them are extremely curious.)[16]

Still unsated in his desire to hear the work and share his pleasure, Dugas
planned a third reading of the book in the company of his friend Bottu de
Saint-Fonds, who lived in Villefranche-sur-Saône and to whom his letter is
addressed. For this purpose he asked M. de la Font to lend him the book
for the day Bottu was to come to Lyon, and he declares to the latter: "Je
sens que je serai charmé de le relire avec vous" ("I feel that it will be a
delight to reread it with you").

But reading aloud was not practiced exclusively among those who knew
each other and saw one another frequently. In the midst of the uncertainties of travel, it could foster a temporary bond among fellow travellers. On
26 May 1668, Samuel Pepys returned from Cambridge to London with his
young servant Tom:

Up by 4 a-clock; and by the time we were ready and had eat, we were
called to the coach; where about 6 a-clock we set out, there being a man

and two women of one company, ordinary people, and one lady alone that is tolerable handsome, but mighty well spoken, whom I took great pleasure in talking to, and did get her to read aloud in a book she was reading in the coach, being the King's Meditations; and then the boy and I to sing.[17]

Along with conversations and song, the reading heard as a group—in this case, a reading of the prayers and meditations of Charles I before his execution—created an ephemeral togetherness, a feeling of being together that remains anonymous, thereby heightening the pleasure of the trip's forced congeniality. The socializing initiative taken by Pepys seems, moreover, to have had its effect, as he notes: "we dining all together pretty merry."[18]

Readings thus took place during travel; they took place at taverns as well. These have been depicted, among others, by the Dutch painter Ludolf de Jongh in a painting dated 1657 (Mittelrheinisches Landesmuseum, Mainz). In an inn, a man, a long horn hanging from his shoulder, reads aloud to three listeners: an old man seated across from him listening attentively, a girl, leaning on the back of the chair in which the old man is seated, and another man, who is looking intently at the reader. The latter, probably a public crier, is reading what appears to be a letter. The positions of the three, so absorbed in their listening that they are straining so as not to lose any part of the words being read, as if understanding it required a great effort, no doubt indicate that the reading aloud is being performed here by someone who knows how to read, to others who do not. The painter thereby brings our attention to the time and place of these mediated readings, in which the spoken word of the other constitutes the necessary condition for a relation with the written word.

The peasant evening gathering (or *veillée*) has often been considered a typical illustration of this sort of reading, allowing country illiterates to hear popular books. But such a view seems to have confused two quite different practices: reading aloud that implies the presence of the written or printed word on the one hand, and the recitation of tales or stories learned by heart and narrated from memory on the other. If ample evidence exists substantiating the latter practice as one of the customs of these evening gatherings, there is scant evidence to support the former. In the *Propos rustiques de Maistre Léon Ladulfi*, Noël du Faïl depicts one such evening gathering, held in the home of the laborer Robin Chevet:

Voulentiers apres souper, le ventre tendu comme un tabourin, saoul comme Patault, jazoit le dos tourné au feu, teillant bien mignonnement du chanvre, ou raccoustrant à la mode qui couroit ses bottes (car à toutes modes dordinaire saccoustroit l'homme de bien), chantant bien melodieusement, comme honnestement le sçavoit faire, quelque chanson nouvelle, Jouanne, sa femme, de l'austre costé, qui filloit, luy respondant de mesmes. Le reste de la famille ouvrant chascun en son office, les uns adoubans les courroyes de leurs fleaux, les autres faisans dents à Rateaux, bruslans hars pour lier (possible) laixeul de la charrette, rompu par trop grand faix, ou faisoyent une verge de fouet de mesplier ou meslier. Et ainsi occupés à diverses besongnes, le bon homme Robin (après avoir imposé silence) commençoit un beau compte du temps que les bestes parloyent (il ny ha pas deux heures): comme le Renard desroboit le poisson aux poissonniers; comme il feit battre le Loup aux Lavandieres, lors quil lapprenoit à pescher; comme le Chien et le Chat alloyent bien loing; de la Corneille, qui en chantant perdit son fromage; de Melusine; du Loup garou; de cuir d'Asnette; des Fees, et que souventesfois parloit à elles familiairement, mesmes la vespree passant par le chemin creux, et quil les voyoit dancer au bransle, pres la fontaine du Cormier, au son dune belle veze, couverte de cuir rouge.

(Often after supper, his stomach stretched like a drum, drunk as Patault, he liked to chat with his back to the fire as he cut hemp or remade his boots to the current fashion [for a proper man usually adjusts to all fashions], singing most melodiously—for he sang well—some new song, while Jouanne, his wife, on the other side answered him in like manner as she spun. The rest of the household was working, each on his own task, some mending the thongs of their flails, the others making teeth for rakes, scorching faggots to reconnect (possible) the wagon axle broken by an overload, or making a stick whip out of medlar wood. [When they were] thus occupied with their various tasks, goodman Robin, after imposing silence, would begin a fine story about the time when the animals talked (it was just two hours before); of how Renard the fox stole a fish from the fishmongers; of how he got the Washerwomen to beat the Wolf when he was learning how to fish; of how the Dog and the Cat went on a voyage; about Asnette's hide; about fairies and how he often spoke with them familiarly, even at vespers as he passed through the hedgerows and saw them dancing near the Cormier fountain to the sound of a red leather bagpipe.)[19]

Clearly Robin is not reading; rather he is telling stories and tales that belong to the oral tradition. Certain ones, if not all of these tales, have already been the subject of several printed versions, which Robin may very well have been able to read, but during this gathering, he is telling them by heart and from memory to his wife and household, in the absence of all books:

Que si quelcun ou une se fust endormie daventure, comme les choses arrivent, lors quil faisoit ces haults comptes (desquelz maintesfois jay esté auditeur), maistre Robin prenoit une chenevotte allumee par un bout, et souffloit par lautre au nés de celuy qui dormoit, faisant signe dune main quon ne lesveillast. Lors disoit: "Vertu goy! jay eu tant de mal à les apprendre et me romps icy la teste, pensant bien besongner, encores ne daignent ilz me escouter."

(And if by chance one of them fell asleep, as such things happened when he was telling these old tales [to which I often listened] master Robin would take a piece of straw lit at one end and would blow through the other at the nose of the sleeper, making a sign with his free hand that no one was to wake him. Then he would say, "S'truth! I've gone to so much trouble to learn these and I'm breaking my head here so that everybody will keep at his work, and they don't even deign to listen to me.")[20]

In part one of *Don Quixote,* chapter 20, Cervantes also evokes these tales or stories (the *consejas*) told during the gatherings. They are learned by heart and narrated according to traditional formulas. To Don Quixote, who asks him to tell him some story, Sancho replies:

Yo me esforzaré a decir una historia, que, si la acierto a contar y no me van a la mano, es la mejor de las historias; y estéme vuestra merced atento, que ya comienzo. Érase que se era, el bien que viniere para todos sea, y el mal, para quien lo fuere a buscar. . . .

(I will endeavour to tell you a story and, if I manage to tell it without interruption, it'll be the best story in the world. Pay good attention, your worship, for I'm going to begin. "Once upon a time; may good befall us and evil strike man who seeks it.")[21]

While narrating, Sancho constantly digresses and repeats himself, and includes reprises and parenthetical remarks. These techniques annoy his master very much indeed:

"Si desa manera cuentas tu cuento, Sancho"—dijo don Quijote—"repitiendo dos veces lo que vas diciendo, no acabarás en dos días; dilo seguidamente, y cuéntalo como hombre de entendimiento, y si no, nos digas nada."
"De la misma manera que yo lo cuento"—respondió Sancho—"se cuentan en mi tierra todas las consejas, y yo no sé contarlo de otra, ni es bien que vuestra merced me pida que haga usos nuevos."

("If you tell your story that way, Sancho," said Don Quixote, "and repeat everything you have to say twice over, you will not be done in two days. Tell it consequentially, like an intelligent man, or else be quiet."
"The way I'm telling it," replied Sancho, "is the way all stories are told in my country, and I don't know any other way of telling it. It isn't fair for your worship to ask me to get new habits.")[22]

Through his fiction, Cervantes gives substance to a culture of oral recitation that is at once fixed and free-form, spontaneous and encoded, based on techniques of narrating that are totally different from the techniques of reading implied by the written text. In so doing, he shows us scenes of the peasant gathering where the tale has its place, but where reading aloud, so it would seem, is extremely rare.

This, at least, is what is taught in ecclesiastical writings, in synodal and episcopal statutes that condemn such evening gatherings. The latter are always described as assemblies in which there is singing and dancing, where people work and play, where boy meets girl, but never as places where reading is practiced, be it silently or aloud, in groups or alone. Generally, village culture of the Early Modern period is not one in which reading is performed aloud or in which the written word is present and mediated by a reader who vocalizes it. It is a culture of recitation, one of narratives or tales, and in which those who know how to read memorize the written tale in order to tell it, thus assimilating the written narrative to oral tradition. One can cite as proof the *Mémoires* of Valentin Jamerey Duval, born in 1695 near Tonnerre, who after a childhood spent wandering, became a shepherd in a village in Lorraine-Clézantaine, near Epinal, at the beginning of the eighteenth century. There he learned how to read, and he devoured the "libraries of the village":

> J'engageay mes confrères dans la vie bucolique à m'aprendre a lire, ce qu'ils firent volontiers au moyen de quelques repas champetres que je leur promis. Le hazard m'occasionna cette entreprise par l'inspection d'un livre de fables, ou les animaux, qu'Esope introduit pour instruire ceux qui croyent avoir la raison en partage, étoient représentés en fort belles tailles douces. Le dépit de ne pouvoir comprendre leurs dialogues sans le secours d'un interprète m'irrita contre l'ignorence ou je croupissais, de sorte que je résolus de mettre tout en usage pour en dissiper les ténèbres. Mes progrès dans la lecture furent si rapides qu'en peu de mois les acteurs de l'apologue n'eurent plus rien de nouveau pour moi. Je parcourus avec une extrème avidité toutes les bibliothèques du hameau. J'en feuilletay tous les auteurs et bientot, grace à ma mémoire et a mon peu de discernement, je me vis en état de raconter les merveilleuses prouesses de Richard sans peur, de Robert le Diable, de Valentin et Orson et des quatre fils Aimon.

(I engaged my companions in the bucolic life to teach me to read, which they did willingly, thanks to a few outdoor repasts that I promised them. I embarked on this enterprise through the chance examination of a book of fables, in which the animals, which Aesop introduces in order to instruct those who think reason is theirs alone, were represented in very beautiful copperplate engravings. My vexation at not being able to understand their dialogue without the help of an interpreter made me become irritated at the ignorance in which I was wallowing, so I re-solved to do my utmost to dissipate the darkness. My progress in reading was so rapid that in only a few months the actors in the apologue held no surprises for me. I went through all the libraries of the village with extreme avidity. I leafed through all the authors they contained and so, thanks to my memory and to my eclecticism, I found myself capable of recounting the marvelous feats of Richard the Fearless, Robert the Devil, Valentin and Orson, and the four sons of Aimon[23] [these being four novels of chivalry printed by publishers in Troyes who specialized in popular books at the beginning of the seventeenth century].)

To thank those who had taught him to read, Jamerey Duval narrates the best passages of his recent reading for them in theatrical style:

J'invitois les jeunes gens dont j'avois été le disciple a recevoir le change de leurs instructions et montant sur une tribune de gazon, je leur déclamois, avec cette emphase qui caractérise si bien l'ignorence, les plus beayux traits de Jean de Paris, de Pierre de Provence et de la merveilleuse Mélusine.

(I invited the young people who had first taught me, and, mounting a rostrum of grass, I declaimed to them, with the pompousness so characteristic of ignorance, the most beautiful passages from Jean de Paris, Pierre de Provence, and the marvelous Mélusine[24] [three other books from the *Bibliothèque bleue*].)

"To recount," "to declaim": the vocabulary clearly indicates that it is not a question of reading aloud but rather of reciting texts learned by heart and told like tales. It would seem as though reading aloud—which takes for granted the presence of the text read and listened to—were more a city than a rural practice, normal in urban culture where the printed word is a sight familiar even to illiterates incapable of decoding it, but exceptional in a peasant culture, for which the book would remain a rarity for a long time to come and where not all the harvesters enjoyed the same good fortune as those amused by the three works so jealously guarded by Juan Palomeque, the innkeeper in *Quixote*.

Although it may not have been standard practice in communal gatherings, reading aloud has been attested to in certain kinds of intimate family groups. In the first place, it can be a reading conducted by one person on behalf of another. The servant reads for the master: thus we see Pepys who often bids his valet read him some text—and this even before his sight has gone bad. For example, on 22 September 1660: "To bed, not well of my last night's drinking yet. I had the boy up tonight for his sister to teach him to put me to bed, and I heard him read, which he doth pretty well";[25] on 9 September 1666, after the great fire that forced him to leave his place of dwelling: "Anon to Sir W. Penn to bed, and made my boy Tom to read me asleep."[26] The same sort of ancillary reading was to take place on Christmas Day, 1668:

So home and to dinner alone with my wife, who, poor wretch, sat undressed all day till 10 at night, altering and lacing of a black pet-ticoat—while I by her, making the boy read to me the life of Julius Caesar and Des Cartes book of music—the latter of which I understand not, nor think he did well that writ it, though a most learned man. Then after supper made the boy play upon his lute, which I have not done twice before since he came to me; and so, my mind in mighty content, we to bed.[27]

But readings were also acts of conjugal reciprocity, conducted between spouses. On 22 December 1667, Samuel Pepys's wife suffered from an inflammation of the cheek and was forced to keep to her room:

After dinner, up to my wife again, who is in great pain still with her tooth and cheek; and there . . . I spent the most of the afternoon and night reading and talking to bear her company, and so to supper and to bed.[28]

Three days later, on Christmas Day, it is his wife's turn to do the reading: "all the afternoon at home, my wife reading to me the history of the Drummer of Mr. Monpesson, which is a strange story of spirits, and worth reading indeed."[29]

Such readings also bound niece and uncle, as Teresa de Avila attests:

Estaba en el camino un hermano de mi padre, muy avisado y de grandes virtudes, viudo [. . .] Su ejercicio era buenos libros de romance, y su hablar era los mas ordinario de Dios y de la vanidad del mundo: haciame le leyese, y aunque no era amiga de ellos, mostraba que si.

(On the road lived one of my father's brothers, a widower, who was a very shrewd man and full of virtues [. . .] It was his practice to read good verse novels and his conversation was ordinarily about God and the vanity of the world. He made me read to him; and, although I did not much care for his books, I acted as though I did.)[30]

And there were readings between father and son, as Dugas from Lyon reports in his letters: "je passais un temps considérable avec mon fils à lire du grec et quelques odes d'Horace" ("I spent considerable time with my son, reading Greek and some odes of Horace") (22 July 1718); "Je lis avec mon fils aîné le *Traité des Lois* de Cicéron et Salluste avec le second" ("With my eldest son, I am reading Cicero's *Treatise on Laws* and with my younger son, Sallust") (14 September 1719); "c'est le soir que je joue aux échecs avec mon fils. Nous commençons par lire un bon livre, c'est-à-dire un livre de piété, pendant une demi-heure" ("it is the evening that I play chess with my son. We begin by reading a good book—that is, a book of piety—for a half hour") (19 December 1732).[31]

Reading aloud for another person, or with another, was thus a practice that entailed a host of different relationships: the service due a master, conjugal exchange, filial obedience, paternal education. Whether arranged or spontaneous, reading aloud was one of the duties—and sometimes one of the pleasures—of the domestic and filial bond. In any case, it perpetuated a rapport with books, which, insofar as they are heard, inscribes the printed word within a culture of the spoken word. Reading was considered not as some privileged solitary retreat, but rather as the very articulation of one person's rapport with others, with all the complexity such relations imply.

But domestic readings could also assemble the family in its entirety around the book. The model here is clearly a religious one, observed by the Protestant reformers. Reading the Bible aloud is an obligation of the head of the family. We are continually reminded of this in Luther's writings, in the reformed catechisms or postils (such as, among others, Dietrich's *Kinder-Postilla* published in Nuremberg in 1549: "in the evening, once work is finished [. . .] read them [the children and servants] a passage or two from the Bible and commend it to their memory"). At times books themselves included illustrations of such required readings being performed. This is true, for example, of Justus Menius's treatise *Ein kurzer ausszug auss der christlichen Oeconomia,* in an edition published at Regensburg in 1554 (the Latin text dates from 1529). On the title page, a vignette depicts the paterfamilias conducting a reading to his entire household: his wife and children seated on his right, his servants in another corner of the room (two are standing and a female servant is holding a distaff in her hand). On the table is a heavy Bible, another smaller book (perhaps the *Oeconomia* itself ?), a pair of glasses, and an hour glass.[32]

True, this paternal, biblical reading was not actually practiced by all brands of Protestantism—and often pastoral visits deplored its absence—but its practice has been authenticated in many areas. One example of this occurred in sixteenth-century Switzerland: Felix Platter remembered in his childhood listening to his father, Thomas, who conducted such readings: "It was my father's custom, before we went to church, to read us the Holy Scripture and to preach from it." Another example is to be found in London of the seventeenth century, where the Puritan artisan, Nehemiah Wallington, assembled his family at six o'clock on Sunday mornings around sacred writings, spiritual readings, and domestic catechism:

One did read Leviticus 26, of which I did speak what God put into my mind; then I went to catechizing, and then to read out of *The Garden of Spiritual Flowers,* very useful to our souls, and some others read out of the Psalms. And so to prayer with my family wherein I did find some comfort.[33]

The same situation applied in New England in the seventeenth and eighteenth centuries.[34]

Such oral and familiar readings set up a lasting reference and a tenacious ideal. And it was a model adhered to throughout eighteenth-century France, for example, from Greuze's painting exhibited in the salon of 1755 to which Diderot gave various titles, some biblical, others not *(Father Reading the Holy Scripture to His Children, Peasant Reading to His Children)*, to the frontispiece engraved in 1778 for the second volume of *La Vie de mon Père* by Rétif de la Bretonne. Leisure became instruction through this religiously inspired imagery, and the spoken word edified, exposing the frivolity or license of solitary reading. Readings conducted aloud to the assembled household promised morality and utility.

The goal of this initial and somewhat summary collection of a few depictions (literary, iconographic, or autobiographical) of reading aloud during the first two centuries of the modern period has been to sketch out the lines of potential future research. The present study has deliberately left aside three forms of vocalized reading because they lie outside the pale of privacy and are not linked to leisure time. The first involves ecclesiastic readings conducted by the priest or the pastor during religious services. The second involves both political and legal readings, inscribed in the ancient custom that links a document's authority to its verbal proclamation. The third involves academic, professorial readings, as performed in the college and to an even greater extent in the university, the essential act by which knowledge is transmitted.

In spite of the inroads made by personal readings pursued in privacy and silence and practiced by an increasing number of readers between the sixteenth and the eighteenth centuries, listening to readings remained a frequent practice, one customarily indulged in on any number of different occasions. It was also a practice whose goal was not only to allow illiterates to share a little in the culture of the written word: often, both in representations and in practice, reading aloud was conducted by those who knew how to read to others with the same knowledge, for the twin pleasures of the exchange and the relationships it secured. It was a pastime and an amusement, and the sociability fostered by these readings performed and listened to is a figure of the social bond itself. This is doubtless why reading aloud, to one person or to many, remains a familiar gesture of the men and women of older societies. It is also why in the eighteenth century, this kind of reading was to become the sign of convivialities lost and sought for.

Notes

This article, which makes use of certain material presented at the symposium "Forms of Play in the Early Modern Period" held in April 1984 at the University of

Maryland at College Park, was developed into its present form during an NEH Postdoctoral Interdisciplinary Seminar that I taught at the Newberry Library in Chicago in 1985. I would like to thank those people who shared their opinions and criticisms with me—particularly Barry Wind who brought the painting by Ludolph de Jongh to my attention.

Since I have written it, I have read two articles devoted to the same topic, which give some other data: William Nelson, "From 'Listen, Lordings' to 'Dear Reader,'" *University of Toronto Quarterly* 46 (Winter 1976–77): 110–24; and Margit Frenk, "'Lectores y oidores': La difusión oral de la literatura en el Siglo de Oro," *Actas del Séptimo Congreso de la Asociación Internacional de Hispanistas,* 25–30 August 1980 (Rome; Bulzoni Editore, 1982), 1:101–23.

1. Michel de Montaigne, *Essais,* ed. Pierre Villey (Paris: Presses Universitaire de France, 1978), 2:36. Translation: *The Complete Works of Montaigne,* trans. D. M. Frame (Palo Alto, Calif.: Stanford University Press, 1967).

2. William Shakespeare, *The Tempest,* act 1, lines 109–10, The Illustrated Stratford Shakespeare (London: Chancellor Press, 1982), 110.

3. Tristan L'Hermite, *La Mort de Sénèque,* 1644, act 1, lines 197–200 (Paris: Comédie Française, 1984), 19–20.

4. Paul Saenger, "Silent Reading: Its Impact on Late Medieval Script and Society," *Viator: Medieval and Renaissance Studies* 13 (1982): 367–414.

5. *La Celestina: Tragicomedia de Calisto y Melibea / La Célestine ou Tragi-Comédie de Calixte et Mélibée,* attributed to Fernando de Rojas, preface and translation (into French) by Pierre Heugas (Paris: Aubier-Flammarion, 1980), 2:522–23. English translation: *Celestina: A Play in Twenty-two Acts,* attributed to Fernando de Rojas, trans. M. H. Singleton (Madison: University of Wisconsin Press, 1958).

6. Ibid, 1:118–19.

7. Miguel de Cervantes, *El Ingenioso Hidalgo Don Quijote de la Mancha,* ed. John Jay Allen (Madrid: Ediciones Cátedra, 1984), 1:376. Translation: *The Adventures of Don Quixote,* trans. J. M. Cohen (Harmondsworth, Eng.: Penguin Books, 1984).

8. Ibid., 1:382.

9. Henri de Campion, *Mémoires,* ed. Marc Fumaroli (Paris: Mercure de France, 1967), 95.

10. Ibid., 95–96.

11. Frances Yates, *The French Academies of the Sixteenth Century* (London: Warburg Institute, 1947); and Daniel Roche, *Le Siècle des Lumières en province: Académies et académiciens provinciaux, 1660–1789* (La Haye: Mouton, 1969).

12. Letter from Brossette to Nicolas Boileau-Despréaux, 16 July 1700, in *Lettres familières de Messieurs Boileau-Despréaux et Brossette* (Lyon: Cizeron-Rival, 1770).

13. Molière, *Les Femmes Savantes,* 1672, act 3, lines 955–58, in *Théâtre Complet de Molière,* ed. Robert Jouanny (Paris: Editions Garnier, n.d.), 2:720. Translation: *The Learned Ladies,* trans. R. Wilbur (New York and London: Harcourt Brace Jovanovich, 1978).

14. Ibid., act 3, lines 988–90, 721.

15. Letter from Dugas to Bottu de Saint-Fonds, 23 March 1733, in *Correspondance littéraire et anecdotique entre Monsieur de Saint-Fonds et le Président Dugas* (Lyon, 1900). Translated by L. Cochrane.

16. Ibid.

17. Samuel Pepys, *The Diary,* ed. Robert Latham and William Matthews (Berkeley: University of California Press, 1970), 9:213.

18. Ibid.

19. Noël du Fail, *Propos Rustiques de Maistre Léon Ladulfi Champenois,* 1548, in *Conteurs français du XVIe siècle,* Bibliothèque de la Pléiade (Paris: Gallimard, 1965), 620. Translated by L. Cochrane.

20. Ibid., 621.

21. Miguel de Cervantes, *Don Quijote,* 1:237.

22. Ibid.

23. Valentin Jamerey Duval, *Mémoires: Enfance et éducation d'un paysan au XVIIIe siècle,* ed. Jean-Marie Goulemot (Paris: Editions Le Sycomore: 1981), 191–92.

24. Ibid., 193.

25. Samuel Pepys, *Diary,* 1:251.

26. Ibid., 7:251.

27. Ibid., 9:400–401.

28. Ibid., 8:586.

29. Ibid., 589.

30. Santa Teresa de Jesús, *Su Vida* (Madrid: Espasa-Calpe, 1960), 27.

31. Letters from Dugas to Bottu de Saint-Fonds, 22 July 1718, 14 September 1719, and 19 December 1732, in *Correspondance littéraire et anecdotique.*

32. Gerald Strauss, *Luther's House of Learning: Indoctrination of the Young in German Reformation* (Baltimore: The Johns Hopkins University Press, 1978), 108–31. The title page of the *Oeconomia christiana* by Menius is reproduced on p. 114.

33. Paul S. Seaver, *Wallington's World: A Puritan Artisan in Seventeenth-Century London* (Palo Alto, Calif.: Stanford University Press, 1985), 40.

34. David Hall, "Introduction: The Uses of Literacy in New England, 1600–1850," *Printing and Society in Early America,* ed. W. Joyce, D. Hall, R. Brown, and J. Hench (Worcester, Mass.: American Antiquarian Society, 1983), 1–47.

5

Trickery, Gender, and Power:
The *Discorsi* of Annibale Romei

Werner L. Gundersheimer

Many historians in recent times have taken a strong interest in processes of economic and social decadence, degeneration, and decline. As a result, we know far more than we used to about such issues as how families preserve their wealth as the public resources around them diminish, and how political regimes tend to respond to perceived reductions in their economic and military strength.[1] It is clear that historians have overlooked evidence of continuing vitality, or at least viability, in groups or societies that are being outclassed, surpassed, and left behind as a result of processes of change or shifts in what one sixteenth-century writer called "the vicissitude and variety of things in the universe."[2] This essay considers an example of vitality amidst decline in the late Italian Renaissance.

In the late sixteenth century, the Duchy of Ferrara, long celebrated for its continuity and stability, was in the midst of a prolonged process of decadence, decline, and ultimately destruction.[3] Yet, surprisingly, very few scholars in this century have bothered to look at the Este city during the long reign of Alfonso II (1559–1597) as a significant case of an established early modern regime responding to stresses and challenges that recurrently battered and ultimately overwhelmed it. *Fin-de-siècle* Ferrara, to borrow Carl Schorske's apt term, reveals a complex, engrossing society, one that is just beginning to be understood.[4] The first major step forward took place in 1980 with the publication of Anthony Newcomb's two-volume study *The Madrigal at Ferrara, 1579–1597.*[5] While that book seeks mainly to explain the stages in the stylistic evolution of a musical form, it clarifies many neglected or unknown aspects of Estean patronage and court life, and links them effectively to specific historical developments. Above all, Newcomb brings to life large sectors of a courtly world of secular *divertissements*—fun and games of all kinds and degrees—in which dancing and singing came to play an important part. As to their precise role, he suggests that

The overall impression that one draws from accounts of conditions in Ferrara in the last ten years of Este rule is that of a court that had walled itself off from the turmoil and trouble in the world outside. Increasingly frustrated, even threatened by that world, it had determined to create an artful and artificial world of particular pleasures to enjoy in its declining years.[5]

One is tempted to state the case even more strongly. Historically, Ferrara had for centuries been comprised of two separate and distinct social worlds. On the one hand, there were the Este rulers, their secretaries, counsellors, chancellors, ambassadors, and agents; their squires, pages, men-at-arms, and servants; their humanists, physicians, musicians, librarians, astrologers, painters, sculptors, and weavers; and of course, their women, most of whom had similar, if smaller, staffs and households. These people, together with various other retainers scattered about Ferrara and the various Estean rural retreats, comprised the social world of the court, and numbered from five hundred to one thousand people, depending on the inclusiveness of our categories. With the exception of noblemen whose terrains provided them with dependable incomes, they were dependent on the Estean payrolls.[6] On the other hand, there was the rest of the population of Ferrara, its many dependent cities, and its approximately 3,200 square miles of countryside. This was a world in which peasants comprised the bulk of the population, supplemented by artisans, tradesmen, and a smattering of more specialized workers, such as fishermen, Po River boatsmen, and a few people in the traditional professions like teaching, banking, medicine, and low-level local administration.[7] Between these two worlds, but more closely tied to the second than the first, were a few special groups—the clergy (particularly those in orders); the Jews; and the usual deviants such as brigands, prostitutes, criminals "on the lam," and others whose marginality disposed them to drift as inconspicuously as possible in what Mao Zedong used to call "the ocean of the people."[8]

What might be termed the social distance between these two cultures—the one small, prosperous, and controlling; the other immense, often destitute, and subject—was never small. But throughout the fifteenth century, a succession of Este rulers consistently made at least symbolic, and occasionally even substantive, efforts to acknowledge and serve the interests of the multitudes under their sway. I do not know when the Estensi abandoned their practice of manifesting concern for their subjects in popular and palpable ways. But Alfonso II was most assuredly an aristocrat whose isolation from the people was as absolute as the small world of Ferrara could afford. Even foreign observers remarked upon the callous indifference of the duke toward the welfare of the people, citing his fiscal exactions, his reliance on forced labor, and his arbitrary confiscations of property.

The same observers also bear witness to the refined and elegant life of the court. The exemplary and didactic functions of courtly magnificence, so prominent an aspect of conspicuous consumption in the *Quattrocentro,* seem entirely absent from Alfonso's circle. In *fin-de-siècle* Ferrara, the central purpose of life in the ducal household would appear to have been the pursuit of pleasure. The men and women of the court, many of them extremely bright, highly educated, and talented, seem literally to have retired—drawn back—from the world, and to have confined themselves happily to the institutional setting that existed for them and for which they existed. Within the sumptuous houses and manicured gardens where they spent their days, they were free to amuse and entertain themselves and one another, provided only that they were available to pay court to duke and duchess on request, and that they remained within the bounds of Counter-Reformation propriety in their verbal and actual behavior. Life at court, so full of vitality and innovation in an earlier time, seems stylized and constricting for the fortunate few of the late sixteenth century.[9]

However limited its opportunities and circumscribed its pleasures, the late Renaissance court offered a sheltering space, happily distanced from the cruel world beyond. And for those who ruled Ferrara, that world had become as never before a source of anxiety, trouble, and danger. In the late 1560s and throughout the 1570s, a series of bad harvests had brought the region repeatedly to the edge of famine and the brink of serious social upheaval. Storms, floods, and droughts succeeded one another in an unprecedented pattern of destruction. On the night of 16 November 1570, Ferrara and its territories were struck by a terrible earthquake. One observer reported:

> The castle is all broken up; the churches of S. Giovanni Battista and S. Francesco, part of S. Polo, Sta. Maria in Vado, the Duomo, all wrecked with their bells fallen; similarly, the bell-towers of S. Giorgio, the Certosa, the church of the Angels, that of Sta. Anna are down, almost all the convents of nuns are in ruins, and all in all the whole city is a miserable, heartbreaking sight to see.[10]

Fearing the aftershocks, the duke and most of the court slept outdoors for some time thereafter, in the damp, freezing fogs of a northern Italian winter. Despite numerous casualties, witnesses agreed that many thousands would have been killed had there not been some premonitory tremors.

Challenges from other quarters faced the Estensi during these years. Perhaps the most serious was the problem of succession, for Alfonso II appeared (and in fact proved) incapable of producing a legitimate male heir. It was not for want of trying, and with a succession of three wives.[11] Since the Estensi ruled Ferrara under a papal vicariate, transmittable by law only through direct descent, Alfonso's problem promised to bring the Este dynasty in Ferrara to an inglorious end.

This beclouded, preoccupied time witnessed, not coincidentally, an indian summer in the life of the court. Never had its nobles been more distinguished, its guiding intellects more fastidiously intelligent, its visitors more exalted, its women more elegant, its performers more accomplished, its venues more hospitable or beautiful. The pastimes and diversions of the court survive in the records as a sugary veneer. Rare are the cracks that allow the tensions and stresses to show through. In *fin-de-siècle* Ferrara, living well had become the best revenge on a mutable world, a threatening fate.[12]

The source that in many ways both illustrates and exemplifies these characteristics is a work simply called *Discorsi*.[13] Its author, Annibale Romei, was a somewhat obscure descendant of a noble family of Spanish origin that had settled in Ferrara three centuries earlier. One of their fifteenth-century houses, the Casa Romei, survives more or less intact today as a museum. Although Annibale's name does not appear regularly on the salary rolls, Alfonso II used him for at least three diplomatic missions, and he can be securely placed in the circle of *familiari,* a contemporary term signifying both the inner circle of the duke or his household. A few letters and a brief treatise on earthquakes would seem to round out Romei's literary remnants; his reputation, such as it is, therefore rests on the *Discorsi*.

Neither a philosophical treatise, nor a book of manners, nor a description of life at court, Romei's *Discorsi* partakes of all of these forms. It is most commonly cited in discussions of the influences of Castiglione's *Il Cortegiano,* on which it depends in important formal and substantive ways. The book reports a series of conversations among men and women of the court that Romei says took place during the early autumn of 1584 at the palace of La Mesola, a hunting retreat that had recently been constructed near the Adriatic, east of Ferrara.[14] While the first edition (published in Venice, in 1585) divides the discussion into five days, the second (from Ferrara, in 1585) and subsequent versions expand them into seven. The topics will seem all too familiar to readers of sixteenth-century moral texts: beauty; human love; honor; the duel; nobility; riches; and finally, the question of precedence between arms and letters.[15]

Romei's book enjoyed a modest success in its own time, benefitting both from the perennial popularity of its topics to contemporary readers and the aura of prestige that still surrounded the court of the Este. A third edition appeared in Verona in 1586, followed by at least four more Italian editions. In 1595, a very decent French translation was produced by the

Sieur DuPré. His epistle dedicatory, addressed to Gillonne de Matignon, Dame de Beauron et de la Motte Harcourt, simply plagiarized Romei's original dedication to Lucrezia d'Este, duchess of Urbino, Alfonso's sister. Three years later, the book appeared in England bearing the title *The Courtier's Academie,* in a translation by John Kepers dedicated to Sir Charles Blunt, better known as Lord Mountjoy, knight of the Garter and captain of the fortress and town of Portsmouth.[16]

Kepers omitted Romei's letter to Lucrezia d'Este but put in its place two letters of his own. The second of these, "To the courteous and benevolent reader," reveals an entirely justified diffidence as to the quality of the translation, while reviewing its methods, problems, and inadequacies. The first letter, to Lord Mountjoy, sets forth Kepers's claims for the interest of the book in terms of its philosophical content:

> These worthie discourses written by no unwoorthie gentleman in Italian, grounded on the firm foundations of Aristotelian, and Platonical discipline, and yet accompanied with a lively touch and feeling for these times, I thought no less woorthie to be offered to the view and censure of noble and courteous constructions.[17]

Notwithstanding the qualities Kepers perceived in Romei's work, it has not fared well in the hands of its most recent critics, and understandably so. There are far more impressive examples of "Artistotelian and Platonical discipline."[18] Intellectually, the book lacks originality, while stylistically it offers little of the liveliness, the *sprezzatura* of its celebrated predecessor. Thus Thomas Frederick Crane, writing of the *Discorsi* in his own useful and unjustly neglected *Italian Social Customs of the Sixteenth Century* (1920) paraphrased the entire work and then, as though to reward himself for the tedium he had voluntarily both endured and inflicted, noted:

> Romei's work is evidently an imitation of Castiglione's *Cortegiano,* but it is an uninteresting and colorless one. . . . As a work of literary art it does not stand high, and cannot be compared with its original except to its great disadvantage. . . . There is not a gleam of wit in the entire work, which never rises above a certain mediocre seriousness.[19]

Professor Alice Shalvi's verdict is similar, and she also notes Romei's "stiff, heavy prose."[20]

These reservations, which it would be absurd to challenge, do not bear in any way upon the second of John Kepers's motives for making the *Discorsi* available to English readers—"a lively touch and feeling for these times." What gives the work its interest is not so much the dutiful transcription of philosophical debates (though these are far from sterile). It is the pedestrian accuracy, the authoritative realism with which the settings for those debates are recreated. That is to say, the book's primary interest is not as a text in intellectual history, but as a source for the cultural anthropology of the court. Through Romei's painstakingly detailed settings, reconstructed out of deep knowledge and without apparent artifice, modern readers may still find that special quality of authenticity that moved the Elizabethan translator.

The philosophical discussions in this book take place within a series of nicely delineated frames in which the author describes settings at court. The physical spaces, the weather, and the days' and nights' activities all figure in the debates and the narratives that surround them. Romei evokes a labile world that shifts from room to room, from palace to seaside, finally even to the ducal *bucintoro*, the elaborately decorated, gilded launch that transported the courtiers and ladies back up the Po to Ferrara.

While Castiglione also provided a persuasive *mis-en-scène,* there are some major differences between the circumstances in which the two authors composed their works. *The Boke of the Courtier* was written at an indeterminate time long after 1507, when its purported discussions were said to have occurred. Even later, Castiglione edited and revised the text, and it did not appear in print until 1528, by which time most of the participants were dead. Upon its appearance, it was therefore addressed to people who were ignorant of its setting and could hardly have known more than one or two of the interlocutors.

Romei's situation was almost precisely the opposite of Castiglione's. The Ferrarese courtier published his work the year after the events in it purportedly took place. All of the participants were still on hand. The dedicatee herself had for many years been a permanent resident and an active force at court; she was well placed to judge the accuracy of the reportage. There was, then, little chance for time, memory, or literary skill to work their subtle changes in Romei's text. That enhances its documentary authority. Moreover, to the extent that other sources provide data on the people involved and the events alluded to in the *Discorsi,* Romei's descriptions and characterizations are supported. Finally, there is a single, extremely striking instance of the suppression from all later editions of an anecdote that appeared in the first, Venetian edition, of 1585, a fact that suggests that this portion of Romei's text received an unfavorable reception at court, and that omission needs to be examined in detail.

This account appears at the beginning of the second day, as Romei describes the activities leading up to the afternoon's discussions. As he tells it:

Early the next morning the Queen with all the court went to the sea, where the nets were prepared and the fishermen ready. Entering a large and sumptuous vessel with the Duchess, his Highness, Signor Don Cesare, the ladies and other noble cavaliers were towed to their great pleasure over the calm sea, while the fishermen drew the nets. Suddenly from one of the towers guarding the harbor two shots were heard signalling that two corsairs had been sighted. At the same moment, a bark belonging to the fishermen from Comacchio was seen rowing eagerly, and was said to be returning to port to avoid the pirates. When the ladies heard this news, they grew as pale as death *(si tinsero i volti de le dame di color di morte)* and, all trembling, commended themselves to the cavaliers, and would willingly have fled, had they known how.

The Signor Giulio Cesare Brancaccio, a noble and valiant warrior, advanced before the Queen and spoke in a bold voice in this manner: "It would be a great shame, most serene Queen, to your Majesty and to all the cavaliers who serve here, if after the fashion of the infamous Cleopatra you should flee, distrusting our will and your strength. . . . Here are twelve barks, each with ten oars, well armed, with which . . . I boast that as soon as I shall have provided them with musketeers, I will capture and bring before you those two galleys with all those robbers. But your Majesty must give the order at once, so that our delay may not expose us to the danger of being outstripped before this slow and tardy boat of ours is brought back to the harbor." His Highness praised the opinion of Signor Brancaccio, and so encouraged the Queen, who although she was very brave was rather inclined to flight than to battle, that she entrusted the undertaking to Signor Giulio Cesare. He entered a little boat with some of the cavaliers, had himself rowed to the harbor, and presently came forth with ten vessels well provided with musketeers, and made his way towards the galleys. Nor was it long before the battle began, within sight of the royal vessel, which was being towed toward the harbor. The storm of artillery and muskets was heard, to the great terror of the ladies *(grandissimo spavento delle dame),* who raised vows and prayers towards heaven. Finally, the battle having lasted over an hour, the galleys were captured, and the victors towed them into the harbor to the sound of drums and trumpets, and all the corsairs were brought in chains before the Queen. Then the joke was discovered *(E allora si scoperse la burla):* for these were all courtiers, and the galleys were those which his Highness keeps for a guard while he is at the seashore. . . . The joke was secretly arranged the evening before by his Highness and Don Cesare; but the Duchess and some other ladies who were suspected of being pregnant were informed of it.

The noblemen who had played the part of the corsairs were then ordered to serve as slaves to the ladies of the court, complete with chains and sailors' clothes. And, Romei adds,

These ladies could not treat their slaves cruelly enough in revenge for the fright they had had, and for the many vows they had offered in vain. So that day passed in great pleasure and laughter, and in very fine fishing of many kinds of fish.[21]

Both Crane and Angelo Solerti in his 1891 edition of the *Discorsi* preserve this passage in footnotes. But neither pauses to ask why it was deleted after the first edition.

The quoted passage illustrates the disjunctive, almost paradoxical (not to say schizoid) relationship between the two poles of attention in Romei's view of the court. The interior passages—those that exist within the previously cited frames of which our anecdote was an original example— represent an ongoing intellectual game, played according to formal rules by a group of cultivated, witty, and thoughtful men and women. Each day a queen is chosen, to decide the topic for discussion and serve as moderator.[22] She in turn appoints the first speaker, always a man, whose position is intermittently challenged by one or more of the other men. The women then ask questions, which sometimes amount to sustained statements, and the principal speaker and/or his opponent(s) seek to answer. The discussion either plays itself out, whereupon the queen finds a way of gracefully concluding it, or it is interrupted by the arrival of the duke, returning from a day spent at his own games.[23]

Thus the play of intellect, with its well-defined sex roles, its ludic and agonistic structures, and its polite and uplifting doctrinal antiphonies, goes on in the quiet interior spaces of Alfonso II's fall vacation schedule— ultimate questions amidst trivial pursuits. The paradox of Romei's frame is real, not a literary device. At Mesola in 1584, the duke was happily doing what he most loved to do. He was playing a game in which his predecessors were quite accomplished, but which he had completely mastered. Let us call it "Carefree Ruler." Like most games that have come down to us from traditional societies—chess, backgammon, queen for a day, even conversation—some strategies and behaviors may change over time, but the essential modes, styles, and functions of the game do not. "Carefree Ruler" is the game of the powerful, played by Macedonian princes and Indian rajahs, by medieval monarchs, and the presidents of modern republics.

In its classic form, "Carefree Ruler" has three requirements—getting out of the office; killing animals for the fun of it; being surrounded by a goodly number of people more or less like one's self, but less powerful. In "Carefree Ruler," the act of getting out of the office has a delicious kind of ambiguity, because while one is apparently leaving responsibilities behind, the act of abdication actually enhances one's power. Subordinates maintain the lines of communication, so that one can deal with sudden developments while angling for eels in Comacchio, snagging salmon in the highlands, or horseback riding in the Santa Barbara hills. In these settings, one's ability to exercise control over creation appears guiltless and victimless, indeed in harmony with the natural order. The feeling of accomplishment is enhanced by the presence of peers and near-peers, who provide a chorus of admiration and approval, as well as a modicum of competition.

Alfonso II was a cardplayer and knew his way around a chessboard, but he strongly favored large motor activities, especially "Carefree Ruler."[24] In his younger days he had been a notable jouster. By 1584 he was in his early fifties and had turned all his equestrian skills to the hunt. If contemporary portraits are to be believed, and if the splendidly decorated suit of ceremonial armor in the Wallace Collection was really his, as has long been thought, he must have been extraordinarily fit. Well into middle age he played a vigorous game of *pallone*. He seems to have liked nothing better than to work up a good sweat.[25]

While Romei puts this almost compulsive physicality a bit more delicately, there is no concealing the fact that with Alfonso's court, as in the Ferrarese state itself, there were two distinct cultures, characterized by extremely different forms of play. The play of intellect, which provides the central focus of the *Discorsi,* must have seemed too much like work to Alfonso and many of his courtiers. To sit around talking about beauty was unthinkable when one could be riding through the forests in search of stag and boar or watching one's favorite falcon hurtle out of the sky to force a gangling heron into gunshot range. For them, the more cerebral games that engaged the ladies and humanists were at best mere pastimes, to be pursued in the absence of alternatives, or during periods of disability; trivial pursuits, women's work. One could construct a simple chart of the polarities that seem to distinguish the two distinct ludic cultures in the court of Alfonso II. On one side is the large motor, macho side, which tends toward the physical, sporting, expensive, aristocratic, noisy, and public. On the other is the small motor, feminine side, which tends toward the intellectual, contemplative, bourgeois, quiet, and private.

These two sides wake up and go to sleep together. During the day, they are effectively separated, each pursuing its own paths. In the late afternoon and into the evening, they meet on a common ground, where they share such activities as dining, dancing, and performing at or attending concerts, plays, and ballets. These pastimes provide a kind of median space, energizing and enlivening for one group, soothing and relaxing for the other, on some level spiritually as well as physically nourishing for both. In the first instance, we see the relentless pursuit of the ancient and enduring prerogatives of the rich, the well-born, and the powerful.[26] Alfonso in the field surrounded himself with a glittering panoply of titled grandees, a who's who of the Ferrarese nobility. In contrast, the verbal jousts that Romei reports seem to prefigure something like the salon culture of eighteenth-century France and Germany. Here, the role of the women, while formally controlling, remains limited and deferential in practice. Yet there is no doubt that in some ways they ruled, choosing the topics, moderating the discussions, steering the development of the debate through questions, and finally acting as referees. However, the fact that this is a game, that it is bracketed within forms of play rather than opened out into the free flow of life, sets it apart from salons (which are nevertheless much indebted to these courtly institutions).

Another way in which the women's circle at La Mesola anticipates the *embourgeoisement* of court interests and styles is in the presence of commoners and foreigners, men and women whose talent provides them with a high degree of social acceptability. To cite a few examples, the cast of characters in the *Discorsi* includes Giulio Cesare Brancaccio, a Neapolitan of great military attainments, but who owed his presence at Ferrara to his vocal gifts as a *basso*. A furious Alfonso once dismissed him from the court because Brancaccio refused an order to sing for the Duc de Joyeux, to whom he insisted on talking about war. Laura Peverara was a commoner from Mantua who was regarded as one of the great madrigal singers of the time. Celebrated by Tasso and immortalized in several madrigal books, her talents led her to an advantageous marriage to a member of a distinguished Ferrarese family. Tarquinia Molza, also a commoner, came from Modena. One of the remarkable women of the late sixteenth century, she wrote poetry, translated some Platonic dialogues, and inspired Tasso's dialogue *La Molza or vero de l'amore* (1583). She was also a singer. Antonio Montecatini, whom Romei perhaps optimistically calls the principal philosopher of his age, succeeded the historian Gian Battista Pigna as Alfonso's principal secretary. Francesco Patrizzi da Cherso, indeed one of the leading philosophers of his time, came from Dalmatia to teach at the *studium* of Ferrara, and became a favorite at court. Gian Battista Guarini, author of *Il Pastor Fido,* owed his place at court to talent, not birth. Finally, although this does not exhaust the list, there is Signor Antonio Barisano, "Il Greco," a refugee from the Turkish occupation of Skios who taught Greek in Ferrara and was welcomed at the court for both his learning and his wit. One can readily see that this is a group of gifted and cosmopolitan men and women with an agenda distinct from that of the other courtly culture.[27]

It is now timely to return to the *burla,* or practical joke, which Romei described at the beginning of the second book of *Discorsi* in the 1585 edition. Romei's painstaking description of the *burla* represents, for him, a rather sustained narrative effort. It is also carefully constructed, in that the joke is not revealed to the reader until its effects on the victims have already been recounted. At that point, the reader is quickly informed that the ladies made a quick recovery, "enslaving" their deceivers, and spending the rest of the day in "great pleasure and laughter."

Why, then, did Romei delete the episode completely? That it took place cannot be doubted. Only Alfonso himself could have orchestrated such a complex trick, requiring the coordination of hundreds of men-at-arms and much equipment, and the collusion of the duchess and other women thought to be pregnant. Nor would a court writer like Romei have dared to attribute a stratagem of this kind to his ruler if it were nothing more than an *invenzione* on the part of the author. Indeed, the duke's direct responsibility for the event may have something to do with the care with which it is recounted.

In the absence of direct evidence, one is driven to speculate on the possible causes of such a suppression. My own hunch is that once the book was published, the account fixed in black and white for all to see, someone in the duke's circle realized how incongruous, even cheap, Alfonso's game seemed, especially in the context of high-minded discussions of beauty, love, and honor. Here we see the strong using their power in a despicable parody of its normally mock-chivalric form. Clearly it was not the duke's intention that anyone be hurt, but the success of the game lay in the deception, and the only test of the deception was the unfeigned terror of the women, as manifested in their pallor, their screams, their prayers, and their vows. Flushed with the triumph of one of the greatest *beffe* of the Renaissance, Alfonso might have been flattered by its celebration in Romei's pages. Given the benefit of hindsight, the duke must have discovered the great truth that awaits all practical jokers: that in hurting others, one hurts oneself. He therefore moved to limit the damage. As a result, later editions of the *Discorsi* offer a somewhat less extreme contrast between the two courtly cultures.

However, this elaborate *burla* is not the only instance in which the courtly play of intellect and the courtly game of chivalry come perilously close to confrontation. In a later episode, after a long, intense, and very interesting discussion about love (ending in Guarini's demonstration that love cannot survive if it is not supported by hope), the women turn to some guessing games, as was their habit ("piacevoli giuochi da indovinare, come si costuma fra donne" ["pleasant guessing games, such as are customary amongst women"]). Meanwhile, the duke and duchess return quietly, having netted a deer in the woods. Releasing the terrified deer amongst the ladies, they regale themselves as the ladies scatter in confusion.[28] Shortly thereafter, the rest of the hunting party arrives, and Alfonso orders them to bring the catch into the hall. Romei says: "si videro distesi molti cinghiali, ed alcuni così grandi e d'aspetto così orribili, che le donne di marar non si ardivano" ("many wild boars were laid out there, some so big and of such horrible appearance that the women couldn't stand to look at them.")[29] Here, in rapid succession, are two incidents that seem expressly designed to cause discomfiture to the women, to play on their less robust sensibility, and to enforce the dominance of "Carefree Ruler" over the play of intellect at court. It is not easy to find in these actions traces of the manly protectiveness over women that some have seen as the altruistic justification of chivalry.

Yet, these women can hold their own in the company of the huntsmen, even as the court is preparing for its return to the capital.[30] Indeed, their role becomes more influential during the final day's conversation, which takes place on board the ducal *bucintoro,* this time in the presence of an invited company of officials most of whom are distinguished jurists and/or men of letters, along with a number of musicians. In a very festive setting, after lunch and time for checkers, chess, and card games, the day's queen, Tarquinia Molza, introduces the topic:

> As there are two ranks of men deemed worthy of true honor, the profession of letters and of arms, so often it has been disputed to which of these the preference should be given. Considering, therefore, that in this noble band are to be found on the one hand the flower of the scholars of this age of ours, and on the other, cavaliers who excel in the military art, seizing this fine occasion, I mean that for the diversion of our journey today we should decide by debate which is worthy of greater honor, the scholar or the soldier. . . . The sentence shall be pronounced by the prudent and immaculate judgment of the Countess di Sala.[31]

Upon discussion, the scholars choose Francesco Patrizzi to represent their cause, and the men of action place their trust in our old friend, Giulio Cesare Brancaccio, the venerable warhorse who played the shill in the corsair caper.

Thus the final debate in Romei's book is a staged confrontation between two prominent figures, who not only embody, but agree to defend, the antithetical strands in the life of the court that the author presents as two courtly subcultures living in a tense equilibrium. I have argued that the imbalance between them is one of physical power. And indeed, this is clearly recognized by both speakers at the very outset of the debate. Patrizzi agrees to the contest on the condition that the weapons be limited to those with which men of letters normally overwhelm their opponents. Brancaccio smilingly yields, with the observation that his victory will be all the more glorious for having been achieved with Patrizzi's weapons. Mock heroically, he urges Patrizzi to begin his warlike charge—"movete ormai la lingua, signor Patrizio, al bellicoso assalto" ("move your tongue now, Signor Patrizio, to the warlike attack").

Of all the commonplaces that comprise the stock in trade of sixteenth-century humanist dialogues, arms and letters is perhaps the most shop-worn. But it seems important that Romei placed this topic in such a conspicuous spot in the book and conferred upon it a unique dramatic prominence, whether by way of reportage or artifice. The competition between Patrizzi and Brancaccio opposed two admired and very distinct courtly types, each charged with demonstrating the superiority of his own way of life. On one level, what is at stake is merely a day's play of wit, the winning or losing of a *jeu d'esprit*. On another, the contest is an open acknowledged enactment of the ongoing joust between antithetical styles, of which Romei deliberately provides examples. The debate is a classic case of a serious form of play, in Huizinga's terms.[32]

Patrizzi in fact begins by underlining this very point. He stresses the extreme difficulty of the subject, the nobility and excellence of both professions, and their ultimate interdependence. It's immediately clear that he is not out to offend the knightly culture. He seeks to ensure himself against any such interpretation of his future remarks by indicating that he realizes that this contest is a mere pastime, an "ingenious and enjoyable dispute, with which to surmount the trip's boredom."[33] It is as if Patrizzi knows that of all topics, this one could be taken seriously, with disastrous consequences. How would Alfonso and his circle respond to a convincing demonstration of the superiority of letters over arms? Surely Patrizzi, with his superior intellectual firepower and mobility, had to take this possibility into account.

For this reason, I believe, he offers a transparently bland and tepid statement of the case, very abstract, allusive, and low-keyed. He appears not as the incisive contemporary philosopher of the earlier dialogues, but as a learned pedant, staggering through the thickets of ancient allegories. When Brancaccio's turn comes, he immediately asserts that warriors are in no imminent danger from such attacks. He proceeds to develop a clear, tough, and convincing argument that the military art precedes and in important social respects transcends the life of the mind. He makes deft use of the same ancient sources that in Patrizzi seem dragged in by the teeth. He even demonstrates that warfare subsumes thought and knowledge in an uniquely useful and productive way.[34]

Patrizzi, far from responding with energy to Brancaccio's vigorous arguments, seems pleased to have been put on the defensive. He smilingly suggests that Brancaccio's praise of arms does nothing to refute the previous praise of letters, as if to show Brancaccio exactly what he has to do to win the argument. The old warrior seizes on this right away, and develops arguments to show that achievement in war is more honorable, more public and visible, and more praiseworthy than the life of scholarship and learning. This develops into a defense of the active over the contemplative life, and of civic over intellectual commitments. He has made an overwhelming case, and it seems that Patrizzi has nothing more to say. "It seemed," writes Romei, "to the Queen and to all of the spectators that victory hung from the flag of cavaliers."[35]

At that point, however, Renato Cato rises to his feet in defense of learning. He claims that Patrizzi's argument was "rather partial," not a true advocacy of all *letterati*. He unsheathed only the very weak sword of contemplative philosophy, leaving aside the "ferocissime arme de'giurisconsulti" ("most ferocious weapons of the lawyers"). Brancaccio responds that it's typical of a lawyer like Cato to break the rules of battle as he has just done, interjecting himself into the game; but that Cato deceives himself if he thinks Brancaccio is not ready to take him on. Cato then delivers a long speech against war, attacking its destructiveness, and holding that only peaceful governance under law can create a decent world. This is a passionate attack on every form of militarism. Rebutting Brancaccio's claims point by point, he states that "weapons are the world's biggest burden, using up people's wealth, placing free cities under the yoke, forcing wise men to obey the madness of the most atrocious tyrants."[36] He goes on to state that it is an abuse to devote statues, crowns, and triumphs to victorious soldiers (an ancient practice that Brancaccio has used in support of their superiority). "What could be a bigger abuse, or a more inhumane thing, than to seek to aggrandize and glorify killings, burnings, rape, sacrileges, looting, and then gloating over human misery?" The only just war, he argues, is in defense of the *patria;* any other is contrary to natural law. Thus, it is illegitimate to use force to acquire territory or indulge a desire to rule.

But Cato goes even further, examining the case of someone who may for some reason be in a position to pursue a just war. "What," he asks, "are the injustices that follow from this justice?" He goes on to describe these attendant horrors—innocent people imprisoned, mutilated, murdered, houses looted, women violated; whole towns, castles, and cities battered, sacked, and burned; "that which nature, art, and human prudence made over many years one sees destroyed in the shortest moment by the virtue of arms."[37] The ringing irony of this phrase, "per virtù dell'arme" should not be lost in translation. For Cato, there is no way even a good prince can wage war without doing untold damage to good and innocent people. No prince, in fact, has ever conferred lasting benefit upon his people in this way. His exemplar of political virtue is the Emperor Justinian, who by force of law brought about "a universal wellbeing, which the whole world enjoyed for ages to come." Compared to him, Julius Caesar's fifty-four victorious battles helped only the Roman people, while killing hundreds of thousands of men and destroying their countries. So much for Brancaccio's namesake.

Lightening his tone a bit, Cato suggests that warriors are also much inferior to professors of law. In cities, the former are merely guardians, while the latter serve as rectors. This, he says, is so obvious as to require no further comment. But now it appears that Brancaccio is restless, "impaziente d'ascoltare, e avidissimo di parlare," so Cato yields the floor.

Brancaccio begins his speech with an acknowledgment of the universally recognized fact that lawyers know how to make the worse appear the
better cause.[38] He then develops a new line of argument. Human beings
are born into the world nude and defenseless. In the first instance, they
have been given weapons so as to be safe among more ferocious animals,
and laws so as to live a perfect and civil life. Thus, it is wrong to claim, as
Cato did, that laws come from God and arms from the abyss. Both are
"divine inventions." Brancaccio then seeks to demonstrate the falsity of
Cato's argument that the world would be better off without weapons on
the grounds both that military force is needed to support the legal system,
and that without it we would again be prey to more ferocious animals.

The next stage in his counterargument is to show that Cato's assessment
of the role of jurisconsults is greatly exaggerated. They are merely technicians of the laws. The real authorities with respect to laws are princes,
and, in republics, other magistrates. It is they who decide how the laws are
to be applied and protected; and through their powers of appointment,
they (like generals in warfare) determine the direction of the state. Lawyers are the technicians of the legal system, men whose function it is to
apply the laws and resolve disputes. Far from being rectors—whose task it
is to command—they are mere *mecanici,* unless of course, transcending
the mere knowledge of Ulpian, they have the virtues of Ercole Cato and
the other exceptional jurisconsults who are really worthy to be counsellors to a prince. But such men deserve to be called legislators, not
lawyers. As applied justly by such men, arms are universally beneficent.
Brancaccio argues further that in the divine order, the evildoers ultimately
are punished by force of arms. And of all malefactors, the unjust jur-iscon-
sult is the worst, for he allows injustice to flourish under the law.

Concluding his argument, Brancaccio indicates that his intent is to
recognize the positive contributions of the legal profession, but to insist
that it is subordinate to the military. In this context, he cannot help
observing that dukes, kings, and even emperors are addressed as knights,
but never as doctors; and that the latter never present themselves in such
highly honorable contests as jousts and tournaments; and that in processions in which precedence expresses rank, the learned invariably come
after the great captains and warlords. Finally, and this is his concluding
and most damning proof, most ladies are more inclined to the love of
knights than of *letterati.* They love seeing their men in jousts and tour-
neys, all dressed up, breaking lances and whacking each other around.
That is because such men are demonstrating their prowess "non con
scritture o parolette vane, ma con vero valore, con sangue e con sudore"
("not with writings or vain little words, but with true bravery, with blood
and with sweat").[39] Renato Cato is more than ready to defend jurisco-
sults at this point, but the queen raises a finger to impose silence, and then

asks the Countess of Sala to deliver her verdict. After taking a few minutes to think things through, she pronounces the following judgment:

> Having heard, and well considered the reasons on one side and the other, we judge that civil honor, which is the reward to excellent and heroic works, should mainly be accorded to men of war; and that veneration, an attribute of divine things, belongs to wise and learned men.[40]

All the courtiers and ladies admire this judicious sentence, and well they might. For the Countess di Sala has, with one dextrous sentence, defused a potentially explosive issue. Having candidly and heatedly acknowledged their differences, the men of the court were exposed to a ruling that, even in the context of a game, could have resulted in humiliation to one of the parties. But this would have been a bitter outcome.

Too often during the vacation, the traditional patterns of social tolerance and mutual respect had been breached, if only in fun. Cato's speech in response to Brancaccio's first-round victory over Patrizzi dangerously reversed the process. Moreover, attacking the very idea of armed conflict and exposing its horrors so evocatively, he challenged the central ethos of Alfonso II and his circle. Brancaccio's valiant reply was designed precisely to defend this ethos. His concluding sentences conjured up the underlying assumptions meant to buttress the world in which "Carefree Ruler" is the main game in town—the values of jousts, tournaments, processions, and courtly love. To allow him to lose would be the most dangerous game in town. On the other hand, Patrizzi and Cato had constructed a strong case. For a court lady who depended on them and was one of their strongest allies to rule against them would have been treacherous and spineless, in addition to letting down the side of the weak at court. That would have been the most self-defeating game in town. No wonder we are told that Cato was not allowed a second rebuttal, and that the contessa remained for a while "alquanto pensosa."

Like the brilliant and accomplished figure everyone says she was, the Countess di Sala to the palpable relief of all came up with the perfect solution. As the anxiety dissolved, so too did the party. The book ends with the *bucintoro* docking outside the gates of Ferrara, where it is met by carriages that convey the group back to the ducal palace and then each to their own houses. That they part friends, or in some measure estimable equals, is essential to this rapid and successful closure.

Romei's picture of the court in late sixteenth-century Ferrara reveals some of the tensions underlying Estean pretensions of valor and intellect. Among these tensions we have identified gender-based stress between the ladies and those courtiers whose primary allegiances were to the duke and his late- and also mock-chivalric conception of noble living. In their physical weakness and political subordination, these women formed alliances with the court's intellectuals. Like many of the women, these too are largely commoners, closer to a *noblesse de robe* than to the boisterous noblemen surrounding the duke. Thus a serious, if playful, rivalry emerges between these two male factions. In life, as in the discourses themselves, the women play a pivotal role. Only Brancaccio dares to present them as the objects of sexual competition between the two groups of men, owing to his boastful confidence that here too arms rather than words will carry the day.

Yet, in the long history of this court, it had not always been so. The incidents examined here, whether historical or fictional, expose the same kind of brutality that appears implicit in Brancaccio's argument. The contempt expressed toward the life of the mind may alert us to the presence in *fin-de-siècle* Ferrara of decadence and decline in both the military and intellectual sphere, with neither arms nor learning taking precedence. A collective intellectual life that lacks vitality and influence can hardly hope to command respect in a universe of carefree rulers, once they have lost touch with the needs and aspirations of lesser folk.

Perhaps there is some masculine anxiety in Brancaccio's assertive insistence on might over mind, especially in a setting where the ruler's sexual impotence was reflected in his increasing inability to compete in the new world of national territorial states. The corrective voice comes from the women, who, symbolized by the Countess di Sala's judgment, preserve a perilous balance, refusing openly to tilt toward one side or the other. But we may also consider this balancing act as a reflection of the moral uncertainties, the corrosive inner relativism of a court declining amid its traditional outward pursuits. The court ladies of Ferrara could have had no illusions about their future course. The play of intellect alone offered them a pathway out of the gilded cage of courtly life.

Notes

1. J. C. Davis, *The Decline of the Venetian Nobility as a Ruling Class* (Baltimore: Johns Hopkins University Press, 1963); and, with reservations, H. G. Koenigsberger, "Decadence or Shift? Changes in the Civilization of Italy and Europe in the Sixteenth and Seventeenth Centuries," *Trans. Royal Hist. Soc.*, 5th Ser., 10(1960): 1–18, reprinted in Koenigsberger, *Estates and Revolutions: Essays in Early Modern European History* (Ithaca and London: Cornell University Press, 1971), 278–97; and "Republics and Courts in Italian and European Culture in the Sixteenth and Seventeenth Centuries," *Past and Present*, no. 83(1980): 32–56.

2. The phrase is Louis Le Roy's. See his *De la vicissitude ou variété des choses en l'Univers* (Paris, L'Huillier, 1575); and, on the sense of decline among late sixteenth-century thinkers, W. L. Gundersheimer, *The Life and Works of Louis Le Roy* (Geneva: Droz, 1966), chs. 10–12. Several studies by Eric Cochrane provide telling evidence for the ongoing intellectual vitality of Italy in a period of

alleged decline, esp. *Tradition and Enlightenment in the Tuscan Academies* (Rome: University of Chicago Press, 1961); *Florence in the Forgotten Centuries* (Chicago: University of Chicago Press, 1973). E. L. Goldberg, *Patterns in Late Medici Art Patronage* (Princeton: Princeton University Press, 1984) contains important implications for this subject, as does W. J. Bouwsma, *Venice and the Defense of Republican Liberty* (Berkeley and Los Angeles: University of California Press, 1968).

3. L. Chiappini, *Gli Estensi* (Varese: Dall'Oglio, 1967), esp. chs. 10, 12 and the good bibliography, 511–52; also L. Marini, *Per una storia dello stato Estense, I: Dal Quattrocento all'ultimo Cinquecento* (Bologna: Patron, 1973) and "Lo stato Estense," in *I Ducati Padani, Trento e Trieste* (Turin: Unione Tipografico–Editrice Torinese, 1979), 3–211 (vol. 17 of G. Galasso, ed., *Storia d'Italia*).

4. Carl Schorske, *Fin-de-Siècle Vienna* (New York: Alfred A. Knopf, 1979).

5. Anthony Newcomb, *The Madrigal at Ferrara, 1579–1597*, 2 vols. (Princeton: Princeton University Press, 1980), 108. The second volume is devoted to musical examples; all references in this article are to the first volume. Studies of the musical culture of Ferrara are flourishing. For the early period, see now L. Lockwood, *Music in Renaissance Ferrara, 1400–1505: The Creation of a Musical Center in the Fifteenth Century* (Oxford: Oxford University Press, 1984), and numerous articles cited in the appended bibliography. P. Macey is opening up the rich field of liturgical music under Alfonso I; see his "Savonarola and the Sixteenth-Century Motet," *Journal of the American Musicological Soc.*, 36, 3 (1983): 422–52; Jessie Ann Owens is preparing a study of the period of Ercole II (1535–69).

6. The general structure of the court underwent only minor changes from 1470 to the end of the sixteenth century. For a brief overview of its administrative forms in the late fifteenth century, see W. L. Gundersheimer, *Ferrara: The Style of a Renaissance Despotism* (Princeton: Princeton University Press, 1973) Appendix I: The Administration of the Estensi, 285–96.

7. The paucity of serious studies of Ferrarese society below the level of the ruling group is to be lamented. Some initial soundings appear in M. Zucchini, *L'agricoltura ferrarese attraverso i secoli* (Rome: G. Volpe, 1967); L. Marini, *Per una storia dello stato degli Estensi,* (Bologna: Patron, 1973); and some suggestive passages in A. Piromalli, *La cultura di Ferrara al tempo di Ariosto* (Florence: La Nuova Italia, 1953; rev. ed. Rome, Bulzoni, 1975). For the region in general, see G. L. Basini, *L'uomo e il pane: Risorse, consumi e carenze alimentari della popolazione modenese nel Cinque e Seicento* (Milan: Giuffre, 1970).

8. Deviant and marginal groups in Ferrara require study. With respect to criminality, there is W. L. Gundersheimer, "Crime and Punishment in Ferrara, 1440–1505," in *Violence and Disorder in Italian Cities, 1200–1500,* ed. L. Martines (Berkeley and Los Angeles: University of California Press, 1972), 103–28. The only recent work on the Jews of Ferrara is the intellectual biography by D. Ruderman, *The World of a Renaissance Jew: Abraham Farissol* (Columbus: Ohio State University Press, 1981). A. Samaritani's work on religious institutions opens a vast, neglected terrain. See, for example, his Ferrarese studies in *Medievali e altri studi* (Codigoro; Giari, 1970).

9. That is not to say that Ferrarese behavior struck contemporary observers as epicene or overcivilized. It conforms only partially to the patterns suggested by N. Elias, *Die höfische Gesellschaft* (Neuwied and Berlin: Luchterhand, 1969); trans. as *The Court Society,* transl. E. Jephcott (Oxford: Basil Blackwell, 1983); also his *This Civilizing Process,* trans. E. Jephcott (New York: Pantheon, 1978). Indeed, the Florentine ambassador commented unfavorably on more than one occasion on

table manners and other mores at the Ferrarese court. See especially the documents appended to P. de Nolhac and A. Solerti, *Il viaggio in Italia di Enrico III re di Francia e le feste a Venezia, Ferrara, Mantova, e Torino* (Turin: L. Roux, 1890), esp. 171–79.

10. Nolhac, *Il viaggio,* 173–75; Chiappini, *Gli Estensi,* 293ff; A. Solerti, *Ferrara e la corte estense nella seconda metà del secolo XVI: I discorsi di Annibale Romei* (Citta di Castello: S. Lapi, 1891; 2nd rev. ed. 1900), ch. 12: Il terremoto del 1570. I have used the first edition.

11. Chiappini, *Gli Estensi,* 265ff.; Newcomb, *The Madrigal,* 105; W. L. Gundersheimer, article on Alfonso II d'Este in *A Concise Encyclopaedia of the Italian Renaissance,* ed. J. R. Hale (London: Thames & Hudson, 1981), 125.

12. Cf. Newcomb, *The Madrigal,* 108, who dates the court's increased social distance to the 1590s. Here I take issue slightly with his splendid interpretation. Della Rena's *Cronaca di Ferrara,* on which these observations rest, was written in 1589, but it documents an ongoing, evolutionary process in the life of the court. Della Rena's descriptions of Alfonso and his circle, wonderfully translated by Newcomb (109–12), seem entirely consistent with the elegant, remote world depicted by other observers, most notably Annibale Romei, in the early 1580s. By the 1590s, the mood seems to become more elegiac, but the behavior, allowing for some aging, has changed very little.

13. For the modern Italian edition, see Solerti, note 10.

14. The only study of the Estean villas taken as a group is the antiquated work by G. Pazzi, *Le 'Delizie Estensi' e l'Ariosto: Fasti e piaceri a Ferrara nel Rinascimento* (Pescara: Jecco, 1933). La Mesola's exterior remains substantially intact, although the great, walled hunting preserve is gone. A recent description is in U. Malagu, *Guida del Ferrarese* (Verona, 1967). Della Rena's description of it as in "a swampy location and the air . . . very unhealthy" (Newcomb, *The Madrigal,* 110) is true. The *bosco* of Mesola, a national park still known for its wild boar, harbors some of the largest and most aggressive mosquitos in Italy.

15. The *Discorsi* have received little attention from scholars. They are cited by R. Kelso, both in *Doctrine for a Lady of the Renaissance* (Urbana: University of Illinois Press, 1939), and in *Doctrine of the English Gentleman of the Renaissance* (Urbana: University of Illinois Press, 1929). V. Arullani, "I Discorsi di Annibale Romei," *Vita Nuova* 2, 39 (1890): 112–14 is a three-page synopsis. A more detailed summary appears in T. F. Crane, *Italian Social Customs of the Sixteenth Century* (New Haven: Yale University Press, 1920), 219–39.

16. The 1968 facsimile edition contains an introduction by Alice Shalvi and includes full bibliographical details on earlier editions.

17. Romei, *The Courtier's Academie,* fol. 3r.

18. For the best recent discussion of Aristotelianism in the sixteenth century, see C. B. Schmitt, *Aristotle and the Renaissance* (Cambridge, Mass.: Harvard University Press, 1983), with bibliography and capsule biographies of 124 Aristotelian thinkers, mainly from the sixteenth century.

19. Crane, *Italian Social Customs,* 239.

20. Shalvi, *The Courtier's Academie,* xi.

21. Solerti, *Ferrara e la corte,* 35–37; Crane, *Italian Social Customs,* 225–6. I have used Crane's translation, with a few minor emendations.

22. This device derives directly from Boccaccio's *Decameron,* in which each of the women is crowned with laurel to signify her dominant role in the day's entertainments. By the late sixteenth century, such a coronation, whether actual or metaphorical, had become a conventional part of certain popular Italian parlor

games. These may be sampled in Girolamo Bargagli's *Il dialogo dei giuochi che nella vegghia si usano di fare* (Siena: Luca Bonetti, 1572) and many later editions. For useful discussion, see R. Bruscagli, "Les Intronati 'A Veglia': L'Académie en Jeu," *Lew Jeux à la Renaissance* (Paris: P.U.F., 1982), 200–12. According to Newcomb, *The Madrigal*, 84–85, the laurel was accorded a heightened significance in Ferrara in the 1580s owing to the dominance of Laura Peverara among the singers at court. The wreath was conferred each day in Romei's *Discorsi*. For an illuminating discussion of *Il Cortegiano*, in some respects parallel to this one, see T. M. Greene, "*Il Cortegiano* and the Choice of a Game," *Renaissance Quarterly* 32, 2 (Summer 1979); much additional discussion of courtly values is in twenty-two papers edited by C. Ossola and A. Prosperi, *La Corte e Il Cortegiano*, 2 vols. (Rome: Bulzoni, 1980), and esp. P. Floriani, "Il dialogo e la corte nel primo Cinquecento," 1: 83–96.

23. Sometimes the duke's arrival is heralded by a surrogate, such as the dwarf who appears at the end of the first day's discussion. In any case, whether appearing in person or merely in anticipation, the duke functions as a *deus ex machina*, completely preempting other activities in progress.

24. As Della Rena put it, "In the swamps and lakes of his territory, and even in the air, he kills a huge quantity of water birds, which he stalks with such pleasure that he pays no attention to extremes of heat and cold. He also enjoys all other hunting, both of birds and of other animals, and he pursues it with violent exertions and extreme energy" (Newcomb, *The Madrigal*, title 110).

25. "He has always had a tendency toward soldiery. . . . Indeed, his activities are not at all far removed from that profession and, both as regards physical strength and mental alertness, he is up to any undertaking, even the largest" (Newcomb, *The Madrigal*, 111).

26. On the role of hunting and related pursuits, see J. C. Margolin and P. Aries, eds., *Les Jeux à la Renaissance*, 119ff, and particularly G. Innamorati, ed., *Arte della Caccia*, 2 vols. (Milan: Il Polifilo, 1965). A useful collection of essays on elites is F. C. Jaher, *The Rich, the Well-Born, and the Powerful: Elites and Upper Classes in History* (Urbana: University of Illinois Press, 1974).

27. All of these personages would figure prominently in a general history of late sixteenth-century Ferrarese culture. They have begun to receive needed attention from Newcomb, *The Madrigal*, esp. chs. 2 and 3, who is especially helpful on Brancaccio, Peverara, and Molza.

28. Solerti, *Ferrara e la corte*, 79.

29. Solerti, *Ferrara e la corte*, 79. The passage continues: "Il restante del giorno fu dispensato in discorrer sopra gli accidenti della caccia, pigliandosi non men piacere le donne nell'udire, di quello che ci facessero li cacciatori in raccontare le prove da lor fatte nell'affrontare ed uccidere quei ferocissimi animali." ("The rest of the day was spent in talking about events of the hunt, with the women taking no less pleasure in hearing about what had been done than did the hunters themselves in recounting their deeds in confronting and killing those very ferocious animals.") It appears that a gender-related protocol implicitly governed the relationship of women to the hunt. Exposing them to the kill itself was somewhat uncouth and indecorous, a kind of practical joke—masculinity carried too far. On the other hand, they were prepared to respond appreciatively to tales of male prowess in the field.

30. Il Greco has a fool's, or a foreigner's, license. He can tease the women without causing offense; but his jokes reflect an underlying sympathy for their position. Thus, he criticizes one speaker who claims that women may partake of

nobility, and states that reason and common sense impute nobility only to men. This produces a long argument in praise of women from his adversary. When Tarquinia Molza tells Il Greco that the women he has angered may, like the Bacchae, make him into a new Orpheus, Il Greco replies that it was only his condemnation that elicited such eloquent praise of women. Il Greco also defends poverty in the book on riches, clearly a losing cause in the Ferrarese circle.

31. Solerti, *Ferrara e la corte,* 258–59.

32. Jehan Huizinga, *Homo Ludens: A Study of the Play Element in Culture* (New York: Roy Publishers, 1948; first Dutch ed. Haarlem, Tjeenk Willink, 1938). For other theorists of play, see R. Caillois, *Les Jeux et les Hommes, le Masque et le Vertige* (Paris: Gallimard, 1967); also, A. Cotta, *La Société Ludique* (Paris: Grasset, 1980), E. M. Avedon and B. Sutton-Smith, *The Study of Games* (New York: Wiley, 1971), with extensive bibliography, and J. Ehrmann, *Literature and Revolution* (Boston: Beacon Press, 1971).

33. Solerti, *Ferrara e la corte,* 261–66. That Patrizzi was deliberately making a weak case is suggested by the language with which he begins his oration on a topic that cannot have posed the slightest challenge to an accomplished philosopher. Indeed, he indicates that he is compelled to argue this case—"mi sforzero di mostrare . . . che la bilanza trabocca dalla banda nostra."

34. Ibid., 267 ff.

35. Ibid., 275.

36. Ibid., 277: "E io diro allo incontro, che l'arme sono al mondo di maggior travaglio, che d'ornamento, sendo elle principio dell'occupar i beni altrui, e di metter le citta libere in dura servitu, sforzando il piu delle volte uomini savi obedir alla pazzia degli atrocissimi tiranni."

37. Ibid., 279.

38. Ibid., 280ff.

39. Ibid., 286. It is significant that here, in the concluding argument of the book, the ethos of the carefree ruler is again juxtaposed with, and placed above, the play of intellect.

40. Ibid., 286.

6

Minstrels and Their Repertory in Fifteenth-Century France: Music in an Urban Environment

Howard Mayer Brown

Minstrels were the quintessentially urban musicians of the late middle ages and the Renaissance in France, and it is important to understand the role they played in everyday musical life and to know as precisely as we can what sorts of music they normally performed, if we are to understand how the urban environment shaped the course of music in fifteenth-century France. At least a part of the answer to the question of the influence of the city on fifteenth-century secular music is immediately and strikingly obvious, for it has been well studied. For the first time in the late fifteenth and the early sixteenth centuries, a large repertory of urban songs—"popular" in very much the same way present-day entertainment music is "popular"—began to appear in musical manuscripts (albeit courtly musical manuscripts) and a number of scholars have already shown how this repertory of monophonic tunes profoundly influenced the character of polyphonic French song from that time on.[1] These are the songs Noël du Faïl called "chansons plus ménéstrières que musiciennes," songs more fit for a member of the minstrels' guild than for a church musician, a courtier, or a member of the intelligentsia.[2]

Paradoxically, some literary people in the fifteenth and sixteenth centuries called these songs "chansons rurales" or "chansons rustiques," which makes explicit an anomaly underlying any study of music in the urban environment during the Renaissance.[3] In the abstract, most of us would contrast "urban" with "rural," but in fact a more meaningful distinction in considering the secular musical life of the Renaissance can be made in contrasting "urban" with "courtly" or "learned," since questions about the way in which cities shaped the musical life of the times inevitably involve asking how, when, where, and why music was made available to ordinary citizens, members of the middle classes.[4] Their music is more difficult to study than the music of the ruling elite, because relatively few middle-class manuscripts have survived, and because their music may have well included a much larger component of orally transmitted music, never written down; but it is nevertheless easier to study than music associated with the urban lower classes or with peasants, which has disappeared almost completely.

Musical life in French towns and cities in the fifteenth and sixteenth centuries centered around two institutions: the church choir and the town minstrels. Choirs, whether attached to a cathedral, a collegiate church, or a princely chapel, have been much studied in the recent past, at least partly because they were the principal sources of supply for composers, and because their records are relatively well kept and easy to get at.[5] And little by little we are beginning to see how choirs grew and changed, how they were organized, who their members were, just what and when they sang, and how their duties related to the repertories of music that survive. Perhaps it is premature to make any general statements about the nature of choirs in the fifteenth and sixteenth centuries—the evidence is far from in—and yet certain things do begin to be clear. Gradually, a picture has emerged of a repertory centered around chant, with polyphony reserved for the larger churches, and then only for important feasts, special occasions, and certain regular ancillary functions.[6] We begin, too, to see how churches gradually came to be specialized musical organizations, and this institutionalization seems to have coincided with a gradual change from the composer of polyphony as an anomaly—a member of the intelligentsia and perhaps even of the bureaucracy or the ruling elite with very special tastes and abilities (I think of men like Philippe de Vitry and Guillaume de Machaut, the two leading composers of fourteenth-century France)—to the specialist composer of polyphony, a professional musician whose principal activities were musical and whose duties involved little else but singing, composing, and educating choirboys.[7] In France and the Low Countries, this consolidation of duties and specialization seems to have been a gradual development over the course of the fourteenth and fifteenth centuries.[8]

Town minstrels and minstrels' guilds have been much less thoroughly studied in the recent past, and we must turn to nineteenth-century local historians for much of the detailed information we have about them.[9] In trying to summarize my own understanding of this class of musicians, I shall in fact offer a series of questions formulated as statements. Almost everything I say about minstrels in general can be challenged and may need to be modified for particular times and places. And yet it is important to attempt a synthesis of what we know, however prematurely, so that the details we gain from the investigation of individual situations can be more easily fit into a larger picture of the life of the time.

The history of minstrels in the fourteenth and fifteenth centuries in France and the Low Countries shares one central feature with the history of church and chapel choirs. Both institutions gradually established over a two-hundred-year period a fixed and regular place within society for the specialized activities of both kinds of musicians, and they defined more clearly than before the scope of their professional activities, in the case of minstrels by creating for them an established institution, the guild. The turning point in the history of minstrelsy in France came in 1321, the year the Confrérie de St. Julien des Ménétriers was formed in Paris, the guild that transformed the often vilified and otherwise unprotected freelance secular musicians into regular members of the artisan classes.[10] From that time on, professional urban instrumentalists (and singers) were protected by guild statutes and regulations.

The original eleven statutes of 1321, it is true, mostly dealt with regulations that protected clients and maintained good business and professional standards.[11] Minstrels were not allowed to enter into contracts through middlemen; they could not send substitutes to performances; they were not allowed to cancel a contract because they had received in the meantime a better offer; they could not bargain competitively against fellow members of the guild; and apprentices, who could play only in taverns and not for weddings and other honest assemblies, were more closely controlled than master players. Only one of the eleven articles deals with the administration of the guild itself, and that merely specifies that two good men and true should be in charge of enforcing the regulations.

The statutes were revised in 1407,[12] partly to increase the size of the fines levied against those who broke the rules, fines that were divided among the royal treasury, the head of the guild, and the hospice and chapel in Paris that the minstrels had in the meantime erected, and partly to make more explicit the internal management of the guild. One of the new regulations defines the role of the head of the guild, the so-called king of the minstrels. He was to see that the rules were obeyed; he served as the final arbiter of who could be admitted to full membership in the guild; and he was responsible for various other administrative decisions. He had to decide, for example, whether apprentices could be admitted as master players before their full time of learning was finished, and he had to give special authorization to master players who wished to open schools, an activity otherwise forbidden under guild statute. From the incomplete list of heads of the guild in the fourteenth century, it is clear that the king of the minstrels was not elected by the membership, but appointed by the king from among his own minstrels.[13] So there was and continued to be a close connection between royal minstrelsy and urban minstrelsy. And, with the centralization so characteristic of the French kingdom, the king of the Paris minstrels had the right to appoint the kings of the various guilds in provincial towns, guilds that gradually grew up during the fifteenth and sixteenth centuries in many of the larger cities of France.[14]

The other new statutes in 1407 have to do with conditions of apprenticeship. Apprentices had to stay with their masters for six years, the longest term of servitude of any of the Parisian guilds of the time, a regulation that may say more about the monopolistic instincts of the guild members than about the difficulty of the minstrels' professional activity. Although the statutes are silent on the subject, it may have been, too, that each master could have no more than one apprentice, as in so many other craft guilds, a way of keeping the number of professional musicians in Paris within reasonable bounds. Nor, alas, do the statutes say more about the examination required for an apprentice to be accepted as a master player, beyond the fact that the king of the minstrels or his deputies had to hear and approve him personally.[15] The statutes of 1407 stayed in effect in France throughout the fifteenth and sixteenth centuries. They were revised in 1658 under Louis XIV, but not radically, and they stayed in force from then until the fall of the ancien régime at the time of the French Revolution.[16]

The formation of minstrels' guilds in Paris and eventually in other cities and towns in France and the Low Countries doubtless increased dramatically the stability of the lives of professional secular musicians of the time and assured them a more or less fixed place in the society of the time. But we should not forget that there continued to exist throughout the fifteenth and sixteenth centuries also some nomadic players who roamed the countryside, getting whatever engagements they could in each small town they passed through. Because of the nature of their lives and work, we can never know much about this vagabond class of performers. Indeed, we know about their existence largely through occasional illustrations, or from sporadic archival documents.[17] In 1454, for example, Queen Marie of Anjou paid some "comédiens ambulants qui couraient le pays."[18] Moreover, musicians "de passage" and theatrical troupes who included some musicians sometimes addressed petitions to town councils, requesting permission to rent the town hall for a day or two in order to give performances, requests sometimes granted on condition that the performance first be given to members of the town council, so that they could censor the contents.[19] It is not likely that wandering musicians, actors, and other entertainers enjoyed the protection of any guild, and even those provisions, so frequently found in guild regulations, about conditions imposed on visiting musicians who required permission from the guild in order to exercise their profession in a strange city, probably did not apply to wanderers, who may well have belonged to a class largely outside society, the kind of demimonde familiar to us from the works of François Villon and others.

We should not suppose, either, that the guild members themselves were a completely homogeneous group, each with similar skills and talents. One obvious way to distinguish among various kinds of minstrels is to divide them according to the job opportunities that awaited them once they had finished their apprenticeship. Professional secular musicians could earn their living in one of three main ways: they could be hired by a town to serve as the civic band and watchmen's society; they could work as freelance musicians in a large city, earning what money they could by playing for weddings and other honest assemblies, and by teaching private citizens; or they could be employed by some member of the ruling elite, the king, a prince, a bishop or some other wealthy and powerful man to serve as part of a domestic household.[20]

There is another equally important classification that needs to be made before we can understand the nature of the professional musician in fifteenth- and sixteenth-century France. We also need to take account of whether they were players of *haut* or *bas* instruments, that is, loud winds or softer chamber instruments.[21] Again, there seem actually to have been three kinds. Some minstrels played the trumpet or the kettledrums (the nakers); they would have been the men who made ceremonial noises on public occasions: heralds, town criers, and the players of fanfares when the ruler or the town council entered a hall formally or walked in procession.[22] At some times and in some places, they may have had their own guilds, but in France and the Netherlands in the fifteenth and sixteenth centuries, they seem to have belonged to the same regulatory agency as the more obviously "musical" of the musicians. Indeed, it may be that some of them actually played slide trumpet ("minstrels' trumpet"?) as well as the long straight trumpet used for fanfares, military signals, and civic occasions.[23] There were also players of shawm and sackbut, members of the loud winds bands that came to be such a stable feature of fifteenth-century civic and courtly life, the groups of three, or at most four men, who played for courtly dances, for daily or weekly concerts outside the town hall, and for many other outdoor celebrations, and who some of the time may also have had the job of keeping watch at the city's gates and in the streets at night.[24] And finally, there were the singers and the players of soft instruments, the harpers, vielle players, and players on the flute, the psaltery, the lute, and so on.[25]

A part of the difficulty of interpreting the surviving documents and of understanding therefore just what musical life was like in the late middle ages and the Renaissance comes from ambiguities about just which individuals performed which tasks. From sixteenth-century French accounts, and from fifteenth-century records in other countries, it seems clear that individuals often specialized not in a particular instrument but in a particular part.[26] There were players of various soprano, alto and tenor instruments, rather than specialists on shawm, harp, or flute (although some virtuosi did indeed seem to have specialized). But there are few documents that make so clear the versatility of a small band of musicians as the petition from the four members of the town band of Verona—admittedly an Italian rather than a French document—which begs the town councillors to hire them on a regular basis, and points out that they have been supplying the town with "tuta l'arte nostra musica: cioè piffari: trombeti: fiauti: arpe: lauti: organo: e canto" ("all our art of music, that is, shawms, trumpets, flutes, harps, lutes, organ, and singing").[27] The Veronese document is tantalizing, for we really do not know enough to be certain whether it reflects a normal or an exceptional situation. Is it in fact normal practice for the players of shawms and sackbuts to perform as well on soft instruments and to sing? The players from Verona suggest that we can answer the question with a tentative Yes. But we also need to continue our search for answers that will give us a more general picture and possibly modify our conclusion with respect to particular times and places.

In the fifteenth century, town bands seem normally to have consisted of three or four musicians. We can perhaps take the Arras city ordinance of 1501 as typical.[28] It specifies that the city council should hire four musicians, a trumpet player and three players of loud winds who were to play in the belfry every morning when the town gate was opened, and every evening when it was closed. In addition, of course, the trumpet player would announce all the public proclamations, as a number of manuscript illuminations from the fifteenth century show us. An ordinance from Lille lists rather more duties for the town band.[29] Although undated, it was probably passed late in the sixteenth century, for the ordinance begins by stating that there had always been five minstrels in Lille—a standard number for the sixteenth century—and it goes on to say that they were to give concerts from the belfry every Saturday and on the evenings before feast days. Moreover, they were to play in the livery supplied to them by the town for the solemn processions that were so characteristic a part of town life in the late middle ages and the Renaissance, and they were required as well to give serenades to each of the town councillors on New Year's Eve and also in front of the city hall on All Saints' Day.

Such regulations give us a general idea of the normal duties of the town bands, and the picture can be filled in a bit by considering other sorts of archival documents that make clear, for example, that many towns had regular annual celebrations at which the members of the town band were expected or required to play. In Abbeville, for example, in 1416 the town band got their regular New Year's gift—their *estrennes*—for playing.[30] And the research of Pierre Pansier has made clear that in Avignon there was a regular schedule of annual processions at which the town band marched, as well as an annual banquet on Mardi Gras for all the town councillors in which the civic musicians regularly took part.[31]

Public concerts, official serenades, processions, banquets, and some duty as watchman or herald made up the staple fare of the civic musician. Playing for weddings and other private parties made up the staple fare of the freelance secular musician in the fifteenth and sixteenth centuries, although no one, so far as I know, has yet made a serious study of precisely what musical duties an instrumentalist or singer was expected to perform at a citizen's marriage. François Lesure has made clear the terms of their employment, though, in studying the contractual arrangements of ad hoc sixteenth-century bands, those groups of three, four, or five musicians who banded together for a few days or for many years.[32] Their contracts protected the individual's rights within the group, and also established the group's authority over the individual; that is, their salaries had to be divided equally among them all, in some cases even when only a part of the band was engaged to play, but each player had to agree not to perform with other bands. Lesure describes, too, the many sorts of occasions when freelance musicians could find employment: engagement parties, weddings, serenades, royal entries, processions, public feast days, holidays sponsored by confraternities and guilds, university celebrations, theatrical performances, and so on. At least one document, though from late fifteenth-century Lille, makes clear how dependent these freelance musicians were on weddings and public festivals, for the Lille minstrels complain that they can no longer survive since the town council cancelled its annual civic festival because of the wars, a national calamity that also helped to destroy their livelihood, since military duty and the disruption of peace had kept many people from marrying.[33]

Freelance musicians played for some of the same kinds of festivities as civic musicians, for certain celebrations called upon all of the resources of a town and not just its band of three or four loud winds. In Arras in 1489, for example, when the duke of Burgundy entered the city, the choirboys from the cathedral sang motets, but at the tournament that served as a climax to his visit, there were mounted trumpeters with pennants displaying the town's coat of arms, as well as other musicians made up not only of freelance minstrels but also members of the bourgeoisie.[34] Indeed, even the bands from neighboring towns were pressed into service when the need was great enough. Whenever a town council decided to put together one of those great mystery plays that took several days to perform and probably owed their production more to the commercial instincts of the merchants than to their piety, the town band would perform as well as freelance musicians, the cathedral choir, and the bands from the neighboring towns. In Montbéliard in 1503, for example, the magistrates sent to Altkirch and Neufchatel for trumpet players, and to Porentruy, Souchau, and Granvilliers for drummers (or pipe and tabor players) when they put on a mystery celebrating Saint Sebastian.[35] Royal entries and civic theater were not the only times, either, when all sorts of minstrels and church singers were engaged in a display of civic or national pride, for the birth of a royal child, a particularly momentous military victory, or the signing of a treaty might also inspire a city to outdo itself in organizing a holiday to entertain and impress its citizens.[36] In addition, both freelance and civic musicians gave private lessons to citizens.[37]

Minstrels of all kinds—those self-employed as well as those hired by a town, a member of the aristocracy, or the church hierarchy, or even by the king—came together in yet another context during the fourteenth and early fifteenth centuries. Once a year, usually during Lent when business was otherwise bad, schools were held for minstrels in many cities in France and the Low Countries. We know, unfortunately, very little about those schools. We have little concrete information about precisely how such annual conventions worked, who taught, who learned, and how and what. Putting together the fragments of information from a number of archival documents, however, it seems clear that these professional meetings were often organized by the guild administration, by the *roi des ménestrels,* and that they were organized to help professional musicians to learn new repertory and new techniques of performance and to give them an opportunity to buy and sell instruments.[38] Whatever went on in them, the schools were important enough so that the traveling expenses of the individual minstrels were often borne by town councils, who subsidized not only their own civic musicians, but often the minstrels attached to various private individuals within their jurisdiction as well. Thus, Abbeville in 1401 sent not only their own town band to school at Soissons, but also paid for the minstrels of Messrs. de Dampierre, de St. Pol, de Bourbech and de Reyneval.[39]

Civic musicians and those in domestic service had more than one occasion, then, to associate with the royal minstrels. But probably the most important points to be made about the third category of stable professional musicians—those in royal service—as well as the minstrels in private employ are that they were the most socially mobile of all minstrels, and they are those whose identities and professional expertise are the most difficult to determine with any degree of precision. Certainly, royal households hired minstrels who were very much like those who played in town bands; players who, whatever else they did, concentrated, perhaps chiefly, on the performance of loud wind music, or on playing fanfares, military signals, and other ceremonial noises on their trumpets and drums.[40]

But there was as well another category of secular musicians in royal service, and they are the most vaguely defined, and for us the most

tantalizing of all the minstrels. I refer, of course, to the chamber musicians, those few virtuosi who worked in the immediate presence of the
ruler and his family and courtiers. They were presumably responsible for
the performance of whatever repertory of secular music the nobility cultivated. One of the difficulties of summarizing and describing this sort of
performer is that he did not normally fit into any preconceived pattern of
employment in the same way that wind bands or trumpet corps did. Steven
Bonime reports, for example, that Charles VIII in 1490–91 hired six
musicians to serve him in chambers: three singers (presumably trained as
church musicians), as well as players of the organ (another church musician?), lute, harp, cornet, and drum (or, more probably, pipe and tabor).[41]
Almost certainly, some of the instrumentalists were minstrels of precisely
the sort I have been describing, trained in the apprenticeship system, but
more expert than most and therefore at the very top of their profession.
Such musicians, it will be seen, probably performed regularly with some
of the king's singers, at least those who specialized in secular music.
Sometimes, too, these sorts of virtuosi had other nonmusical duties as
well. They might be used by the king in diplomatic service and they might
even aspire to be appointed *valet de chambre,* or even ennobled.[42]

It is virtually impossible to try to disentangle those of the chamber
musicians who did come up through the ranks of minstrelsy from those
who were clerics, with an education in a cathedral school, who had a
special bent for secular music, or even from some courtiers who were not
professionally trained in music but whose talents were great enough to
permit them to perform with the chamber musicians or even to compose.
If my interpretation is correct, some minstrels then could have risen quite
high in the social hierarchy. They became the intimates of princes and
joined the ranks of the intelligentsia. Some of these men might even have
been composers. Craig Wright has made a convincing attempt to associate
the composer Baude Cordier with the harper to the duke of Burgundy,
Baude Fresnel.[43] If he is correct, it is by no means beyond the realm of
possibility that we have in Baude Cordier an example of a minstrel risen
quite beyond normal expectations, a harper turned intellectual.

In short, minstrels in the fifteenth century in France were not all of a
kind. From the wandering vagabond, presumably outside the protection of
the guild system, leading a marginal existence on the fringes of society to
the *valet de chambre* of the king, enjoying a position of respect and
stability at the very center of political power, professional secular musicians were nevertheless in the main an urban phenomenon, or rather their
new economic stability in the fourteenth century made the base of their
influence and their activities the towns and cities that gave them opportunities to earn a regular living by taking part in the private and public
celebrations of the citizenry.

The trickiest question of all, though, about the minstrels, and the one that must be confronted if we are ever to associate the activities of this important class of musicians with the musical monuments that have come down to us is, of course, what their repertory was. More particularly, could minstrels cope in one way or another with the repertory of polyphonic music that makes up the largest portion by far of the surviving music from the fifteenth and sixteenth centuries? A number of different kinds of evidence needs to be brought under scrutiny in order even to suggest what the minstrels played: contracts between students and teachers, archival documentation of one kind or another, literary references, and, most important, the surviving manuscripts themselves, if indeed any of them can be associated with minstrels.

In the first place, three kinds of music can fairly clearly be associated with minstrels, even though the evidence is not always absolutely clear-cut in differentiating one kind of repertory from another or associating one class of musician with a particular repertory. But it does at least seem likely that minstrels performed whatever narrative songs still survived in fifteenth-century France, that they played dance music of various kinds, including those dances improvised over *cantus firmi,* and that they incorporated into their repertory some at least of the monophonic *chansons rustiques* that I have already identified as a specifically urban repertory, even though such songs appeared in great quantities for the first time only in courtly manuscripts of the very late fifteenth and early sixteenth centuries.

It would appear that the unwritten tradition of narrative song occupied a much less important position in French than in Italian society in the fifteenth century. To be sure, there is some record of narrative singing, of singing long tales, romances, or even possibly *chanson de gestes,* presumably to melodic formulas or otherwise quite simple but completely lost music, in France in the fifteenth century, but what few records there are seem quite restricted in scope, and they seem to diminish in number and importance as the century progresses. The greatest concentration of notices about narrative song known to me comes from Beauvais in the fifteenth century. One man held the so-called "fief de la jonglerie" and presumably in return for an annual fee he sang, or, by the fourteenth century, sent someone else to sing in the cathedral "historias de gestis."[44] The tradition continued at least until the late sixteenth century, for in 1579 the chapter of the cathedral had become the possessor of the fief and the notice explaining the transfer of power specifies that by then the fief had been transformed into an instrumental concert held on St. Peter's Day in June and on four other feast days of the year in front of the church portal.

Various other archival notices from the fifteenth century reveal that *chanteurs en place,* or whatever else they were called, were sometimes rewarded for what may have been narrative singing. On the one hand, there can be little doubt that Mahieu Siffait, paid by the town of Abbeville in 1409, was such a singer, for he is called a *chanteur en place,* and he is rewarded for having performed "son roumant au bos"; that is, he sang "with his voice" ("au bos") a romance.[45] On the other hand, it is not so clear that Jehan Ostran and his companions, who were paid for having sung before the town councillors of Amiens about the victory that the duke of Lorraine had had over the Burgundians in 1476, performed some version of narrative song, a monophonic historical song, or even some sort of polyphony.[46] Nor is the nature of the *estampie* that was played (but apparently not sung) in Chaumont in 1487 clear.[47] In any case, such notices that can be interpreted to imply narrative singing are quite rare in France; they seem mostly to be associated with the more nomadic of the minstrels, or else with civic endowments whose character gradually changes as the century wears on, and they seem to cease almost completely by 1500. I would conclude that the older fashion of declaiming long tales lingered on only in such marginal ways as the traditional performances endowed at the cathedral of Beauvias. Narrative singing was not, I would suppose, an important part of the musical scene or of the minstrels' repertory in fifteenth-century France.

Dances, on the other hand, made up a central part of the minstrels' repertory, a fact that hardly needs to be stressed, since the sources and the nature of the fifteenth-century basse dance has been so thoroughly studied.[48] Scholars have clarified the way in which the surviving slow-moving dance tenors served as *cantus firmi* for upper-class dances, and they have inferred from the tenors and from the few written-out examples of polyphonic dances the character of the melodic lines instrumentalists improvised above, below, and around the given voice. While it is true that most of the surviving tenors and choreographies—and especially the elegant manuscript of *cantus firmi* now in the Bibliothèque Royale in Brussels[49]—associate the basse dance with the ruling elite, there can be little doubt that the music was the province of minstrels, and that an important part of their professional training consisted precisely in learning how to invent counterpoints against a given melody.

Further research may well sharpen our sense of the difference between *cantus firmus* dances associated with the upper classes and other kinds of dances (for example, monophonic dance tunes played on pipe and tabor, more commonly performed in the fifteenth century by ordinary citizens), but the ability of the minstrels to improvise arrangements of dance tunes will almost certainly not be challenged. On the other hand, we must keep in mind the prevalence of monophonic dances in the fifteenth century, a repertory that scarcely survives at all but whose existence can be inferred from archival documents attesting to the presence of a *tabourineur*—a term I take to mean pipe and tabor player rather than merely a drummer—among the musicians at court or performing for some urban celebration, and from the many pictures that actually show pipe and tabor players accompanying dancing and other kinds of merrymaking.[50]

Monophonic songs may also have made up an important part of the minstrel's repertory, and especially those songs described as "plus mén-éstrières que musiciennes," that is, the repertory of urban songs I have already mentioned. But the truth is that there are precious few fragments of popular monophonic songs from the earlier part of the fifteenth century, and the existence of a vast repertory of such songs can only be guessed at. The most concrete evidence of monophonic popular songs from the first part of the fifteenth century comes from the occasional reflections found in polyponic chansons, songs like *La belle se siet* by Dufay and *Filles à marier* by Binchois.[51]

It should be stressed, however, that this French monophonic repertory seems to be popular in mode of expression—whoever actually wrote the song texts and melodies—and that evidence of any sort of courtly or upper-class monophonic song in France is entirely lacking for the fifteenth century. Craig Wright has discovered a single monophonic *lai* from the period, a highly suggestive piece, but one that may well reveal the very end of a medieval tradition rather than signalling a repertory in common use but unwritten and hence lost to us.[52] The notices that I have already mentioned concerning the *fief de la jonglerie* in Beauvais and the continuation of a courtly monophonic tradition there likewise appear to reflect a dying tradition, and in any case the activities in Beauvais probably involved narrative rather than lyric song, an important distinction to keep in mind. And courtiers would have known and enjoyed a repertory of monophonic dances. But any French equivalent of the Italian courtly improvised songs, the *rispette, strambotti,* and *barzellete* of the Italian *improvvisatori,* seems to be completely unknown in France. In its place, we can suppose, although without any very definite proof for the earlier part of the century, that the French urban dweller had an unwritten repertory of "popular" songs that may well have made up an important part of what minstrels played in their belfry concerts, their serenades, and their share of wedding celebrations.

In addition, it seems to me, various kinds of evidence make clear the fact that minstrels, at least some minstrels, could and did play composed polyphony. I should stress that the question of the extent to which minstrels could read notation, or notation of the most complex kinds, is really irrelevant to the central issue of what their repertory consisted of. In the first place, we simply do not know enough and probably never will about the literacy of this kind of musician to be able to know for certain the extent to which they did rely on written notation. In the second place, there is no reason to suppose a uniform level of ability among all minstrels, as I have taken some pains to try to demonstrate. If Baude Cordier were in fact by training a minstrel, he certainly would have been able to read the most complicated kinds of notation. Even if he were not, the chamber musicians of the king almost certainly would have needed to learn polyphonic songs, even in the unlikely event that they could not read music or could not read it very well. On the other hand, the sort of minstrel who earned a marginal living as a wandering vagabond almost certainly had very different gifts and abilities from the relatively highly paid minstrel in royal service. And in the third place, we do not know, although we need to try hard to find out, just how the surviving manuscripts were used in performance. The small size of many chansonniers suggests that they cannot have been used for performance by many people at a time. Most of them show little or no signs of use, and most of them are filled with uncorrected errors of a sort that makes it seem more likely that such written documents were used more as reference books or simply as luxurious items for display rather than as practical tools for regular performance.

We can know something of the minstrel's repertory from one or two archival documents that give us welcome glimpses of the nature of the musical life of the past. Thus, when a student at the University of Avignon decided he wanted to learn the harp in 1449, he secured for himself a teacher, Mosse of Lisbon, a Jewish cloth dyer and hence not properly a minstrel at all, and they drew up a contract in which Mosse agreed to teach his student a number of "carmina sive cantinellas," which are listed in the contract and that all turn out to be dances and hence a part of the unwritten tradition.[53] When the British wool merchant, George Cely, studied harp with Thomas Rede, a harper, at Calais, on the other hand, the notes he made about his lessons seem to suggest that he not only learned the harp, but also French, singing, and dancing from his teacher, and that the repertory they worked on included not only dances but also polyphonic courtly songs, including *Mine heartys lust* and *Go heart hurt with adversity,* both of which survive in polyphonic settings by Walter Frye, an English musician in Burgundian service.[54] Even less ambiguously, in 1484 the city of Bruges commissioned Nicasius de Brauwere, a priest and singer at the church of Saint Sauveur, to write some motets for the minstrels to play at instrumental *Salve* concerts,[55] clear evidence that in the Low Countries at the time, the repertory of the civic musicians encompassed composed polyphony.

Indeed, a few books prepared for minstrel bands survive from the sixteenth century, and sporadic archival notices make clear that even more such books once existed. I think, of course, in the first place of the Copenhagen wind band manuscripts, partially edited in a modern edition by Henrick Glahn, which preserve the repertory of the instrumental musicians from the court of King Christian III of Denmark in 1541.[56] Although the relevance of the wind band part books to the practices of fifteenth-century French minstrels may rightly be questioned, the fact remains that this precious document tells us more than we can know from any other source precisely what a mid-sixteenth-century instrumentalist played at court: namely, Mass movements, motets, sacred and secular music originally composed as settings of German, French or Italian lyric poems, dances, and a few pieces that seem to have been originally conceived for instrumental ensemble, in short, a conspectus of all the genres of composed, polyphonic music in use at the time.

The late fifteenth-century chansonnier probably prepared for the wind band of Isabella d'Este in the 1480s and now housed in the Biblioteca Casanatense in Rome is less comprehensive in its coverage of all the genres of polyphony in use at the time.[57] It contains French chansons almost exclusively by the leading composers of the time—Martini, Isaac, Busnois, Compère, and so on—plus a handful of pieces with incipits in Flemish or Italian, and a handful that were probably conceived originally for instruments. The Casanatense manuscript is particularly interesting for the evidence it displays of a highly active editorial intervention. Many of its special readings—not found in any other source—can be explained by the necessity to adapt written polyphony to the practical requirements of a set of wind instruments tuned a fifth apart.[58] Thus, in some instances, the lowest notes, presumably not attainable on the instruments in question, have been deleted or changed, and in a few passages two voices actually exchange parts to put them both in playable range. The Casanatense chansonnier, then, is not only a highly important source of information about the kind of polyphonic music performed by Italian wind bands, but also about the kind of adjustments in musical detail that were required for such performances.

But, it can be argued, the repertory of the wind band at the Danish court in 1541 and that of the Ferrarese and Mantuan courts in the 1480s might well have been quite different from the repertory of urban minstrels in fifteenth-century France, no matter how clearly their existence demonstrates that written polyphony was within the purview of some minstrels of the time. Unfortunately, no manuscript known to me survives that actually belonged to French minstrels in the fifteenth or early sixteenth centuries, but that fact can hardly be regarded as surprising in the view of the great rarity of any kinds of French manuscript music of the period. Wars and the ravages of time have taken a heavy toll of French Renaissance artifacts of all kinds, and one of the central problems of musicologists interested in French music of the fifteenth and sixteenth centuries is precisely the difficulty of studying a repertory that has largely been preserved in peripheral sources, far from the center of musical activity at the French royal court or the capital city of Paris.

There are, however, two manuscripts that come at least part way to answering the objections that nothing survives to instruct us about the repertory of specifically urban or at least more ordinary sorts of minstrels than those in aristocratic service. Daniel Leech-Wilkinson has recently reported on a manuscript now in the British Library that was prepared by an Italian ship's trumpeter in the 1440s,[59] and Jozef Smits van Waesberghe has claimed for some fragments now in the city archives of Maastricht dating from the last quarter of the fifteenth century that they originally belonged to one of the civic musicians in that town.[60] Leech-Wilkinson stressed the poor readings in the British Library manuscript and the naive and simplified notation in order to discourage the notion that minstrels took part in performances of polyphonic music. But the fact remains that the manuscript contains mostly polyphonic chansons of a sort we are accustomed to think of as courtly—*Jour à jour la vie, Une fois avant que mourir* and *Puisque m'amour* among others—as well as three tenors that may well have served as the starting point for some sorts of improvisation.[61] However bad the readings and however poor the notation, a quite ordinary sort of minstrel included polyphonic chansons in his repertory. Even, I would be inclined to say, a ship's trumpeter knew some polyphonic chansons. And precisely the same conclusion is to be drawn from the Maastricht fragments, which include polyphonic parts to some well-known chansons such as *De tous bien plaine,* along with a number of arrangements of Flemish *chansons rustiques,* such as *Tandernaken,* and even a motet, *Salve regina,* that might have been played at a Salve service, along with a handful of plainchants that might well have served a minstrel as melodic material for processions or other church-related services.[62]

In short, what pathetically few fragments do remain to instruct us about the repertory of minstrels in the fifteenth century suggest that their repertory encompassed polyphony as well as monophony, and at least a few courtly chansons as well as arrangements of one kind or another of popular monophonic music. Such conclusions should modify our notions somewhat of what precisely we mean when we speak of courtly or popular culture in French-speaking countries in the fifteenth and sixteenth centuries. For these concepts are simply convenient abstractions that enable us to distinguish one style, one mode of expression, from another.

In real life, of course, such distinctions are less clear-cut and more complex. We know almost exclusively from "courtly" sources about the existence of a middle-class urban music in the late fifteenth and early sixteenth centuries. But it has been harder to discover that quintessentially urban musicians such as minstrels also doubtless included in their repertory some pieces that we rightly call "courtly." Indeed, our distinc-

tions must be flexible enough to encompass a variety of kinds of excep-
tions to the categories that seem to constitute the rule. We are doubtless
correct, for example, to stress that the subject of courtly poetry set to
music is almost invariably love, and almost always that kind of courtly love
that many literary scholars would like to believe never existed. But our
conception of courtly needs to be adaptable enough to include, for example, those songs in celebration of May and of the new year that the young
Guillaume Dufay, a cleric at Cambrai, may well have written as his contribution to town life; as urban songs, in short, but in a courtly style.[63] Only
by using such abstractions as "courtly" and "popular" to help us separate
phenomena of different kinds that in real life touched one another and
even influenced one another can we begin to understand the complexities
of the distant past. And only by beginning to understand that minstrels
were of different qualities and had different kinds of talents, and that their
repertory of music encompassed more than merely some now-lost and
dimly understood unwritten tradition, can we begin to avoid the sort of
oversimplifications that will badly distort our view of the late middle ages
and the early Renaissance in France.

Notes

1. The dominant characteristic of these urban songs is that they circulated,
and were presumably conceived, as one-line tunes. Two courtly manuscripts from
Paris, Bibliothèque Nationale, MS fonds fr. 9346, published in a modern edition in
Théodore Gérold, *Le manuscrit de Bayeux* (Strasbourg: Librairie Istra, 1921); and
Paris, Bibliothèque Nationale, MS fonds fr. 12744, published in a modern edition
in Gaston Paris and Auguste Gevaert, *Chansons du XVe siècle* (Paris: Société des
anciens textes français, 1875), comprise the largest collection of these monophonic
"popular" melodies. In the early sixteenth century, anthologies of such texts
without their melodies were issued in inexpensive editions; they have been reprinted in a modern edition in Brian Jeffery, *Chanson Verse of the Early Renaissance,* 2 vols. (London: Tecla Editions, 1971–76).
  On the influence of these *chansons rustiques* on the *chanson musicale,* see
Howard Mayer Brown, "The *Chanson rustique:* Popular Elements in the 15th- and
16th-century Chanson," *Journal of the American Musicological Society* 12 (1959):
16–26, and more recently, Lawrence F. Bernstein, "Notes on the Origin of the
Parisian Chanson," *The Journal of Musicology* 1 (1982): 275–326.
  2. Noël Du Faïl, *Oeuvres facétieuses,* ed. Jules Assézat, 2 vols. (Paris: P.
Daffis, 1874), 1:35.
  3. Fifteenth- and sixteenth-century references to *chansons rurales* or *rustiques* are listed in François Lesure, "Éléments populaires dans la chanson française au début du XVIe siècle," in *Musique et poésie au XVIe siècle* (Paris, 1954),
169–85.
  4. I mean, of course, members of the lower middle class, for the educated,
upper middle class would, presumably, have aped the nobility. Manuscript anthologies of secular music prepared for members of the upper middle class, such
as Dr. Hartmann Schedel's Liederbuch: Munich, Bayerische Staatsbibliothek,

Cgm 810, published in facsimile in *Das Erbe deutscher Musik,* vol. 84, Abteilung Mittelalter, vol. 21 (Cassel and Basel: Bärenreiter, 1978); Johannes Heer's Lieder- buch: St. Gall, Stiftsbibliothek, Cod. 462, published in a modern edition in Arnold Geering and Hans Trumpy, eds. *Das Liederbuch des Johannes Heer von Glarus,* Schweizerische Musikdenkmäler, vol. 5 (Basel: Bärenreiter, 1967); and Fridolin Sicher's Liederbuch: St. Gall, Stiftsbibliothek, Cod. 461, published in a modern edition in Franz Julius Giesbert, ed., *Ein altes Spielbuch aus der Zeit um 1500,* 2 vols. (Mainz: B. Schott's Söhne, 1936), to cite but three examples, are indistin- guishable in content from the manuscript anthologies prepared for princes or members of the aristocracy.

    5. A number of recent studies have concentrated on the personnel and the polyphonic manuscripts of a particular cathedral or court, for example, Stephen Bonime, "Anne de Bretagne (1477–1514) and Music, an Archival Study," Ph. D. dissertation, Bryn Mawr College, 1975; Frank A. D'Accone, "The Singers of San Giovanni in Florence during the 16th Century," *Journal of the American Musi- cological Society* 14 (1961): 307–58; Frank A. D'Accone, "The Musical Chapels at the Florentine Cathedral and Baptistery during the First Half of the 16th Century," *Journal of the American Musicological Society* 24 (1971): 1–50; Iain Fenlon, *Music and Patronage in Sixteenth-Century Mantua,* 2 vols. (Cambridge: Cam- bridge University Press, 1980); Lewis Lockwood, *Music in Renaissance Ferrara, 1400–1505. The Creation of a Musical Centre in the Fifteenth Century* (Oxford: Oxford University Press, 1984); William Prizer, *Courtly Pastimes, The Frottole of Marchetto Cara* (Ann Arbor, Mich.: University Microfilms, 1980); Christopher Reynolds, "The Music Chapel at San Pietro in Vaticano in the Later Fifteenth Century," Ph. D. dissertation, Princeton University, 1982; Richard Sherr, "The Papal Chapel ca. 1492–1513 and its Polyphonic Sources," Ph. D. dissertation, Princeton University, 1975; Andrew Tommasello, *Music and Ritual at Papal Avig- non, 1309–1403* (Ann Arbor, Mich.: University Microfilms, 1983); and Craig Wright, *Music at the Court of Burgundy, 1364–1419, A Documentary History* (Henryville, Ottawa, and Binningen: Institute of Mediaeval Music, 1979).

    Many of these studies include some information about minstrels, but they all place their main emphasis on the composers of polyphonic music associated with the institutions they describe. Reinhard Strohm, *Music in Late Medieval Bruges* (Oxford: Oxford University press, 1985) is a recent archival study that does include extensive information about civic minstrels.

    6. On this point, see Anthony M. Cummings, "Toward an Interpretation of the Sixteenth-Century Motet," *Journal of the American Musicological Society* 34 (1981): 43–59. The place of polyphony in sacred services during the Renaissance is a topic that badly needs further study.

    7. This point is made in Christopher Reynolds, "Musical Careers, Eccle- siastical Benefices, and the Example of Johannes Brunet" (forthcoming). I am grateful to Prof. Reynolds for allowing me to read his essay before publication. See also Nino Pirrotta, "Music and Cultural Tendencies in Fifteenth-Century Italy," in his collected essays, *Music and Culture in Italy from the Middle Ages to the Baroque* (Cambridge, Mass. and London: Harvard University Press, 1984), 83–86, who points out that early fifteenth-century composers were employed in a variety of administrative, political, or diplomatic tasks, whereas later composers were inclined to be "mercenary professionals."

    8. The situation seems to have been rather different in Italy, where in many institutions polyphonic choirs seem to have been established for the first time or

reorganized drastically beginning about 1470, as some of the studies cited in note 5 show. Moreover, musicians' guilds seem not to have existed in sixteenth-century Italy. The singers described in Jonathan Glixon, "A Musicians' Union in Sixteenth-Century Venice," *Journal of the American Musicological Society* 36 (1983): 392–421, organized themselves to address a particular situation. Their group resembled a guild in some ways, but it was not intended as a regulatory agency for all professional musicians from a certain region, like the guilds of northern Europe.

9. The most complete study of minstrelsy in France in the fifteenth and sixteenth centuries remains B. Bernhard, "Recherches sur l'histoire de la corporation des ménétriers ou joueurs d'intruments de la ville de Paris," *Bibliothèque de l'Ecole des Chartes,* Series 1, vols. 3 (1841–42): 377–404, 4 (1842–43): 525–48, and 5 (1843–44): 254–84 and 339–72. See also G. van Doorslaer, "L'éducation artistique des anciens musiciens instrumentistes," *Gedenkboek aangeboden aan Dr. D.F. Scheurleer op zijn 70sten jaardag* (The Hague: M. Nijhoff, 1925), 89–98; François Lesure, "Les joueurs d'instruments et la musique instrumentale à Paris au XVI siècle," *Bibliothèque d'humanisme et renaissance* 12 (1950): 373–75; and François Lesure, "Les orchestres populaires à Paris vers la fin du XVIe siècle," *Revue de musicologie* 36 (1954): 39–54.

10. See Bernhard, "Recherches," 3:382–88.

11. The statutes of 1321 are printed in Réné de Lespinasse, *Histoire générale de Paris. Les métiers et corporations de la ville de Paris,* vol. 3: *XIVe–XVIIIe siècles. Tissus, Étoffes, Vêtements, Cuirs et peaux, Métiers divers* (Paris: Imprimerie nationale, 1897), 580–83.

12. The statutes of 1407 are printed in Lespinasse, *Métiers,* 3:584–85. They are discussed in Bernhard, "Recherches," 4:527–31.

13. See Bernhard, "Recherches," 3: 395–96.

14. See Bernhard, "Recherches," 4:534–35. On the minstrels' guilds in Brussels, see Joseph Cuvelier, "La confrérie des musiciens instrumentistes de Bruxelles sous l'ancien régime," *Académie royale de Belgique. Bulletin de la classe des beaux-arts* 28 (1946): 39–43. For statutes from various minstrels' guilds in the Low Countries, see Edmond van der Straeten, *Les ménestrels aux Pays-Bas du XIIIe au XVIIIe siècle* (Brussels: A. et F. Mahillon, 1878; reprint, Geneva: Minkoff Reprint, 1972).

15. The earliest notice known to me to give details about the examination required to become a master player comes from the statutes of the Corporation de Saint-Job et de Sainte-Madeleine in Antwerp and is dated 1676. It is summarized and discussed in van der Straeten, *Ménestrels aux Pays-Bas,* 145–46. The statutes specify that the candidate must bring his instruments to the jury already tuned. They then untune them, and require him to retune them to a pitch suitable for playing with other musicians. Then the candidate must play some dances and his part in three motets or other pieces. Clearly in the seventeenth century minstrels needed to be able to read music, or at least to play composed polyphony.

16. On the later statutes of the confraternity, see Bernhard, "Recherches," 4:532–33. The statutes of 1658 are printed in Lespinasse, *Métiers,* 3: 587–89.

17. Nomadic freelance minstrels are better documented for earlier periods. A number of archival notices about them appear, for example, in Edmond Faral, *Les jongleurs en France au moyen age* (Paris: H. Champion, 1910), Wolfgang Hartung, *Die Spielleute. Eine Randgruppe in der Gesellschaft des Mittelalters* (Wiesbaden, Steiner, 1982), and Walter Salmen, *Der fahrende Musiker im europäischen Mittelalter* (Cassel: Johann Philipp Hinnenthal-Verlag, 1960). For iconographical evi-

dence of the activities of wandering minstrels, see Edmund A. Bowles, *Musikleben im 15. Jahrhundert,* Musikgeschichte in Bildern, vol. 3, pt.8 (Leipzig: Deutscher Verlag für Musik, 1977), 164–65.

18. Quoted in the notes of Émile Picot in Paris, Bibliothèque Nationale, MSS nouv. acq. fr. 12.633–12.634, after Auguste Jal, *Dictionnaire critique de biographie et d'histoire,* 2nd ed. (Paris, 1872), 412.

19. For notices of itinerant performers renting town halls for theatrical and musical performances, see, for example, the notes of Émile Picot in Paris, Bibliothèque Nationale, MSS nouv. act. fr. 12.633–12.634 for information about Amboise; Georges Lecocq, *Histoire du théâtre en Picardie* (Paris: H. Menu, 1880), 145–75, for information about Amiens; and other similar studies of local theatrical activities.

20. Some minstrels were hired on a regular basis by one of the larger stable civic organizations of the time, such as the association of law clerks, the Basochiens, in Paris. On the Basoche and their entertainments, see Louis Petit de Julleville, *Les Comédiens en France au moyen âge* (Paris: L. Cerf, 1886), 88–142.

21. On this distinction, see Edmund A. Bowles, " 'Haut' and 'Bas': the Grouping of Musical Instruments in the Middle Ages," *Musica Disciplina* 8 (1954): 115–40.

22. On trumpet players as heralds announcing public news "à son de trompe," see, for example, *Le journal d'un bourgeois de Paris sous le règne de François 1er (1515–1536),* ed. V. L. Bourrilly (Paris: A. Picard et fils, 1910), 8, 32, 38, 84, 95, 101, 128, 130, and so on. Such examples could easily be multiplied; archival documents of the fifteenth and sixteenth centuries mention trumpets as heralds or as accompaniments to royal or civic processions and entrées more often than any other kind of instrument. On trumpeters' guilds in Germany, where they seem to have been common especially among court trumpeters, see Abram Loft, "Musicians' Guild and Union: A Consideration of the Evolution of Protective Organization Among Musicians," Ph. D. dissertation, Columbia University, 1950, 101–6.

23. On these distinctions, see Edmund A. Bowles, "Unterscheidung der Instrumente Buisine, Cor, Trompe, und Trompette," *Archiv fur Musikwissenschaft* 18 (1961): 52–72, and Vivian Safowitz, "Trumpet Music and Trumpet Style in the Early Renaissance," M. A. thesis, University of Illinois, 1965.

24. The best study of the more or less fixed shawm bands of the fifteenth and sixteenth centuries remains Keith Polk, "Flemish Wind Bands in the Late Middle Ages: A Study of Improvisatory Instrumental Practices," Ph.D. dissertation, University of California, 1968. See also Keith Polk, "Wind Bands of Medieval Flemish Cities," *Brass and Woodwind Quarterly* 1 (1968): 93–113, and Keith Polk, "Municipal Wind Music in Flanders in the late Middle Ages," *Brass and Woodwind Quarterly* 2 (1969): 1–15.

25. Since soft instruments were not played in fixed groups in the fifteenth century, it is difficult to study the musicians who played soft instruments as a group. For some notion of the sorts of *bas* instruments played by minstrels, see, on the one hand, Bernhard, "Recherches," 3:380–93, and on the other hand, sixteenth-century wills of minstrels published in François Lesure, "La facture instrumentale à Paris au seizieme siècle," *Galpin Society Journal* 7 (1954): 11–52, which lists the instruments possessed by several musicians at the time of their death.

26. On this point, see François Lesure, "Les orchestres populaires à Paris vers la fin du XVIe siècle," *Revue de musicologie* 36 (1954), 50–52.

27. The petition is printed in Enrico Paganuzzi, "Medioevo e Rinascimento," in

Giovanni Battista Pighi, ed. *La Musica a Verona* (Verona: Banca Mutua popolare di Verona, 1976), 79–83.

28. Printed in Adolphe de Cardevacque, *La musique à Arras depuis les temps les plus reculés jusqu'à nos jours* (Arras: Imp. Rohard-Courtin, 1885), 63–64.

29. See Léon Lefebvre, *Notes pour servir à l'histoire de la musique à Lille: les ménestrels et joueurs d'instruments sermentés du XIVe au XVIIIe siècle* (Lille: Impr. Lefebvre-Ducrocq, 1906), 6.

30. See the notice printed in August Breuil, "La confrérie Notre-Dame-du-Puy d'Amiens," *Mémoires de la société des antiquaires de Picardie*, series 2, vol. 3 (1854): 658.

31. Pierre Pansier, "Les débuts du théâtre à Avigonon à la fin du XVe siècle," *Annales d'Avignon et du comtat Venaissin* 6 (1919): 5–52. On the instrumentalists who played at banquets for the city councillors of Cambrai in 1493 and 1494, see Achille Durieux, "Le théâtre à Cambrai avant et depuis 1789," *Mémoires de la société d'émulation de Cambrai* 39 (1883): 156–57.

32. See Lesure, "Orchestres populaires." Jacques Levron, "Une association de musiciens au XVIe siècle," *Euterpe*, 7 (July 1949): 123–38, reports a contract drawn up in 1557 that even specifies rehearsals. Whenever one of the three musicians in the band expressed the desire, they had to meet at the home of one of the players "pour se raccorder et jouer autant de fois et quantes qu'il sera besoin" ("to come together and play as much as and whenever they had need").

33. The document of 1491 is discussed in Lefebvre, *Musique à Lille*, 7.

34. See Cardevacque, *Musique à Arras*, 29 and 57.

35. See A. Tuetey, *Étude sur le droit municipal du XIIIe et du XIVe siècles en Franche-Comté et en particulier à Montbéliard* (Montbéliard: Impr. de H. Barbier, 1864), 134–41 and 285–92. The citation is given in the notes of Émile Picot in Paris, Bibliothèque Nationale, MS nouv. acq. fr. 23.193. On the participation of bands from neighboring towns in civic celebrations in Besançon, see Ulysse Robert, *Les origines du théâtre à Besançon* (S. 1., 1900), 67–68; for Cambrai, see Durieux, "Théâtre à Cambrai," 22, and 158–65 (and 25 for notices of visits the town band of Cambrai made to other towns).

36. See Michel Brenet, *Les concerts en France sous l'ancien régime* (Paris: Fischbacher, 1900), 12, for a document recording the participation of all the available instrumentalists in Orléans for the celebration in honor of the birth of a son to Louis XI in 1470. On 16 Brenet describes the annual festivities in Orléans that were initiated in 1482 to commemorate Joan of Arc and the siege by the English. For the civic celebrations in Rheims for the treaty of Arras in 1482—a *fête* that included dancing and the performance of a *Te deum*—see Louis Parris, *Le théâtre à Reims depuis les Romains jusqu'à nos jours* (Reims, 1885), 20–21. Almost all the local studies cited in the notes describe the festivities attendant on the formal *entrée* into a town of a prince or ruler, most of which included some music.

37. We know very little about the arrangements made by private citizens who wished to take lessons from a minstrel. That they did teach can be inferred from the prohibition against holding schools without permission of the guild authorities cited in the ordinances of 1407 and 1658 (see notes 12 and 16 above). The composers Jean Tapissier and Jean Vaillant were said to have organized schools of music in Paris in the late fourteenth century, but their schools may have been oriented toward a more formal training for choirboys; on this point, see Wright, *Music at the Court of Burgundy*, 45 and 129–30. For some contracts between private students and teachers, see notes 53 and 54 below.

38. For some typical documents recording payments by town councils to minstrels to attend annual schools, see Breuil, "Confrérie Notre-Dame-du-Puy d'Amiens," 657–68; E. Charvet, *Recherches sur les anciens théâtres de Beauvais* (Beauvais, D. Pere, 1881), 20–23; Durieux, "Théâtre à Cambrai," 142–45; and Lefebvre, *Musique à Lille,* 5. These and other historians report that notices of such schools disappeared in the middle of the fifteenth century.

39. See Breuil, "Confrérie Notre-Dame-du-Puy d'Amiens," 656.

40. See, for example, the classic study of secular singers and instrumentalists at the French royal court in the first half of the sixteenth century, Henri Prunières, "La musique de la chambre et de l'écurie sous le règne de François Ier: 1516–1547," *L'Année musicale* 1 (1911): 215–51, and, for a recent study of French royal minstrels at a slightly earlier time, Steven Bonime, "The Musicians of the Royal Stable Under Charles VIII and Louis XII (1484–1514)," *Current Musicology* 25 (1978): 7–21.

41. Bonime, "Anne de Bretagne and Music," ch. 3, "Musicians of the *Chambre* of Charles VIII and Louis XII."

42. See, for example, Albert Jacquot, *La musique en Lorraine,* 3d ed. (Paris: Fischbacher, 1886), 21, for a notice that Duke Réné II ennobled his *tabourin* and his *trompette* in 1493.

43. See Wright, *Music at the Court of Burgundy,* 132–34.

44. See Charvet, *Théâtres de Beauvais,* 11–19 and 109–15. On the concert in 1579 and the *fief* in the late sixteenth century, see Lecocq, *Théâtre en Picardie,* 171.

45. See Breuil, "Confrérie," 656. For other notices of *chanteurs en place* in Abbeville, see Breuil, "Confrérie," 658, and Lecocq, *Théâtre en Picardie,* 174.

46. See Lecocq, *Théâtre en Picardie,* 175.

47. See Émile Jolibois, *La diablerie de Chaumont* (Chaumont and Paris, 1838), 144–48, where the festivities on the day of the "grand pardon" are described. After mass, an *estampie,* was played "again" ("l'on commence de rechief à sonner une estampie"), at noon there was another ("au midi une autre sonnerie"), and after Vespers and Compline, still others ("apres vespres une aultre estampie, et a complie une autre pareillement").

48. See Daniel Heartz, "The Basse Dance: Its Evolution cira 1450 to 1550," *Annales musicologiques* 6 (1958–63): 287–340; James L. Jackman, ed., *Fifteenth Century Basses Dances,* The Wellesley edition, 6 (Wellesley, Mass.: Wellesley College, 1964); and the sources listed in Frederick Crane, *Materials for the Study of the Fifteenth Century Basse Danse* (Brooklyn, N.Y.: Institute of Mediaeval Music, 1968).

49. Brussels, Bibliothèque Royale, MS 9085, reproduced in Ernest Closson, ed., *Le manuscrit dit des basses danses de la Bibliothèque de Bourgogne* (Paris, 1912; reprint, Geneva: Minkoff, 1976).

50. For some pictures of pipe and tabor players accompanying dances, see Bowles, *Musikleben im 15. Jahrhundert,* 57, 63, and 160.

51. Published in modern editions, among other places in Guillaume Dufay, *Opera omnia,* ed. Heinrich Besseler, vol. 6 (Rome: American Institute of Musicology, 1964), 27–28, and Gilles Binchois, *Chansons,* ed. Wolfgang Rehm (Mainz: B. Schott's Söhne, 1957), 52. For monophonic melodies of the early fifteenth century, some of them arguably "popular" in character, found in the margins of archival documents in Namur, see Ernest Montellier, "Quatorze chansons du XVe siècle extraites des Archives Namuroises," *Annuaire 1939. Commission de la*

vieille chanson populaire. Ministère de l'instruction publique (Antwerp: Druk-ekerij Holthof, 1939), 153–211.

52. Craig Wright, "A Fragmentary Manuscript of Early 15th-Century Music in Dijon," *Journal of the American Musicological Society* 27 (1974): 306–15. On the evidence for the survival of *chansons de gestes* into the fourteenth century, see also Bernhard, "Recherches," 3:398–99. It is just possible that a learned mono-phonic style was cultivated in civic *puys* in the fifteenth and sixteenth centuries, those musico-literary societies organized in various towns in France that gave prizes for the best poems and musical compositions composed by their members or by contestants who sent in entries. So far as I know, no recent study has been made of music in the *puys*. For a brief discussion of these sorts of societies and a bibliography of some of the standard works on the subject, see Howard Mayer Brown, *Music in the French Secular Theater, 1400–1550* (Cambridge, Mass.: Harvard University Press, 1963), 35–36.

53. The contract is published in Pansier, "Théâtre à Avignon," 42; see also Crane, *Basse Danse,* 91.

54. The contract between Cely and Rede is published in Alison Hanham, "The Musical Studies of a Fifteenth-Century Wool Merchant," *The Review of English Studies,* new series, 8 (1957): 270–274. Frye's music is published in his *Collected Works,* ed. Sylvia W. Kenney (American Institute of Musicology, 1960).

55. See van der Straeten, *Ménestrels aux Pays-Bas,* 33, and also Strohm, *Music in Bruges,* 86, who identifies the composer as Nicasius de Brauwere, succentor of St. Savior's church in Bruges. Polk, "Flemish Wind Bands," 76–79, mentions Brauwere, and gives several other notices mentioning written music prepared for minstrels' use. G. van Doorslaer, "La chapelle musicale de Philippe le Beau," *Revue Belge d'archéologie et d'histoire de l'art* 4 (1934): 40, prints a notice reporting that the minstrels of Brussels played for the duke of Burgundy "plusieurs chansons de musique" (that is, composed polyphonic songs) in 1490. According to Camille Mellinet, *De la musique à Nantes* (Nantes: Impr. de Mellinet, 1837), 11, Pierre II of Britanny had among his players of *bas* instruments two "joueurs de vielle" who in 1455 played in the Magnificat at Vespers; we cannot even rule out altogether, therefore, the occasional participation of minstrels in liturgical ser-vices.

56. Copenhagen, Det kongelige Bibliotek, G1. kgl. Samling 1872.4°, partially published in a modern edition in Henrik Glahn, ed., *Musik fra Christian IIIs tid, Dania Sonans* 4 (Copenhagen: Dansk Selskab for Musikforskning, 1978).

57. On Rome, Biblioteca Casanatense, MS 2856, see Arthur S. Wolff, "The Chansonnier Biblioteca Casanatense 2856, Its History, Purpose, and Music," Ph. D. dissertation, North Texas State University, 1970, and the studies cited in *Census-Catalogue of Manuscript Sources of Polyphonic Music, 1400–1550,* vol. 3 (American Institute of Musicology, 1984), 112–14.

58. For evidence of the sorts of editorial changes made to these pieces to accommodate instrumental performances better, see Howard Mayer Brown, *A Florentine Chansonnier From the Time of Lorenzo the Magnificent, Florence, Bilblioteca Nazionale Centrale, MS Banco Rari 229,* 2 vols. (Chicago and London: University of Chicago Press, 1983), music volume, footnotes to nos. 3, 5, 7, 11, 13, 15, 17, and so on (that is, all those chansons that appear in both Florence 229 and Rome 2856).

59. Daniel Leech-Wilkinson, "Il libro di appunti di un suonatore di tromba del quindicesimo secolo," *Rivista italiana di musicologia* 16 (1981): 16–39.

60. Jozef Smits van Waesberghe, "Een 15ᵉ eeuws muziekboek van de stads-minstrelen van Maastricht?," in *Renaissance-Muziek, 1400–1600, Donum natalicium René Bernard Lenaerts,* ed. Jozef Robijns (Louvain: Katholieke Universiteit. Seminaire voor Muziekwetenschap, 1969), 247–73. It must be admitted that Smits van Waesberghe does not present any firm evidence that the manuscript was really prepared for the use of the town minstrels.

61. The contents are given with lists of concordances in Leech-Wilkinson, "Il libro di appunti," 31.

62. The contents are listed, and modern editions of some of the compositions are given in Smits van Waesberghe, "Muziekboek," 254–68; facsimiles of the pages with music are given there, opp. p. 252.

63. See, for example, Dufay, *Opera omnia,* 6:34–35, 49, 51, 54–55, and 57–58, for some examples of May songs and new years' songs. On this repertory, see David Fallows, *Dufay* (London: J. M. Dent 1982), 54, who points out that most of these songs predate 1440 and therefore are not likely to have been written in Cambrai.

7

History, Politics, and the Portrait of a City: Vermeer's *View of Delft*

Arthur K. Wheelock, Jr.

In the stillness of early morning light, the tower, roofs, and walls of Delft stretch across the imposing view of the city by Johannes Vermeer (fig. 1). Beyond the darkly weathered city walls and fortress-like gates that guard the entrance to the city, light falls on the orange tile roofs of the houses and the tower of the Nieuwe Kerk, as though life were awakening within the city if not without. For although a few figures stand and converse near a transport boat on the near shore of the harbor before the city, and a few are seen walking on the quay on the far shore, their forms are no less quiet and subdued than the walls themselves. The painting tells no story, describes no event, and does not even allow access to the town itself, yet it is one of the most memorable city views ever created. So extraordinary is the image that it is difficult to place it within an art historical perspective.[1] Writers have frequently commented that the painting, executed around 1660, has no direct precedents and that it is an anomaly within Vermeer's *oeuvre*. Yet it comes with such fullness of expression that no one doubts the conviction with which it was conceived. This conviction, I believe, stems to a greater degree than heretofore recognized from pictorial traditions, but it also draws on Vermeer's inherent sense of the dignity, power, and purpose of the city that is represented. This study will explore these underlying bases for Vermeer's image both in terms of the political and social role of cities in the Netherlands in the seventeenth century and in relation to the nature of city views upon which he drew for inspiration.

Delft was a venerable city with a long and distinguished past. The view depicted by Vermeer was in the mid-seventeenth century the primary entrance to the city by virtue of the harbor that had been built in 1614.[2] The harbor before the city walls fed into a waterway from Schiedam and Rotterdam, and the fourteenth-century city gates to the left and right of the bridge with the arched opening were named respectively the Schiedam and Rotterdam gates. By the mid-seventeenth century, the city was attrac-

Figure 1. Johannes Vermeer, *View of Delft,* **ca. 1660, oil on canvas.** *(Courtesy of the Mauritshuis, The Hague.)*

tive and prosperous. Its Delftware factories, tapestry-weaving ateliers, and breweries were thriving, but the city attracted travellers more for its charm, monuments, and historical associations than for its mercantile importance. One Englishman wrote that "Delft has as many bridges as there are days in the year and a like number of canals and streets with boats passing up and down."[3] Another traveller admired the great marketplace in the center of the town flanked by the imposing town hall and the soaring steeple of the Nieuwe Kerk, the sunlit tower seen in Vermeer's painting.[4] This same traveller also praised the tomb of Admiral van Tromp in the Oude Kerk, Delft's other major church, the tower of which is barely visible in the distant left center of the *View of Delft.*

Most visitors, however, whether they were countrymen or foreigners, focused their attention on the Nieuwe Kerk and the imposing tomb of William the Silent in its choir. In 1667 the local Delft historian Dirck van Bleyswijk wrote with pride that this tomb, built by Hendrick de Keyser in 1622, was famous throughout Europe.[5] Not only was it the most magnificent tomb in the Netherlands, it also had enormous symbolic importance because it was the burial place of the father of the Dutch republic, William of Orange, as well as of his successors, Prince Maurits, Prince Frederik Hendrik, and Prince Willem II (fig. 2).

The political associations Delft had with the house of Orange through the presence of the tomb of William the Silent in the Nieuwe Kerk gave enormous prestige to the city. Whatever one's political affiliations, the role of the house of Orange in the great struggle for independence was never

Figure 2. Gerard Houckgeest, *The Tomb of William the Silent in the Nieuwe Kerk in Delft*, 1651, oil on panel. *(Courtesy of the Mauritshuis, The Hague.)*

forgotten, and even in the Stadtholderless period after 1651 the leaders buried in the tomb were greatly revered (see fig. 2).[6] The tomb, moreover, served a civic function. It was a constant reminder of the important role Delft had played in the revolt against Spain and the early support the city had given to William the Silent's cause. Delft had been the seat of government under William of Orange because The Hague was not a walled city and was considered unsafe for that function during those turbulent times. Delft emphatically supported William of Orange's policies in the Union of Delft, signed on 25 April 1576, a contract that in many ways anticipated the treaty known as the Pacification of Ghent.[7]

The Pacification of Ghent, signed on 8 November 1576 at the instigation of William of Orange by both the States General of the southern Netherlands and the provinces of Holland and Zeeland from the northern Netherlands, represented the ideal to which William aspired: a cooperative effort to expel the Spanish troops and a hope for a reunited Netherlands. Unfortunately, the mutual trust between north and south was short-lived and the Pacification of Ghent was supplanted only three years later in 1579 by the Union of Utrecht. This pact established a confederation that formed the political basis for the separate Dutch republic, consisting of the seven northern provinces. Although William did not fully embrace the concepts of the Union of Utrecht, since it threatened his ideal of cooperation among all provinces, he continued to lead the northern forces until he was assassinated in Delft on 10 July 1584.[8]

The important role assumed by Dutch cities in the seventeenth century resulted from the complex political structure of the Netherlands that evolved in the late sixteenth century. This structure had at its roots a fear of strong centralized authority such as the Dutch had endured under the rule of Philip II of Spain. Only limited authority was given to the Stadtholder, primarily that of military leadership. The economic and social welfare of the republic was the responsibility of the States General, to which each province sent representatives. This body, which met in The Hague, was dominated by the most important province, Holland, and its most important city, Amsterdam. The leaders of the major cities in Holland advocated a course of peace that would enhance trade, and hence, the economic prosperity of the bourgeoisie. The Stadtholders who followed William of Orange, Prince Maurits, Prince Frederik Hendrik, and Prince Willem II were all capable leaders who possessed great military abilities. Since their role in state affairs was clearly augmented during periods of military conflict, they advocated a policy of military intervention, but their desires were often stymied by debate in the States General. Thus, unlike the absolute monarch in other countries of the period, national policy was determined by a body that represented many segments of Dutch society.

Primary among these, as has been mentioned, were the cities of the province of Holland, including Delft, which forcefully guarded their independence and economic interests. At the end of the sixteenth and the beginning of the seventeenth centuries, these interests were effectively represented by Johan van Oldenbarnevelt, who was first appointed *Advocaat van den Lande* in 1586.[9] From this position, which effectively meant that he was chief minister of the States General and hence of the Republic, he sought a policy of peace and eventually negotiated a Twelve-Year Truce with Spain in 1609. In the intervening years he continued his efforts to establish a lasting peace, but he was unsuccessful, not only because of the intransigence of Spain, which insisted on at least a formal recognition of the sovereignty of the King of Spain, but also because Prince Maurits, who had succeeded his father Prince William I as Stadtholder, favored a continuation of the war.

The political differences represented by Oldenbarnevelt and Prince Maurits were aggravated by religious ones. Oldenbarnevelt favored the milder form of Calvinism practiced by the Remonstrants to that of the orthodox belief advocated by the Reformed Church. The Remonstrants also appealed to Oldenbarnevelt's political instincts, since they allowed civil authority to have authority over church doctrine. Since the Remonstrants were particularly strong in the province of Holland, the issue became one of local versus national control, and it paralleled the existing conflicts between the political role of Holland in the States General and the leadership ambitions of Prince Maurits. These issues came to a head when the orthodox ministers called for a national synod to be held in Dordrecht in 1618 to settle the dispute. Prince Maurits eventually sided with the Counter-Remonstrants, arrested Oldenbarnevelt, and had him and his followers executed in 1619.

The Synod of Dort upheld the Counter-Remonstrant position and left Prince Maurits as undisputed leader of the Dutch republic. The issues underlying the conflict between Oldenbarnevelt and Maurits, however, did not disappear. The end of the Twelve-Year Truce came all too quickly in 1621 and the internal conflicts between the house of Orange with its militaristic orientation and that of the States General with its desire for peace continued unabated for the next thirty years. One of the outgrowths of these conflicts was a renewed sense of the political and social importance of the major Dutch cities, an awareness that manifested itself in poems, books, atlases, wall maps, prints, drawings, and paintings.

The political significance of the cities is evident in one of the most remarkable propaganda statements on the advantages of peace, Claes Jansz. Visscher's map of *Leo Belgicus* (fig. 3). Visscher took over an older, allegorical image of the United Netherlands shaped in the form of a lion and transformed it from a roaring and striding figure representative of the country's alertness and strength to a seated lion resting his paw on a sword

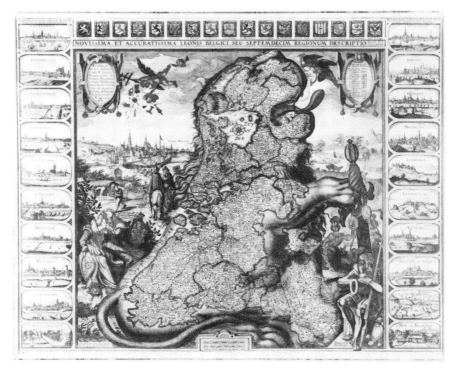

Figure 3. Claes Jansz. Visscher, *Leo Belgicus,* ca. 1620, copper engraving.

thrust into the ground. As the lion looks up with mouth open and tongue extended, he is fed the Twelve-Year Truce (Bestant von 12 Jaer) from the horn of a flying cupid. At the same time, an armored figure at the lower right, Sleeping War (Slapende Oorlogh), rests his arm on the lion's paw. Around the lion, dotted across the landscape are the fruits of the peace: prosperity, in the form of grazing cows (t'Overvloelich Ver) and merchant ships at a city's harbor (t'Lant Velvaert); commerce (Coop handel) being conducted by traders on the shore; fertile crops (t'Vredich Lantbouwen) being sown and reaped by active farmers; freedom of travel (t'Veylich Reysen) illustrated by two mounted riders, and finally, expanding cities (t'Vergrooten der Steden) as seen by the construction of an imposing entrance gate to the city in the far distance. A flying cupid on the left distributes blessings (Zegen) that further enrich the land in such periods of peace: art and science, knowledge, and riches (Const en Wetenschap, Kennisse, Ryckdom).

The political solution that would ensure the continuation of this prosperity is also clearly indicated by Visscher in the right and left middle ground: alert defense of the frontiers (Frontier Wacht), and reconciliation between the two Netherlands, the south and the north. This union is symbolized by two allegorical figures (t'Neerlandt onder d'Aertshertogh Alberts, and t'Vrije Neerlant) who hold shields containing the coats of arms of the individual provinces of the south and the north and who sit on a dishevelled figure representing their former discord (t'Oude Twist).

Along the top edge of the map are the coats of arms of the seventeen provinces, and significantly, along the sides are views of the most important cities of the provinces. Those on the left are identified as principal cities under the jurisdiction of the States General of the united provinces (Hooft Steden onder t'gebiet der HM Herren Staten van de Verenichde Provin.), those on the right as the principal cities under the jurisdiction of the Enfante Isabella Clara Eugenia (Hooft Steden onder t'gebiet van den Infante Isabella Clara Eugenia). The bottom view on each side represents the site of their respective courts, on the left t'Hof van Hollant and on the right t'Hof van Brabant.

The underlying message of the central allegorical image is immediately clear, but perhaps less evident is the political statement implied by the bordering material. Visscher explicitly equates the ruling authority of the States General in the united provinces with that of the Regents Albert and Isabella in the southern Netherlands. Nowhere does he mention the house of Orange or the Stadtholder Prince Maurits. Moreover, it is evident that the underlying strength of the proposed union of the two Netherlands comes from the individual provinces, and even more specifically, from the capital cities, shown bordering the map, under the respective leadership of Amsterdam and Antwerp.

The desire for peace in the face of the renewal of hostilities seems to have been strong throughout the following decades. Hendrick Terbrugghen's painting *Sleeping Mars,* 1625 (Centraal Museum, Utrecht) (fig. 4) so closely parallels the figure of "Slapende Oorlogh" in Visscher's map that one can conclude that the same motivations underlay this image.[10] Small scenes of cavalry engagements by Esaias van de Velde, Gerrit Claez. Bleeker, Pieter Post and others from the 1620s or 1630s likewise should be seen as negative commentaries on the political situation rather than merely as neutral observations of events occurring in the Dutch countryside.

Political efforts toward a peaceful settlement were made after the resumption of hostilities by the Spanish Netherlands but, because of the strong Calvinistic character of the States General in the years immediately following the Synod of Dort and because of Prince Frederik Hendrik's own dynastic interests, these efforts remained unsuccessful. Peter Paul Rubens, while on a diplomatic mission in England for the Infanta Isabella to help negotiate a peace treaty between England and Spain, indepen-

Figure 4. Hendrick Terbrugghen, *Sleeping Mars*, 1625, oil on canvas. *(Courtesy of Centraal Museum, Utrecht.)*

dently approached the Dutch diplomat Albert Joachimi in the winter of 1630 to encourage him to advise the Dutch to forge a peaceful settlement with Spain. Rubens had a settlement in mind that would be premised on accepting the sovereignty of Spain.[11] Joachimi, however, tersely replied that any reunification of the Netherlands would have to be based on the Pacification of Ghent. A more official plea came in the fall of 1632 when a delegation sent by the States General of the Spanish Netherlands travelled to The Hague to meet with the Dutch States General. This attempt likewise failed.[12]

With the appointment of Cardinal-Infante Ferdinand as regent in the Spanish Netherlands at the end of 1634, the political relations between the united provinces and the Spanish Netherlands changed. Ferdinand, a triumphant military leader who had defeated the Swedish army at Nordlingen in 1634, was seen as a military threat by the Dutch. Almost immediately in February 1635 the Dutch entered into a political alliance with France. The alliance was essentially a treaty of partition that stated that once the Spanish had been driven from the Netherlands the French-speaking segments of the Spanish Netherlands would be taken over by France and the Dutch-speaking regions would come under the jurisdiction of the Dutch republic. The treaty was thereby built upon a different principle than that envisioned by the Pacification of Ghent. Although its goals were not achieved, it did deal a death blow to the old aspirations for a united Netherlands consisting of seventeen provinces.

As already evident in the 1635 alliance with France, by the late 1630s sentiment had turned away from the ideal of a political reunification of the seventeen provinces in favor of the principle of separation established in 1579 at the Union of Utrecht. An additional reason for this shift in attitude was Amsterdam's desire to maintain its economic and political power over Antwerp, whose position had been weakened through the blockade of the river Scheldt. Thus it is noteworthy that in 1641, when Rembrandt painted his allegorical work *The Concord of the State (De Eendracht van het Land,* Museum Boymans-van Beuningen, Rotterdam) (fig. 5), the lion in the foreground no longer represents the Leo Belgicus but the Leo Hollandicus. The lion is chained to a mound on which the coats of arms of Amsterdam are prominently displayed, surrounded by the coats of arms of the other cities of the province of Holland. Antwerp and the southern cities are no longer represented. The exact meanings of Rembrandt's allegory have never been totally unravelled; however, it is almost certainly an appeal for concord under the leadership of Holland and, by implication, Amsterdam.[13]

When the Treaty of Münster was finally signed in 1648, the conditions established were those determined by the States General and in large part by the province of Holland and its major cities. Prince Frederik Hendrik

Figure 5. Rembrandt van Rijn, *The Concord of the State (De Eendracht van het Land),* **1641, oil on panel.** *(Courtesy of Museum Boymans-van Beuningen, Rotterdam.)*

was actually opposed to the signing of a separate peace with Spain, and had he not died the year before the culmination of the negotiations, it is likely that no treaty would have been forthcoming. Almost in celebration of the supremacy of the province of Holland and of its leading cities in these negotiations, Claes Jansz. Visscher published in 1648 a map called *Het Graafschap Holland (The Countship of Holland)* (fig. 6). Although dedicated to Prince Maurits for his military defense of the province until his death in 1625, the map is clearly intended to stress the vigor and might that Holland had assumed in the succeeding decades. In this map Visscher adapted the lion metaphor from his map of *Leo Belgicus* of the 1620s. The lion, however, is now rampant, not seated; his sword stresses his role defending the country. Along the sides of the map are once again the profiles of cities, in this instance the cities of Holland: Dordrecht, Delft, Amsterdam, Rotterdam, Alckmaer, Enkhuizen, Haerlem, Leyden, Dergon (Gouda), Den Briel, Hoorn, and the court in The Hague. The standard format of the city profiles stresses their united front, but each city is distinctly recorded and its visual characteristics are unmistakable.

The city views on Visscher's maps, while integral to the symbolic meaning he wished to impart, are derived from a long tradition that originates with Ludovico Guicciardini's masterful *Descrittione di Tutti i Paesi Bassi,* first published in Antwerp in 1567. Guicciardini described the essential characteristics of the major urban centers and even included two views of the major buildings of Antwerp drawn from life, the town hall and the cathedral. More elaborate maps and city profiles were provided by Braun and Hogenberg in the *Civitates Orbis Terrarum,* first published in Cologne in 1574 (fig. 7). These city profiles established precedents for those that appeared in later editions of Guicciardini (fig. 8), in the borders of Visscher's maps, and to a large extent for painters of topographic views, in particular, Esaias van de Velde (fig. 9), Hendrick Vroom (fig. 10), Aelbert Cuyp (fig. 11), and even Johannes Vermeer in his *View of Delft* (fig. 1). Both of these early publications were reprinted and revised frequently in the first half of the seventeenth century by the Dutch publishing houses of Hondius and Blaeu. The most remarkable publication on Dutch cities, however, is clearly Joan Blaeu's city atlas, *Tooneel der Steden der Verenighde Nederlanden,* Amsterdam, published in 1649, just after the signing of the Treaty of Münster. Blaeu's remarkable bird's eye views of the cities give precise information about the houses, gardens, roads, and canals, as well as the major public buildings.

Figure 6. Claes Jansz. Visscher, *Het Graafschap Holland (The Countship of Holland),* 1648, engraving.

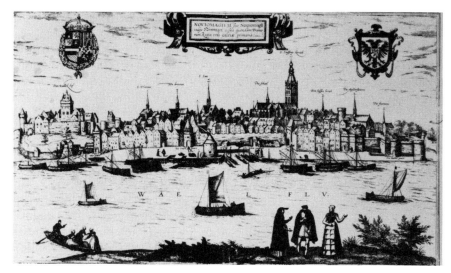

Figure 7. *Nijmegen*, woodcut in Braun and Hogenberg, *Civitates Orbis Terrarum*, Cologne, 1574, from Braun and Hogenberg, *De Hollandse Steden*, Groningen, n.d. (facsimile edition).

Figure 8. *Amsterdam*, woodcut in Ludovico Guicciardini, *Description de touts les Pays-Bas*, Amsterdam, 1613.

Figure 9. Esaias van de Velde, *View of Zierikzee,* **1648, oil on canvas.** *(Courtesy of Staatliche Museen, Berlin-Dahlem.)*

Figure 10. Hendrick Vroom, *View of Delft,* **1615, oil on canvas.** *(Courtesy of Municipal Museum Het Prinsenhof, Delft.)*

Figure 11. Aelbert Cuyp, *View of Nijmegen*, ca. 1648, oil on canvas (*Courtesy of The Duke of Bedford.*)

Figure 12. *De Stadt van Haerlem,* **woodcut accompanying Karel von Mander's poem,** *Beeld van Haarlem,* **Haarlem, 1596.**

These cartographic views emphasize the pride the Dutch took in their carefully ordered, well-kept cities. This pride, obviously, was also felt locally, and writers, historians, poets, and painters, either by choice or commission, glorified their cities on many occasions during the course of the seventeenth century. One of the earliest examples is Karel van Mander's poem in honor of Haarlem, *Beeld van Haarlem,* published in 1596, which was accompanied by a woodcut print of the city (fig. 12).[14] Books describing and illustrating the history, famous citizens, wonders, and virtues of cities, specifically Haarlem, Leiden, Delft, and Dordrecht, became increasingly popular after the conclusion of the twelve-year truce when cities were consciously emphasizing their importance within the social fabric of the Netherlands. Perhaps the most famous of these is Samuel Ampzing's *Beschrijvinge ende lof der stadt Haerlem in Holland (Description and Praise of the Town of Haarlem in Holland)* published in Haarlem in 1628. The first print in the book is a city profile of Haarlem by Pieter Saenredam, under which is included a poem that reads in part:

> See here an old town born thousand years ago, / . . . How many beautiful churches! how many high towers! / How many noble Houses! Justly formerly chosen / because of her ornament and glory, because of her virtue and praise, / And a good site as court of our Count.[15]

Topographic prints, drawings, and paintings of these and other cities, above all Amsterdam, are numerous and attest to the great popularity of this type of visual record. Presumably most of these views were made to satisfy market demands, both public and private. One artist who exploited this market was Hendrick Vroom (fig. 10). In 1615 he painted two views of Delft, each of which followed the scheme devised by Braun and Hogenberg. Vroom placed the city, with its major monuments plainly visible, beyond a foreground filled with activities one might find in the surrounding countryside. In 1634 he "donated" these views to the municipality because of his "deep affection" for the city. In exchange for his generosity he was offered a gift of 150 guilders.[16] Whether or not he had offered these paintings to the city in 1615 is not known; significantly, however, the municipality accepted these glorifications of the city at a time when the cities in Holland were asserting their importance within the political and social structure of the country.

Vroom's style of painting was by the 1630s rather old-fashioned. Most of the younger landscape artists of the day, Jan van Goyen, Salomon van Ruysdael, and Aelbert Cuyp were less interested in careful topographical depictions than in placing the cities they represented into a broader pictorial context. Most of their city views of the 1630s and 1640s place the city less centrally in the composition and further back into depth. The city as well as the land is bathed in atmosphere and light. Another clear shift of emphasis, however, is noticeable in the late 1640s at about the time of the Treaty of Münster and the renewed focus on the vitality of the city in maps and atlases by Visscher and Blaeu. Dramatic silhouettes of church spires, city walls, and windmills against the sky are emphasized by bringing the point of view closer and by bathing the structures in strong light. At just this time the city with the most dramatic skyline in the Netherlands, Nijmegen, with its massive fortress the Valkhof, built by Charlemagne, became a favorite subject for Van Goyen, Ruysdael, and Cuyp (fig. 11). Each suggested the massive stone walls with a variety of short strokes and dabs of paint, thus giving a solidity to the forms not seen in earlier views.

The artists may have chosen to paint the Valkhof at this time merely because its silhouette satisfied their compositional needs at this stage of their careers, but one wonders as well if the choice was not also political. Nijmegen had been the home of the Batavians, the ancient forefathers of the Dutch. The city had been the site of one of Prince Maurits's earliest major victories against the Spanish. At a time when the Dutch were finally freeing themselves of the Spanish yoke, these views of an old and distinguished city with a highly significant cultural and political heritage may have held special nationalistic meaning.

Paintings of Delft around 1650 may have been significant in comparable ways. Delft was an important, if not leading city within the province of Holland and thus for a number of political and economic reasons it was necessarily allied to that faction of the political spectrum. Orangist sympathies in Delft, however, were present because of its historical associations with William of Orange, ones that were visually reinforced by the presence of the tomb of William the Silent in the Nieuwe Kerk. Delft citizens must have felt strong conflicting emotions, ones that partly explain why the city did not take an assertive political or cultural role during the first half of the century.

Almost simultaneously with the unexpected death of Prince Willem II on 6 November 1650 and the subsequent decision of the seven provinces to assume all the sovereign powers of the state, Delft experienced a remarkable creative outburst. Gerard Houckgeest (fig. 2), Emanuel de Witte, and Hendrick van Vliet introduced new forms of architectural painting by means of unusual vantage points and strong contrasts of light and shade. Their works, which captured the sense of the dramatic interior spaces of the two Delft churches, focused on views of the significant tombs and monuments, in particular that of William the Silent. For the first time since it was erected in 1622 the tomb was portrayed in its actual setting in the choir of the Nieuwe Kerk, surrounded by those who had come to view this famous memorial, not only to contemplate death, but also to reflect on the role the house of Orange had played in their national heritage. Ironically, only with the death of Willem II and the establishment of the Stadtholderless republic did Delft artists feel free to acknowledge and even celebrate the important historical presence of the house of Orange in Delft.

The unusual nature of the political situation at the time, and the complex character of Delft's historical relationship to the house of Orange clearly affected the types of scenes represented by Delft architectural painters. Although Houckgeest, De Witte, and Van Vliet insisted on the physical reality of their church views by emphasizing the rich textural effects of stone and marble in these vast structures, the subjects they chose—figures looking at and contemplating monuments and tombs—were imbued with profound symbolism.[17]

A slightly different relationship between symbolism and reality is apparent in Carel Fabritius' evocative *View in Delft with a Musical Instrument Seller's Stall*, 1652 (National Gallery, London) (fig. 13). Here the exterior of the Nieuwe Kerk is visible in the distance, beyond the pensive figure of the seated man in the foreground. The strangely distorted perspective in the foreground, and the exaggeratedly small and distant appearance of the church are effects that probably derive from his use of a wide-angle lens in conceiving the scene. These modifications of the site make it clear that Fabritius was not primarily interested in recording an exact equivalent of reality.[18] Fabritius was searching for a different type of symbolism than that expressed by the architectural painters. Of primary importance for him was the suggestive mood of the scene and the way in which it brought together the diverse components of man, musical instruments, and church. Musical instruments often suggest the transitoriness of life, and this theme may be the underlying one for the painting. It certainly would

Figure 13. Carel Fabritius, *View of Delft with a Musical Instrument Seller's Stall,* **1652, oil on canvas.** *(Courtesy of National Gallery, London.)*

not have escaped the notice of contemporaries, moreover, that the choir of the Nieuwe Kerk was the site of the tomb of William the Silent, the most poignant monument in the Netherlands.[19]

Transitoriness of life, indeed, became a very real concern in Delft shortly thereafter. On 12 October 1654, the gunpowder warehouse in Delft exploded, devastating a large northeastern section of the town and killing many citizens, including Fabritius. The explosion and its aftermath became the subject of many city views by Delft artists, particularly Daniel Vosmaer and Egbert van der Poel. In most paintings of Delft from the 1650s, however, particularly those by Pieter de Hooch, *A Dutch Courtyard,* c. 1658 (National Gallery of Art, Washington, D.C.), Jan Steen, *The Burgher of Delft and His Daughter,* 1655 (private collection, Great Britain), and Johannes Vermeer, *The Little Street,* c. 1657 (Rijksmuseum, Amsterdam), this disaster plays no role. The destruction is never hinted at in their courtyard scenes or views across or along canals. On the contrary, these paintings are conscious statements about the prosperity and well-being of the citizens of this town and the carefully manicured and maintained world in which they live.

Vermeer's *View of Delft,* painted about 1660, stands as the culmination of these pictorial traditions in Delft architectural painting. To create his image Vermeer drew heavily from cartographic traditions, but, as had Aelbert Cuyp in his *View of Nijmegen,* Houckgeest in his painting of the *Tomb of William the Silent* and Fabritius in his *View of Delft,* Vermeer sought to convey far more than the physical characteristics of the city. Unlike city profiles on maps and unlike Vroom's earlier views of Delft,

Vermeer did not choose a view in which the main monuments of the city would dominate the horizon. In his painting the Oude Kerk tower is barely seen, and the town hall not at all. Only the tower of the Nieuwe Kerk rises significantly above the rooftops. Even this tower, supremely important to the composition as it is, does not overpower the city; it is part of the dense fabric of towers, gables, and rooftops, shapes that comprise the physical presence and historical character of Delft.

The *View of Delft,* indeed, is not primarily a topographical painting. Vermeer wanted to make a statement about Delft in his work. He carefully modified buildings and perspective effects to enhance the dignified, stately appearance of the city.[20] He also used light symbolically. The darkly weathered walls and fortified gates poignantly stress the city's ancient foundations and the rich heritage of its past. The light that streams down within the city, illuminating the orange tiled roofs and soaring tower of the Nieuwe Kerk, acts as a powerful and positive force, symbolizing as it were the city's strength and optimism, even in the aftermath of the disaster of 1654. Vermeer's symbolism is not complex but it explains a great deal about Delft's perception of itself after the political ferment during the years of the formation of the Dutch republic. Even more significantly, however, the haunting image of this extraordinary painting has a life of its own, and, even if we do not completely understand its full range of meanings, it speaks to every admirer with incomparable force and presence.

Notes

I would like to thank H. Perry Chapman, Sara M. Wages, and Kathleen Pedersen.

1. Aside from discussions that appear in monographs on Vermeer, the pictorial antecedents for the *View of Delft* have been discussed by: Wolfgang Stechow, *Dutch Landscape Painting of the Seventeenth Century* (London: Phaidon, 1966), 125–126; Richard J. Wattenmaker, et al. *The Dutch Cityscape in the Seventeenth Century and its Sources,* exhibition catalogue (Amsterdam Historisch Museum, Amsterdam, and the Art Gallery of Ontario, Toronto, 1977), 19–23; Svetlana Alpers, *The Art of Describing: Dutch Art in the Seventeenth Century* (Chicago: The University of Chicago Press, 1983), 152–65. The most extensive analysis of the painting is the article by Arthur K. Wheelock, Jr., and C. J. Kaldenbach, "Vermeer's *View of Delft* and his Vision of Reality," *Artibus et Historiae* 6 (1982): 9–35.

2. For the alterations made at that time, see W. F. Weve, "Verdedigingswerken," in *De Stad Delft: cultuur en maatschappij van 1572 tot 1667,* exhibition catalogue (Delft: Stedelijk Museum Het Prinsenhof, 1981), 62–65.

3. Williame Crowne visited Delft in December 1636 at the end of his trip through Germany and the Netherlands with the duke of Arundel. Quoted in

Francis C. Springell, *Connoisseur and Diplomat* (London: Maggs Bros. Ltd., 1963), 94.

4. Edward Browne, *An Account of Several Travels Through a Great Part of Germany* (London: Benjamin Tooke, 1677), 3. See also John Ray, *Observations Topographical, Moral, and Physiological Made in a Journey through part of the Low-Countries, Germany, Italy and France* (London: John Martyn, 1673), 25.

5. Dirck van Bleyswijck, *Beschryvinge der Stadt Delft*, (Delft, 1667–[1674?]), 1:264.

6. For the symbolic significance of the tomb of William the Silent, see Arthur K. Wheelock, Jr., "Gerard Houckgeest and Emanuel de Witte: Architectural painting in Delft around 1650," *Simiolus* 8 (1975/76): 167–85.

7. H. J. Ph. G. Kaajan, "De Unie van Delft van 25 April 1576," in *De Stad Delft*, 7–14.

8. For excellent analyses of the political events in the Netherlands of the sixteenth century, see Pieter Geyl, *The Revolt of the Netherlands, 1555–1609*, 2nd ed., (London: Ernest Benn Limited, 1958); A. Th. van Deursen and H. de Schepper, *Willem van Oranje* (Weesp: Fibula-van Dishoeck, 1984); Geoffrey Parker, *The Dutch Revolt* (Ithaca: Cornell University Press, 1977).

9. Two accounts of the events of the period are to be found in Pieter Geyl, *The Netherlands in the Seventeenth Century*, 2 vols. (London: Ernest Benn Limited, 1961), 1: 18–83; J. L. Price, *Culture and Society in the Dutch Republic During the 17th Century* (New York: Charles Scribner's Sons, 1974), 16–40. For a discussion of the evolution of Dutch political theory, see E. H. Kossmann, "The Development of Dutch Political Theory in the Seventeenth Century," in *Britain and the Netherlands*, 4 vols., ed. J. S. Bromley and E. H. Kossmann, Anglo-Dutch Historical Conference (London: Chatto & Windus, 1960), 1: 91–110.

10. Wolfgang Schöne, "Rembrandts Man mit dem Gold Helm," *Jahrbuch der Akademie der Wissenschaften in Göttingen* (1972): 33–99. I would like to thank Dr. Perry Chapman for this reference.

11. C. V. Wedgewood, *The World of Rubens 1577–1640* (New York: Time-Life Books, 1967), 147.

12. The emissaries from the Brussels States General first travelled to Maastricht to negotiate directly with Frederik Hendrik. For a full account see: Geyl, *Netherlands*, 1: 92–107.

13. See J. G. van Dillen, "Amsterdam's Role in Seventeenth-Century Dutch Politics and its Economic Background," in *Britain and the Netherlands*, 4 vols. ed. J. S. Bromley and E. H. Kossmann, Anglo-Dutch Historical Conference (Groningen: J. B. Wolters, 1964), 2:133–47.

14. I would like to thank Dr. Margarita Russell for this reference.

15. Quoted in *Pieter Jansz. Saenredam*, exhibition catalogue, Centraal Museum (Utrecht, 1961), 243–44.

16. The transaction is discussed in John Michael Montias, *Artists and Artisans in Delft* (Princeton: Princeton University Press, 1982), 185–88.

17. See: Wheelock, "Houckgeest"; Walter Liedtke, *Architectural Painting in Delft: 1650–1675* (Doornspijk: Davaco 1982).

18. Arthur K. Wheelock, Jr., *Perspective, Optics, and Delft Artists around 1650* (New York: Garland 1977), 4–11, 191–220.

19. Bleyswijck, *Beschryvinge*, 264.

20. See Wheelock and Kaldenbach, "Vermeer's *View of Delft*," for a full discussion of these changes.

PART III

Authority and Order in the Renaissance Town: The Politics of Ritual

Celebrating Authority in Bristol, 1475–1640

David Harris Sacks

The exercise of authority is a ubiquitous fact of social life. But the problem of authority was raised in a special way in the Renaissance. For this was an era in which the secular state established itself upon new social and intellectual foundations. Authority was also a subject of special significance to English cities in this period. An English city was primarily a legal and political unit, defined by jurisdictional boundaries that offered no real barrier to economic and social change. What held it together was its corporate existence, which in turn depended upon the authority of its governors to act for the urban community.[1] Authority consequently required justification and continuous reinforcement, and its celebration became one of the great subjects of civic culture.

But before we can begin to examine the celebration of authority in the Renaissance English town we need to explore the concept of authority, for our problem is as much an intellectual as an institutional one. We know, more or less accurately, who held authority in England from the end of the fifteenth to the middle of the seventeenth century. We are less clear what it meant for them to do so, and how meanings might have changed during the reigns of the Tudors and the first two Stuarts.

I

By any standard, "authority" is a deeply ambiguous concept.[2] It can refer in a variety of ways to rights. Someone in authority has the right to act and to be obeyed within his jurisdiction. He is at liberty to act, but he need not make the choice on every occasion on which the opportunity arises. In the case of rights, then, authority is a legalistic concept, and we often speak of those holding it as having "legal" or "constitutional" authority. But "authority" also can refer in a variety of ways to capacities or powers. Someone who is exceptionally competent in a given realm is an authority. He has the power to produce results. Through his reputation for expertise, he also has the title to be believed and the capacity to influence the opinions and judgments of others. In this way, he exercises power over their conduct or action, and he is said to have "moral authority." His authority, however, not only enables him to act within the areas of his competence, but it poses the duty upon him to do so. As an authority he has an obligation to perform right actions; he is not morally free to use his skills on some occasions and to withhold them on others.

For some purposes, these two ideas can be thought to complement one another. He who authorizes an action has a right; he who is authorized has a duty. The former works autonomously to perform as he chooses in the realm in which he is authorized to act. The latter works for the good of or interest of those who have granted him his power, and he must perform this service if he is to meet his obligations to them. This formulation, however, assumes that the fundamental unit of analysis is the individual, and that the fundamental question is how individuals come to accept authority. But by its very nature, the concept of authority presupposes the existence of community. It is not enough to claim authority for oneself; it is also necessary that it be recognized by others according to some mutually agreed upon rules. Otherwise, one is applying force, not exercising authority.[3]

The problem of community, however, proves just as troubling as the problem of authority. In everyday language, "community" can mean no more than a collectivity of people having common interests and sharing common activities. But many scholars have come to consider community more narrowly as a bounded social system—a small group or collectivity or neighborhood characterized by multifaceted, face-to-face, and permanent social relationships in contrast to the partial, impersonal, and transitory relationships found in the larger society. In keeping with this understanding it is assumed that authority in a community is what Max Weber called "traditional authority," i.e., authority that rests on an "established belief in the sanctity of immemorial traditions and the legitimacy of the status of those exercising authority under them." Authority in a more broadly gauged modern society is what Weber called "legal authority," i.e., authority that rests on a "a belief in the 'legality' of patterns of normative rules and the right of those elevated to authority under such rules to issue commands."[4]

In this interpretive scheme, the Renaissance often is treated as the period in which the second type of authority first took hold. It is thought to be the era that saw the rise of the bureaucratic state and that consequently produced inevitable collisions between society and the state. But scholars recognize that this new rational form of authority did not succeed all at once. Instead, they tell us that it made itself felt initially only in certain advanced political settings, namely in the great cities of Italy and in the courts of the great northern monarchs. The provinces, and especially the provincial towns, remained centers of the older, sanctified forms of authority.[5]

This interpretation is a classic example of what F. W. Maitland once called "retrospective modernism," the tendency of scholars to view the past through criteria of thought applicable, if at all, only in the present. No one living in the era of the Renaissance could have made distinctions between traditional and legal authority, or between community and society. These are terms of art in modern scholarship. They may help us locate ourselves amidst the complexities we study, but they do so by obscuring the very uncertainties and ambiguities with which contemporaries lived. They make it difficult to see how those who experienced the changes wrought during the Renaissance participated in them. To understand the Renaissance as an historical process, we must delve into these thickets of conceptual confusion, not eliminate them by abstraction. As Maitland said, "we . . . have to think away distinctions which seem to us clear as the sunshine; we must think ourselves back into a twilight."[6]

If we are to grasp this reality, however, we must turn our attention away from the deep structures and sweeping developments that preoccupy most studies of the Renaissance period. Instead we need to look at the ways in which ideas of authority were represented during this era. In the provincial towns, authority was present at every turn, but on certain festive occasions—at the annual election of the mayor, for example—it was given particular notice by townsmen. Here ideas, so difficult to come by in words, were revealed in gestures and actions. By paying close attention to the nuances of meaning on these occasions, much can be learned about the changing history of authority.[7]

In what follows, I shall explore the celebration of authority in Bristol from the end of the fifteenth to the beginning of the seventeenth century. Bristol, of course, cannot be thought to represent the "typical" English provincial town in this era. It was, after all, the kingdom's third most populous urban center and its second most active port. But as a leading corporate town, it shared many political and social characteristics with similar places like Norwich, York, Exeter, Chester, Coventry, and even London. In the fifteenth century it also equalled these places in its devotion to its ancient traditions. Its history, then, can give us insight into the processes of change that affected the major urban centers in provincial England.

II

In the earlier middle ages, when Bristol's merchant guild was transforming the borough into an effective corporate body, the central ceremonial event of the civic year was the annual swearing of the freeman's oath. By the later fourteenth and early fifteenth centuries, however, the fabric of social life in Bristol had begun to alter, as a class of merchant entrepreneurs differentiated themselves from the other members of the old mercantile community, and as local governance fell into the hands of the borough's "better and more worthy men," serving on a select council chosen by cooptation. In this era more than before, the burgesses of Bristol lived according to the ideals of social unity but the realities of social division. They bound themselves into a compact body politic by oaths promising a complete devotion to the city's commonweal and a thorough commitment of their wealth and power to its aid. Yet they resided in a town whose topography segregated them into distinct neighborhoods and whose economy placed them in separate social groupings. During this period a series of ceremonial and festive events emerged to secure the town's internal unity through ritual.[8] The most important of them concerned the community's relations with its mayor, common councillors, and other governing officials.

In the fifteenth century, Bristol's government, established by King Edward III's charter of 1373, was a self-perpetuating, closed institution of forty-two citizens. Its members were chosen by cooptation, and its chief officers, the mayor and sheriff, were elected exclusively from among its own membership, who were themselves the only voters. As described in Robert Ricart's *The Maire of Bristowe is Kalendar,* written in 1479–80,[9] election proceedings began on St. Giles' day, 1 September, when the mayor's four sergeants officially warned the membership of the Common Council of the impending election. The election itself was held on 15 September and failure to appear subjected each councillor to a ten-pound fine.[10] Candidates were nominated and chosen on 15 September and each election was conceived to be a spontaneous judgment about who was best suited to serve the city. The voting proper began with the current mayor, "first, by his reason to name and gyve his voice to some whorshipfull man of the seide hows," i.e., nominating and voting in the same motion. "[A]fter hym the Shiref, and so all the house perusid in the same, euery man to gyve his voice as shall please him." In theory, it was possible for each council member to nominate a new candidate, including himself, when his time came to give his voice. The victor was "hym that hathe moste voices." In fact, contests appear to have been exceedingly rare. But participation by the entire membership in this way helped to bind them in obedience to the new regime, since the councillors were much less free to criticize or oppose the new officers at a later date if they had played a part in selecting them. The vote of every member promoted effective government for the following year. The form of election, then, was based upon the principles of spontaneity and openness. An election was considered the free choice of the assembled civic leadership made according to the community's highest ideals. Reason and good conscience were supposed to find the best person to serve the commonwealth for the coming year.[11]

After the selection of the new mayor began the necessary tasks of raising him into office and of presenting him to the borough community. Having been "in due form electid," the successful candidate was to "rise fro the place he sat in, and come sytt *a dextris* by the olde maires side," there to participate in subsequent deliberations. Once these "communications" had been completed, attention was turned to making the new mayor known to the town. With the adjournment of the election meeting, he was "worshipfully accompanyed, with a certein of the seid hous, home to his place," in effect, publically announcing the election to all who should observe this mayoral party pass through the streets.[12]

Election to the mayoralty was a great honor in the city. It enhanced the social importance of the officeholder both by the deference that his fellow townsmen showed him and by the opportunity his office gave to display his wealth in the city. The office was also a burden, requiring time and the outlays of large sums to support its ceremonial requirements. There was little independent political power, for the mayor's freedom of action was restrained by the legal forms he was obliged to follow and by the council, which acted as a check upon his formulations of policy. But the office brought enhanced status, and status, especially when given official recognition, carried its own political weight. It rewarded the recipient with greater influence and brought his fellow townsmen to him for his wise counsel and good advice.[13]

In the public presentation of the new mayor to the town, all these considerations played a role. The official date for his installation in office was Michaelmas, 29 September, fully two weeks after the election. In the interval, Ricart tells us

> the seide persone so electid maire shalle haue his leysour to make his purveyaunce of his worshipfull householde, and the honourable apparailling of his mansion, in as plesaunt and goodly wise as kan be devised. . . .

When his house was readied for the festivities to come, "the seide new Maire then to come to the Guyldehalle," in a full-scale procession in which he took his proper place as the head of the government,

> accompanyd with the Shiref and all his brethren of the Counseill, to feche him at his hows and bring him to the saide hall, in as solempne and honourable wise as he can devise to do his oune worshippe. . . .

The mayor was the head not only of the government but also of the community, and thus he entered office "to the honour, laude, and preysyng of all Bristol.[14]

Processions were especially well-suited to convey the structure of authority in a community. They represented in the simplest, most abstract, and yet most visible way the particular roles and connections among the various members of the civic government. At the same time they reminded all those who stood along the line of march of their own relationship to the same individuals and with the government at large. No better way could have been devised to inform the people of the town, not only who had been selected to the high office of mayor, but of the significance of this personage in Bristol's social and political structure.[15]

Because of the preeminence of the mayor in the civic hierarchy, the ceremony of his inauguration was extremely rich in meaning and detail. His formal installation into the seat of authority was only accomplished after he was reminded of his responsibilities to the borough community and sworn to his duties. Before swearing the oath-taking, the outgoing mayor made a speech to his brethren and to the others assembled that stressed the commonweal of the city and the maintenance of unity among the citizens. According to Ricart, he apologized to his fellow townsmen for any offense he might have given, and offered to make amends for his errors from his own goods or to "ask theym forgevenes in as herty wyse as I can, trusting verilly in God they shal haue no grete causes of ferther complaynts." But if he could not heal all the wounds that his government might have caused, the "worshipfulle man" chosen to be the new mayor "of his grete wisedome, by goddes grace, shal refourme and amende alle such thinges as I of my sympileness haue not duely ne formably executed and fulfilled." Finally, the outgoing mayor thanked his fellow citizens for their "godeness" according to their "due merits" in showing "trewe obedience to kepe the king our alther liege lorde is lawes, and my commaundment in his name, at all tymes," and he prayed that God reward them with "moche joy, prosperitie and peas, as evir had comens and true Cristen people."[16]

After the utterance of these significant words came the swearing in of the new mayor. The oath, as it was taken in Ricart's time and with some small changes down to at least the end of the sixteenth century,[17] was preoccupied with the formal and specific tasks undertaken by the mayor that had been laid out in the city's charters. Standing at the "high deise of the Yeldehall," before his fellow common councillors and members of the "Comyns," the inaguree swore allegiance to the monarch to "kepe and meyntene the peas of the same toune with all my power." Under this authority he promised to "reproue and chastice the misrewlers and mysdoers in the forsaid toune," to maintain the "fraunchises and free custumes whiche beth gode," to put away "all euell custumes and wronges," to "defende, the Wydowes and Orphans," and to "kepe, and meyntene all laudable ordinaunces. . . ." Most importantly, he also swore "trewely, and with right," to

Figure 1. Illustration from Robert Ricart, *The Maire of Bristowe is Kalendar,* Bristol Record Office Ms. 04720(1), fol. 152v. *Courtesy of the City of Bristol Record Office.)*

trete the people of my bailly, and do every man right, as wel to the poer as to the riche, in that that longeth to me to do. And nouther for ghifte, nor for loue, affeccion, promesse, nor for hate, I shall do no man wronge, nor destourbe no mannes right.[18]

In these clauses the mayor is viewed largely in his capacity as a judge. The underlying theme, even where the enforcement of municipal ordinances is concerned, is one of judiciousness and evenhandedness.[19] By the formula of the oath, then, the mayor's role within the city also rested almost entirely upon his position as the king's viceregent in the city. This fact was reinforced, moreover, at the conclusion of the oath. After kissing the book held for him by the old mayor, he received from the hands of his predecessor the essential symbols of his office, viz., the king's sword and the cap of justice, the casket containing the seal of his office as escheator, the seal of the Statute Staple, and the seal of the Statute Merchant, all signifying the judicial authority that the mayor derived from the crown.

When taken together with the old mayor's speech, however, the inauguration conveys a more complex picture of the mayor's role. Although his authority is derived from a royal grant, its base is local. He is the king's lieutenant in the city, but the borough's servant. In other words, he enjoys both legal and moral authority in Bristol; he is at one and the same time the keeper of traditional and legal authority. As head of the community he could act as a buffer between the crown and the city, protecting it from corrosive outside interference and permitting it the maximum autonomy by carrying out the king's business and maintaining peace in his name. With aid of the Holy Trinity, his duty also was to keep the city "in prosperouse peas and felicite" and to preserve its internal solidarity by maintaining the social fabric against all damage, especially that caused by misgovernment.[20]

Along with the formal oath-taking, which renewed the bonds of authority, there were also informal proceedings that were intended to promote the unity and internal solidarity of the civic body. The first of these festal events occurred immediately after the mayor had taken his oath. Once the symbols of office had been handed over to him, he immediately changed places with his predecessor. With this ritual completed, "all the hole company" were to

> bring home the new Maire to his place, with trompetts and clareners, in as joyful, honourable, and solempne wise as can be devised; and there to leve the new Maire, and then to bring home the olde Maire.[21]

These honorific processionals were followed by communal dinners with the majority of the council dining with the new mayor at his house, and a smaller number, "in especiall all officers," dining with the old mayor.

After they had eaten, "all the hole Counseille" assembled at the High Cross, in the town center

and from thens the new maire and the olde maire, with alle the hole company, to walke honourably to Seint Mighels churche, and there to offre. And then to retorne to the new Maires hous, there to take cakebrede and wyne. And then, euery man taking his leeve of the Maire, and to retray home to their evensong.[22]

This ceremony repeated in symbolic way the transfer of authority from the outgoing to the incoming mayor. First the council was divided, some to honor one man, some the other in separate feasts. The outgoing and the incoming mayors then jointly led a slow and stately procession uphill to St. Michael's church. The mood seems to have been one of reluctant farewell to the outgoing mayor. But after the offering at St. Michael's, the tone changes. The return to the town center, downhill, undoubtedly was more briskly paced and more easily executed. The spirit of an energetic and joyful new beginning, then, would have received added emphasis by the livelier downhill procession. To conclude the celebration, all were united at the new mayor's house where they sealed the transition of power by sharing in his cheerful hospitality.

III

The mayor's mediating role as both the king's and the community's servant received special emphasis when royalty visited the city in this period. For these rare events stressed Bristol's dual character as a legal corporation and moral community. Between 1461 and 1509 there were five such visits, of which only Henry VII's in 1486 is documented in detail.[23] Henry's sojourn in the town was part of a progress through the realm designed to secure the loyalty and obedience of his kingdom's major cities.[24] Hence much attention was bound to have been paid to Bristol's subordination to royal authority. But to a remarkable degree, the performances during his stay also were expressions of the corporate independence of the civic community.

The most important pageant took place amidst "great Melodie and singing," immediately as the king passed through the town gate. Henry was accompanied there by "the Maire, the Shriffe, the Bailiffs with ther Brethern, and great Nomber of other Burgesses al on Horseback," who had ridden three miles out of town to greet him. "But the Mair of Bristow bar no mase, nor the Shrif . . . no rodde, unto the tyme they came to the gate . . . wher beginneth ther Fraunches."[25] Here the mayor and sheriff took up the symbols of their offices as the representatives of royal justice in the borough, accentuating the boundaries of the community and their own special authority within it. When the gate was passed and the king had entered Bristol proper, Henry was greeted at once by a figure representing the legendary British king, "King Bremmius." Bremmius welcomed his "moost dere Cosine of England and Fraunce" to the town, thanking God highly on behalf of the Bristolians "for such a Souveraigne Lorde." But his main purpose was to ask Henry for assistance. "This Towne lefte I in greate prosperitie," he said,

> Havyng Riches and Welth many Folde;
> The Merchaunt, the Artyficer, ev'ryche in his Degre,
> Had great Plentye both of Silver and Golde,
> And lifed in Joye as they desire wolde,
> At my departing; but I have been so long away,
> That Bristow is fallen into Decaye.
>
> Irrecuparable, withoute that a due Remedy
> By you, ther herts Hope and Comfort in this Distresse,
> Proveded bee, at your Leyser convenynetly,
> To your Navy and Cloth-making, wherby I gesse
> The Wele of this Towne standeth in Sikerness,
> May be mayteigned, as they have bee
> in Days hertofor in Prosperitie.
>
> Now farwell, dere Cosyn, my Leve I take
> At you, that Wele of Bountie bee
> To your saide Subjects for Maries Sake,
> That bereth you ther Fidelitie.
> In moost loving wise now graunte ye
> Some Remedye herin, and he wille quit your Mede,
> That never unrewarded leveth good Dede.[26]

This may seem no more than a straightforward petition for aid from the crown, but there is also another, more subtle dimension to the speech.

According to Geoffrey of Monmouth and his followers, King Bremmius, or Brennius as he is more frequently called, was one of the noble race of Trojans who ruled Britain after Brutus had conquered and settled the land. He is identified with the historical Brennus who sacked Rome in 390 B.C. As Geoffrey himself told the tale, there was no mention of Bristol.[27] But in another tradition, Bremmius is identified as the founder of Bristol, just as Brutus founded London, under the name "Trinovantum," and King Ebrancus founded York, under the name "Kaerebrauc."[28] Robert Ricart, who as Town Clerk probably assisted with the pageants conducted on King Henry VII's behalf, preserves this part of the story in his *Kalendar*. Beginning with an account largely based upon Geoffrey's, he writes that after returning from his great victories abroad,

Brynne first founded and billed this worshipfull Towne of Bristut that nowe is Bristowe and set it vpon a litell hill, that is to say, bitwene Seint Nicholar yate, Seint Johnes yate, Seint Leonardes yate, and the Newe yate. And nomore was bilde not many yeres after.[29]

Since Henry Tudor himself claimed descent from the "British" kings,[30] King Bremmius gave Bristol a form of kinship tie to the new monarch, which was of use in requesting assistance from him. At the same time, however, reference to this mythic founder helped avoid the worst implications of the petition, namely the apparent dependency of the borough community upon the royal will for its maintenance. The point is a subtle one. Since Bristol was in existence from the first beginnings of the "British" realm, the Bristolians seem to be saying, its status could hardly depend upon a later royal grant. Any special exemptions or privileges it received, it is implied, were offered not by the king's mere motion and sovereign will, but as a moral obligation to preserve the noble work of his great and famous ancestor. As Bremmius says, he founded the city and "called it Bristow," after himself "For a Memoriall that Folke ne wolde / Oute of Remembraunce that Acte Race ne unfolde."[31]

The point, of course, goes well beyond Bristol's request to Henry for aid. It was clear in law that each of the city's liberties and franchises, including that of its corporate status, required a royal warrant. In this sense, the borough community was founded by the royal will. But the existence of the borough, with its sworn membership and its reciprocal and interlocking social relationships, transcended this dependency, since its citizenry formed a moral community as well as a legal corporation. History was called upon to meet this dilemma. Because the city was obviously the creation of men, it could not be thought a part of the natural landscape. It required a founder. But if the community was to preserve its independence, its foundation had to be set in the distant past. By stressing Bristol's antiquity, King Bremmius not only pointed to the borough community's continuity, but also to its autonomy. Autonomy went hand in hand with unity. To the larger world, the city presented itself as a single, integrated whole, existing independently of its surroundings.

IV

As expressed in ceremony, the unity of late medieval Bristol was a living unity, like that of the human body. Within its boundaries, it was portrayed as a highly structured organism, whose parts worked together to preserve the well-being of its members. But to maintain this unity required constant vigilance, because there were always divisive interests, such as craft rivalries, ready to undermine the general welfare. Bristol's social and political rituals largely sought to overcome these disruptive forces and to reinforce the moral and spiritual foundations of its community by directly confronting the points of stress in the city's political and social structure.[32] The ceremonies and festivities at the annual inauguration of the mayor addressed the yearly transfer of authority from one individual to another. It was also necessary, however, to deal with the more fundamental fact that Bristol's public officials were also private men, who might be tempted to put themselves or their family and friends above the common good. They needed to be reminded, then, of their duties as servants of the community. Hence the promises of fairness in the mayor's oath and the presence of the commons in the guildhall to hear it.

On St. Michael's day, however, the commons played only a passive role, standing in the guildhall outside the ring of councillors merely to observe the oath-taking and thronging the streets to watch deferentially as the processions passed. In other festivities, their involvement was more asser-tive, for they often intervened to mock the civic authorities for their folly, to chastise them for their failures, and to instruct them in their duties. For example, there was St. Katherine's day in late November, when St. Kather-ine's players, probably a group of weavers, performed at the doorfronts of the mayor and the common councillors. And at Christmas, a Lord of Misrule issued satiric proclamations and ordinances endorsing licen-tiousness, approving disorder, and encouraging drunkenness, idleness, and other misdemeanors, standing authority on its head and criticizing its shortcomings.[33] But for our purposes the most intriguing of these celebra-tions is the festival of the boy-bishop.

Much of what we know of this popular custom relates to its use in cathedral chapters, university colleges, and schools such as Eton. At Salisbury Cathedral, for example, a young chorister was elected to serve in this capacity from 6 December, St. Nicholas' day, until Childermas, 28 December. According to a seventeenth-century account, he was not only "to bear the name and hold up the state of a *Bishop* . . . habited with a *Crozier* . . . in his hand and a *Mitre* upon his head," but to perform everything the "very Bishop himself" did, except the Mass. And "his fellows," a group of boy choristers, "were to take upon them the style and counterfeit of Prebends yielding to their Bishop . . . no less than canonical obedience." The Sarum use also provided elaborate processionals and services for this mock bishop, including his giving the sermon and bene-diction on Holy Innocents' day.[34]

But in Bristol the custom had unique qualities that made the municipal authorities as much a focus of the ceremony as the church hierarchy. Ricart describes the festival as follows:

on Seynt Nicholas Eve . . . the Maire, and Shiref, and their brethern to walke to Seynt Nicholas churche, there to hire theire even-song: and on the morowe to hire theire masse, and offre, and hire the bishop's sermon, and have his blissyng; and after dyner, the seide Maire, Shiref, and theire brethern, to assemble at the maires counter, there waytyng the Bishoppes comming; pleying the meane whiles at Dyce, the towne clerke to fynde theym Dyce, and to have I d. of every Raphill; and when the Bishope is come thedir, his chapell there to synge, and the bishope to geve them his blissyng, and then he and all his chapell to be serued there with brede and wyne. And so departe the Maire, Shiref, and theire brethern to hire the bishopes evesonge at Seynt Nicholas chirch.[35]

In most respects, then, the authority of the Bristol boy-bishop corresponds quite closely to the usage at Salisbury. He has a chapter, gives sermons,[36] offers benediction and sings evensong. His blessing of the civic body during its game of dice, however, appears to be unique.

The role of the boy-bishop in this encounter is both satiric and didactic. Although dice-playing was a widely used pastime in the later middle ages, this form of gambling was also understood to be a pernicious vice that indicated the corruption of those who played at it. In the *Canterbury Tales,* for example, it appears time and again as the symbol of folly and evil. The Pardoner speaks of it, together with drunkenness, as the "devels sacrifice"; the Franklin indicates that it is the very opposite of virtue and frugality; the Shipman shows it to be the negation of a merchant's craft. In the "Cook's Tale" it is portrayed as a form of sin that, along with dancing, lechery, and drunkenness, leads to idleness and theft.[37] These views were commonplaces of the moral teaching not only in Chaucer's time but for much of the three centuries following. According to Sir Thomas Elyot writing in 1531, dice-playing was most likely the devil's invention

For what better allective coulde Lucifer deuise to allure or bringe men pleasauntly in to damnable seruitude, than to purpose to them in fourme of a playe, his principall tresory; wherin the more parte of synne is contained, and all goodnesse and vertue confounded?[38]

The governor of the game of dice, of course, is fortune, which by nature is changeable, alternately bringing good and bad to those who are at its mercy.[39] Accordingly, to play at dice is to remove oneself from God's will and moral purpose in order to become the victim of mere chance. At the same time, it is to deny one's capacity to reason and to act. In the words of Elyot again,

there is nat a more playne figure of idlenesse. . . . For besides that, that therin is no maner of exercise for the body or mynde, they which do

playe therat must seme to haue no portion of witte or kunnyng, if they
will be called faire plaiars.[40]

In the Bristol Common Council, however, this understanding of dice-
playing takes on a special significance. By the city's charters, the principal
duties of the councillors were first to establish competent ordinances
"that shall be consonant with reason and useful for the commonalty," and
secondly, to levy local tallages and rates for common purposes and over-
see their proper expenditure.[41] Sitting at the mayor's counter throwing
dice represents in simple terms the absolute abandonment of these responsibilities. Where reason and prudence were supposed to be displayed,
we find chance and profligacy; where the councillors were supposed to act
as the better and more worthy men of the community, we find them idly
playing, without apparent regard to their standing. As Chaucer tells us

> Hasard is verray mooder of lesynges
> And of deceite and cursed forswearings
> Blaspheme of Crist, manslaughtre, and wast also
> Of catle and of tyme, and furthermo
> It is repreeve and contrarie of honour
> For to ben holde a common hasardour
> And ever the hyer he is of estaat
> The moore is he yholden desolaat
> If that a prince useth hasardrye
> In all governaunce and policye
> He is, as by commune opinioun
> Yholde the lasse in reputacioun[42]

The significance of the boy-bishop's visit to the guildhall perhaps may be
better comprehended by looking briefly at a surviving sermon of a boy-
bishop given at St. Paul's, London, in the early 1490s. Beginning with the
exhortation "Prayse ye childerne almyghty God," this sermon likens man
in childhood to animal kind.

A childe fyrste when he is in his infant age is not constreyned unto no
lawes; he is not corrected nother beten; and there is no defaute layde
unto hym, but utterly he is lefte unto the lawe of kynde. Do he what
somever he will no man doth blame hym. Morally the state of man
immedyately after synne was verely the state of chilhode and infans
hauinge no nouryce.

Conversely, life solely under control of the passions is childhood. As the
boy-bishop says

whan that man was utterly left without ony expressyd lawe, havynge no
mayster to his owne naturall inclynacyon as to his lawe, there was no
lawe of God newe put to hym.

The message is a twofold one. Quoting St. Paul in *Corinthians,*

> Be ye not chylderne in your wyttes; but from all synne and malyce by ye childerne in clennesse. And in this fourme all maner of people and al maner of ages in clennesse of lyf ought to be pure as childrine. . . .[43]

Viewed in this context, the presence of the boy-bishop at the mayor's counter offers a telling commentary upon the dice game. For the city fathers are shown to act without a child's cleanness but with his wit. They abandon themselves to the "laws of kynde," and the whims of chance, being for the moment themselves "without a nouryce or guyder." To them comes the child bishop, exercising a supremely adult authority and signifying the high purposes for which they were elected. In this way, the festivity not only criticizes the mayor and his brethren for their periodic failings, but it also purges them of their official sins. It also emphasizes that the civic authorities served the community and thus were subject to the chastisement and approbation of their fellow citizens.

In general, all of Bristol's late medieval festive life encouraged Bristolians to conceive of their city in this way. To the larger world, the celebrations stressed the borough community's noble and ancient origins, its heroic character, and its independent standing. To the borough community itself, they offered a subtle commentary on the nature and distribution of political authority. In ritual and festival, the body politic appeared as a world of reciprocal relations—of harmonies and correspondences—not of absolutes. Structure implied exchange as well as deference. Celebrations like the mayor's inauguration and the feast of St. Nicholas stressed the social limitations on authority, not the sovereignty and power of those who exercised it.

V

The ceremonial practices we have just analyzed survived intact until the middle of the sixteenth century. But they did not go completely unchallenged. One source of resistance was Bristol's large contingent of Lollards, who resided in the cloth-producing southern parishes of the city. These men and women, drawn primarily from among the commons of their crafts, not the leadership, vigorously attacked the main tenets of late medieval Catholicism on which the feasts of the civic year so much depended. By the early fifteenth century, there was also widespread indifference to participation in the great Corpus Christi procession, which had been one of the most popular civic celebrations and the preeminent means of expressing the hierarchical organization and spiritual kinship of the townsfolk. At the same time, authority came under challenge in various ways in guild and government.[44] Even Robert Ricart's loving codification of the annual cycle of processions and feasts may be a sign that some Bristolians—like Mayor William Spencer who had requested it—thought their ancient customs needed to be reinforced among the city's elite. But the ceremonies themselves persisted. By the early 1530s, however, the rejection of the most important aspects of late medieval popular piety became very general in Bristol. Almost at the very outset of the Reformation, for example, Hugh Latimer won the support of large numbers of leading townsmen, including the mayor and the majority of the Common Council, when he preached against them in Lent, 1533. Such attacks carried with them large social and political as well as religious implications. They were the rejection of a regime as well as a theology.[45]

With the combined attack on popish "superstitions," the religious orders, and the chantries, the framework described by Ricart suffered a permanent change. In 1541, Henry VIII ordered the abolition of the "many superstitions and chyldysh obseruances . . . observed and kept . . . vpon Saint Nicholas, Saint Catherine, Saint Clement, the Holy Innocents and such like."[46] Corpus Christi day suffered a similar fate, disappearing from the church calendar with the Edwardian prayer books.[47] At the same time Bristol's reformed ministry offered the hammer blows against idle pastimes and drunken behavior. In 1577, for example, John Northbrooke, sometime "minister and Preacher of the word of God" in St. Mary Redcliffe, at Bristol, published a lengthy treatise against idleness, drunkenness, concupiscence, and other evils associated with plays, gaming, and dancing. Thomas Thompson, who served the city from 1607 to 1612, offered a series of ten Lenten sermons on drunkenness in 1608. His colleague Edward Chetwin often spoke on similar topics. Under these strictures, celebrations such as those that had honored St. Nicholas, St. Katherine, or St. Clement stood utterly condemned for their depravity.[48]

Along with the elimination of many of the great public festivals, the structure of politics also underwent important changes in the sixteenth century. In 1499, new Letters Patent were issued by Henry VII to reform the existing organization of the city's governing body, primarily by creating a bench of aldermen. The mayor and aldermen received a designation as justices of the peace, which brought the city into conformity with the national system of administration then emerging in the counties. At the same time, the recorder—usually an up-and-coming London lawyer—became fully integrated into town government as one of the aldermen. His presence was required at gaol delivery, of which the mayor and aldermen were now to be justices. Since the mayor also served as one of the two justices of assize, the civic body was formally bound into the judicial and administrative structure of the nation. This meant that the status and power of the leading men in town government were increased, whether they were acting at any given moment as royal or purely as local officials; it also meant that the crown through the mayor and aldermen now had a direct and continuous link to the city government upon which both the city and the Privy Council could rely.[49]

The men who exercised the wide powers and responsibilities of local government may have symbolized the community, but they were far from representative of its population. This acquisition of public office was a direct outgrowth of economic and social success. If a man had accumulated riches (£1,500 was the minimum set in 1635),[50] he was expected to accept the burdens of borough government, bearing from his own funds if necessary a portion of the financial charges. Hence as patterns of mobility were altered and the social hierarchy became reorganized, the structure of civic politics would also change.[51]

In the sixteenth century, Bristol had experienced just such a process of social change, as its commercial economy shifted to trade in luxury goods with Spain and the Mediterranean and a new form of merchant community took shape in the city. Access to the merchant leadership, once open to men of quite humble backgrounds—itinerant merchants and small shop-keepers—narrowed as a group of large-scale wholesale dealers differentiated themselves from the city's retailers and handicraftsmen. These "mere merchants," more and more the sons of the country gentry as well as of Bristol's own merchant families, habitually acted as agents, partners, creditors, and brokers for one another, switching roles as circumstances required. They chartered ships together and used each others' servants as factors in overseas trade. But where merchants often appear as both creditors and debtors in their dealings with fellow overseas traders, sometimes borrowing from and sometimes lending to the same individual, relations with domestic dealers were dramatically different. Clothiers, for example, tended to be the creditors of merchants, selling their small quantities of fabric for "half a year and half a year," while vintners and grocers tended to be debtors, paying back their merchant suppliers on a similar schedule. As a result, Bristol's "mere merchants" conceived of the economy as a great chain of being with themselves at the top, mediating between the domestic and international markets.[52]

In the mid-sixteenth century, the most important overseas traders founded the Society of Merchant Venturers to give reality to this view. This body existed to coordinate the activities and protect the interests of these "mere merchants," something it repeatedly attempted to do by excluding retailers and handicraftsmen from overseas trade. By necessity, moreover, the activities of these men depended upon national economic policy. To a large degree, then, the Society was a political "pressure group," operating in the economic interest of its members, as is revealed by the streams of their petitions and letters to the king and his officers for redress of one grievance or another.[53]

We can establish the occupation of nearly all the members of the Common Council in this period, using service as sheriff to determine council membership.[54] For the whole century, almost 80 percent of the council were either overseas merchants or major retailers or soapmakers, but this proportion was on the increase—under 70 percent in the first fifty years, over 85 percent in the second. Among the grocers, drapers, mercers, and vintners, moreover, many had abandoned their shops to deal exclusively by wholesale—that is, as "mere merchants" in the parlance of the period (see table pp. 206–7).

Unfortunately, we cannot determine the membership of the Society of Merchant Venturers before the early seventeenth century. But between 1605, when the Society was put on a new footing by the Common Council, and 1642, when civil war events disrupted election procedures, over 60 percent of the common councillors were associated with the Merchant Venturers during their careers. Moreover, almost 90 percent of these served at one time or another as the Society's master, treasurer, or warden, indicating that their connections were close.

VI

These changes had profound effects upon the conception of political authority in Bristol. No longer was the city conceived as a quasi-religious brotherhood in which authority was celebrated and legitimized at feasts and on holy days. Rather the ideals of godly rule, linking the authority of the local governors to the monarchy and from thence to God Himself shaped the new conception of officeholding. Thomas Thompson, lecturing his Bristol congregation upon the virtues requisite of a magistrate, best articulates this viewpoint. Government officials, he says, are to be

> such as are most perfect in knowledge, hence in conscience, and expert in practice. . . . But since all the praise of virtue is in action, we cannot make knowledge only; the Magistrates complement: and therefore with those Intellectual abilities they must adioyne those morall vertues of *Fortitude* and *Iustice*: that: both: to endure the troubles, looses and dangers of gouernment . . . in warres, and . . . in peace. . . .[55]

Thus a magistrate was expected to be a Christian exemplum of civic virtue, not only living according to God's law and with the blessing of His grace, but also endowed with a practical understanding of worldly affairs and the courage to use it wisely and well.

There was no doubt that governmental service for such a man was conceived as a duty. As Thompson says,

> it is not . . . for him to refuse it as either too base or too troublesome, vnlesse hee will bee accounted either an idle, or a proud man . . . since hee is a member of that body politique which by all meanes hee must preserue, and since he must not hide what grace God hath given him for the benefit of the Common-wealth vnlesse he will partake of the punishment inflicted vpon the idle seruant, whose talent was given vnto another. For (as *Chrysostome* saith well) *hee that receiveth the grace of learning for the profit of others, and doth not use it, doth wholly loose that grace.*[56]

Thompson also makes clear the principal responsibilities of the city's officers. As his lecture reminded them, "they were to keep order," without which there is "Anarchie, wherein every man is king in his owne conceite, vndertaking what him list to doe as when there was no King in Isreal." And, in proper fulfillment of the judicial duties, they were to "both scatter the wicked, *and Iudge the poore in truth.*"[57] Their failure to accept these responsibilities, or to neglect them in their rule, would only bring ruin to the commonwealth.

> For I pray you shall not all the body bee troubled, when the head is shaken a sunder? As shall not the tree be subiect to falling, whē the root is bared? Some flatter the great men telling them, that they by reason of their wealth, and high estate neede not doe any thing else, but to live at ease, eat and drinke, and take their pastime, as the retchlesse rich glutton said to his secure soule. But the wisest king that euer liued said Wo bee to thee O Land when thy King is a child and thy Princes eate in the Morning.[58]

To a very large degree these are commonplaces of late medieval and early modern political thought; little about them would have been foreign to the viewpoint of Ricart's time. But in the Elizabethan and early Stuart period, the mechanisms of communal control that the citizens previously had imposed upon their governors had been replaced by a different form of ritual, whereby the common councillors reminded *themselves* of their high calling. To open each council session, they prayed:

> Especially (O Lord) wee beseech thee in they great and infinite mercyes to look uppon this Citye and uppon us nowe assembled and uppon all the corporacōn and comōns here that wee both for our selves and for them may consulte of those thinges wch concern our dutyes towards thee our gratious God and towardes the Kinge under our gratious Lorde that both wee and all the people of this Citye may glorifie thy name [and] may live in brotherly love, and charitye one toward another.[59]

OCCUPATIONS OF BRISTOL SHERIFFS, 1500–1600

	1500–1549/50		1550–1599/1600		1500–1600	
	#	%ª	#	%ª	#	%ª
Merchants	30	33.71	39	41.49	69	37.70
Major Retailers						
apothecary, grocer	12	13.48	8	8.51	20	10.93
draper	6	6.74	15	15.96	21	11.48
fishmonger	—	—	1	1.06	1	0.55
haberdasher	4	4.49	—	—	4	2.19
mercer	7	7.87	9	9.57	16	8.74
vintner	—	—	2	2.13	2	1.09
Subtotal	29	32.58	35	37.23	64	34.97
Soapmakers, Chandlers	2	2.25	7	7.45	9	4.92
Total: Leading Entrepreneurs	61	68.54	81	86.17	142	77.60
Textile Industries						
capper	2	2.25	—	—	2	1.09
tailor	—	—	2	2.13	2	1.09
tucker, clothier	3	3.37	1	1.06	4	2.19
upholsterer	—	—	2	2.13	2	1.09
Subtotal	5	5.62	5	5.32	10	5.46
Leather Industries						
shoemaker	—	—	1	1.06	1	0.55
tanner	4	4.49	2	2.13	6	3.28
whitawer, glover, pointmaker	5	5.62	1	1.06	6	3.28
Subtotal	9	10.11	4	4.26	13	7.10

	No.	%[a]	No.	%[a]	No.	%[a]
Metal Industries						
bellfounder	1	1.12	—	—	1	0.55
cardmaker	1	1.12	1	1.06	2	1.09
goldsmith	—	—	1	1.06	1	0.55
pewterer	1	1.12	—	—	1	0.55
smith	1	1.12	—	—	1	0.55
Subtotal	4	4.49	2	2.13	6	3.28
Woodworking						
hooper, cooper	—	—	1	1.06	1	0.55
Food Production						
baker	2	2.25	—	—	2	1.09
brewer	6	6.74	1	1.06	7	3.83
Subtotal	8	8.99	1	1.06	9	4.92
Professional and Service Trades						
scrivener	1	1.12	—	—	1	0.55
tidewaiter	1	1.12	—	—	1	0.55
Subtotal	2	2.25	—	—	2	1.09
Total Known	89	—	94	—	183	—
Unknown	13	—	6	—	19	—
TOTAL	102	—	100	—	202	—

[a] Percentage of total known for period.

Prayer, of course, could bind political actions as forceably as social obligation. But it involved a very different kind of ritual exchange than the one
that had regulated political authority in late medieval Bristol. It linked the
prayer-giver directly to God, not to a community—a microcosm of the
universe—that mediated between the individual and his Maker.

Not surprisingly, then, these Renaissance magistrates set themselves
into the wider world of the nation by the principle of hierarchy. Indeed,
much of Bristol's ceremonial life in the later sixteenth and early seventeenth century conveyed precisely this quality. Its most characteristic form
remained the processional. Eleven major feast days were recognized, and
on them the mayor and his brethren were to wear the scarlet robes
signifying their particular rank in the civic body, cloaks with fur and felt
trimming for the mayor and former mayors, gowns alone for the rest.
These so-called scarlet days were Michaelmas—when the new mayor was
installed, preceded and followed by solemn processions as in the past[60]—
All Hallows, Christmas, St. Stephen's, Twelfth Day, Easter Sunday, Easter
Monday, Ascension, Whitsunday, Trinity Sunday, and Saint James, for the
great summer fair. On every one of these important religious festivals, with
the exception of St. James, there was a full-scale procession of the city
government, wherein all could observe the civic hierarchy in its proper
order making its way through the town. Except perhaps for the absence of
St. Clement, St. Katherine, St. Nicholas, Corpus Christi, St. John and St.
Peter, all of this would have been familiar enough to Ricart and his
contemporaries. But there is perhaps one all-important difference. In the
later sixteenth and early seventeenth centuries, the corporation members
dressed themselves in their scarlet garments not to hear mass and take the
Eucharist, still less to participate in a drunken revel, but to attend a lecture
by one of the city's preachers interpreting the Word of God.[61] Sitting
together in church, the mayor and councillors must have stood out as a
distinct and honored elite among the congregation.

Not only did these changes bring a new earnestness and sense of
sobriety to officeholding, but they raised the magistrates above criticism
from their inferiors. No longer was emphasis placed primarily upon their
membership in the borough community. Instead, their roles as the agents
of royal authority were given special attention. Authority now meant
sovereignty; it conveyed rights and yielded majesty and power. The magistrates revealed this viewpoint especially in the symbolism they chose to
assert their position. In 1606, for example, the Common Council agreed
that a convenient place ought to be built in the cathedral church where
they and their wives might "sytte . . . to heare the sermons on the
Sabaothe and after festival dayes."[62] After some discussion the dean and
chapter agreed to the proposal and a gallery was built "over against the

pulpit." William Adams, who no doubt saw the finished work himself, gives the following description.

> It was not only a fair and comely ornament to the church, but also a fit and convenient place for the council to sit and hear the word preached, leaving the room below for gentlemen and others. They placed there our King's arms gilded, and under [it] reserved a fair seat for the King or any nobleman that should come to this city: and under the same [gallery] also fair seats for the council's and clergy's wives, and other fit places also for the bishop, dean and others of the clergy.[63]

There could be no clearer hierarchical symbolism, nor a more revealing insight into how the Bristol corporation viewed their place in God's order. Seated in honor above the pulpit, with the bishop, dean, and even the king sometimes among them, they were to hear the holy word preached. This self-image was a powerful one. Less than two years later, Bishop Thornborough, returning to Bristol from a long absence at York, where he was dean of the Cathedral chapter, found this symbolism so much an affront to his dignity that he ordered the gallery removed.[64]

VII

These new attitudes were given added depth when royalty appeared in the city. There were two such visits between 1558 and 1640, one by Queen Elizabeth I in 1574, and the second by Queen Anne of Denmark, James I's wife, in 1613. Both were occasions for magnificent displays of civic pomp. Since much honor came from these rare opportunities to entertain royalty, every effort was made to put forward the best face of the city. But these two events show a very different face than had been displayed to Henry VII. In both instances, the celebrations took the form of massive military displays in which the prowess of the city's Trained Bands went hand in hand with their show of loyalty and obedience to royal rule. Instead of stressing the city's antiquity and independence, the mayor and his brethren emphasized their city's place in the larger organization of the state and their own subordination to the monarchy.[65] We can see this clearly in the description of Queen Elizabeth's visit.

When Elizabeth came to Bristol in August 1574, "the mayor and all the council riding upon good steeds, with footcloth, and pages by their sides, . . . received her Majesty within Lafford's gate," just inside the boundaries of the city. There an interesting series of exchanges took place, for "the mayor delivered the gild mace unto Her Grace," thus relinquishing the symbol of his authority as her lieutenant, "and she delivered it unto him again," reinforcing his dependence upon her favor. After an oration by John Popham, the recorder, and the delivery of one hundred pounds in gold to her

> the mayor himself rode nigh before the Queene, betweene 2 serjeants at arms, and the rest of the council rode next before the nobility and trumpeters, and so passed through the city unto M[r]. John Young his house on S[t]. Augustine's Backe.[66]

This procession, with each rider holding his proper place in the order of march, set the tone for the military displays that occupied the queen's time for the rest of her stay.

To give these displays added meaning, the city hired Thomas Churchyard, the poet, to supply an allegory, which was presented to the queen in speeches and in a little book interpreting the action for her.[67] The allegory pitted peace against war and put the city on the side of peace.

> Dissenshon breeds the brawll
> and that is Pomp, and Pried.
> The Fort on law and order stands
> and still in peace would bied.
> The Warrs is wicked world
> as by his fruets is seen:
> The Fortres representith peace,
> and takes thy part O Queen.[68]

Later we learn that the fort, founded on law and order and representing peace, in fact stands also for the "Citie."[69] The "Citie" resists war and shows "what follies and conflicts rise in Ciuill broyls, and what quietnesse coms by a mutual loue and agrement."[70] "Our traed doth stand on Siuill lief / and thear our glory lies," says this character representing Bristol,

> Wee Marchants keep a mean vnmixt.
> with any iarrying part:
> and bryng boeth Treble and the Baess,
> in order still by art.[71]

However, it required human will to tune the parts of a community into harmony with one another. For order is an active principle; it must be created and not merely preserved. "Our orders maks the roister meek," says the "Citie,"

> and plucks the prowd on knees
> The stif and stobborne kno the yoek,
> and roets vp rotten trees.

> That may infect a fruetfull feeld,
> what can be sweet or sownd:
> But in that soyl whear for offence,
> is due correction fownd.
> Wee make the siuill laws to shien,
> and by example mield.
> Reform the rued, rebuek the bold,
> and tame the contrey wyeld.[72]

Nevertheless, vanity could undermine this harmony by encouraging people "to prowl about for pens and piuish pealf" to the neglect of their fellows. But selfishness was shortsighted; it bred dissension and blinded one to danger.

> You wold not, moue, nor seek your selus to saue
> On drosse and dong, sutch deep desiers you haue.
>
> You heer not how, the enmies at your noes,
> Aer vp in aerms, and cawls your cowards still
> You caer not mutch, abroed how matters goes
> Whan that at hoem, ye want no wealth nor will[73]

To overcome this threat, it was necessary for citizens to move beyond their petty, private interests into the service of the queen and the nation. All were members of her "staet," and hence must be "a true and loyal stock . . . reddy . . . with losse of lief" to battle her foes.[74] Thus the "Citie" declares that "though our ioy be most in peace, and peace we do maintain . . . Yet haue we soldyars" that

> . . . daer blaed hit with the best,
> when cawse of contrey coms
> And cals out courage to the fight,
> by sound of warlike Droms.[75]

It was only from the monarch, however, that peace and order could come to the city. She was "[a] Prince in deed of princely minde . . . the toutchstoen . . . the Pillar, Prop and stay o[f] eury region far or neer." She was the "noble Judge" who stood above the fray to decide great quarrels. Hence, her "helpyng hand" was needed "to corb disorders" wherever they appeared.[76]

> And blest be God we haue a Prince,
> by whom our peace is kept:
> And vnder whom this Citie long,
> and land hath safly slept.

> From whomliekwyse a thousand gifts,
>   of grace enioy we do:
> And feell from God in this her rayne
>   ten thousand blessyngs to.
>   .   .   .   .
> And mark how mad Dissension thriues,
>   that would set warres abroetch:
> Who sets to saell poer peoples liues,
>   and gets but viell reproetch.
> And endless shaem for all their sleights:
>   O England ioy with vs:
> And kis the steps whear she doth tread,
>   that keeps her countrey thus.
> In peace and rest, and perfait stay,
>   whearfore the god of peace:
> In peace by peace our peace presarue,
>   and her long lief encreace.[77]

This dependence upon the queen, so clearly articulated in these verses, was repeated in the mock battle itself. The third and last day of the maneuvers ended with three assaults upon the fort, but the enemy being repulsed agreed to a parley. The attackers offered the "good Citizens and Soldiors" of the fort a chance to surrender and "depart with bag and bagaeg," honorably, but in defeat. "To which the Fort maed answer, that the Cortaynes nor Bulwarks was not their defence, but the corrage of good peple, & the force of a mighty prince (who saet and beheld all these doyngs) was the thyng they trusted to." With this the enemy was defeated and peace was declared. "[A]t which pece boeth the sides shot-of their Artillery, in sien of a triumphe, and so crying God saue the Queen, these triumphes and warlik pastimes finished."[78]

Throughout these three days, the underlying theme was the city's place in the royal chain of command. The queen came to town "with princely trayn and power," and to honor her the city called out its Trained Bands to guard and wait upon her. The citizens thus fell "with all orders of marshall manner" into line with this princely train. Churchyard's allegory, moreover, gave added stress to the queen's position as commander. He arranged, for example, to have the gentlemen waiting upon the queen join with the citizens in defense of the fort. In addition, during one of the mock engagements, John Robarts, a common councillor, came to the queen to crave her aid "in their defence that peace desiers." Later "nue suckors commyng from the Court to the Forts great comfort" turned the tide of battle on the third day. To cap this symbolism, the queen exercised the prerogative of commander in rewarding the Trained Bands with two hundred crowns for a banquet.[79] Where Henry VII's stay in Bristol had stressed the city's independence of the ruling monarch, Elizabeth's accomplished just the reverse. Instead of arising from autonomy as was claimed in the fifteenth century, civic unity now required the authority of the monarch.[80]

VIII

The spirit of this new urban order is captured in a sermon given in 1635 by Thomas Palmer, vicar of St. Thomas and St. Mary Redcliffe in Bristol. "This honorable City," he says,

> may be compared unto the sea-fairing Tribe of Zebulon, that was a Haven for ships. . . . And so is this. The men of that Tribe were expert in warre: they could keepe ranke, they were skilfull at all the Instruments of warre. . . . And so may the men of this City.[81]

Warfare is understood to be the scourge of God upon the wicked; it "is sent into the world for our sinnes, to correct us for them, to deterre us from them." In consequence, military service is a divine calling. "As warre is from the Lord," Palmer says,

> so let it be for the Lord. If *Caesars* honour was touched, his souldiers were so prodigall of their blood, so desperately furious, that they were invincible. They gave unto *Caesar* that which was *Caesars:* let us give unto God, that which is Gods; the expense of our dearest blood for the maintenance of his Cause.[82]

This militant Christianity is highly political, with the soldier being viewed as the counterpart of the government official; each in his own realm battles in God's name against iniquity and evil. As their roles are conceived by Palmer,

> The sword of the Warrior findes an honourable Parellel with the sword of the Magistrate. They are both drawn for the execution of Justice. Experience and skill are requisite to the managing of them both. Let the Magistrate countenance the souldier in the time of Peace. And the souldier shall defend the Magistrate in the time of warre.[83]

Both coexist under the Lord of Hosts,

> That as the God of peace hath taught us those thinges which belong unto our peace, so that man of warre would teach our hands to warre, and our fingars to fight; that neither the sword of the Magistrate, nor of the warrior may bee drawne wrongfully, or in vaine. That the end of our temporall warfare may be a blessed peace upon earth; and of our

spirituall, an eternal peace in the heavens. Unto which Peace the God of Peace brings us all.[84]

In contrast to the social vision of the late medieval community, whose hierarchical structure was mediated by a series of ritualized exchanges and mocking reversals of role, this new model of society is a military one, with sharply defined ranks, rigid organization, and harsh discipline. There is no room here for the carnival spirit of abandon that Mikhail Bakhtin argues offered "a second world and second life outside officialdom," through which "all hierarchical rank, privileges, norms and prohibitions" are suspended, and people are permitted to enter "for a time . . . the utopian realm of community, freedom, equality, and abundance."[85]

For Englishmen in the Renaissance, the controlling social metaphor was the idea of the body politic. A body politic is a commonwealth; its component parts form an integrated whole and cannot exist separately from one another. In consequence, not only must there be a head to rule, but everything else must be proportionately organized and in its proper place. The vision is one of a hierarchical division of labor. Some parts have greater importance or value than others, but each performs a vital function for the rest. If this commonwealth should fall into "distemper" or become "distracted"—political terms that themselves depended upon the metaphor of the body—the ruling authority was to restore it to health by reestablishing the proper arrangement of organs and limbs.

This hierarchical image of political society rests, however, on two competing ideals. On the one hand, there was the ideal of reciprocity by which ruler and ruled worked together for the common good, thereby creating a moral community. On the other, there was the ideal of rank or function by which each member of the community contributed according to his station, but only established rulers had responsibility for government. Implicit in this Renaissance picture of the body politic, then, was a division between the commonwealth and the state. The commonwealth involved the mutual relations each member of society had with the others; the state involved the use of authority by rulers to bring order and security to them. Proper coordination of the commonwealth with the state produced an harmonious polity. But at bottom, these concepts offered alternative visions of order. In the former, every member of the polity had an obligation to uphold justice, the foundation of order; in the latter, the governors alone had the right to dispense it.

Authority in late medieval Bristol had arisen from within the community of burgesses, which as a microcosm of the world replicated the order of the universe and displayed in small its harmonies and correspondences. Those who ruled the borough did so by virtue of their moral leadership in it, which was sanctioned not only by the legalities of election but by rituals of recognition and acceptance that criticized and purified as well as exalted those in power. In Queen Elizabeth I's time, authority arose in a much wider field. Those who held it were no longer merely citizens of their borough. They participated in the larger hierarchy of the nation. Their community could no longer be thought a microcosm of the world. It was instead a part of a larger commonwealth; it did not stand alone. Those who governed it, then, were agents of royal rule, subject to the tutelage of the Crown and privileged to associate themselves with its majesty and power. Long ago, F. W. Maitland taught us to think of the medieval borough as both an organ and organism—an agency for the government of an urban place and a community with a life of its own.[86] In the medieval polity, these two aspects carried equal weight. The early modern English city was also both an organ and organism, but those who ruled now identified themselves with the national regime and took pride in their places in the organization of the state.

Notes

The author thanks Yehoshua Arieli, John Brewer, Natalie Zemon Davis, Sigmund Diamond, and Wallace MacCaffery for comments and criticisms offered at various stages of research for this article.

1. This theme is pursued in David Harris Sacks, *Trade, Society and Politics in Bristol: 1500–1640* (New York: Garland, 1985), chs. 1–4; see also my article "The Corporate Town and the English State: Bristol's 'Little Businesses,' 1625–41," in *Past and Present* 110 (February 1986): 69–105.

2. This paragraph and the following depend upon the discussion in "Authority," a symposium conducted by R. S. Peters and Peter Winch in *Proceedings of the Aristotelean Society,* supp. vol. 32 (1958): 207–40, reprinted in Anthony Quinton, ed., *Political Philosophy,* Oxford Readings in Philosophy, ed. G. J. Warnock (Oxford: Oxford University Press, 1967), 83–111; see also Richard Tuck, "Why Authority is Such a Problem?" in *Philosophy, Politics, and Society,* fourth series, ed. Peter Laslett, W. G. Runciman, and Quentin Skinner (Oxford: Blackwell, 1972), 194–207.

3. Winch, "Authority," 99; Tuck, "Why Authority," 200–07.

4. Max Weber, *The Theory of Economic and Social Organization,* trans. A. M. Henderson and Talcott Parsons, ed. with intro. by Talcott Parsons (New York: Oxford University Press, 1947), 328; R. S. Peters, "Authority," 86–87.

5. The classic expression in English of this view can be found in A. F. Pollard's chapter on "The New Monarchy," in his *Factors in Modern History* (New York: G. Putnam's Sons, 1907), ch. 3. Among contemporary historians, G. R. Elton has done the most to explore the bureaucratic character of the emergent English state in the sixteenth century; see especially his *The Tudor Revolution in Government: Administrative Change in the Reign of Henry VIII* (Cambridge: Cambridge University Press, 1953) and *England under the Tudors,* 2nd ed. (London: Methuen, 1974), ch. 7. More generally, see H. R. Trevor Roper, "The General Crisis of the Seventeenth Century," in Trevor Aston, ed., *Crisis in Europe, 1560–1660* (Garden

City, N. Y.: Anchor Books, 1967), 63–102. The implications of this view of the state for the treatment of provincial or local history are summarized in H. P. R. Finberg, *The Local Historian and His Theme* (Leicester: University of Leicester, Department of English Local History, Occasional Papers, 1 1952), 5–8; Alan Everitt, "The County Community," in E. W. Ives, ed., *The English Revolution, 1600–1660* (New York: Harper and Row, 1971), 48–63; idem, "The Local Community and the Great Rebellion," reprinted in K. H. D. Haley, ed., *The Historical Association Book of the Stuarts* (London: Sidgwick and Jackson, 1973), 76–99; and Conrad Russell, *Parliaments and English Politics, 1621–1629* (Oxford: Clarendon Press, 1979), 5–26. For a stimulating critique of the anachronisms inherent in Pollard's views, see J. H. Hexter, " 'Factors in Modern History'," in his *Reappraisals in History: New Views on History and Society in Early Modern Europe*, 2nd ed. (Chicago: University of Chicago Press, 1979), 26–44. For a useful commentary on Elton's treatment of bureaucracy, see Arthur J. Slavin, "G. R. Elton and His Era: Thirty Years On," *Albion*, 15 (1983): 221–22. On Elton, see also David Harris Sacks, "The Hedgehog and the Fox Revisited," *Journal of Interdisciplinary History*, 16 (1985): 267–80. For criticism of Finberg's, Everitt's, and Russell's views of "localism," see Sacks, "The Corporate Town and the English State," 69–105.

6. Maitland, quoted by C. H. McIlwain, "The Historian's Part in a Changing World," *American Historical Review, 42* (1936–37): 212.

7. I have discussed the methodological difficulties inherent in this enterprise and suggested some approaches in David Harris Sacks, "The Demise of the Martyrs: The Feasts of St. Clement and St. Katherine in Bristol, 1400–1600," *Social History* 11 (1986): 141–69.

8. Sacks, "The Demise of the Martyrs," 146–55.

9. Robert Ricart, *The Maire of Bristowe is Kalendar,* ed. by Lucy Toulmin Smith (Westminster, Eng.: Camden Society, new series 5, 1872) hereafter cited as Ricart, *Kalendar.*

10. Ibid., 70; see also Ordinance 40 Edw. III (1366) in *The Little Red Book of Bristol,* ed. F. B. Bickley, 2 vols. (Bristol: W. C. Hemmons, 1900), 2:46–47 (hereafter cited as *L.R.B.*).

11. Ricart, *Kalendar,* 70.

12. Ibid.

13. See Charles Phythian-Adams, "Ceremony and the Citizen: The Communal Year at Coventry, 1450–1550," in Peter Clark and Paul Slack, eds., *Crisis and Order in English Towns, 1500–1700* (London: Routledge & Kegan Paul, 1972), 57–85.

14. Ricart, *Kalendar,* 70–71.

15. Phythians-Adams, "Ceremony and the Citizen," 62.

16. Ricart, *Kalendar,* 71.

17. Ibid., 72n; for the much simpler oath used before 1373, see *L.R.B.*, 1: 46. Ricart's manuscript depicts the oath-taking in an illustration at fol. 151ᵛ (see fig. 1 on p. 193). Here Ricart shows the incoming mayor, in this case wearing robes to indicate that he had served previously, wearing with his right hand touching a closed book—probably the Bible—held by the outgoing mayor, while the common councillors sat or stood around the council table. A number of citizens appear standing at the periphery of this group. Also shown are the town clerk reading the oath, the swordbearer holding sword and cap, and an assistant holding the seal mentioned by Ricart. On the council table we see a large pouch, probably containing monies to be received into the new mayor's care, a scroll, and an account book. The room itself is decorated by a tapestry showing the royal arms in the

center, the cross of St. George to the left, and the arms of the town of Bristol to the right.

18. Ibid., 72–74.

19. Ibid., 71.

20. Ibid., 72.

21. Ibid., 74.

22. Ibid., 74–75.

23. See William Adams, *Adams' Chronicle of Bristol*, ed. F. F. Fox (Bristol: J. W. Arrowsmith, 1910), 69–80; Ricart, *Kalendar*, 42–49; "A shorte and brief memory by licence and correcon of the first progress of our souueraigne lorde King Henry VIIth," in John Leland, *De rebvs Brittanicus, Collecteanea*, ed. Thomas Hearne, 3 vols. in 4 (London: Gvl. and J. Richardson, 1770), 4:185–203. A somewhat sketchy account of King Edward IV's visit to Bristol in 1461 also survives; see F. J. Furnival, ed., *Political, Religious and Love Poems from the Archbishop of Canterbury's Lambeth Ms. no. 306 and other sources*, Early English Text Society, original series no. 15 (London: K. Paul, Trench, Trübner, 1866), 5–6.

24. John C. Meagher, "The First Progress of Henry VII," *Renaissance Drama*, new series, 1 (1968): 45–73; Sydney Anglo, *Spectacle, Pageantry and Early Stuart Policy* (Oxford: Clarendon Press, 1969), 21–45.

25. Leland, *De rebvs Brittanicus*, 4: 199.

26. Ibid., 4: 199–200. Bristol's petition was not without effect. Two days after King Bremmius' speech, the king summoned the mayor, the sheriff, and other burgesses to inquire about the city's poverty and to offer aid in various ways. According to the herald, who recorded these proceedings, "the Meyre of the Towne towlde me they Lorde not this hundred yeres of noo King so good a Comfort. Wherfor they thanked Almighty God, that hath them soo good and gracious a Souueraigne Lord." Ibid., 202; see also Anglo, *Spectacle*, 34; Meagher, "First Progress," 72.

27. Geoffrey of Monmouth, *History of the Kings of Britain*, trans. Sebastian Evans, rev. Charles W. Dunn, intro. Gwyn Jones (London: Folio Society, 1958), 46 ff; Acton Griscom, *The Historia Regum Britanniae of Geoffrey of Monmouth, with contributions to the study of its place in early British History, together with a literal translation of the Welsh Manuscript No LXI of Jesus College, Oxford by Robert Ellis Jones* (London: Longmans, Green and Co., 1929), 276 ff; Helaine H. Newstead, *Bran the Blessed in Arthurian Romance* (New York: Columbia University Press, 1939), 155–67; Anglo, *Spectacle*, 33.

28. Bodleian Library Rawl. Ms. B. 171, printed in Frederich W. D. Brie, ed., *The Brut or The Chronicles of England*, Early English Text Society, original series 131 (London: K. Paul, Trench, Trübner, 1906), 26–27; *Eulogium (historiarium sive temporis): Chronicon ab orbe condito usque ad annum Domini MCCCLXVI., a monacho quodam Malmesburiensi exaratum. Accedunt continuationes duae, quarum una ad annum MCCCXIII., altera ad annum MCCCXC. perducta est*, ed. F. S. Haydon, 3 vols. (London: Longman, Brown, Green, Longman and Roberts, 1858–63) 2:242. According to this tradition, Brennius first named the city "Brenstou." On the founding of London and York, see Geoffrey of Monmouth, *Kings of Britain* 1:7, 2:7; Brie, ed., *Brut*, 11, 15.

29. Ricart, *Kalendar*, 10.

30. See Sydney Anglo, "The *British History* in Early Tudor Propaganda," *Bulletin John Rylands Library*, 44 (1961–62): 17–48. Henry VII's "British" origins also played an important part in the pageants arranged for him at York and Worcester in 1486; see ibid., 27–28.

31. Leland, *De rebvs Brittanicus,* 199.

32. Ricart gives us a vision of the city as a microcosm of the universe in the plan he provides of Brennius' Bristol. It is reproduced facing p. 10 in the printed edition of the *Kalendar.* This plan conveys the image of Bristol as "the navel of the world," a cross within a circle, representing a heavenly Jerusalem in which the four main streets divide the world into its four component parts. For a discussion of this plan and of the characteristic forms of public ritual in late medieval Bristol, see Sacks, "The Demise of the Martyrs," 146–55. See also Mervyn James, "Ritual, Drama and Social Body in the Late Medieval English Town," *Past and Present* 98 (February 1983): 1–29.

33. Ricart, *Kalendar,* 80, 85–86.

34. [John Gregory], *Episcopus Puerum in die Innocentium. Or, A discovery of an Ancient Custom in the Church of Sarum making an Anniversary Bishop among the Choristers,* first published 1649, in John Gurgany, ed., *Postuma of John Gregory* (London, 1671), 113–16; Christopher Wordsworth, ed., *Ceremonies and Processions of the Church of Salisbury* (Cambridge: Cambridge University Press, 1901), 52–59; Daniel Rock, *The Church of Our Fathers as seen in St. Osmund's Rite for the Cathedral of Salisbury,* ed. G. W. Hart and Witt Frere, 4 vols. (London: J. Hodges, 1903–04), 4: 250–55. Christopher Wordsworth and Douglas MacLean, *Statutes and Customs of the Cathedral Church of the Blessed Virgin Mary of Salisbury* (London: W. Clowes and Sons, 1915), 264–65, see especially "Roger de Mortivale's Code" (1319). Gregory prints on the title page of this work and again at p. 117 a sketch of the boy-bishop statue found at Salisbury. It shows a youth in a bishop's robes with mitre and crozier offering a benediction while standing atop a dragon. The ceremony was not only practiced in the church but also at schools and colleges. For a useful survey of St. Nicholas' career as a saint from the days of the early Christians to the present, see Charles W. Jones, *Saint Nicholas of Myra, Bari, and Manhattan: Biography of a Legend* (Chicago: University of Chicago Press, 1978). In general on the boy-bishop in England, see John Brand, *Observations on Popular Antiquities: Chiefly Illustrating the Origin of our Vulgar Customs, Ceremonies and Superstitions,* ed. by Sir Henry Ellis, 3 vols. (London: C. Knight and Co., 1841–42), 1: 421 ff; Joseph Strutt, *The Sports and Pastimes of the People of England from the Earliest Period,* new ed. by J. Charles Cox (London: Methuen, 1903), 272–73; G. L. Gomme, ed., *The Gentleman's Magazine Library: Manners and Customs* (London: Stock, 1883), 89; A. R. Wright, *British Calendar Customs: England,* ed. T. E. Lones, 3 vols. (London: W. Glaisher, 1936–40), 3: 194–97; J. G. Nichols, ed., "Two Sermons preached by the Boy Bishop at St. Paul's Temp. Henry VIII [sic!] and at Gloucester, Temp. Mary," with an introduction by Edward F. Rimbault in *Camden Miscellany* 7 (Westminster: Camden Society, new series 14, 1876): v–xxxii; E. K. Chambers, *The Mediaeval Stage,* 2 vols. (Oxford: Clarendon Press, 1903), 1: ch. 15; R. T. Hampson, *Medii aevi Kalendarium, or Dates, charters and customs of the Middle Ages,* 2 vols. (London: H. K. Causton and Son, 1841), 1: 80. See also, Natalie Zemon Davis, "The Reasons of Misrule," in her *Society and Culture in Early Modern France: Eight Essays* (Stanford, Calif.: Stanford University Press, 1975), 97–123; Keith Thomas, "Rule and Misrule in the Schools of Early Modern England," *The Stenton Lecture 1975* (Reading: University of Reading, 1976).

35. Ricart, *Kalendar,* 46. It is not clear from which church or ecclesiastical house in Bristol this boy-bishop was selected. He might have been a chorister at St. Nicholas Church or attached to one of the monastic houses in the city. Bristol did not become a bishopric in its own right until 1542.

36. Unfortunately, no boy-bishop sermon has survived for Bristol. But at least three such sermons do exist, viz., *"In die innocentium sermo pro Episcopo Puerum,"* first printed by Wynken De Worde in the 1490s, about which time it was written; Desiderius Erasmus, *De Concio de puero Iesu,* written at John Colet's request for St. Paul's School, circa 1504; and "Sermon of the Child Bishop, pronownsyd by John Stubs, Querster on Chidermas Day, at Glocester, 1555" (British Library Cotton MS, Vesp. A xxv, 173–79). Erasmus' sermon was given in Latin, but survives in an English edition dating from 1540. The other two are printed in J. G. Nichols, ed. "Two Sermons," 1–29.

37. Geoffrey Chaucer, *The Works of Geoffrey Chaucer,* ed. F. N. Robinson, 2nd ed. (Boston: Houghton Mifflin, 1957); Geoffrey Chaucer, *Canterbury Tales,* "The Pardoner's Tale," ll. 463–76, 621–28; "The Franklin's Tale," ll. 682–91; "The Shipman's Tale," ll. 1492–96; "The Cookes Tale," ll. 4365–422.

38. Thomas Elyot, *The Boke named The Gouernour,* ed. H. H. S. Croft, 2 vols. (London: K. Paul, Trench and Co., 1883), 1: 275. See also, John Northbrooke, *Spiritus est Vicarius Christi in terra. A Treatise wherein Dicing, Dancing, Vaine playes, or Enterluds, with other idel pastimes, &c., commonly vsed on the Sabboth day, are reproued by the Authoritie of the word of God and auncient writers* (London, 1577, reprint ed. J. P. Collier, Shakespeare Society, vol. 16, 1843), 130 ff.; Philip Stubbes, *The Anatomy of Abuses* (London: R. Jones, 1583), 172–77.

39. Chaucer, *Works,* "Troilus and Criseyde," bk. 2, lines 1347–51; bk. 4, lines 1093–99; *Canterbury Tales:* "The Knights Tale," ll. 1238–50.

40. Elyot, *The Boke,* 1: 272–73.

41. Bristol Record Office (hereafter B.R.O.), doc. no. 01208 (1373), printed in *Bristol Charters, 1155–1373,* ed. N. Dermott Harding, Bristol Record Society, (Bristol, 1930), 1: 136–37.

42. Chaucer, *Works, Canterbury Tales,* "The Pardoner's Tale," ll. 591–602.

43. Nichols, ed., "Two Sermons," 5–6.

44. Sacks, "The Demise of the Martyrs," 165–69. Bristol supplied six chaplains and forty other men, most of them weavers and clothworkers to Sir Thomas Oldcastle's army in 1414; K. B. McFarlane, *The Origins of Religious Dissent in England* (New York: Collier Books, 1966), 187–89. Some of their names are available in Public Record Office K.B. 9/205/1 mm. 82–83. For Bristol Lollardy after 1414, see J. A. F. Thomson, *The Later Lollards, 1414–1520* (London: Oxford University Press, 1965), 20–28, 33–35, 37, 44, 46–47, 54, 65–66, 68, 99, 109, 114, 155, 209, 221, 240, 246. The ideas of Wycliffe and his early followers can be gleaned from *Selections from English Wycliffite Writings,* ed. Anne Hudson (Cambridge: Cambridge University Press, 1978); see also K. B. McFarlane, *Origins of Religious Dissent,* ch. 4; Herbert B. Workman, *John Wyclif: A Study of the English Medieval Church,* 2 vols. (Oxford: Clarendon Press, 1926), 2: 3–45, 149–55. On later Lollard beliefs, see Thomson, *Later Lollards,* 239–50; A. G. Dickens, *Lollards and Protestants in the Diocese of York, 1509–1558* (London: Oxford University Press, 1959), chs. 1–2; A. G. Dickens, *The English Reformation* (New York: Schocken Books, 1964), ch. 2; Margaret Aston, "Lollardy and the Reformation: Survival or Revival?" *History* 41 (1964): 149–70. For evidence of challenges to religious and governmental authority in guilds and corporations in fifteenth-century Bristol, see *L.R.B.* 2: 117–22, 147–53. For Wycliffe's own criticism of the craft guilds, see John Wycliffe, *The Grete Sentence of the Curs Expounded* in his *Select English Works,* ed. Thomas Arnold, 3 vols. (Oxford: Clarendon Press, 1869–71), 3: 333–34.

45. See Hugh Latimer, "Articles untruly, unjustly, falsely, uncharitably im-

parted to me by Dr. Powell of Salisbury," in *The Works of Hugh Latimer*, ed. George Elwes Corrie, 2 vols., The Parker Society Publications, vols. 26 & 27 (Cambridge: Cambridge University Press, 1844–45), 2:233; see also "Letter of Hugh Latimer to Ralph Morice, Mayor, June, 1533," in ibid., 2:357 ff. Much additional material bearing upon Latimer's preachings in Bristol and the controversies that followed is printed in John Foxe, *Acts and Monuments of the Christian Martyrs*, 8 vols. (New York: AMS Press, 1965), vol. 7, appendix 9. For a discussion of these events and a review of the religious issues raised, see Harold S. Darby, *Hugh Latimer* (London: Epworth Press, 1953), ch. 5. For analysis of the official reaction to these disturbances, see G. R. Elton, *Policy and Police: The Enforcement of the Reformation* (Cambridge: Cambridge University Press, 1972), 110–20. See also, Sacks, "The Demise of the Martyrs," 168–69.

46. Proclamation of 22 July 1541 in *Tudor Royal Proclamations*, ed. Paul L. Hughes and James F. Larkin, 3 vols. (New Haven: Yale University Press, 1964–69), 1: 301–02.

47. F. E. Brightman, *The English Rite, being a synopsis of the sources and revisions of the Book of Common Prayer*, 2nd rev. ed., 2 vols. (London: Rivingtons, 1921), 1: 98–101.

48. Northbrooke, *Treatise;* Thomas Thompson, *A Diet for a Drunkard, Deliuered in two Sermons at St Nicholas Church in Bristoll Anno Domini 1608* (London: R. Bankworth, 1612), which prints the last two sermons in the series; Edward Chetwin, *The Strait Gate and Narrow Way of Life opened and pointed out in certain sermons upon Luke 13, 23, 24* (London: W. Hall, 1612), see esp. p. 4; Edward Chetwin, *Votiuae Lachrymae, A Vow of Teares for the losse of Prince Henry in a Sermon Preached in the Citie of Bristol, December 7, 1612, being the Day of his funerall* (London: W. Welbys, 1612), 24–32. For the effects of the Reformation and other sixteenth-century developments on popular festivities and practices, see Imogen Luxton, "The Reformation and Popular Culture," in Felicity Heal and Rosemary O'Day, eds., *Church and Society in England, Henry VIII to James I* (London: Macmillan, 1977), 57–77; Phythian-Adams, "Ceremony and the Citizen," 70–80; Peter Burke, *Popular Culture in Early Modern Europe* (London: T. Smith, 1978), ch. 8. Mervyn James, relying on the work of Charles Phythian-Adams, attributes many of the changes to the so-called urban crisis in the late fifteenth and early sixteenth centuries, "Ritual, Drama, and Social Body," 26; see Charles Phythian-Adams, "Urban Decay in Late Medieval England," in Philip Abrams and E. A. Wrigley, eds., *Towns in Society: Essays in Economic History and Historical Sociology* (Cambridge: Cambridge University Press, 1978), 159 ff; Charles Phythian-Adams, *Desolation of a City: Coventry and the Urban Crisis of the Late Middle Ages* (Cambridge: Cambridge University Press, 1979). I have expressed some reservations about Burke's and James's arguments in "The Demise of the Martyrs," and about Phythian-Adams's view of "urban crisis" in my review of his book, *Journal of Modern History* 54 (1982): 105–07.

49. B.R.O. doc. no. 01230 (1499) printed in *Bristol Charters, 1378–1499*, ed. H. A. Cronne, Bristol Record Society, (Bristol, 1945), 11: 163–91. This paragraph is based on evidence presented in Sacks, *Trade, Society and Politics*, chs. 1–4; see also Sacks, "The Corporate Town and the English State," 76–96.

50. B.R.O., *Common Council Proceedings* (hereafter *C.C.P.*), 3 fol. 122^r.

51. B.R.O. doc. no. 01230 (1499) in *Bristol Charters, 1378–1499*, 167, 183; *Bristol Charters, 1508–1899*, ed. R. C. Latham, Bristol Record Society (Bristol, 1947), 13: intro., 6–7; J. H. Thomas, *Town Government in the Sixteenth Century*

(London: G. Allen & Unwin, 1933), 34; Sacks, *Trade, Society and Politics,* 692–708.

52. This paragraph and the two following it are based on Sacks, *Trade, Society and Politics,* chs. 6–14. For a statement in verse of the merchants' hierarchical views, see I[ohn] B[rowne], *The Merchants Avizo,* ed. Patrick McGrath, Publications of the Kress Library of Business and Economics, no. 11 (Boston: Baker Library, Harvard Graduate School of Business Administration, 1957), 5. These views did not go unchallenged by the retailers and craftsmen whom the merchants sought to exclude from foreign trade. Unfortunately, space does not allow treatment of this theme here, but see e.g., "Letter of the Master and Company of Tuckers to William Pepwell, Mayor of Bristol, 1568," printed in *Some Account of the Guild of Weavers in Bristol: Chiefly from Mss.,* ed. F. F. Fox and John Taylor (Bristol: J. Wright, 1880), 92–93; more generally, see Sacks, *Trade, Society and Politics,* chs. 13–14; Sacks, "The Demise of the Martyrs," and Sacks, "The Corporate Town and the English State," 85–96.

53. The phrase is Patrick McGrath's, see *Records Relating to the Society of Merchant Venturers of the City of Bristol in the Seventeenth Century,* ed. Patrick V. McGrath, Bristol Record Society (Bristol, 1952), 19: intro., 37; see also, Patrick McGrath, *The Merchant Venturers of Bristol: A History of the Society of Merchant Venturers of the City of Bristol from its Origins to the Present Day* (Bristol: The Society of Merchant Venturers of Bristol, 1975), 62–70; Sacks, *Trade, Society and Politics,* 634–39. For the history of the Merchant Venturers during the sixteenth and early seventeenth centuries, see also John Latimer, *The History of the Society of Merchant Venturers of Bristol with some Account of the Anterior Merchants' Guilds* (Bristol: J. W. Arrowsmith, 1903), chs. 1–2; McGrath, *Merchant Venturers,* chs. 1–5; Sacks, *Trade, Society and Politics,* chs. 12–13.

54. After 1499, two sheriffs were elected annually from among the council members who had not previously served. In practice, the office was filled by the most recently coopted council members, nearly all of whom served; see Sacks, *Trade, Society and Politics,* 694–98.

55. Thompson, *Diet for a Drunkard,* 74–75.

56. Ibid., 76–77.

57. Ibid., 59–60, 75.

58. Ibid., 25.

59. B.R.O. *Seventeenth-Century Ordinance Book,* frontispiece; this prayer dates from early in the reign of James I, not later than 1612.

60. Adams, *Chronicle,* 182.

61. B.R.O. *Old Ordinance Book,* fol. 20v (1563). At regular meetings of the council held after 1564 on the first Tuesday in each month, proper dress was gowns "of the gravest sort" and caps; ibid., ff. 61v, 67r–v Scarlet was reserved for formal occasions only and was worn primarily to attend church services; B.R.O., *C.C.P.,* 1: 139; Adams, *Chronicle,* 185.

62. B.R.O., *C.C.P.,* 1: 167; John Latimer, *Annals of Bristol in the Seventeenth Century* (Bristol: William George's Sons, 1900), 30.

63. Adams, *Chronicle,* 182.

64. Ibid., 183–84; Latimer, *Annals,* 30–31.

65. Adams, *Chronicle,* 113–14, 188–200; Thomas Churchyard, *The Firste parte of Churchyardes Chippes, contayning twelue seuerall Labours* (London: T. Marshe, 1575), fol. 100v–110v. Queen Anne of Denmark's visit is recounted in a long poem written by Robert Naile and copied into his *Chronicle* by Adams, who

describes its author as an apprentice in the city.

66. Adams, *Chronicle,* 113–14.

67. Churchyard, *Chippes,* fol. 100v, 106v. Bristol paid Churchyard £6-13-4 for his efforts, and in all the city laid out almost a thousand pounds on this three days of festivity; B.R.O., *Mayor's Audits, 1570–1754,* 290; David M. Bergeron, *English Civic Pageantry, 1558–1642* (Columbia: University of South Carolina Press, 1971), 26–27. Churchyard reports that some of the speeches at the end of the celebration "could not be spoken, by means of a Scholemaister, who enuied that any stranger should set forth these shoes," Churchyard, *Chippes,* fol. 110v. But in most cases the speeches were given, and in any case all were contained in the book which the Queen was presented.

68. Ibid., fol. 102r.

69. Ibid., fol. 103r.

70. Ibid., fol. 107r.

71. Ibid., fol. 108r, misnumbered in the text as fol. 118, 109r.

72. Ibid., fol. 108v.

73. Ibid., fol. 104r–v.

74. Ibid., ff. 101v, 102v.

75. Ibid., ff. 108v–109r.

76. Ibid., ff. 101v, 102r, 102v, 103v.

77. Ibid., fol. 109r–v.

78. Ibid., fol. 109v.

79. Ibid., ff. 101r, 103r, 105r, 106r–v, 109v–110r.

80. On this theme in general, see Bergeron, *English Civic Pageantry,* ch. 1; Roy Strong, *Art and Power: Renaissance Festivals, 1450–1650* (Berkeley: University of California Press, 1984); Stephen Orgel, *The Illusion of Power: Political Theory in the English Renaissance* (Berkeley: University of California Press, 1975); Frances A. Yates, *Astraea: The Imperial Theme in the Sixteenth Century* (London: Routledge and Kegan Paul, 1975), pt. 2; R. Malcolm Smuts, *The Culture of Absolutism at the Court of Charles I* (Ph. D. dissertation, Princeton University 1976), 20–112. The author thanks Professor Smuts for permission to consult his dissertation.

81. Thomas Palmer, *Bristol's Military Garden: A sermon Preached unto the worthy Company of Practitioners in the Military Garden of the well Governed Citie of Bristoll* (London: F. Kyngston, 1635), 31.

82. Ibid., 7–8.

83. Ibid. 31–32.

84. Ibid., 32.

85. Mikhail Bakhtin, *Rabelais and his World,* trans Hélène Iswolsky (Cambridge: M.I.T. Press, 1968), 6, 9, 10; see also Victor Turner, *The Ritual Process: Structure and Anti-Structure* (Chicago: Aldine Pub. Co., 1969), especially ch. 3 and 168–70, 177–78, 200–03; Davis, *Society and Culture,* 122–23. In this light, the history of Bristol's midsummer watches of St. John's night and St. Peter's night is especially instructive. In the fifteenth century, these were convivial guild events, involving candlelight processions through the town and guild drinkings; see *The Great Red Book of Bristol,* ed. E. W. W. Veale, 5 vols., Bristol Record Society, 2, 4, 7, 16, 18 (Bristol, 1931–53), 2: 125–26, Ordinance of 20 May, 28 Hen. VI (1450); Phythian-Adams, "Ceremony and the Citizen," 64–65. In 1572–73, however, Mayor John Browne ended the drunken revellings and "the delightful shows" that traditionally had accompanied these festive occasions and "turned the same into a general muster in war-like sort; and all the burgesses being fully armed with all sorts of warlike weapons, every craft and science several by themselves with their

drums and colours, which was well used and made a comely show," Adams, *Chronicle,* 112–13. In making this change, Browne might have been following the guidance of John Northbrooke, who in his treatise against vain plays of 1577 argued that military exercises "trayning vp men in the knowledge of martiall and warrelike affaires and exercising" and imparting "knowledge to handle weapons" were acceptable forms of play; Northbrooke, *Treatise,* 107.

86. Frederick Pollock and Frederic William Maitland, *The History of English Law before the Time of Edward I,* 2nd ed., 2 vols. (Cambridge: Cambridge University Press, 1968), 1: 635; see also Sacks, "The Corporate Town and the English State," 74–75, 85–86.

9

The Palio of Siena: Game, Ritual, or Politics?

Sydel Silverman

Any inquiry into public life in Siena, whether that of the Renaissance or of today, inevitably leads to the Palio, then as now the central event of the festive calendar, a focus of social energies the year round, and a symbolic repository of the city's multiple images of itself. The Palio of Siena is unique among festivities of its kind in central Italy for its uninterrupted continuance as a vital form for centuries—from the time of the Sienese Republic (1260–1555) up to the present day—evolving and changing but never "revived." Yet if it is to yield to analysis it must be understood in terms of social and cultural processes that are not unique to Siena. Its continuity makes it a valuable case for the comparative study of ritual, ceremony, and play, for its present-day manifestation is accessible to direct observation, while its history reveals a long series of responses to changing circumstances. To explore the case, this paper first describes the Palio as it exists today, then outlines its historical trajectory. Finally, it asks how we may begin to understand the Palio: what kind of phenomenon is it, and what processes might have been entailed in its development?[1]

The Palio of today is a bareback horse race around the Campo, the great central piazza of Siena, run twice each summer—on 2 July in honor of the Madonna del Provenzano and on 16 August as the culmination of the celebration of the Assumption of the Virgin, Siena's patroness. The Palio is run by the seventeen *contrade* or wards of the city. It is this *contrada* structure, which extends beyond the Palio to form a basic patterning of social life in Siena throughout the year, that makes the Palio fundamentally different from horse races and tournaments elsewhere in Italy, including those that are called a "palio" because they offer a painted banner as the prize. Such events, featuring revived or reinvented medieval or Renaissance games, have proliferated in central Italy over the past fifty years or so, and typically the units of competition are territorial divisions (often called "contrade"); but nowhere do these units have the corporate identity, internal organization, and continuity of functioning that mark the Sienese contrade.[2]

The contrade of Siena are legal entities with fixed boundaries, owning property and holding rights and obligations as corporate bodies. Each contrada takes its name from a quasi-totemic figure, usually an animal, and each is associated with particular colors and with a complex array of symbols—distinctive songs, myths, numbers, and traditions of many kinds. Membership in the contrada is theoretically ascribed and permanent; once based exclusively upon place of birth, today it is generally determined by the contrada identity of a parent (which is then formally conferred on the child by a secular contrada baptism) or, increasingly, by voluntary adhesion. The contrada has an elaborate structure of governing bodies and officials (headed by a prior), elected by and responsible to an assembly of the citizenry. In addition to this civic administration, there is a separate "wartime" apparatus for the period leading up to the Palio, when an elected captain is given full powers. The contrada also maintains external relations as an autonomous body with other contrade, with communal authorities, and even with political entities outside of Siena. Among contrade there are formal alliances and relations of friendship that are sustained through diplomatic exchanges on certain occasions, and there are paired enmities, most of them between adjacent contrade. Such relations, both of alliance and of enmity, are extremely important elements of strategy in the Palio.

The contrade are a major focus of recreational life in Siena. The contrada seat is a frequent gathering place; the society affiliated with each contrada organizes social activity the year round; and the variety of events that make up the contrada calendar bring *contradaioli* together regularly. The contrade are internally stratified, but social interaction among contradaioli is governed by conventional forms of intimacy, such as the use of familiar terms of address, and by sanctions against potentially divisive behavior. The contrada also has a religious identity. Each has its own church and priest (separate from the parish structure) and its own patron saint, whose annual celebration is marked with a week-long round of festivities that are at once ritual, political, and social occasions.

While the contrade thus have institutional form and a range of functioning beyond the Palio, the Palio is at the center of contrada life, and everything that goes on in the contrada has reference, directly or indirectly, to the Palio. In a sense, the Palio is never over; each Palio leads into the next, and both the reliving of Palii past and preparations for the next one go on continually. However, the Palio begins officially about a month before the event with a ceremony for the designation of the contrade that will run. Ten contrade run in each Palio; these include the seven that did not run in the last Palio of that cycle (the July and August Palii constituting separate cycles), and three others that are chosen by lot, by means of a special mechanical device. When "extraordinary" Palii are held—which are fairly frequent events, to honor some special occasion—lots are drawn to choose all ten. Like a number of other ceremonies of the Palio, the drawing of lots takes place in the precincts of the city hall before the mayor and the captains, while the populace gathers outside to await the results that will be announced through a display of contrada flags.

The "four days of the Palio" begin with the assignment of horses to the contrade. Early in the morning the horses (around thirty in number) that are offered by private owners are brought to the Campo, where they are inspected by the municipal veterinarians. Then, sorted into groups of about six and ridden by jockeys wearing the colors of the commune, they are raced around the piazza under the scrutiny of the captains, who will vote to select the ten horses to run in the Palio. Generally, the aim of the captains is to obtain ten evenly matched horses, although many factors enter into their selection. Around noon the crowd assembles in the piazza; the names of the horses selected are posted, and as the tension mounts, the lots are drawn to match up horses and contrade. Once a contrada draws a horse, it cannot be changed or replaced. The contradaioli, exultant or disheartened by the draw, lead their horse to the stable deep inside contrada territory ("the horse's house"), guarding it carefully until the Palio. That evening, the first of six *prove* or trial races takes place. The others follow on the morning and evening of the next two days, with the last coming on the morning of Palio day.

The jockeys, most of them from outside of Siena, are hired by the contrade for each Palio. The contrada may be in contact with prospective jockeys throughout the year, often continuing negotiations through the days of the trial races, and a final commitment may not be made until the captains formally register their jockeys in a ceremony at the city hall following the last trial. While some jockeys have special relationships with particular contrade, in general they are regarded as mercenaries, never entirely trustworthy.

As the trial races unfold, Palio fever engulfs the city. Every new development is discussed at length, there is growing speculation about intrigues, and the intensity of excitement escalates. People wear their contrada emblems, contrada banners are displayed throughout each territory, and groups of contradaioli parade about the city singing their songs and insulting their enemies. The young men of the contrada accompany their horse to and from each trial in a mood of increasing militancy, and violent encounters between contrade are common. After the final evening trial (the *prova generale*), each of the ten competing contrade comes together for a propitiatory dinner, with tables set for hundreds (sometimes thousands) in the streets or main piazza of the contrada.

The only prize to the winner of the race is the "palio" itself, the banner painted for each Palio by a different artist on commission of the commune. Regardless of its material value or opinions as to its artistic merit, each banner is treasured beyond measure, to be carried about in triumph by the victorious contrada for days after the Palio and then displayed in its museum along with others won in the past. Each banner bears the image of the Madonna in whose honor the race is run, and on the evening before her feast-day, following the trial race, the banner is carried to her church to be consecrated. The procession is led by the municipal authorities, the Palio officials, and representatives of the contrade. During the August Palio it forms part of a larger ceremony for the offering of candles at the cathedral, the collective act of submission of Siena to her patroness.

Early in the morning of Palio day, the bishop officiates at a mass in the outdoor chapel of the Campo, where he blesses the jockeys. The last trial race follows—the *provaccia* or bad race, because the jockeys will try to hold the horses back. At three in the afternoon a ceremony is held in each contrada church, where the horse is taken to be blessed. Meanwhile, the *comparse*, the groups of costumed men who represent the contrade in the Palio procession, gather at the contrada seats to dress up in their finery; the splendid medieval costumes and regalia used in the *corteo* are owned by the contrade, along with a store of other costumes worn by many of the men and boys when the contrade parade on their saints' days and other festive occasions. The different comparse make their way through the streets to the rhythm of their drummers, the flag-bearers performing flag-throwing feats at various stops in homage to the important institutions of the city. Then the comparse, those of the competing contrade each escorting its horse and its jockey (who rides in medieval attire on a parade horse), all assemble for the entrance of the corteo into the Campo.

This spectacular procession, which includes over five hundred people in costume, presents the participants in the Palio as part of a symbolic reenactment of the historic Republic of Siena. Led by the banner of Siena and representatives of the communal government, the corteo displays the communities and territories that were subject to the Sienese state, the military orders of the Republic with their commanders, and the major institutions and officials of the state. The comparse of the seventeen contrade make up the largest part of the procession, each one bearing the symbols of the military companies associated with its territory under the Republic. At four points around the piazza, the comparse stop for performances of flag play; a prize, the *masgalano,* will later be given to the contrada making the best presentation. Also represented are six contrade that no longer exist (having been excluded from the partitioning of contrada territories in the early eighteenth century). At the end of the corteo comes the ox-drawn cart representing the triumphal chariot of the Republic, which bears the palio banner.

Finally the Palio itself begins. The horses, ridden by the jockeys now wearing the contrada colors, emerge from the courtyard of the city hall. The order of the ten at the starting line is determined at the last minute, again by a procedure of drawing lots. The start is adjudicated by an official, the *mossiere,* and false starts are frequent. Then the race: three circuits clockwise around the piazza, in the time of a little over a minute. Falls are common, especially at the two points where the track makes right-hand downhill and uphill turns; but a riderless horse may win, provided its head ornament displaying the contrada emblem remains intact. The three Palio judges declare the winner—and their decision is irrevocable, regardless of the outcome of disputes that may arise after the race—but the victorious contradaioli will already have swarmed onto the track to claim the palio banner from the judges' stand. Accompanied by the contrade friendly to them, they take the palio to the church of its Madonna in thanks and then pass the night in jubilation and triumphant procession around the city.

The celebration and noisy parades continue all the next day. The victors suck on baby bottles and pacifiers to symbolize their rebirth, spread leaflets with celebratory odes or mockery of their enemies around the city, and add this Palio to their ongoing count of victories achieved. The losers—which include the contrada that came in second, the enemy of the winning contrada, and the contrada that has gone longest without a victory—suffer their defeat, by purging themselves it is said. The victors hold another more elaborate parade on the Sunday following the Palio. Later, during the fall, there will be a victory celebration with a weekend of festivity, including a lavish spectacle staged in the Campo by the victorious contrada and a great banquet in the streets of the contrada, with the horse in the place of honor.

The fascination of the Palio lies in the fact that each one plays out a unique and intricate set of elements, yet each forms part of a continuing saga of the contrade and their interrelations. The Palio is a ferocious race demanding extraordinary skills of horsemanship on a perilous course; but it is more than that. It is also a competition among the contrade carried out through arrangements of byzantine complexity and a politics of alliance, negotiation, and quasi-military tactics. Each contrada promises its jockey a specific bonus if he wins, but in addition each contrada and each jockey also enter into *partiti,* secret agreements to further a contrada's own efforts to win, to prevent an enemy from winning, or to help an ally. There are a great many ways in which the race can be manipulated through such agreements, but the outcome is always unpredictable—for chance plays a large part—and the precise arrangements that determined a particular result are invariably matters of debate. Only the winning contrada pays off its partiti, after the race. Victory is costly; the large sums of money required are raised by the contrade throughout the year and through special contributions of the members.

The Palio is supervised by the communal administration, which officiates over every phase, appoints the various Palio officials, and adjudicates disputes. The detailed regulations of the Palio are instituted as laws of the city, and each Palio is followed by formal reviews of all irregularities and complaints. Violations are subject to sanctions on a graded range of severity, including the exclusion of a contrada or jockey from the Palio for specified periods of time. Contrary to the caricature of the Palio as a chaotic race where anything goes, it is regulated to an extreme degree and in an often finely legalistic manner. It is, moreover, a particularly subtle form of regulation, which recognizes distinctions between law and custom, between rules that may be broken and those that may not be, and between acceptable and unacceptable ways of breaking rules.

While the rules and customs of the Palio are backed by the force of tradition of almost mythic proportions, they are not frozen traditions; they have evolved over time and are continually reexamined and renegotiated. Yet locating the Palio historically is more than a matter of tracing the evolution of its rules and practices. It entails, in the first instance, theoretical judgments about which aspects of this complex pattern are to be regarded as defining features. Thus, one might well trace the passion for horses to the Etruscans and brutal competitive games to the Roman circuses. Public games between territorial divisions of the city and horse races run for a decorative banner in conjunction with Siena's major festivals go back to the beginning of the Republic. If, however, the contrada structure is regarded as definitive, then the modern Palio can be traced to contrada-organized horse races in the piazza dating from the beginning of the seventeenth century, which in turn had their roots in other forms of festival competition among totemic contrade that go back about a century earlier.[3]

Leaving aside the debate over the relationship of the modern contrade to territorial divisions of the city that preceded them, the major phases in the development of the contrada-based Palio may be summarized. Groups defined by totemic emblems appear first in a few scattered references from the late fifteenth and early sixteenth centuries in the context of games or displays of rivalry at public festivals. By the 1540s all the emblems of the seventeen modern contrade are present.[4] The nature of the groups that bear these emblems is not entirely clear, but they are seen mounting floats in the procession preceding the "palio" horse race for the Assumption and staging public games such as fist-fighting on that and other festival occasions. The palio race at that period was run on an open track (*palio alla lunga*) and was limited to thoroughbreds entered by gentlemen. It was held on 15 August as part of Siena's great politico-religious festival, which served both as a celebration of the Virgin patroness and as a demonstration of the sovereignty of the Republic.

Following the fall of the Republic, the explicitly political aspects of the festival—the expressions of state sovereignty—were prohibited, but the festival continued to be the most important event of the Sienese year. The city's religious ritual of submission to the Virgin was sufficiently apolitical on the face of it to be tolerated by the new Medici overlords, although for the Sienese it was still a symbol of autonomy, if only an autonomy of spirit. While the open-track horse race continued, the contrada games in the Campo became increasingly central to the festival. In the second half of the sixteenth century, totemic contrade held animal-baiting games, bull-fights (until they were outlawed by the Council of Trent), water-buffalo races, and races with donkeys or with horses (packhorses, in the main, rather than thoroughbreds). Such games also took place on festive occasions other than the Assumption. During the early seventeenth century, the contrade began to organize horse races in the piazza on 2 July in honor of the Madonna del Provenzano, a cult that had been founded in the territory of the Giraffe during the 1590s. In 1656 this race became a fixed annual event, and this date is customarily taken for the establishment of the modern Palio of the contrade.

By this time the contrade denoted by totemic names were established entities with limited administrative as well as festival functions, in the process of supplanting local units with other designations.[5] However, they were loosely organized, with fluid boundaries, and lacked the resources and structure for systematically managing the Palio. Upper-class "protectors" in each contrada provided the financing and represented the contrada in its relations with authorities and with other contrade. The number of contrade participating varied from one Palio to another, depending upon their ability to mobilize a sufficient number of people and sufficient funds, and the right (or obligation) of contrade to participate was frequently called into question, as was the very status of some contrade.

The development of the contrada structure and of the Palio went hand in hand. As the Palio became more regular and more complex, it fostered a more formal internal organization of the contrade and an expansion of their functions. An important impetus in the formation of the modern contrade came in 1729, when, following a series of territorial disputes, a decree of the governess Violante established the status and boundaries of the contrade.[6] This act set the number of contrade permanently at seventeen, confirmed their legal status, and fixed their boundaries (following a plan drawn up by an appointed commission, which modified customary boundaries so as to achieve a better balance of population). This consolidation of the seventeen contrade encouraged the elaboration of their structure, which in turn made it possible for them to assume a more systematic role in the Palio. At the same time, they were able to expand their economic base through the acquisition of property, a process aided by the 1784 action of Grandduke Pietro Leopoldo to confer expropriated ecclesiastical properties upon them.

Once the July Palio was regularized, it became common for the contrada winning in July to organize a second race during the festival of the Assumption, on 16 August. The gentlemen's open-track race of 15 August continued alongside it until the nineteenth century; abolished under the French occupation, it was later revived and run sporadically until shortly after the Unification. However, the Palio "in the round" run by the contrade along the same pattern as the July race became increasingly the focal point of the festival of August.

At the beginning of the nineteenth century the municipal government took over much of the financing of the Palio. This change led to a redefinition of the category of "protectors" and a shift in the role of high-status members from one of personal patronage of the contrada to institutionalized leadership through election to the major offices. The nineteenth century also saw a series of changes in the rules of the Palio designed to modify practices that were sometimes criticized as barbaric; for example, there were new rules forbidding jockeys to knock each other off their horses.[7] The general result was to make the event more a race than a jousting match and to emphasize the role of the contrade themselves as the active competitors, with the jockeys taking on their current status as hired mercenaries. Along with this change came the growing practice of partiti, a mechanism that enabled corporate entities to wage the competition through political arrangements and financial maneuver.

The nineteenth century also brought modifications in the costuming and other explicit symbolism used in the festival, conferring upon the Palio its striking "medieval" aspect. The forms that today tempt the observer to see the Palio as a continuation of medieval patterns in fact date from the ideological climate of the post-Unification period. In the earlier Palio, the contrade made their appearance in the most diverse costumes, drawing—according to the epoch—on allegorical, mythological, biblical, or various military themes. Uniformity of costuming dates only from 1813, and it was only in 1878 that a medieval (fifteenth-century) theme was fixed. It was during the late nineteenth century that the "Myth of the Republic"—as Alessandro Falassi has called it—became the dominant symbolism of the festival, and the procession molded into an explicit recreation of the Sienese Republic.[8]

Much of the elaboration of social and ritual activity surrounding the Palio is even more recent. One factor has been the growing role of the Monte dei Paschi bank as financial underwriters of the Palio. While the bank had long given vital support to the festival, its contribution escalated during the twentieth century—including, since World War II, full coverage of the enormous costs of replacing the costumes every twenty-five years.

Another basic factor has been the florescence of the contrade in the post-World War II period. Recent decades have seen the revival or development of the contrada recreational societies, a vast expansion of associational activity (both related to the Palio and extending beyond it), and the creation of new ritual and symbolic forms underlining contrada identity (such as the contrada baptism). This revitalization is in large part a response to changes in residential patterns that have led to a separation between residence and contrada membership. The contrade have shown extraordinary resilience and inventiveness in the face of this challenge, themselves changing in the process and at the same time accelerating the pace of cultural creativity in the Palio.

How, then, is the Palio to be understood—what theoretical approaches can be enlisted in its analysis? At the outset, it might appear to be a game, a form of play.[9] While it clearly conforms to many of the characteristics set forth in theories of play, a number of problems confront this approach. For one thing, the native view of the Palio rejects any definition of it as sport; for the Sienese the Palio is intensely serious, at the center of "real life" and not something apart from it, more akin to war than to play. Moreover, it would be perilous to apply conventional notions of sport to the Palio. Indeed, the case of the Palio shows just how culturally specific such concepts as "sportsmanship" and "fair play" are—concepts that have entered into sociological analysis as well as into common discourse in the Anglophone world. "In the Palio," the Sienese say, "it's not the best man who wins; the man who wins is the one who comes in first."[10] If the Palio is to be analyzed as a game, it must be in terms of the principles that actually guide it, not those taken from other cultural systems.

Game analysis, however, may be useful if one takes "game" to mean a structure of action that can accommodate a wide range of cultural content. From this viewpoint, a game may be defined as a bounded competition among designated participants, which is governed by rules—"bounded" meaning that there is a separation between the game itself and that which occurs outside it. The anthropologist F. G. Bailey takes the concept further by using the game as a model for a universal theory of politics.[11] Bailey defines the game (including the game of politics) as action governed by a set of rules: rules about prizes, personnel, leadership, teams, competition, and control; there are normative rules for regulating the competition, and pragmatic rules (tactics) for winning.[12] According to these criteria, the Palio has all the elements of a game. Furthermore, it lends itself to a game analysis of politics. That is, not only can the politics internal to the Palio be unraveled along the lines of game strategy, but the Palio might also be seen as a replication of some political "game" beyond it. Thus, it has sometimes been compared with the forms of competition the Sienese Republic engaged in with other city-states.[13] Whether one treats the Palio as the game itself or thinks of it as modeled after a larger political game, what game analysis yields is the rules of the game, both codified and implicit—the rules for playing, the rules for winning, even the rules for "cheating." One benefit of this approach to the Palio is that it can specify precisely how the competition is ordered and rational, and thus dispel the gross misunderstanding inherent in such depictions of the Palio as "the world's wackiest horse race" or "the world's crookedest horse race."

The limits of game analysis, however, are precisely in the boundedness of the game, which presents the problem of relating the game to the world outside it. Above all, there is the problem of accounting for the game itself. We know how the Palio is "played" but not why it is played in the first place, what is at stake in it, or what forces external to it might be involved in its formation or persistence. In short, what is the game all about?

A second approach to the Palio might be to view it as ritual. Ritual, for present purposes, can be defined as patterned and repetitive, noninstrumental behavior, which entails the indirect communication of socially meaningful messages. The Palio is clearly surrounded by ritual. The elaborate procession preceding the race, the blessing of the horses and jockeys, the contrada feasts and parades, the cycle of ceremonies that make up each Palio—all are ritual performances; and ritual marks out all the phases of contrada life, indeed gives the contrade their identity. Whether the race itself can be thought of as ritual is less clear, since it is never repeated in precisely the same way. Yet the race is only a moment in a much larger enactment, which unquestionably has a large ritual component.

A number of anthropologists have looked at the Palio as ritual, emphasizing the messages communicated by it, or as a symbolic enactment in a more comprehensive sense. One analysis, for example, treats the Palio as a metaphor, containing many levels of implicit meanings that in their totality constitute the Sienese "world view."[14] Another, taking its departure from the work of Clifford Geertz and James Peacock, sees the Palio as a cultural performance, a ritualized public activity in which the Sienese demonstrate their identity to themselves and to others.[15] The Palio is a "rite of traditionalization," which symbolically reproduces the Sienese Republic and thereby defines Siena as a separate cultural community in continuity with its past.

Such analyses allow one to inquire into the social meanings that are dramatized in the ritual performance, exposing the relationship of the symbolism in the Palio to a social structure and the commonly held values underlined by the performance. Their limitation, however, is that they cannot account for the performance or the social structure enacting it or represented by it. If, to paraphrase Geertz, the Palio is a story the Sienese like to tell themselves about themselves, that story cannot be read as the history of the Palio. It is an ideological construction of the past, a mixture of history and myth, and it is the analyst's job to untangle the mixture: to understand why people invented their story and what its relationship is to what happened in their history. The symbolic representations in the Palio emphasize continuities with the medieval Republic—the autonomy, civic virtues, and military power of the city-state. Yet the history of the Palio-contrada complex places it in the period of the defeat of the Republic and Siena's incorporation into a Tuscan territorial state. To account for this complex as more than cultural construction demands going beyond the native view (the story they tell), to try to specify the conditions under which it emerged and developed.

The Palio is a game; but it is more than that. It is ritual, but it is more than that too. It is also politics, as several of its features suggest: the contrade are quasi-political bodies in their form and functioning; the idiom of Palio and contrada has a political cast, employing a language of warfare, alliance, and diplomacy; the running of the race itself is managed through relationships and maneuvers that resemble larger politics. But what kind of political phenomenon is the Palio-contrada complex? The concept of politics, in the broadest sense, has to do with who gets what. An operational definition might be the organization of power in a society and action within that organization, which can be translated into access to resources.[16] By this token, the contrade would not be considered political entities, for there are hardly any issues of power or resources in the larger society that are negotiated through the contrade.[17] The contrade jealously guard their apolitical stance, excluding any involvement in party politics as divisive. They play no role in economic activities beyond those concerning the contrade as such, nor do they appear to have had greater political or economic significance in the past. As for the Palio, the Sienese are united in their defense of it from any taint of politicization or commercialization, that is, the intrusion of political or economic interests not intrinsic to the Palio itself.[18]

The Palio-contrada complex, however, can be analyzed as a political phenomenon in this broad sense, if one shifts the focus from the cultural complex to the context in which it is embedded. If, as I have argued, it is the contrada structure that defines the Palio, the beginning point for analysis needs to be that structure, understood in its relationship to a larger society and polity. The Sienese contrade are territorial divisions within higher levels of organization—city, commune, region, state (the particular organization varying by historical period). Analogous territorial divisions existed in Siena before the totemic contrade, and they occur in towns and cities throughout central Italy. In comparison with other such divisions, the modern contrade of Siena are marked by an unusually high degree of corporateness, internal organization, and functionality. Like some, but not all, analogous territorial divisions in the region, the Sienese contrade contain the full range of social and economic differentiation within the city. Thus, they crosscut the lines of strategic class interests, the lines of potential class alliances. The question might then be posed: what are the implications of territorial divisions of this kind, and how might these have shaped their historical development? In posing the question in this way, the problem of Siena—and what is unique to Siena—is placed in a larger framework of processes common to the region as a whole.

I would propose three lines of inquiry in pursuing this question. First, one needs to look at the relationship between territorial divisions and the overarching units—especially the commune, which has long continuity as the strategic unit of local government in central Italy, and the larger systems that challenged or incorporated it. I would suggest that strong, corporate territorial divisions existed historically in inverse relationship to the strength of the commune. In part, this is a question of the allocation of functions to units at different levels, but it may also be a measure of a strategy of control, as external powers sought allies in their efforts to weaken the commune. During the heyday of the Sienese Republic, the commune absorbed most functions to itself, using component units as means of administering its own policies. Territorial divisions within the city during this period are best described as neighborhoods, neither bounded nor corporate, and with limited functions.[19] Then, the defeat of Siena reduced the commune to an administrative arm of the territorial state that Cosimo I was constructing. It is precisely in this context that the modern contrade emerged and subsequently developed corporate form and internal structure.

The transformation of the festival of August reveals a political struggle played out on a ritual stage. The festival, which had served to underline the power and legitimacy of the commune, had its political component dismantled. Not only did Siena lose this demonstration of the supremacy of the Republic, but the commune was now obliged to perform a ritual of submission to the Medici state, at the cathedral of Florence on the day of its patron St. John; at least in the beginning, legend has it, this was done in a manner that expressed the involuntary nature of Sienese participation.[20] At the same time, the contrade moved to the center of Sienese public ritual, representing both local tradition (a memory of autonomy, but in a harmless form) and Siena's acceptance—indeed, glorification—of the new order. As the festival role of the contrade grew, fostered both by the local authorities and the Medici princes, so also did the structure of the contrade, enabling them to expand their nonfestival functions and eventually absorbing other territorial units that had coexisted with or overlapped them.[21]

A second line of inquiry would focus on the multiclass composition of territorial divisions like the contrade, and pursue the hypothesis that the contrade were encouraged for their role as a counterforce against class-based alliances. While the contrade were always vigorous popular associations, the upper-class members retained dominance in them and a spirit of *interclassismo* prevailed. At the same time, the contrada structure as a whole created a seventeen-way division of class interests. The question of whether this structure actually impeded class action that might otherwise have occurred may not be answerable. However, virtually every government of Siena, from the Medici on, was supportive of the contrade, seeing them not only as a uniquely Sienese tradition but also as a stabilizing force, and the local "protectors" who bestowed their patronage on the contrade clearly had a stake in this structure.

Finally, there is a line of inquiry that asks about Siena's uniqueness within central Italy: why is it only in Siena that there is an enduring structure of strong, corporate, territorial divisions, and why is it only in Siena (and in a very few other special cases) that the competitive festival has been maintained continuously for over three centuries? A clue may lie in an institution that makes Siena unique among towns of its size in another way: its status as the seat of the Monte dei Paschi, one of the largest banks in Italy and the world. Founded in 1472, its rise linked to the emerging territorial states and with major international operations since the seventeenth century, the Monte dei Paschi always retained its base in the city of Siena and cultivated a public image inextricably woven with the image of Siena and the prime symbol of Siena, the Palio. It was the wealth of the bank that underwrote the costs of the Palio, indirectly at first through the upper-class protectors of the contrade and officials of the festival, and later directly, through grants to the commune and the contrade. The relationship between the bank and the city and its festival is complex and reciprocal. The Palio served in the forging of Monte dei Paschi's expansion: an event that attracted the most stellar visitors, it brought advantageous connections that translated into good business for the bank, which in turn guaranteed the perpetuation of the Palio and the contrade on which it rested. Since the Unification, the close identification of Monte dei Paschi with Siena has enabled it to operate on terms that have benefited both the bank and the city. The Palio is the linchpin of that identification.

The Palio, therefore, is game, ritual, politics, and more—for this paper has only touched upon the many dimensions of this remarkable complex. To understand it adequately requires multiple approaches. It is useful, as we have seen, to analyze it in terms of how the game is played; in terms of what its performance communicates symbolically; in terms of the politics internal to the Palio. But something can be learned also from considering the larger political and economic implications of the Palio and of the contrada structure that underlies it. That approach may allow us to move beyond speculation over what the Palio is, and begin to ask why—why Palio and contrade developed, why they persisted, and why in Siena.

Notes

1. The description of the contemporary Palio is based on observations in the course of several field trips between 1980 and 1985, on newspaper accounts, and on sources in the voluminous but extremely uneven literature on the Palio. The most comprehensive description of the present-day Palio is Alessandro Falassi, "Siena's Festival," in A. Falassi and G. Catoni, *Palio* (Milan: Electa, 1983), 9–88, which expands on and updates Alan Dundes and Alessandro Falassi, *La Terra in Piazza* (Berkeley: University of California Press, 1975). Other useful sources for the twentieth-century Palio are: Virgilio Grassi, *Le contrade di Siena e le loro feste* (Siena: U. Periccioli, 1972); Dario Neri, "The Palio in its Contemporary Form," in G. Cecchini and D. Neri, *The Palio of Siena* (Siena: Monte dei Paschi, 1958); Giulio Pepi, *Le contrade e il Palio* (Siena: La Diana, 1967); Luca Luchini, *Il Palio nel XX secolo* (Siena: Tipografia Senese, 1985); Arrigo Pecchioli, ed., *Il Palio di Siena* (Rome: Editalia, 1974); and Gerardo Righi Parenti, *L'anima del Palio di Siena* (Pisa: Giardini, 1979). On the history of the Palio, the standard work is Giovanni Cecchini, "Palio and Contrade: Historical Evolution," in G. Cecchini and D. Neri, *The Palio of Siena,* but other basic sources include: William Heywood, *Palio and Ponte* (New York: Hacker Art Books, 1969, orig. 1904); Giuseppe Zazzeroni, *Le contrade di Siena negli spettacoli anteriori al Palio* (Siena: Tipografia Combattenti, 1931); Agostino Provedi, *Relazione delle pubbliche feste* . . . (Siena: Bindi, 1791); Riccardo Brogi,*Il Palio di Siena* (Siena: Torrini, 1894); and A. Rondini, *Il Palio di Siena* (Florence: Società Editrice Toscana, 1932).

2. The literature on the contrade obviously overlaps that on the Palio, but additional important works specifically on the contrade and their history include: Guilano Catoni, "Factious Harmony," in A. Falassi and G. Catoni, *Palio,* 225–72 (the most authoritative recent study); Virgilio Grassi, "Le Contrade," *La Balzana* 3–7 (1929–33); V. Grassi, *I confini delle Contrade secondo il bando di Violante Beatrice di Baviera* (Siena: Tipografia Ex-Cooperativa, 1950); Flaminio Rossi, *Le Contrade della Città di Siena* (Bologna: Forni, 1981, orig. 1839–52); Alessandro Lisini, "Notizie su le Contrade di Siena," *Miscellanea Storica Senese* 4 (1896): 67–78, 85–88; Giuseppe Zazzeroni, *Le Contrade di Siena secondo il cronista Gio. Antonio Pecci* (Siena: Tipografia Ex Combattenti, 1929), incorporating the full text of Pecci, *Relazione distinta delle quarantadue contrade* (1723); Giuseppe Valsecchi, *Le Contrade di Siena* (Siena: Turbanti, 1928); Alberto Comucci, *Le Contrade di Siena e la loro autonomia* (Siena: Tipografia Ex Combattenti, 1938); Alberto Tailetti, *Aneddoti contradaioli* (Rome: Olimpia, 1967); Sandro Rossi and Augusto Mattioli, *Ci si vede in società* (Siena: Nuovo Corriere Senese, 1978). There is also a rich literature of contrada publications dealing with their own histories and traditions as well as Palio lore in general.

3. In arriving at this overview I have drawn selectively on the large historical literature on the Palio, which contains a number of controversies. With regard to the important question of the origin of the contrade, I have found it useful to define the modern totemically marked contrade as distinctive entities whose relationship to other local units cannot be assumed but remains an open question, particularly

their relationship to the smaller divisions identified with place-names that were linked to military companies under the Republic and that appear in documents as late as 1723. Clearly, these units overlapped in reality, and the distinctions between them were never sharply drawn. However, my reading of the evidence suggests that the two kinds of units coexisted during the sixteenth and seventeenth centuries and that the level of organization represented by the totemic contrade superseded the other, as opposed to the common explanation that "the forty-two contrade became further and further reduced in number until by 1729 there were only seventeen" (Dundes and Falassi, *La Terra in Piazza*, 15).

4. A number of writers refer to a document of 1513 as evidence of the first appearance of all seventeen modern contrade. However, Catoni identifies three notaries who appear in the document and the years each one practiced (Catoni, "Factious Harmony," 259). According to this calculation, the date of the document could not be earlier than the 1530s. The seventeen, identified by their animal names, are thoroughly described in well-documented accounts of a bullfight of 1546 (Zazzeroni, *Le Contrade . . . negli spettacoli anterior . . .* , 1931; A. Lisini, "Una Caccia di Tori in Siena nel 1546," *La Diana* 2 [1927]: 90–102).

5. In general, before 1650 documents dealing with administrative matters refer to the smaller units identified by place-names, while the totemic names occur in festival contexts. After that time, the modern contrada names appear almost exclusively in all contexts.

6. This famous governess of Siena was Violante Beatrice of Bavaria, daughter-in-law of the Medici grandduke.

7. Catoni sees the changes of the nineteenth century as part of a process whereby a new Sienese ruling class, guided by the rationalistic, utilitarian, and bourgeois ideology of the period, attempted to sterilize the Palio; for him, the contrade represented a "plebeian" culture that was a focus of local resistance to integration into the national and popular culture advocated by the Tuscan moderates (Catoni, "Factious Harmony," 249–54). Catoni's very useful and provocative analysis understates, however, the ideological differences within the Sienese upper class, as well as the extent to which upper-class interests were allied with the contrade.

8. In Falassi's summary of the evidence on the transformation in the costumes over the history of the Palio, he identifies 1839 as a significant time marker—when the Palio pageant began "to celebrate itself and its own origins." The pageant of 1829 introduced the uniform "medieval" costuming, and when the costumes were redesigned for the extraordinary Palio of 1904, the corteo included representations of Republican Siena treated as a mythical golden age. (Falassi, "Siena's Festival," 68.)

9. For purposes of this discussion, "game" and "play" are treated as roughly synonymous, but they actually address different kinds of interests: "play" focuses on the behavior and motives of actors, while the notion of "game" concerns the structure of their interaction. The two phrasings lead in different theoretical directions.

10. This quotation, a paraphrasing of a Sienese saying, is from the mayor of Siena as recorded in the 1972 Granada Television film "The She-Wolf and the Caterpillar."

11. F. G. Bailey, *Stratagems and Spoils* (Oxford: Basil Blackwell, 1969).

12. Ibid., 1, 19–20.

13. Dundes and Falassi, *La Terra in Piazza*, 42, 90 and *passim*.

14. Ibid., 185–240.

15. Alice Pomponio Logan, "The Palio of Siena: Performance and Process," *Urban Anthropology* 7 (1978): 45–65.

16. This definition borrows Morton Fried's use of the criterion of differential access to strategic resources as the defining mark of stratified societies, as opposed to those societies in which status does not carry preferential access to resources, Morton H. Fried (*The Evolution of Political Society,* [New York: Random House, 1967]). It is, therefore, a definition limited essentially to politics within state societies.

17. There are indications, however, that the contrade are moving into limited arenas of political activity in their efforts to defend the interests of the contrada as a whole, for example in the involvement of some contrade in the commune's planning for urban redevelopment.

18. The definition of what is intrinsic to the Palio is, of course, a matter of debate. In general, the Sienese are unified in their objective, and new developments and proposals are measured against the criterion of their effect upon the integrity of the festival.

19. The major debate on the status and function of these "contrade" under the Republic concerns their relationship to the military companies. The points that appear to be clear are that the military companies were drawn from neighborhoods, i.e., were territorially based, and that military companies and contrade were formally distinct. That the contrade were not clearly bounded or corporate is evident from such definitions as that given in an early fourteenth-century statute, which stated that "a person's contrada" is a distance of two hundred feet from his house (William M. Bowsky, "The Anatomy of Rebellion in Fourteenth-Century Siena," in Lauro Martines, ed., *Violence and Civil Disorder in Italian Cities, 1200–1500* [Berkeley: University of California Press, 1972], 234–35).

20. The story is that when the Sienese representative made the required offering of wax at the cathedral of Florence, he added (loudly) to the formula of homage, "Siena per forza!" (Niccolo Piccolomini, *Il Monte dei Paschi di Siena e le aziende in esso riunite,* [Siena: Tip. Sordomuti Di L. Lazzeri, 1891], 2 : 15).

21. This discussion is indebted to Richard Trexler's analysis of the transformation of public festivals in Florence during the sixteenth century, which he sees in terms of a process whereby the Medici enlisted marginal social groups in their task of reorienting the major urban festivals so as to undermine their civic character (Richard C. Trexler, *Public Life in Renaissance Florence* [New York: Academic Press, 1980], 491–547).

10

"Thou Idol Ceremony": Elizabeth I, *The Henriad,* and the Rites of the English Monarchy

Richard C. McCoy

Something happened at the coronation of Elizabeth I, something potentially scandalous that subverted the rite's sacrosanctity and symbolic hierarchy. For centuries, the coronation had been a virtual sacrament as well as a "clerical monopoly" administered by bishops.[1] Traditionally, the highest-ranking primate presided over the solemn oath, the anointment, and the investiture, and the monarch's inaugural subordination to a higher power was symbolized by his literal prostration at various points in the service. The coronation ordo of Richard III and Henry VII prescribes that the king shall lie "groveling afore the high aulter" before the administration of the oath and the unction, and that the king and his queen "wᵗ a great devocion receive the sacrament" at the subsequent Mass.[2]

From the beginning of her reign, Elizabeth displayed little reverence toward the clergy or their solemnities. She excluded the most staunchly Catholic primates such as Heath and Bonner from the coronation service; the timely death of Cardinal Pole, archbishop of Canterbury, relieved her of the need to eliminate him as well. She retained the lower-ranking bishop of Carlisle, Owen Oglethorpe, to crown and anoint her, but she insisted on making Protestant changes in the ensuing Mass. The bishop balked at such changes several weeks before the coronation. According to Il Schifanoya, an Italian resident in London, "on Christmas day, the Bishop of Carlisle sang high mass, and her Majesty sent to tell him that he was not to elevate the host; to which the good Bishop replied that thus he had learnt the mass, and that she must pardon him as he could not do otherwise."[3] Offended by his intransigence, Elizabeth walked out after the reading of the gospel, replacing Oglethorpe at the next day's service with a more pliant royal chaplain.

How then did Elizabeth conduct herself at her coronation? There are hints in the records of scandalous irregularities, but these accounts are so elliptical and inconsistent that certainty is impossible.[4] The only official version is an unusually brief and fragmentary paragraph in the archives of the College of Arms that is much less detailed than the herald's earlier accounts of coronation proceedings. Its cryptic summary may reflect an effort to play down if not cover up a troublesome inaugural occasion. There are also two unofficial versions of the event: a letter from a Mantuan resident, Il Schifanoya, and a report by an anonymous English eyewitness. The herald's account and the letter from Il Schifanoya agree on one significant alteration. Each indicates that, while Bishop Oglethorpe crowned and anointed the queen, the Mass was celebrated by the Dean of the Chapel Royal, George Carew, a man who could be trusted to refrain from elevating the host. Faced with the prospect of such a sacrilegious alteration, several Catholic dignitaries boycotted the service, including, apparently, Il Schifanoya; his version is filled with errors and gives the impression of being second-hand.

The anonymous eyewitness account raises an even more scandalous possibility. In this version, the bishop celebrated the Mass, presumably elevating the host as he said he would. The report says that "her Grace retorned unto her Closset hearing the Consecration of the Mass." Similarly, the herald's proclamation notes the queen's withdrawal during the Mass "to her traverse," a curtained pew or closet. Finally, a heraldic drawing used for planning the service locates a traverse behind the high altar in St. Edward's chapel, but the instructions indicate that she was to go there only "after the ceremonyes and Service [were] doon" (see fig. 1). Evidently, the queen withdrew to a traverse midway through the Mass, where she abstained from receiving communion and hid herself from sight for the duration of the service. The Spanish ambassador had refused to attend a church service that omitted the elevation; now he had a new scandal to report to Philip II:

> By last post I wrote your Majesty that I had been told that the Queen took the holy sacrament *'sub utraque specie'* on the day of the coronation, but was all nonsense. She did not take it at all.[5]

These tantalizing clues and enigmas have inspired considerable speculation, prompting some historians to conclude that Elizabeth impulsively walked out on her own coronation. One even accused her of committing "a striking breach of the ritual of centuries."[6] Others doubt that such behavior would excite so little remark. H. A. Wilson proposes the less dramatic possibility of a second traverse on the altar to which she withdrew deliberately rather than impulsively.[7] Tudor monarchs often heard

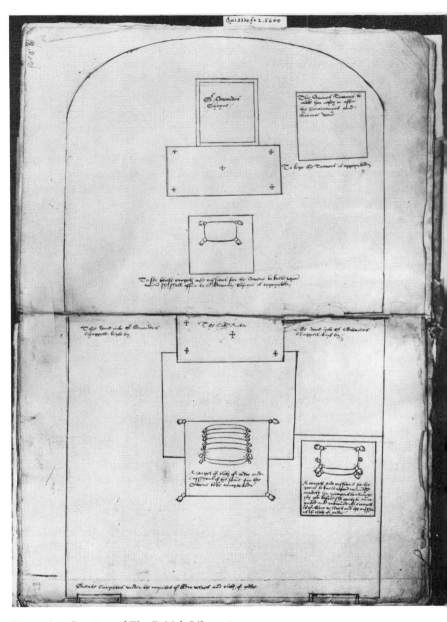

Figure 1. *(Courtesy of The British Library.)*

Mass from the privacy of a curtained pew, a practice going back at least to Edward's coronation.[8] Moreover, a memorandum prepared before the coronation anticipates that "her Matie in her closett may use the Masse without lyfting up above the Host according to the Ancient customs."[9] Nevertheless, even if Elizabeth's withdrawal to her traverse were decorously deliberate, her treatment of the bishop and her abstention from communion still suggest a lapse from the "great devocion" toward the "sacrament" enjoined by the coronation ordo of her predecessors. Indeed her diminished regard for the entire sacred rite is manifest in her subsequent remarks to the French Ambassador, Fénélon. Legalism rather than piety prompts her to assure him that "she had been crowned and anointed according to the ceremonies of the Catholic church, and by Catholic bishops, without, however, attending the mass."[10] Less flippant than the witticism attributed to Henri IV that Paris was worth a Mass, Elizabeth's remark still reflects the same *politique* spirit of calculating pragmatism.

The real historical significance of Elizabeth's coronation finally has little to do with the actual events or the rumors surrounding it. Since the records are scanty and contradictory, the facts can never be determined with any certainty; Elizabeth's coronation is one of those historic occasions that recedes from view as one learns more about it. Many religious sectarians on both sides were certainly scandalized: Catholics were shocked by her liturgical alterations and her treatment of Bishop Oglethorpe, while the Geneva exiles were distressed by her employment of a Catholic bishop and the traditional Latin rite.[11] Nevertheless, none of these scandals or controversies stirred up much excitement. The most extraordinary features of Elizabeth's coronation were its obscurity and ultimate irrelevance. The event's real historical significance consists in the deliberate subordination of the church service to the civic progress the day before.

The civic progress from the Tower to Westminster was a secular procession, traditionally a mere preliminary to the coronation the next day. The progress included popular entertainments and allegorical pageants sponsored by the city guilds, and, at various points along the way, the monarch and his entourage would stop for an exchange of gifts and formal tributes. The progress allowed the London populace their first glimpse of the new monarch as well as an opportunity for stylized dialogue. The citizens may have written their own speeches that promoted their own agenda, but the queen probably previewed them. Nevertheless, this carefully controlled dialogue could generate feelings of spontaneity and "intimate give-and-take."[12] The civic progress was, in Eric Hobsbawm's suggestive phrase, an "invented tradition."[13] Its speeches and spectacles were newly and variously devised for each reign, addressing contemporary political concerns. During Elizabeth's progress, the pageant at the Little Conduit depicted the "decayed common weale" of the previous regime and the "florishing commonweale" expected from her benign rule.[14]

In comparing these two events, a distinction made by some anthropologists is useful. The civic progress was a ceremony, secular and popular, whose pageants were freshly improvised and performed in London's streets and civic spaces; while still formal and "ceremonious," its procedures were varied, open, and genuinely dramatic. By contrast, the coronation was a ritual, sacred and hierarchical, and its procedures were fixed and mystical; these rites were performed within the confines of Westminster Abbey and they directly invoked God's authority.[15] According to Percy Schramm, the coronation was paradoxically jeopardized by its privileged status and aura of ritual mystery:

> only an illustrious and select circle could get near it, and so it became a question whether it would not lose its central position and become a mere episode in a long series of festivities.

The civic progress, on the other hand, was more of a crowd-pleaser because of its greater visibility and malleable theatricality. It included

> manifestations of royal power that could be abandoned, changed, or devised anew. After the Middle Ages, the danger threatening the coronation was precisely that it might be degraded into a pageant of this sort.[16]

The danger hardly bothered Elizabeth, who made the civic progress the main event, one that completely overshadowed the sacred ritual. She clearly appreciated the political value of secular pageantry and sought to exploit it in several ways. First, she helped to subsidize the civic progress by loaning costumes from the Revels Office, as David Bergeron discovered.[17] Secondly, she deployed her considerable skills as an actress to sustain a dazzling performance in which she won the hearts of her people. A commemorative tract records a variety of inspired gestures, such as clasping the English Bible to her breast, accepting humble "nose gaies" from "poore womens hands," and earnestly attending to all the exhortations addressed to her.[18] Her performance enacted a drama of reciprocity and affection in which the queen

> was of the people received merveylous entierly, as appeared by thassemblie, prayers, wishes, welcomminges, cryes, tender woordes, and all other signes, which argue a wonderfull earnest love of most obedient subiects towarde theyr soveraygne. And on thother syde her grace by holding up her handes, and merie countenaunce to such as stoode farre of, and most tender and gentle language to those that stode

nigh to her grace, did declare her selfe no lesse thankefullye to receive her people's good wille, than they lovingly offred it unto her.[19]

The essentially theatrical nature of these ceremonies is manifest in the claim that they transformed London into "a stage wherin was shewed the wonderfull spectacle, of a noble hearted princess toward her most loving people, and the peoples excading comfort in beholding so worthy a soveraign."[20] Finally, and most significantly, the government capitalized on the success of this performance by authorizing the prompt publication of the tract itself. *The Quenes Maiesties Passage through the Citie of London to Westminster the Day before her Coronacion* was an unprecedented publication that made the event accessible to an even larger audience and preserved its glorious memory for all time (see fig. 2). Thus, the published record reinforced the primacy of the civic progress by shifting the focus entirely from the sacred rite to the secular pageant.[21]

The visual records are similarly distorted. There is one drawing of the procession to the church and it is clearly intended as a planning device. There are three heraldic drawings of the civic progress.[22] One of these is somewhat crudely and hastily drawn and was also probably intended for planning purposes: the queen's litter is simply indicated by a rectangle and the words, "The Queens most excellent majesty." The archbishops of Canterbury and York are included, despite the death of the first and the exclusion of the second, but there are x's and lines drawn beneath them, which probably indicate their absence and the need to replace them with those next in line, the Norroy and Clarenceux Kings of Arms (see fig. 3). In the other two drawings, Elizabeth's problems with her bishops are blithely ignored, and the two primates are shown without marks in the proper places. The drawing of the church procession shows the "bishops in their pontificalibus" with miters and crosiers; in the civic progress, they are arrayed in respectably Protestant academic caps and gowns (see fig. 4). The later drawings pay more attention to ornament and dress: the queen is portrayed in her litter surrounded by a throng of noble and courtly attendants and the effect is one of sumptuous display (see fig. 5). The drawings had a practical, prescriptive purpose since they depicted the order of precedence to be observed when "Procydyng to ye parlement or coronacion," but they also serve the same commemorative function as *The Quenes Maiesties Passage*.[23] They preserve an image of social harmony, while suppressing evidence of religious difficulties.[24]

The drawings of the civic progress and *The Quenes Maiesties Passage* present the opening scenes of an enormously successful and long-running stageshow. The show lasted for most of her reign, developing into the nearly idolatrous "cult of Elizabeth."[25] Yet for all its devotional fervor, the cult was a self-consciously theatrical enterprise in which secular cere-

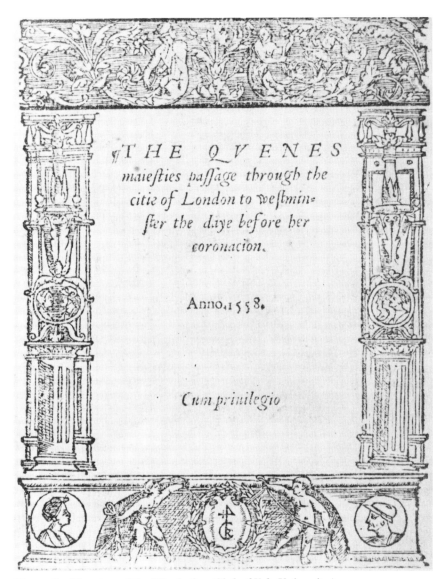

THE QVENES
maiesties passage through the
citie of London to westmin=
ster the daye before her
coronacion.

Anno.1558.

Cum priuilegio

Figure 2. *(Courtesy of the Elizabethan Club of Yale University.)*

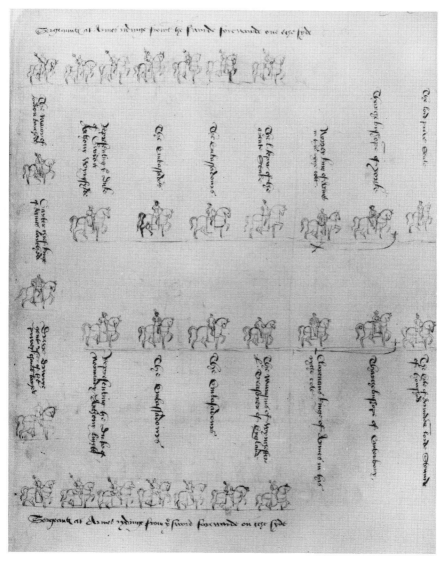

Figure 3. *(Courtesy of The College of Arms, London.)*

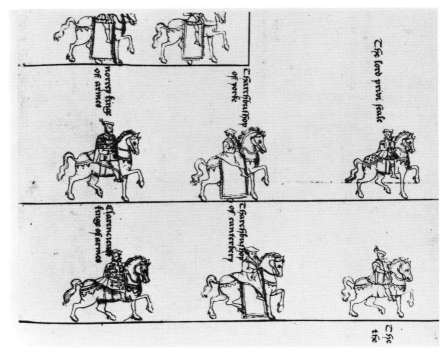

Figure 4. *(Courtesy of The College of Arms, London.)*

mony and printed propaganda affirmed royal authority more effectively than sacred ritual. The Accession Day Tilts, like the civic progress, were "invented traditions," and their adaptations of Catholic symbolism and ritual were, as Stephen Greenblatt explains, stylized improvisations, designed to exploit the residual powers of the old forms and customs. Sir Henry Lee and other courtiers staged elaborate pageants in which altars and candles, hermits at their beads, and hymns in praise of virginity became the theatrical props of temporal power. According to Greenblatt, these stylized ceremonies exemplify

> two of the characteristic operations of improvisation: displacement and absorption. By displacement I mean the process whereby a prior symbolic structure is compelled to coexist with other centers of attention that do not necessarily conflict with the original structure but are not swept up in its gravitational pull; indeed, as here, the sacred may find itself serving as an adornment, a backdrop, an occasion for a quite secular phenomenon. By absorption I mean the process whereby a symbolic structure is taken into the ego so completely that it ceases to exist as an external phenomenon; in the Accession Day ceremony, instead of the secular prince humbling herself before the sacred, the

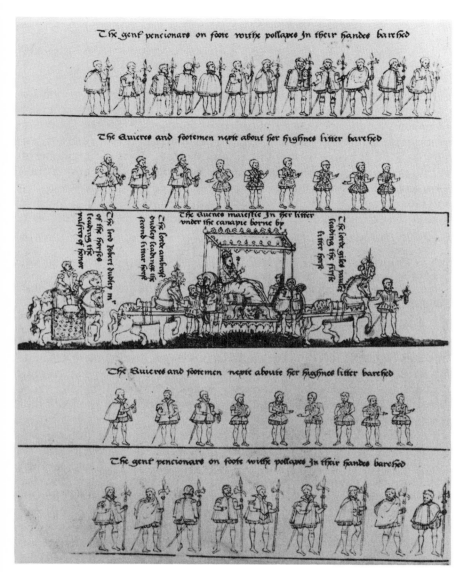

The genf pencionars on foote withe pollares In their handes bareshed

The Quieres and footemen nexte about her highnes litter bareshed

The lord Robert dudley mr
of the horsse
leadeyng the
palfrey of honor

The lorde chamberlayn
oveley leadeng the
seconde litter horse

The Quenes maiestie In her litter
vnder the canapie borne by

The lorde giles pawlet
leadeing the fyrste
litter horse

The Quieres and footemen nexte aboute her highnes litter bareshed

The genf pencionars on foote withe pollares In their handes bareshed

Figure 5. *(Courtesy of The College of Arms, London.)*

sacred seems only to enhance the ruler's identity, to express her power.[26]

At her coronation Elizabeth resisted "humbling herself before the sacred" either by replacing the celebrant of the Mass or by absenting herself completely, and she focused all attention on herself by the shows of secular pageantry. The increasingly elaborate celebrations of her Accession Day, the principal feast of the cult of Elizabeth, dates the beginning of her reign from her accession and reduces the coronation to a superfluous formality.[27] Later in her reign, the queen timed her return from her summer progresses partly to coincide with her Accession Day, and her formal reentry into London reenacted the stately scenes of her first civic progress:

> The Queen came by night with the Master of the Horse leading her palfrey by the bridle and a great noble carrying the sword. Ambassadors were invited to be present, and the Lord Mayor and citizens were called upon to don their rich gowns and chains and give a torch light welcome[28]

The Accession Day Tilt itself was celebrated with increasingly elaborate tilts and pageants recalling the traditional feast and tournament that followed the coronation. Thus, the Accession Day festivities reenacted only the secular ceremonies of her reign's beginning, while displacing them from their original occasion; in the meantime, the sacred rite sunk still further into oblivion.

Ceremonial pragmatism was an essential technique in the Tudors' consolidation of their power. Nevertheless, the secularization of ceremony entailed losses as well as gains. The "divinity [that] doth hedge a king" was inevitably diminished by the desacralization of the rites of majesty, and the dependence of authority on theatrical artifice created problems as well as advantages. In royal pageantry, the alienation effect of ceremonial displacement was offset by the monarch's actual presence, which invested these shows with genuine authority and the aura of sacred ritual. However, when royal pageantry was transposed from the civic or courtly stage to the stages of London's theaters, yet another displacement occurred, removing it still further from its original sacred context. In the theaters, the links to ritual became more attenuated and the effects of displacement more unsettling. In fact, dramatic representation occasionally highlighted contradictions of form and function at the heart of ceremonial improvisation.

Royal ceremony in practice served purposes that were potentially incompatible, because it made the sovereign visible to men at the same time that it distanced him. Jonathan Goldberg emphasizes the contradictions of such performances: "what the sovereign displays in public [is] his own unobservability, observed in his spectacles."[29] In Goldberg's view, royal pageantry retains an aura of ritual mystery and limited accessibility. On its stage, the monarch is inscrutable, standing "not as an actor but as a spectacle . . . distinguished . . . by his penetrating glance, and by his invisibility and his obscurity."[30] By contrast, the theater provided a place

> where the audience saw kings treading the stage, where the public assembled to see itself. The theater, that tragic scaffold, was a place for self-knowledge precisely because its re-presentation duplicated public life. It is there that Renaissance man went to know himself.[31]

The risk was that, presented on the common stage, the monarch became too visible and too commonplace. A desire to prevent this overexposure and demystification of majesty was probably a factor in those commands forbidding "that princes should be played on the stage in their lifetime."[32]

The dangers of overexposure became apparent even in plays that celebrated a monarch's rule. As nostalgia for the good old days of good Queen Bess flourished under James, several plays reenacted the pageantry and events of Tudor history. The implicitly critical contrast between the two regimes proved less disturbing to some than the staging of royal pageantry in a public theater. In his description of *Henry VIII,* Sir Henry Wotton complained that the

> many extraordinary circumstances of pomp and majesty . . . the knights of the Order with their Georges and Garter, the Guards with their embroidered coats and the like [were] sufficient in truth within a while to make greatness very familiar, if not ridiculous.[33]

Wotton's description focuses on the splendid costumes and insignia of the royal retinue. Many of these outfits were undoubtedly obtained through the Revels Office, which frequently gave clothing from the royal wardrobe as payment to the actors' companies. This policy of "translation" made profitable use of outfits no longer "serviceable," some of them passed on because "to moche knowen."[34] Wotton's misgivings suggest some of the troubling consequences of this otherwise perfectly sensible displacement. Within the court, the rites and accoutrements of royal ceremony could inspire awe and sustain distance between subject and sovereign. Translated to the common stage and repeated daily by common players, these ceremonious forms lost their singularity and became "to moche knowen."[35]

These same risks are still more obvious in Thomas Heywood's *If You Know Not Me, You Know Nobody.* The play's first half reenacts the coronation of Mary, whose reign is dominated by murderous bishops and friars, bent on securing their hold on power and doing away with Elizabeth. Their chicanery is defeated by Elizabeth's accession. Following her civic progress, the new queen simply accepts the regalia from her temporal peers, dispensing with the bishops and their rituals. *If You Know Not Me* perpetuates and embellishes many of the myths of Elizabethan propaganda. Its title and title page with its stereotyped engraving of an instantly recognizable personage project an image of a monarch well known to all her subjects and to Englishmen of all ages (see fig. 6). Yet even as Heywood's play perpetuates the cult of Elizabeth, it also reveals some of its problems, particularly in the action of the second half, which features an encounter between Queen Elizabeth, Thomas Gresham, her finance minister, and a comical sidekick named Hobson. Hobson is the epitome of brusque, bourgeois common sense, and, when the queen fails to recognize him, he applies the titular phrase to himself, exclaiming:

> Knowest thou not me Queene? then thou knowest no body.
> Bones a me Queen. I am Hobson . . . I am sure you know me

When she still does not know him, Gresham interjects that "He is a rich substantiall Citizen" and Hobson blurts out:

> Bones a me woman send to borrow money
> Of one you do not know, there's a new trick:
> Your Grace sent to me by a Pursuevant
> And by a Priuie Seale to lend your Highnesse
> An hundred pound: I hearing that my Queene
> Had need of money, and thinking you had known me,
> Would needes vpon the bearer force two hundred.[36]

The queen graciously thanks him and then proceeds to knight Gresham and dedicate the royal exchange.

Amidst the stylized artifice of an actual civic progress, the dialogue between subject and sovereign was carefully controlled. Here, on the public stage, these authoritarian controls and the ceremonial distance between subject and sovereign were partially diminished, despite the efforts of the censors. The inherent vulgarity and levelling tendencies of the public theater were recognized and deplored by an aristocrat like Sir Philip Sidney, who condemned its "mongrel tragi-comedy" for "mingling kings and clowns" and then thrusting in these "clowns by head and shoulders, to play a part in majestical matters with neither decency nor discretion."[37] *If You Know Not Me* confirms Sidney's worst fears: Hobson's presumptuous bluster insists with insulting accuracy on the queen's debts and her dependence on her common subjects. The playwright's treatment of Elizabeth, however positive, is no less impertinent, and one can see why this play would not have been tolerated during her lifetime.

Figure 6. *(Courtesy of The Huntington Library, San Marino, California.)*

As Stephen Orgel says of Jonson's *Every Man Out of His Humor,* the play "overstepped its bounds, making the monarch subject to the whim of the playwright."[38]

There is still another, graver risk attached to the displacement of royal ceremony on to the public stage. This is the "ultimate danger" inherent in all ceremonies, according to the anthropologists Sally Moore and Barbara Meyerhoff:

> the possibility that we will encounter ourselves making up our conception of the world, society, our very selves. We may slip in that fatal perspective of recognizing culture as our construct, arbitrary, conventional, invented by mortals. Ceremonies are paradoxical in this way. Being the most obviously contrived forms of social contact, they epitomize the made-up quality of culture and almost invite notice as such. Yet their very form and purpose is to discourage untrammeled inquiry into such questions.[39]

Shakespeare's later histories, written near the end of Elizabeth's reign, enforce this heightened awareness. Ceremony is a central preoccupation in these plays. Nearly every scene in Shakespeare's *Henriad* undercuts the majesty of royal ceremony in subtle but unsettling ways, exposing its "made-up quality" and the void behind its illusions.[40]

Upon his return to his kingdom, Richard II proclaims his belief in his own sacramental invulnerability with majestic assurance:

> Not all the water in the rough rude sea
> Can wash the balm off from an anointed king
> The breath of worldly men cannot depose
> The deputy elected by the Lord;
> For every man that Bullingbrook hath press'd
> To lift shrewd steel against our golden crown
> God for his Richard hath in heavenly pay
> A glorious angel; then if angels fight,
> Weak men must fall, for heaven still guards the right.[41]

Richard's belief in the sufficiency of sacred unction, the "golden crown," and the divine right of English kingship is swiftly shattered by his abrupt and ignominious defeat. His disillusion is painful and absolute because what had been everything becomes nothing: the regalia, a "hollow crown," and royal ceremony, a macabre farce in death's court (*Richard II.* 3.2.160–70). He bitterly enjoins his rebellious subjects to "throw away respect / Tradition, form, and ceremonious duty" (*Richard II.* 3.2.172–73), but they refuse to obey even this command for their own ulterior motives. First, the rebels require his formal self-deposition, and Richard obliges them, unable to resist the chance for a ceremonial grand finale. Secondly, "tradition, form and ceremonious duty," though insufficient in themselves, are still necessary to the usurper's own accession and rule.

The actual Henry IV "had himself anointed with the sacred oil which Thomas Becket was supposed to have received from the Virgin" in order to enhance his shaky legitimacy, and its "propaganda value" may have been as important to him as the oil's miraculous origins.[42] Shakespeare's Henry IV is more explicitly pragmatic in his manipulation of the rites of royalty. As James Calderwood explains, Henry does not jettison "the panoply of ritual, ceremony, and verbal display with which Richard girded kingship;" instead, he exploits it "with a clear awareness that it is a means and not an end. . . . Bolingbroke's plays of state are directed exclusively to an audience of men, not God."[43] He also uses ceremony to ingratiate himself with the groundlings, while still dazzling them from a distance. Noting how Bullingbrook doffs "his bonnet to an oyster-wench" in "his courtship to the common people," Richard enviously concedes the effectiveness of these theatrics even as he sneers at their falseness (*Richard II.* 1.4.31 and 24):

> How he did seem to dive into their hearts
> With humble and familiar courtesy,
> What reverence he did throw away on slaves,
> Wooing poor craftsmen with the craft of smiles.
> (*Richard II.* 1.4.25–28)

At the same time that he courts popularity, Bullingbrook tries to preserve royalty's ceremonial mystique. As he later tells Hal:

> Thus did I keep my person fresh and new,
> My presence, like a robe pontifical,
> Ne'er seen but wond'red at, and so my state,
> Seldom but sumptuous, show'd like a feast,
> And wan by rareness such solemnity.
> (*1 Henry IV.* 3.2.55–59)

Henry realizes the dangers of overexposure: the royal presence like the robes of state can become "to moche knowen."

Henry's public performances closely resemble Elizabeth's civic theatricals. With both rulers, the same illusion of warmth and spontaneity, of intimate connection with the lowliest "oyster-wench," is conveyed by their passages among the people; during her civic progress, Elizabeth "gentlie receiued presentes offered by base and low personages."[44] Yet the sense of intimate connection is projected from an immense distance, and the monarch usually has the last word in these artfully regulated dialogues. Joseph Porter describes the exchange well when he calls it a "genuine interaction controlled entirely by the king;" in the *Henriad*, Henry's subjects resemble, as Porter says, "those model children who speak when spoken to."[45] A similar interaction occurs at the beginning of Elizabeth's civic progress, when the noise of the crowd drowned out the speech of the official *vox populi*, a small boy deputed to explain the first pageant's meaning. Before she proceeded further, Elizabeth sent a resonant double message ordering "all the other pageants to require the people to be silent for her majestie was disposed to heare all that should be said unto her."[46]

The problem with Henry IV's "plays of state" is that too many of his subjects see through them and through him. Indeed, once he obtains the throne, the aims and the artifice of his ceremonial pretensions become even more obvious. Yet, for all his shrewd cynicism, Henry succumbs to pathetic hypocrisy, making the same accusations against his enemies that Richard made against him. His spokesman chastens the rebels for their "stand against anointed majesty," but Hotspur coldly rebukes such flagrant sanctimony:

> The King is kind, and well we know the King
> Knows at what time to promise, when to pay.
> My father and my uncle and myself
> Did give him that same royalty he wears.
>
> (*1 Henry IV*. 4.3.52–55)

Henry's subjects know him all too well, and their familiarity undermines all his efforts to preserve the mystified distance of "anointed majesty." Indeed, Hotspur explicitly recalls the "covenant" Bullingbrook made in *Richard II* (2.3.50) with those who welcomed him home from exile and pledged to join him in treason. Then he vouched that "All my treasury / Is yet but unfelt thanks, which more enrich'd / Shall be your love and labor's recompense" (*Richard II*. 2.3.60–62). Hotspur subsequently sneers at Henry's claims to sacramental supremacy and insists on his debts and dependence. His claim to "know the King" is a more hostile version of Hobson's impertinent familiarity with Elizabeth in *If You Know Not Me,* but here the reciprocal "covenant" between sovereign and subject leads not to the jocular banter of Hobson or the autocratic stability of Hobbes— but to threats of blackmail and rebellion.

Hal surpasses his father because he places himself beyond all such covenants and all familiarity. He secretly vows to "pay the debt I never promised" and can say to his confederates "I know you all," while no one knows him (*1 Henry IV*. 1.2.209 and 195). Indeed, upon his accession, he uses the ceremonial forms and guises of majesty to thwart knowledge of his character and claims upon his person. Confidently assuming the "new and gorgeous garment, majesty," he assures all that he will "deeply put

the fashion on / And wear it in my heart" (*2 Henry IV.* 5.2.44 and 51–52).
On returning from his coronation, Hal says to Falstaff, "I know thee not
. . . Presume not that I am the thing I was" (*2 Henry IV.* 5.5.56).

Hal's mastery of his sovereign role also derives paradoxically from his
profound skepticism toward its pretensions. That skepticism pervades the
Henriad, but it achieves its sharpest expression in *Henry V.* In that play,
the chorus simultaneously deflates and inflates the illusions of both the
theater and the state, apologizing for the "flat unraised spirits that hath
dar'd / On this unworthy scaffold to bring forth / So great an object"
(*Henry V.* Prologue 9–11) while urging us to "mind true things by what
their mockeries be" (*Henry V.* 4.Cho.53). The second part of *Henry IV*
concludes with Hal's coronation, a solemnity we do not see, but we do
witness an oddly somber mockery of that event when Hal crowns himself
prematurely beside his father's sick bed. The dying king awakens and
bitterly rebukes him: "For now a time is come to mock at form. Harry the
Fift is crown'd! Up, vanity! / Down, royal state!" (*2 Henry IV.* 4.5.118–20).
Here we see another way in which Hal surpasses his father, for he
succumbs to none of majesty's illusions. In *Henry V,* he realizes the
unsettling truth suggested by the chorus: mocking at form is finally redundant, because all forms, no matter how solemn, are mockeries, de-
sacrilized representations of truth and power.

That view receives its clearest expression in Hal's only soliloquy in
Henry V, his desolate address to "thou idol Ceremony" on the eve of
Agincourt:

> What infinite heart's ease
> Must kings neglect, that private men enjoy!
> And what have kings, that privates have not too,
> Save ceremony, save general ceremony?
> And what art thou, thou idol Ceremony?
> What kind of god art thou, that suffer'st more
> Of mortal griefs than do thy worshippers?
> What are thy rents? What are thy comings-in?
> O Ceremony, show me but thy worth!
> What is thy soul of [adoration]?
> Art thou aught else but place, degree, and form,
> Creating awe and fear in other men?
>
> (*Henry V.* 4.1.236–47)

Henry's sumptuously detailed inventory of his regalia dismisses all these
accoutrements as components of a "proud dream" that prevents sleep:

> No, thou proud dream,
> That play'st so subtilly with a king's repose,
> I am a king that find thee; and I know

'Tis not the balm, the sceptre, and the ball,
The sword, the mace, the crown imperial,
The intertissued robe of gold and pearl,
The farced title running 'fore the king,
The throne he sits on, not the tide of pomp
That beats upon the high shore of this world—
No, not all these, thrice-gorgeous ceremony,
Not all these, laid in bed majestical,
Can sleep so soundly as the wretched slave.
                                        (*Henry V.* 4.1.257–68)

Hal exposes an obvious but still disturbing secret of state. The rites of "anointed majesty" have no sacramental efficacy or "soul of adoration," nor are they divinely sanctioned. Up to a point, these sentiments echo the moderate Protestantism of Archbishop Cranmer, who preached at Edward VI's coronation that the

> solemn rites of coronation have their ends and utility, yet neither direct force or necessity: they be good admonitions to put kings in mind of their duty to God, but no increasement of their dignity.[47]

Earlier, Cranmer advised Henry VIII that ceremonies

> ought neither to be rejected, nor yet to be observed with this opinion, that they of themselves make men holy, or that they remit sin . . . not the laws and ceremonies of the church at their first making were devised for that intent . . . but for a common commodity, and for a good order and quietness among your subjects.[48]

However, Hal's speech moves beyond Cranmer's pragmatic traditionalism toward Puritan iconoclasm in its use of the provocative word "idol." Radical Puritans saw ceremony as a form of idolatry, "creating awe and fear in other men" and enslaving them through its mystifications. They deplored what Cranmer endorsed—its subtle capacity to keep subjects in thrall—and they regarded its affirmations of "place, degree, and form" not as a means to "good order and quietness," but as a fraudulent imposition. Shakespeare's startling exposition of sovereignty's mystifications may have caused its suppression. Like the deposition scene of *Richard II,* it was omitted from contemporary printed versions.[49]

The impact of both scenes is, nevertheless, more poignant than directly subversive, illuminating the pathos of sovereignty even as it exposes the artifice of its impostures. Shrewder than Richard and less susceptible to histrionics, Henry yearns to escape for a moment from ceremonial deception. He is well positioned to see through it ("I am a king that find thee") and exempt from the "awe and fear" engendered in other men. His soliloquy allows us to share in his privileged perspective and provides, momentarily, one of those "intimations . . . of a release from the complex narrative orders in which everyone is inscribed."[50] When Hal first assumed the "gorgeous garment, majesty" he eagerly embraced the responsibilities that accompanied it: "I'll be your father and your brother too / Let me but bear your love, I'll bear your cares" (*2 Henry IV.* 5.2.57–58). Now he wants to put aside the mantle and the burdens of sovereignty: "I think the king is but a man as I am. . . . His ceremonies laid by, in his nakedness he appears but a man" (*Henry V.* 4.1:101–05).[51]

He is, of course, incognito when he makes this confession of his common humanity, and he finally never puts his disguise aside.[52] Williams's subsequent reproach confirms this on several levels: "Your majesty came not like yourself" (*Henry V.* 4.8.50). During their encounter, the king's two bodies were both hidden from sight, the physical by the night's darkness and the political by his lowly disguise. The charge also rings true at a more basic level. Henry can never appear as himself, despite his professed desire to do so, nor can any of the successful monarchs depicted in the histories: as A. P. Rossiter sardonically remarks: "By and by he will 'be more himself.' Hal says it; Father says it. None does it."[53] Both the role and its disguises prove inescapable and Henry grudgingly submits to majesty's "hard condition": "We must bear all" (*Henry V.* 4.1.223). Indeed, for the remainder of the play, Henry immediately pulls back from the unsettling depths of his soliloquy, seeking to renew his fraternal connection with others in battle by promising that "he to-day that sheds his blood with me / Shall be my brother; be he ne'er so vile" (*Henry V.* 4.3.60–62). Public confidence in his own sovereignty is renewed by his conquest of France and his enforced dynastic marriage. Critics of the play still argue over the success of these solutions, but, for many, Henry's triumphs are still haunted by the doubts and misgivings of his soliloquy.[54] In that speech, Henry regards his submission to the role and rites of majesty as an exercise in futility and he despairs over amending "the fault / My father made in compassing the crown" (*Henry V.* 4.2.293–94). His profound skepticism toward ceremony extends to the penitential prayers sung by "sad and solemn priests" in chantries that he built and will continue to support: "More will I do; / Though all that I can do is nothing worth" (*Henry V.* 4.1.300–03).

Shakespeare's later histories coincided with the decline of the cult of Elizabeth, and the last one came on the very eve of the event that precipitated its collapse: the return against orders of the earl of Essex, "the general of our gracious Empress . . . from Ireland coming" (*Henry V.* 5.cho.30–31), not, as the chorus anticipates, in triumph over rebellion. Her cult was, as I said earlier, an essentially theatrical enterprise in which secular ceremony affirmed royal authority more effectively than sacred

ritual. It flourished as long as Elizabeth's authority remained firm. However, as she grew older and her authority was challenged by a faction of
increasingly unruly subjects, the artifice of her cult became more brittle
and transparent.[55] The earl of Cumberland, her designated champion in
the Accession Day Tilts had to be "forced to joust" in 1602, and certain
members of the Inns of Court refused to join in the revels traditionally
staged for her pleasure.[56] She had difficulty assembling a suitable entourage for her summer progress of 1600, and, according to one contemporary, "she had just cause to be offended that at her remove to this place
she was soe poorly attended, for I never saw such a dearth of nobility."[57]
Most insulting of all were the theatricals staged during the Essex conspir-
acy. She who had once triumphed by her passage through London's streets
found herself mocked by a tragedy "played forty times in open street and
houses": "I am Richard II. Know ye not that?"[58]

Elizabeth overcame defeat and deposition, the most humiliating aspects
of Richard's fate, but the pathos of his disillusion and the play's mockery of
"tradition, form, and ceremonious duty" must have been galling, as some
of her own subjects let these fall into neglect and worse. There is a terrible
pathos in her final efforts to sustain the cult's illusions through her wigs,
garish make-up, and increasingly threadbare "love tricks." Her "golden
speech" to parliament was perhaps an exception to this decline, for, after
receiving a delegation at Whitehall, she deployed her familiar phrases and
conceits on a somewhat less jaded audience, but, at times, even she
despaired of these pretenses. When one of the ladies at a wedding masque
in 1600 asked her to dance, claiming to represent Affection, Elizabeth
replied "Affection is false."[59] The official portraits of her last years were
perhaps more successful than were courtly performances at sustaining the
old illusions, for the face they present to the world is increasingly youthful,
even ageless, and the figure is heavily encrusted with the mystical trap-
pings of majesty.[60] Yet even here a poignant irony intrudes. One of the last
suggests a reversion to a sacramental idea of kingship. The coronation
portrait that hangs in the National Portrait Gallery has been shown to have
been painted sometime near the end of her reign, possibly even afterward,
but it depicts her reign's beginning (see fig. 7).[61] It shows her as a young
woman clinging to "the sceptre, and the ball" and vested in "the crown
. . . [and] intertissued robe of gold and pearl." It is an icon of that once
obscure and subordinate rite, her coronation.

Notes

1. Percy Ernest Schramm, *A History of the English Coronation,* trans. L. G.
W. Legg (Oxford: Clarendon Press, 1937), 7–9, and Janet L. Nelson, "Inauguration Rituals," *Early Medieval Kingship,* ed. P. H. Sawyer and J. N. Woods (1977;

Figure 7. *(Courtesy of the National Portrait Gallery, London.)*

rpt. Leeds: University of Leeds Press, 1979), 62. For a discussion of the somewhat ambiguous sacramental status of the coronation and the power struggle between clergy and royalty, see Marc Bloch, *The Royal Touch,* trans. J. E. Anderson (London: Routledge & Kegan Paul, 1973), 113–14.

2. The text of the ordo is reproduced by Anne F. Sutton and P. W. Hammond in *The Coronation of Richard III* (Gloucester: Alan Sutton, 1983).

3. *Calendar of State Papers, Venetian,* 7 (1558–1580), ed. Rawdon Brown and G. Cavendish Bentinck (London: Her Majesty's Stationery Office, 1890), 2. To confirmed Protestants, the elevation of the host was the essence of Popish idolatry.

4. C. G. Bayne reproduces and discusses the three extant accounts of the event in "The Coronation of Queen Elizabeth," *English Historical Review* 22 (1907): 650–73. For a discussion of the confusing records of Elizabeth's coronation and the subsequent historical controversy, see my " 'The Wonderfull Spectacle' and Obscure Ordo of Elizabeth's Coronation" (forthcoming).

5. *Calendar of State Papers, Spanish,* 1 (1558–67), ed. Martin A. S. Hume (London: Her Majesty's Stationery Office, 1892–99), 25. Newly consecrated monarchs could receive communion "in both kinds" as an indication of their sacerdotal status, since this was a privilege separating the clergy from the laity. See Marc Bloch, *The Royal Touch,* 120.

6. Bayne, "The Coronation of Elizabeth I" (1907), 661.

7. H. A. Wilson, "The Coronation of Queen Elizabeth," *English Historical Review* 23 (1908): 87–91. Bayne subsequently changed his mind, partly as a result of Wilson's article, concluding that Elizabeth's chaplain probably did say Mass and that Elizabeth remained for the service. See Bayne's "The Coronation of Queen Elizabeth," *English Historical Review* 24 (1909): 322–23. See also William P. Haugaard, "The Coronation of Elizabeth I," *Journal of Ecclesiastical History* 19 (1968): 161–70.

8. *Acts of the Privy Council,* n.s. 2 (1547–50), ed. John Roche Dasent (London: Her Majesty's Stationery Office, 1890), 33. For a description of Elizabeth's "princely travers sumptuously sett forthe" at a later Easter service, see E. K. Chambers, *The Elizabethan Stage,* 4 vols. (1923; reprint, Oxford: Clarendon Press, 1951), 3: 27. When Richard III and his queen received communion after his coronation, two bishops "held before them a long towel of white silk to shield them from the gaze of the congregation" (Sutton and Hammond, *Coronation of Richard III,* 42).

9. Public Record Office, *State Papers Domestic,* Elizabeth I, 68.

10. Bayne, "The Coronation of Elizabeth I" (1909), 322–33, and A. F. Pollard, "The Coronation of Queen Elizabeth," *English Historical Review* 25 (1910): 125–26. Her remark was made in 1571 in the midst of marriage negotiations with Alençon's representatives. It is probably just as dubious as several other claims made during that campaign of diplomatic deception, and Haugaard's suspicions of its accuracy seem justified (166). While the remark's value as evidence is as limited as all the other conflicting claims about what happened at the coronation, it is a good indication of Elizabeth's attitude toward the rites.

11. Patrick Collinson discusses the reaction of the Genevan exiles in *The Elizabethan Puritan Movement* (Berkeley and Los Angeles: University of California Press, 1967), 31.

12. Jonathan Goldberg, *James I and the Politics of Literature* (Baltimore: Johns Hopkins University Press, 1983), 31 and 39.

13. See Hobsbawm's introduction to *The Invention of Tradition,* ed. Eric Hobsbawm and Terence Ranger (Cambridge: Cambridge University Press, 1983).

David Cannadine's excellent essay on the very successful ceremonial adaptations of Victoria and her modern successors, "The Context, Performance, and Meaning of Ritual: The British Monarch and the 'Invention of Tradition,' c. 1820–1977" in the same collection, 101–65, offers intriguing parallels to Elizabeth's ceremonial exercises in public relations.

14. *The Quenes Maiesties Passage through the Citie of London to Westminster the Day before her Coronacion,* ed. James M. Osborn (New Haven: Yale University Press, 1960), 46–47.

15. See Raymond Firth who contends that "Ceremony [is] . . . enforced by mystical sanctions," in *Tikopia Ritual and Belief* (London: Allen and Unwin, 1967), n. 2, 33, and Max and Mary Gluckmans who assert that ritual invokes occult powers while ceremony is secular, in their essay "On Drama, and Games and Athletic Contests" in *Secular Ritual,* ed. Sally F. Moore and Barbara G. Meyerhoff (Assen/Amersterdam: Van Gorcum, 1977), 231–34. They argue that the course and outcome of a ritual is "prescribed and predetermined . . . and conformity to rule and tradition is important;" ceremonies are more improvisational and open-ended (239). Ritual fixity can be exaggerated, and the distinction can become too rigid. Rituals must be relatively flexible for both formal and functional reasons. There are simple mechanical obstacles to unvarying transmission discussed by Richard A. Jackson in a paper presented to the International Conference on Medieval and Early Modern Coronations, Toronto, 31 January–2 February, 1985. See also his *Vive le Roi: A History of the French Coronation from Charles V to Charles X* (Chapel Hill: University of North Carolina Press, 1984). Since many rituals are intended to negotiate conflicts arising at society's liminal stresspoints, they must also allow for flexibility, as Victor Turner has shown; see especially his *Drama, Fields and Metaphors* (Ithaca: Cornell University Press, 1974), 13–15. Richard Trexler's emphasis on the "relative fixity" and "ecologically adaptive" nature of ritual is useful as well; see his *Public Life in Renaissance Florence* (New York: Academic Press, 1980), xxiv.

16. Schramm, *History of the English Coronation,* 93 and 10.

17. David Bergeron, "Elizabeth's Coronation Entry (1559): New Manuscript Evidence," *English Literary Renaissance* 8 (1978): 3–8.

18. *The Quenes Maiesties Passage,* 48, 62, and 36, 37 respectively.

19. *Passage,* 27.

20. *Passage,* 28.

21. In his introduction to the facsimile text, J. E. Neale explains that the Tudor civic progress "became increasingly important until with Queen Elizabeth, it was finally transformed into an occasion in its own right—a popular and secular companion for the subsequent solemn sacrament worthy of commemoration, as commemorated it was, in print" *Passage,* 7. Yet even Neale underestimates the impact of the progress and publication, because they were more than mere companions. The civic progress became the central event, reducing the vexatious coronation to an obscure sideshow whose troublesome irregularities have faded from sight and mind.

22. These drawings are included in British Museum Egerton MS 3320 and College of Arms MS M6.

23. College of Arms MS M6 fol. 86v. There is also a marginal note on fol. 46, "At the parlement the Trompettes take ther place." The more finished of these two sets of drawings resembles drawings of Elizabethan tournaments included in the same manuscript collection. I have discussed this small anthology of chivalric texts and drawings elsewhere, arguing that they were compiled by the herald

Robert Cooke, a protégé of Robert Dudley as a gift to his patron. See my "From the Tower to the Tiltyard: Robert Dudley's Return to Glory," *The Historical Journal* 27 (1984): 425–35. The drawings of the civic progress in which Dudley figured prominently as master of the horse would have been a handsome tribute to both the queen and her favorite. The more traditional ecclesiastical procession was dominated by the older aristocratic families, and Dudley had no special place in it.

24. As a result of these distortions, the sacred and secular processions have become confused in modern accounts of Elizabeth's coronation and our recollection of the event. James Osborn, the modern editor of *The Quenes Maiesties Passage,* reproduces a portion of the Egerton manuscript illustration of the civic progress on the cover and as the frontispiece of the facsimile text. The note says that "the drawing depicts the Queen in her litter on the way from Whitehall to her coronation at Westminster . . . on Sunday, 15 January, the day following her passage through the City of London." The queen actually proceeded from Westminster Hall (not Whitehall) on 15 January, and the dignitaries and their order of precedence in the second day's procession were very different from the first. See Neville Williams, "The Coronation of Queen Elizabeth," *Quarterly Review* 291 (1953): 397–410, especially 402–06.

25. See Frances A. Yates, *Astraea: The Imperial Theme in the Sixteenth Century* (London: Routledge & Kegan Paul, 1975) and Roy Strong, *The Cult of Elizabeth: Elizabethan Portraiture and Pageantry* (London: Thames and Hudson, 1977).

26. Stephen Greenblatt, *Renaissance Self-Fashioning: From More to Shakespeare* (Chicago: University of Chicago Press, 1980), 230; see also 166–68.

27. According to Sutton and Hammond, *The Coronation of Richard III,* the "devaluation" of the coronation had been a trend since the twelfth century, since kings began dating their reigns not "from their coronation and unction but from the day of their accession" around that time (n. 21, 6).

28. Chambers, *Elizabethan Stage,* 1:17–18. The change in schedule from day to night might have been designed to enhance the theatrical impact of these later passages (as well as concealing the changes wrought by age), for as Bishop Goodman says of an equally impressive appearance by the Queen, "shows and pageants are best seen by torchlight" (quoted by Greenblatt, *Self-Fashioning,* 167).

29. Goldberg, *James I,* 150. See also Anne Barton Righter's explanation of royal ceremony that simultaneously distances kings from their subjects while allowing an "outward expression of authority. . . . Through form and tradition, a splendor of ritual and dress, and all those accustomed rites of obeisance and fealty, the nature of kingship is made visible to men" in *Shakespeare and the Idea of the Play* (London: Chatto and Windus, 1962), 114.

30. Goldberg, *James I,* n. 37, 271.

31. Goldberg, *James I,* 150.

32. Chambers, *Elizabethan Stage,* 1:328.

33. The letter is quoted by Herschel Baker in his introduction to *Henry VIII* in *The Riverside Shakespeare,* ed. B. Blackmore Evans (Boston: Houghton Mifflin, 1974), 976.

34. Chambers, *Elizabethan Stage,* 1:76.

35. In his essay entitled "Making Greatness Familiar," Stephen Orgel elaborates on Wotton's apprehensions, noting that "to mime nobility on the stage was to diminish it," because, as Wotton realized, such familiarity could easily breed contempt, *Genre* 15 (1982): 47.

36. Thomas Heywood, *If You Know Not Me You Know Nobody,* 2 vols. (Oxford: Malone Society Reprints, 1934–35), 2: fol. H.1v.

37. Sir Philip Sidney, *An Apology for Poetry,* ed. Geoffrey Shepherd (1965; rpt. Manchester: Manchester University Press, 1973), 135.

38. Orgel, "Making Greatness Familiar," 45.

39. Moore and Meyerhoff, "Introduction: Secular Ritual: Forms and Meanings," *Secular Ritual,* 18.

40. W. Gordon Zeeveld, *The Temper of Shakespeare's Thought* (New Haven: Yale University Press, 1974), 68. Zeeveld's first chapter is devoted to a thoughtful and historically informed discussion of ceremony in the history plays. See also Alvin B. Kernan, "*The Henriad:* Shakespeare's Major History Plays," in *Modern Shakespeare Criticism,* ed. Alvin B. Kernan (New York: Harcourt, Brace and World, 1970), 245–75, and Eric LaGuardia, "Ceremony and History: The Problem of Symbol from *Richard II* to *Henry V*" in *Pacific Coast Studies in Shakespeare,* ed. Waldo F. McNeir and Thelma N. Greenfield (Eugene: University of Oregon Press, 1966), 68–88.

41. *Richard II,* 3.2.54–62. All references are to *The Riverside Shakespeare,* hereafter cited in the text.

42. J. W. McKenna, "The Coronation Oil of the Yorkist Kings," *English Historical Review* 82 (1967): 102.

43. James L. Calderwood, *Shakespeare Metadrama* (Minneapolis: University of Minnesota Press, 1971), 182. Cf. Herbert Coursen's assertion that "ritual becomes the invention of men. . . . Ritual will no longer be the transmitter of deeper spiritual mysteries as it was in the world John of Gaunt recalls" in *Christian Ritual and the World of Shakespeare's Tragedies* (Lewisburg: Bucknell University Press, 1976), 86–87.

44. *Passages,* 62.

45. Joseph A. Porter, *The Drama of Speech Acts: Shakespeare's Lancastrian Tetralogy* (Berkeley and Los Angeles: University of California Press, 1979), 61–62.

46. *Passages,* 36–37.

47. John Strype, *Memorials of Archbishop Cranmer,* 2 vols. (Oxford: Ecclesiastical Historical Society, 1848), 2:8.

48. Thomas Cranmer, *Miscellaneous Writings and Letters,* ed. John Edmund Cox, Parker Society Publications (Cambridge: Cambridge University Press, 1846), 326–27.

49. Zeeveld, *Shakespeare's Thought,* 67.

50. Greenblatt, *Self-Fashioning,* 254. Greenblatt's subtle analysis of these equivocal intimations in Shakespeare is very persuasive, but I think he exaggerates when he concludes that "such a revelation scarcely matters" (253). If that were true in this case, the text would not have been suppressed.

51. Significantly, his effort to evade these burdens begins with a rejection of fraternity, as he dismisses Erpingham and Gloucester, "brothers both": "Go with my brothers to my lords of England / I and my bosom must debate a while / And then I would no other company" (*Henry V.* 4.1.30–32).

52. In her discussion of the disguised king motif, Anne Barton remarks that "most Elizabethan dramatists seem to have accepted the idea that disguise was an essential prerequisite for the ease and success of the meeting between private men and king. Only if the king's identity was concealed could there be a natural conversation, frankness, and a sense of rapport," in "The King Disguised: Shakespeare's *Henry V* and the Comical History" in *The Triple Bond: Plays Mainly Shakespearean in Performance,* ed. Joseph G. Price (University Park: Penn State

University Press, 1975), 98. Henry's disguises thwart rapport in Shakespeare's ironic treatment of this motif, and the king "falls into a series of nonencounters, meetings in which the difficulty of establishing understanding between subject and king is stressed." (99).

53. A. P. Rossiter, *Angels With Horns,* ed. Graham Story (New York: Theatre Arts Book, 1961), 63.

54. E.g., Una Ellis-Fermor's conclusion that "Henry V has transformed himself into a public figure. . . . It is in vain that we look for the personality behind the king; there is nothing else there" in *The Frontiers of Drama* (1945; rpt. London: Methuen and Co., 1964), 45, versus Gary Taylor's assertion that "the final scene of the play is a consummation of union, political and personal" reconciling Henry's "political and his private selves, the king's two bodies" in his introduction to the Oxford *Henry V* (Oxford: Clarendon Press, 1982), 46.

55. For a discussion of the strains on the cult of Elizabeth in its final decade, see my "'A Dangerous Image': The Earl of Essex and Elizabethan Chivalry," *The Journal of Medieval and Renaissance Studies* 13 (1983): 313–29.

56. Strong, *Cult of Elizabeth,* 136, and Philip J. Finkelpearl, *John Marston of the Middle Temple: An Elizabethan Dramatist in His Social Setting* (Cambridge, Mass.: Harvard University Press, 1969), 65.

57. Rowland White to Sir Robert Sydney, 2 August 1600, *Penhurst Manuscripts,* 6 vols., ed. C. L. Kingsford (London: His Majesty's Stationery Office, 1934), 2: 475.

58. See the Arden Shakespeare's *Richard II,* ed. Peter Ure (Cambridge: Harvard University Press, 1956), lvii–lxii. Orgel and Greenblatt each discuss this incident in their respective essays in the special issue of *Genre* 15 (1982): 3–6 and 41–48, respectively.

59. J. E. Neale, *Elizabeth I* (1934; reprint, Garden City, N.Y.: Doubleday Anchor, 1957), 383 and 400–01.

60. See for example the Rainbow Portrait. Roy Strong discusses what he terms "the retreat from reality" and "the mask of youth" in the later portraits in *Artists of the Tudor Court* (London: Thames and Hudson, 1983), 126–32.

61. See John Fletcher, "The Date of the Portrait of Elizabeth I in her Coronation Robes," *Burlington Magazine* 120 (1978): 753. The portrait had been regarded until recently as "contemporary with the Coronation itself," but tree-ring analysis of the panel backing it established that it dates from 1600–1610. "Historical evidence suggests that the events connected with Elizabeth's elaborate funeral in April 1603 might have provided the purpose for this large painting and that it could have been intended to remind one of her 'Second Coronation' after her ascent from earth to heaven" (753). For a detailed comparison of this portrait with the earlier Hilliard miniature and other portraits, see Janet Arnold, "The 'Coronation' Portrait of Queen Elizabeth I" in the same issue of the *Burlington Magazine,* 727–41.

PART IV

Renaissance Urban Identity:
The Uses of Ambiguity and Parody

The Importance of Being Ambiguous: Social Relations, Individualism, and Identity in Renaissance Florence

Ronald F. E. Weissman

This essay is about identity and the urban society of the Renaissance. My remarks stem from a concern about the way Renaissance society is customarily imagined. In much traditional Renaissance social history, man is viewed as something far from a multifaceted "Renaissance man." Instead, the Renaissance sense of self is interpreted as one-dimensional, mechanically reflecting some automatic process of class or status socialization. Scholars rarely propose alternate views of Renaissance society, views that stress the importance of interpersonal interaction, interpretation, and behavior in creating society and forming identity. To paraphrase John Dewey, I believe that society consists as much in its conduct as in its formal categories and sentimental abstractions. This paper attempts to relate certain facets of social conduct in Renaissance Florence to problems of urban social structure and identity.[1]

The oldest conception of Renaissance social identity is that of Renaissance individualism. The most venerable sociological explanation of Burkhardt's individualism is that formulated by Alfred von Martin, who attributed its growth to the growth of Renaissance capitalism. Trade and the development of a money economy, so his argument goes, weakened traditional corporate bonds within Italian city-states. Much in the tradition of Marx, von Martin assumed that relations based on cash replaced relations based on personal obligation. Personal identity was the product of one's own economic class, and one's consciousness of conflicts with other classes.[2] The capitalist revolution of the Renaissance created a society of liberated individualists, free to pursue individual interests without regard to bonds of family, community, or tradition.

Such an interpretation makes certain untenable theoretical assumptions about the priority and importance of economic relations over all other relations. Although economic change may transform social relations, traditional patterns of bonds may themselves serve to constrain what is commonly perceived as the pure economic rationality of the Renaissance economy. Furthermore, in this interpretation, identity is mechanistic and one-dimensional and limited to certain economistic habits of mind: Renaissance society was generally mercantile, thus, bourgeois values such as rationality and impersonality had a preeminent role in shaping the identity of most townsmen.[3]

A second school of Renaissance individualism emerges from the research of Marvin Becker, for whom individualism is an outcome of the collapse of traditional corporate groups during the fourteenth century. Left with a much weakened sense of kinship and the growing unimportance of corporate groups such as guilds and fraternities, the individual turned to the generality and anonymity of the state for a sense of self.[4] Where, in von Martin's view, relations based on money and contract replaced those based on status during the transition from feudalism to modernity, in Becker's interpretation loyalty to abstract principles, to law, and to the state, replaced loyalty to particularist groups or persons.

While acknowledging the creativity and sweep of Becker's thesis, other scholars have advanced a quite different vision of Renaissance society, and they question the very significance of Burckhardtian individualism. For these scholars, traditional groups such as the family maintained their solidarity and cohesion well into the sixteenth century.[5] Those who have described the decline of Renaissance collective identities frequently look for the manifestation of such identities in the existence of formal institutional arrangements such as corporate groupings of the sort displayed in communal processional life. But the presence or absence of corporate arrangements is not necessarily indicative of the strength or weakness of the personal arrangements that bind groups such as family, guild, or neighborhood. According to much recent scholarship, groups maintained their solidarity, in a new form, less political or corporate than before, but no less durable, well into the sixteenth century. In numerous cases, these groups maintained their solidarity not through corporate arrangements but through networks of informal relations. Gene Brucker, for example, argues that the informal relations of kinship, patronage, and influence that flowered in fifteenth-century Florence were neither weaker nor more individualistic than the corporate familial bonds of the preceding century.[6]

In discovering the world of informal yet intense personal relations, the past decade of Renaissance scholarship has profoundly altered our conception of Renaissance society. The current generation of scholars has demonstrated the existence of complex patron-client relations, kinship networks, and neighborhood bonds interlinking the middle- and upper-class citizens of Renaissance Florence. They have offered a corrective to the more traditional Burckhardtian views of the Renaissance city as a center of individualism and social isolation. But often, these scholars have studied individual types of social relations, such as kinship, marriage, or patronage, in isolation, without necessarily considering the totality of personal relations or their combined effect on Renaissance identity.[7] In seeking to demonstrate the continuity of group cohesion, forces leading to group disunity and disorder have sometimes been neglected. And as I shall argue, the total configuration of social networks and personal bonds may imply more about personal identity than discrete types of relations considered separately.

As champions of Renaissance individualism have long argued, identity is not an unself-conscious mirroring of group values or loyalties, but a conscious, reflective process. Whereas those who advance an individualist thesis tend to ignore the persistence of group ties, those who have reminded us of the strength of those ties have often neglected the interpretive and interactive process by which Florentines managed the complexity of their relations with each other. Florence was a socially complex society, characterized by overlapping, conflicting, mutual commitments to kin, neighbors, friends, clients, patrons, and business associates. These ties overlapped in many ways. Thus, social relations were usually mutually supportive, but on occasion, they were also quite competitive. I would argue that the Renaissance urban community was not characterized by anomie, but, if anything, by an excess of intimacy and community.[8]

In the Renaissance, social relations intersected in many ways and loyalty was demanded by the whole spectrum of one's intimates. It was not freedom and isolation that plagued the Renaissance psyche, but rather the problem of managing commitments to diverse groups and individuals. Reading Renaissance memoirs, one notes a strong sense of doubt and conflict, a sense of the difficulty of honoring competing commitments. As historical sociologists, we tend to categorize, to stratify, or to discover "the" relationship (e.g., economic transactions) that accounts for the whole. In our search for greater analytic precision and distinction, we lose sight of a key facet of Renaissance identity that presents problems for almost any schematic analysis of this society: social ambiguity. We want to discern clear patterns of allegiance or conflict, be they around class, neighborhood, or kinship groups. But in the process of seeking to discover such clear patterns of segmentation, Renaissance historians frequently lose sight of the confusion and ambiguity that was as important in shaping Renaissance identity as was each of the diverse loyalties making its claim on the Renaissance psyche.

Renaissance biographies, commentaries on the family, Renaissance diaries, and family memoirs in particular, all devoted special attention to the problem of the behavior required to validate and satisfy diverse loyalties and commitments. The obscurity of motives and the duplicity of social relations were, in particular, common themes. As one of the interlocutors in Alberti's *della Famiglia* observed:

> How can anyone dream that mere simplicity and goodness will get him friends or even acquaintances not actually harmful and annoying? The world is so full of human variety, differences of opinion, changes of heart, perversity of custom, ambiguity, and obscurity of values. The world is amply supplied with fraudulent, false, perfidious, bold, audacious, and rapacious men. Everything in the world is profoundly unsure. One has to be far-seeing in the face of frauds, traps and betrayals.[9]

In this world, as the speaker suggested, the style of social interaction required was anything other than frankness. To be frank with others limited one's ability to respond to their hidden or impenetrable motives. The face value of social exchanges hid many layers of meaning, even during exchanges between friends. And after all, who was a true friend? One was not always completely sure of one's real friends because of the complexity of their commitments. And so, Paolo da Certaldo's guide to fourteenth century etiquette and behavior warned, perhaps a bit over anxiously: "Test your friend a hundred times . . . for he who was your friend earlier has become your enemy because of the trust that you placed in him."[10]

The fifteenth-century diarist Giovanni Morelli echoed Paolo da Certaldo's sentiments:

> Test your friend a hundred times . . . before you trust him, and do not trust him to such an extent that he can be the cause of your undoing. Do not extend your trust easily or lightly; and all the more, he who demonstrated with his words that he is faithful, trust him all the less, and he who offers to help you, do not trust him at all.[11]

This sense of uncertainty is important for understanding much of Renaissance urban social behavior and the rituals and theatrics of everyday life. One key to the Renaissance etiquette of interaction is what one might call the importance of being ambiguous. By this I mean that a high premium was placed on clever, cryptic speech that could take many forms, from double entendre, metaphor, and vagueness, to outright lying and evasion.

Central to the maintenance of the Renaissance sense of self was what one might call impression management. Given competing commitments and uncertain obligations, what sense of self does one project to others? Many projections of self are based on the particular normative roles we are called upon to play: loyal father, generous friend, scrupulous business associate, competitor for political office, or public-spirited neighbor. In modern society, especially that of America and northern Europe, our varied roles are played for different audiences. The fragmentation of modern society allows our different social selves to have different contexts and most incongruities among the roles we play are masked by the segmentation and separation of our audiences. But in the Renaissance city, in which neighborhood and family bounded much of social life, numerous roles had the same audience. And members of this audience were not only present as observers: they themselves placed simultaneous demands upon one for signs of obligation and support.

Given the problem of maintaining honor in the face of competing commitments, one adopted a style of interaction that placed a premium on being ambiguous without appearing to be so, a mode of behavior identified by Irving Goffman as "strategic interaction," or gamesmanship, requiring a high degree of verbal cleverness as well as expert concealment and stage management.[12] It is possible that the importance of classical rhetoric in Renaissance culture had quite popular origins, rooted in the necessary verbal sensitivities required to negotiate the demands of everyday life.

What then should one make of the ambiguous trickster behavior so often noted in the Renaissance? Ambiguity in all its forms—evasion, speech peppered with multiple meanings, and corollary behavior, including deceit and hypocrisy—must be viewed as something other than Renaissance cynicism or immorality. This strategic interaction and manipulative, trickster behavior is not merely a quaint, humorous, distasteful, or colorful aspect of Renaissance culture. I would suggest that it is something more—a repertoire of postures and gestures used to clarify roles, to decipher the intentions and motivations of others, and to protect oneself against excessive obligations and entanglements. Within an intensely public culture that demanded intense loyalty, devious, manipulative behavior was used to protect a coherent sense of self and to project a coherent and trustworthy image.

This publicly projected sense of self that Florentines attempted to protect was of course known as personal honor. And gains and losses in the public management of commitments were tallied according to the public sense of one's reputation, one's honor and shame. Those who managed to maintain a coherent public view of self were considered honorable; those who failed were not.

How did one honor competing commitments and diverse loyalties in a social world in which most of the persons whose commitments demanded attention were present as actors and as observers? The basic strategy for good social encounters was threefold: first, guarding one's own secrets; second, maneuvering one's acquaintances into revealing as much as possible about their own affairs; and finally, appearing at the same time not to pry so as not to lose their trust and friendship. A preliminary strategy to be used in many social encounters was to uncover others' intentions while keeping one's own a secret. "Keep your eyes open and your mouth shut" counseled many a Florentine.[13] Paolo da Certaldo equated his secrets with his liberty and suggested that friends who revealed theirs were mad.[14] Francesco Guicciardini's advice is a perfect description of the techniques and dangers of strategic interaction:

> You have everything to gain from managing your affairs secretly to your friends. For many men feel slighted and become indignant when they see that you refuse to confide in them. Often it is unwise to be open in your conversations, even with your friends. . . . On the other hand, to act with your friends in such a manner that they notice that you are being reserved is to assure that they will do the same with you. For the only thing that makes others confide in you is the assumption that you confide in them. Thus, if you reveal nothing to others, you lose the possibility of knowing anything from them.[15]

One should, at all costs, attempt to stay uninvolved while appearing involved, appearing to agree with everyone even if one must play different roles for different men. For Giovanni Morelli, ambiguity of language was central to the successful adoption of this strategy:

> Stay clear, that through promises or any other means, that you don't get yourself all mixed up in others' affairs; otherwise, you will be regarded as unloyal, a man of scant firmness and stability. Nevertheless, keep discussions open with everyone, and if you need to use different and unworthy words with different men in order to argue your own part, do it, but make sure that your own goals are worth it. Don't allow yourself to lie except when it appears to everyone that a matter of great importance is at hand, and that you lie in order to protect your own position and status. Generally, you should agree with others about everything, otherwise they will suspect you.[16]

Scrutinized by neighbors, one had to guard one's speech and behavior and yet appear trusting. One had to act in accordance with the dual demands of friendship: remaining both relaxed and on guard, inwardly suspicious and outwardly and effusively cordial. As Adovardo and Lionardo Alberti advised, one had to, "Overcome shyness with slyness," since "shrewdness is required for dealing with shrewd people."[17]

When intense public conflict arose, what did one do? Giovanni Morelli advised his reader to stay uncommitted:

> If within your city . . . or rather, your neighborhood, one or more factions springs to life, concerned with the affairs of your commune, as

happens daily . . . try to stay uncommitted, and keep your friendship with everyone. Don't speak ill of anyone, whether to please one man more than another or to satisfy your own anger.[18]

Morelli's advice was probably quite difficult to heed. Caught between conflicting demands and obligations when opposing pressures were irreconcilable, an individual might save his honor by resorting to a second strategy: lying. One fifteenth-century student of Tuscan social behavior analyzed lies in these terms:

There are those who speak with two tongues, who hold one thing in their hearts while they speak another with their tongues, like he who promises something and does not make good of it in order to remain at peace with his family. He will have promised something worthy, and because he sees that it displeases a member of his household, in order to remain at peace with his relatives he will say, "I never promised to do it."[19]

The very ambiguity of situations in which one interacted with others in multiple ways offered possibilities for successful manipulation. Paolo da Certaldo advised that one should attempt to define the interaction situation in terms beneficial to oneself. When seeking favors from a person who otherwise might refuse, for example, one redefined the situation in terms of those roles that are most intimate, or roles that emphasized, through status or patronage, the other's personal or moral obligation to oneself.

Nowhere was the redefinition of situations and the general ambiguity of interaction more evident than in economic transactions. In the familiar interpretation of Florentine society it was the supposed modernizing and rationalizing force of these transactions that changed Renaissance Florence from a closely knit to an impersonal society. Although the sociology of the Renaissance has given greater emphasis of late to the complexity of social bonds, the importance of neighborhood and kinship ties, and the pervasive influence of patron-client ties, the economic history of the Renaissance continues to stress economic individualism, as if economic transactions, at least those that occurred within the local Florentine economy, were somehow freed from the constraints and demands of other social relations.

Florentine economic transaction networks have not been studied in any detail. I have begun, however, to piece together debt and credit networks and the spatial arrangements of property ownership in the quarter of San Giovanni, particularly in the oldest section of Florence, the area between the palace of the priors and the cathedral. One is struck by an impression of extensive indebtedness. The prevalence of uncollectible debts is also striking, even if one discounts an almost certain inflation of such accounts.

In numerous cases, records of defaulted or bad debts are supported by references to private account books submitted in evidence to the commune. And these failed debts frequently tell a story that makes them all the more credible, if not creditworthy.

Some creditors, like the dyer Iacopo di Lippo Doni, were relatively lucky: of his eighty-four debtors, only twenty-seven were listed in default, and these debts amounted to a scant 5 percent of the monies owed him[20] Other creditors were not so fortunate—of Francesco di Gilio Gili's ninety-six debtors, only eight were listed as "good" debts. The remaining eighty-eight debts, amounting to 1,718 of the total 2,620 florins owed him, had already been written off as uncollectible.[21]

Who were these debtors? Frequently, they appear to have been friends, neighbors, and relatives, as in the case of the debts owed Niccolo Baldovini, whose principal debtors included five of his in-laws, three of whose debts he had already written off as uncollectible.[22] What might account for this? As is typical of other face-to-face societies, the clustering of a family's urban property within a restricted social space, as well as the extent to which economic transactions were like other relations bound by many other social ties, generally to family and neighbors, are important factors underlying Renaissance debt and credit networks.

At the center of the territory that I have studied lived Filippo d'Ardengo de'Ricci, whose house and shops clustered in the family enclave around the canto de'Ricci.[23] He shared this house and property with other members of his family, rented his urban residence from relations, and had extensive debt and credit relations with near and far Ricci kinsman.

Iacopo di Guccio Ghiberti was a neighbor of Filippo's.[24] His urban property also clustered around the canto de'Ricci and included a house containing four shops on the bottom floor, the house next door containing two shops, and four other shops, contiguous to one another and to his other houses. Of Iacopo's eleven debtors, six were renters and a seventh debtor was his own brother. And of eight property rentals, six renters owed him money, money far in excess of their rents, usually ranging from between two-and-a-half to four times their annual rent. Although renters remained on the premises, Iacopo had clearly written off several of his renter's debts. Baldo the tailor, he noted, was too poor to pay. The account of his largest debtor, Michele di Bernardo, a carder, appears in 1427 to have been in the process of being written off; "his account isn't worth much," read Iacopo's marginal comment.

Antonio Macci's substantial urban property clustered in the parish of San Bartolomeo al Corso.[25] Each and every one of his wool shops, storerooms, and wineshops belonged to a group of properties next to the Macci inn and family courtyard, all of which formed a family enclave. Much of this property was owned in common with two neighbors, his kinswoman Bandecca di Giovanni Macci, and Nicola di Messer Vieri de'Medici. As was the case with Iacopo Ghiberti, Antonio's renters also owed him sums of money that bore little relation to their annual rents. His largest debtors were, however, his kinsmen: his son-in-law owed him 105 florins, a nephew owed him twenty-seven florins, and other nephews owed him 105 florins. This latter debt Antonio wrote off as uncollectible.

What was it like to provide credit in a social network as interlinked and geographically narrow as that of Antonio Macci or Iacopo Ghiberti? What was it like to provide credit or property to neighbors and kinsmen? In such a network there is scant reason to expect that economic exchanges were not affected by other complex bonds and loyalties. Lenders and debtors shared numerous personal bonds apart from the debtor/creditor relationship. And the extension of credit had numerous purposes and meanings: the maintenance of friendships, the acquisition of clients, and the display of munificence and liberality required by those claiming honor. The use of debt and credit networks to extend friendship and patronage has long been recognized as a key element in the moral economy of small-scale traditional societies and as a key feature of Mediterranean towns.[26] It is not surprising to find evidence of such a moral economy in the face-to-face world of Renaissance Florence. The efficient and impersonal credit arrangements supposedly characteristic of the Renaissance were not always available in a society in which economic transactions took place within the social worlds of friendship, kinship, and patronage.

But how far did one's obligations to friends and kinsmen extend? Under what circumstances could one loan friends money? Florentine moralists all debated these questions. All answered ambiguously. Giovanni Morelli enumerated the possible harmful effects of loaning money to friends and relations.

> First, you might lose your own property, second you might lose your relative or friend, and third, you might become the enemy of your debtor and he might treat you as an enemy if you should ask him twice or more for what is owed you.[27]

But in the end Morelli admitted that one was generally obligated to loan money to friends. Faced with the choice between alienating friends or making them ill-advised loans, Giovanni Rucellai suggested to his sons that they use a variety of delaying tactics, without directly denying the request. If this failed, he further recommended, albeit unenthusiastically, that one should loan the money.[28]

Leon Battista Alberti's discussion of the difficulty of obtaining a long-promised dowry illustrates the difficulties and ambiguities that could affect Renaissance social relations and the use of multiple roles to define situations out of a creditor's moral control:

I know not why everyone, as if corrupted by a common vice, takes advantage of delay to grow lazy in paying debts. Sometimes, in the case of marriage, people are further tempted because they hope to evade payment altogether. As your wife spends her first year in your house, it seems impossible not to reinforce the new bonds of kinship by frequent visiting and parties. But it will be thought rude if, in the middle of a gathering of kinsmen, you put yourself forward to insist and complain. If as new husbands usually do, you don't want to lose their still precarious favor, you may ask your in-laws in restrained and casual words. Then you are forced to accept any little excuse they may offer. If you make a more forthright demand for what is your own, they will explain to you their many obligations, will complain of fortune, blame the conditions of the time, complain of other men, and say that they hope to be able to ask much of you in greater difficulties. As long as they can, they will promise you bounteous repayment at an ever receding date. They will beg you, and overwhelm you, nor will it seem possible for you to spurn the prayers of people you have accepted as your own family. Finally, you will be put in a position where you must either suffer the loss in silence or enter upon expensive litigation and create enmity.[29]

The ambiguities and tensions described by Alberti are characteristic of transactions that occur within a dense social network where roles and relations overlap. Transactions among intimates and friends were not infrequently fraught with conflicting attitudes, distrust, and an overriding sense, nevertheless, of obligation. One's options were constrained by an on-going network of obligations that outlived any specific transaction. Too often, Renaissance economic historians and social historians, taking their cues from economic history, have written as if such economic transactions were separable from other social transactions, or worse, as if economic transactions were somehow logically and psychologically prior to and the primary structurer of other relations.

This discussion of economic transactions is meant to do no more than suggest that single social relations were often constrained and embedded with meanings derived from the entire field of social interaction. And that key to social exchange was the interpretive process of disentangling commitments to diverse groups, each making competing demands on one's sense of obligation. For a society supposedly as individualistic as that of Renaissance Florence, one anomaly stands out: the substantial time that Florentines devoted to discussing the nature of obligations to others. Such discussions, as we have seen, rarely took the individualistic form of denying obligations or renouncing ties. A sense of freedom from traditional social ties is hardly apparent. On the contrary, Florentines thought long and hard about how to honor commitments, how to win friends, and how to expand kinship ties. For a supposedly individualistic society, Florentines devoted much intellectual energy to analyzing the psychology of interpersonal relations.

Perhaps it is time to reevaluate the traditional thesis regarding Renaissance individualism in light of recent scholarship emphasizing the persistence of strong group bonds. An awareness of self, a propensity to reflect on one's identity, a tendency to shape and consciously project one's public image were clearly important facets of the Renaissance urban psyche. If such self-consciousness is a sign of individualism, then, indeed, the Renaissance town was clearly marked by individualism. But what were the roots of such individualism, and how can such individualism be reconciled with current scholarship's vision of a society in which traditional loyalties to family, neighborhood, and friends continued to exercise strong influence?

By now it should be clear that Renaissance self-consciousness, indeed individualism, was not occasioned by the absence or collapse of traditional loyalties to corporate groups, neighbors, or friendship networks. Rather, I would argue, this individualism, this purposeful, intentional use of the mechanisms of ambiguity to define and protect the self, gives evidence not of the absence of ties, but of their very strength, multiplicity, and complexity. Individualism—the capacity to reflect and choose among obligations—was not a product of a clear fragmentation or the absence of strong social bonds; paradoxically, it was itself nurtured by those bonds and reflected the depth of obligations structuring the social order of the Renaissance town.

Notes

1. On methodology supporting other interpretations, see my "Reconstructing Renaissance Sociology: The 'Chicago School' and the Study of Renaissance Society," in Richard Trexler, ed., *Persons in Groups: Social Behavior as Identity Formation in Medieval and Renaissance Europe* (New York: Medieval and Renaissance Texts and Studies, 1985), 39–46, which is a companion piece to the present article.

2. Alfred von Martin, *Sociology of the Renaissance* (New York: Harper and Row, 1963, original 1932), 11.

3. Ibid., 9–19.

4. Marvin Becker, "An essay on the quest for identity in the early Italian Renaissance," in *Florilegium Historiale: Essays in Honor of Wallace K. Ferguson,* ed. J. S. Rowe and W. H. Stockdale (Toronto: University of Toronto Press, 1971), 299, 304–05.

5. On family groups, see F. W. Kent, *Household and Lineage in Renaissance Florence: The Family Life of the Capponi, Ginori and Rucellai* (Princeton: Princeton University Press, 1977); on patronage, see Dale Kent, *The Rise of the Medici: Faction in Florence 1426–1434* (Oxford: Oxford University Press, 1978); on neighborhood, see D. V. Kent and F. W. Kent, *Neighbours and Neighbourhood in Renaissance Florence: The District of the Red Lion in the Fifteenth Century* (Locust Valley, New York: J. J. Augustin, 1982).

6. Gene A. Brucker, *The Civic World of the Early Renaissance Florence* (Princeton: Princeton University Press, 1977).

7. One exception to this practise is Christiane Klapisch-Zuber, who has examined different forms of social relations simultaneously. See her " 'Parenti, amici, e vicini,': il territorio urbano d'una famiglia mercatile del XV secolo," *Quaderni Storici* 33 (1976): 953–82.

8. On this theme, see Ronald F. E. Weissman, *Ritual Brotherhood in Renaissance Florence* (New York: Academic Press, 1982).

9. L. B. Alberti, *I libri della famiglia,* trans. R. N. Watkins as *The Family in Renaissance Florence* (Columbia: University of South Carolina Press, 1969), 266.

10. Paolo da Certaldo, *Libro di buoni costumi* (Florence: Felice Le Monnier, 1945) 241–43.

11. Giovani di Pagolo Morelli, *Ricordi* (Florence: Felice Le Monnier, 1969), 227.

12. Irving Goffman, *Strategic Interaction* (Philadelphia: University Pennsylvania Press Books, 1969).

13. Paolo da Certaldo, *Libro di buoni costumi,* 64.

14. Ibid., 139.

15. Francesco Guicciardini, *Maximis and Reflections of a Renaissance Statesman,* trans. Mario Domandi (New York: Harper and Row, 1965) 88, 101.

16. Morelli, *Ricordi,* 282–83.

17. Alberti, *della famiglia,* 240.

18. Morelli, *Ricordi,* 280–81.

19. San Bernardino da Siena, *Le prediche volgari* (Milan: Rizzoli, 1936), 203.

20. Archivio di Stato, Florence, *Catasto,* vol. 81, fol. 486r.

21. Ibid., fol. 483r.

22. Ibid., fol. 500r.

23. Ibid., fol. 479r.

24. Ibid., fol. 509r.

25. Ibid., fol. 1r.

26. On debt and credit in the Mediterranean, see, for example, J. Davis, *People of the Mediterranean* (London: Routledge & Kegan Paul, 1977), 52.

27. Morelli, *Ricordi,* 237–39.

28. *Giovanni Rucellai ed il suo Zibaldone,* ed. Alessandro Perosa, in *Studies of the Warburg Institute* 34 (1960); 1:10–13.

29. Alberti, *della famiglia,* 117–18.

Ceremonial Play and Parody in the Renaissance

Thomas M. Greene

This study begins with a story that everyone knows but that I recall now for its exemplary value. The city of Florence is stricken with plague; its civic and domestic institutions have broken down; the number of the dead overwhelms the sacramental disposition of their bodies and turns the funeral service into a mockery. Seven young women gather in a church to debate a common course of action and agree to flee the city together with a trio of young men, not without hesitation and misgivings on the part of some of the women. Once they are established in a villa outside the city, the most aggressive of the males makes a short speech in favor of self-indulgence and hedonist freedom, only to be answered by the leader of the women. She expresses her own hopes that the group's life together will be pleasurable though moderated by reason, and to ensure that they all enjoy the highest and most orderly pleasure, proposes that each member take his or her turn as king or queen for a day. Her proposal is accepted and she is elected the first queen. What happens next is spontaneous and unpredictable. After the election of the queen, Pampinea, another young woman, Filomena . . .

> darted quickly to a laurel tree, because she had often heard it said that the branches of this tree possess honor, and also bestow honor on whomever they crown. Having broken off a few sprigs, she made from them a venerable garland which, when placed upon the head, became a visible symbol of royal sovereignty to all as long as their band endured.[1]

Throughout the frame narrative that follows in Boccaccio's *Decameron*, this garland indeed remains as a symbol of authority that is transferred daily from head to head.

In this familiar story, I would like to linger on the incident of the spontaneous coronation. Since my concern is with play, I suppose that the play of the *Decameron* might be said to begin with that little gesture. And yet of course it is not without implications that extend beyond the ludic. The coronation recognizes, among other things, that the new community will be tested by what might be called sexual politics, and indeed has already begun to be so tested by the opening remark of the feisty Dioneo. As the group begins to grope for its bearings, this gesture introduces an element both arbitrary and significant. The laurel crown as an instrument of play is an *ad hoc* makeshift; it is ungrounded by precedent and unsupported by authority. But it does ratify a certain degree of power that is effective within limits, and in the days that follow, the transfer of the crown corresponds to a transfer of circumscribed power. What is unique about the laureation of Pampinea is precisely the uncertainty over the kind and degree of power it confers. That uncertainty can only be dispelled during the lifetime of the microcommunity, in the give-and-take between members and especially between the sexes, where the power of king or queen is challenged and defined. Thus Filomena's improvised ceremony is interesting because it is open-ended; its meaning is not determined by past agreement but by future lived experience, an experience that lasts until the microcommunity, aware of its precarious coherence, returns to Florence.

This little instance of ceremonial play, which anticipates in nucleus much of the play of the centuries to follow, can be contrasted with an episode from an earlier work by Boccaccio, the prose romance *Filocolo.* In that work, still essentially medieval, the hero comes upon a group of elegant young aristocrats of both sexes who pass the day in a flowering meadow reciting case histories of lovers and debating their rights and wrongs. But before proceeding to these *questioni,* questions of lovers' conduct, they choose one of their number, a certain Fiammetta, as queen, and as an emblem of her role they place a coronet of laurel upon her pretty head. The queen thus becomes the arbiter in a court of love, a familiar institution both in medieval society and literature. The scene of her laureation is charming but not surprising, and her prerogatives as queen are well-defined by tradition. Fiammetta's coronation is not open-ended but firmly grounded in precedent; it lacks the improvisatory and experimental character of its counterpart in the *Decameron.* In that shift from the youthful work to the mature work, from one kind of play to another, we can observe Boccaccio entering that civilization we have come to call the Renaissance.

The experimental ceremony that enables all that ensues can be regarded as a response to the failed sacraments of the plague-ridden city. In Florence we are specifically told that the rites for the dead have been travestied or abandoned. As the young men and women plan their departure in the church of Santa Maria Novella, behind them can be heard the ineffectual voices of the Dominican monks singing their paternosters, ignored and irrelevant. The coronation at the villa, and the series of daily re-coronations, provide a minimal simulacrum of order that replaces the ceremonial order that has at least momentarily collapsed. It will collapse again in more than one of the stories to be told, stories that involve abuses of the sacraments in what might be described as playful blasphemy.

The very first story hinges on a fabricated confession by a dying scoundrel, who persuades his confessor of his sanctity and is later canonized. In another story, a lady communicates to a certain gentleman an invitation to her bed by means of invented complaints to her guileless confessor. In others, a monk busies a simpleminded husband with a mock penance in order to enjoy his wife, and a husband is deceived by a fake exorcism. These and similar stories do not reflect a polemical hostility to liturgy but rather an intuitive, unself-conscious skepticism. In effect, the *Decameron* offers us two versions of ceremonial signifiers, neither wholly effective: on the one hand, the millennial repetitions of the church, grounded in dogma and in tradition, too rigid to survive a catastrophe; on the other hand, the extemporized innovations of the *brigata,* ungrounded, hazy, lacking authority and enforcement, holding for a few days without expectation of permanence.

A few key elements can be disengaged from the experimental play of the *Decameron.* First of all there is a ceremonial *breakdown;* next there is *displacement,* a literal, geographical displacement in this case but also a behavioral displacement of one social organization for another; there is *tension*—the brief anxiety of certain young women when the move is proposed, and later the sexual tension provoked by Dioneo's challenge; in response, most crucially, there is an improvised *solution,* ratified by an improvised ceremony, a jerry-built, precarious solution within the empty space opened by the displacement; next, precisely because the improvisation *is* an open-ended makeshift, there is an element of *ambiguity* on which the male aggressor, Dioneo, will continue to play; but there is also finally that element of *creativity,* both social and artistic, which stems from the freedom of improvisation, the creativity that animates the group not only in their stories but also in the fabrication of a communal life.

Although a few examples will not suffice to demonstrate this, versions of the foregoing model seem to me to be recurrent in Renaissance culture. The Renaissance opens up an arena for maneuver in which the individual or the group is obliged to "wing it," and in that space lies the potential, or the compulsion, for play. Improvisation within this arena need not assume, although it may, the oppressive and manipulative character Stephen Greenblatt has associated with that word.[2] Iago improvises, but so does Rosalind; Richard III improvises, but so does Feste. So do many others, in many guises, styles, and contexts. The friends who foregather in Erasmus's *Convivium religiosum,* playfully imitating the ritual of communion, open a space for improvisatory scriptural interpretation where they extem-

porize alternative readings of scriptural cruxes within the reverent amity
of shared understanding. The experience of Brunelleschi's San Spirito or
Alberti's San Andrea does not properly invite the visitor to a liturgical
experience. The architecture moves the visitor away from ritual into what
Alberti conceived as a private, philosophical, unpredictable experience;
the church is a locus for a variable interplay of feeling and reflection, a
space for spontaneous maneuver. *The Book of the Courtier* transforms a
space for closed, medieval games like the *Filocolo*'s into a theater for an
endless, open Renaissance game. The court masque of the Stuart monarchy "wings it" from beginning to end, obliged to explain, interpret, and
justify what it happens to be doing, working up its ceremonial logic as it
proceeds. If then we extend the term "play" to embrace this wide a
spectrum of activities, it is not a peripheral phenomenon of Renaissance
civilization. It goes on at the central core, in that newly available space
that opens as the ceremonial society wanes.

We have difficulty in our time apprehending just how pervasive and
instinctive was the medieval sense of public, formal, communal, repetitive,
symbolic action. Not only was the life of each Christian punctuated by the
great overarching sacraments of the church, but the calendar of the year
was likewise punctuated by a host of holy days and holidays—we tend to
forget the proximity between those terms. But ceremonial was also secular
and it was ubiquitous—at court, in the city, at the university, the court of
law, the guild, the confraternity, the manor house, the peasant village. The
liturgy and the secular ceremony consisted of performed signifiers believed to be effective and thus *de facto* effective. But beyond the particular
concrete power of a marriage, a guild initiation, or a legal judgment, the
more profound effect of a society organized by ceremony was to confirm
personal identity, to inform each individual who he was and why he
existed. This is why the decline of ceremonial power in the early modern
period represented an incipient crisis.

There can be little doubt that this power did begin to decline. The
waning is not only anticipated in a test like the *Decameron,* but by the
sixteenth century the evidence was unmistakable. We can find it, among
other places, in the historical dictionaries of the modern vernaculars,
where for the first time in that century the word "ceremony" and its
equivalents begin to betray negative connotations. In Italian, French, and
English, "ceremony" and its cognates were coming to suggest a lack of
substance or spontaneity, an empty formalism, a tiresome evasion of
realities. In Italy, Della Casa, writing on polite etiquette, denounces "cir-
imonie" as virtual lies. Joachim du Bellay, dismayed by the hollow pageantry of late Renaissance Rome, wrote "je [ne] trouve . . . qu'une
cerimonie." A generation later Montaigne wrote "nous ne sommes que
ceremonie," referring to the stilted formality and prudery of polite con-

versation.[3] In a different register, Shakespeare's Henry V on the eve of Agincourt meditates on the burdensome formality of the social hierarchy and the ponderous regalia of kingship.

> And what art thou, thou idol Ceremony?
> What kind of god art thou, that suffer'st more
> Of mortal griefs than do thy worshippers?
> What are thy rents? What are thy comings in?
> O Ceremony, show me but thy worth!
>
> (*Henry V.* 4.1.257–61)

Usages like these betoken a crisis in certain forms of symbolic experience that was intensified by the antiliturgical thrust of the Reformation. Numerically, the sixteenth century may well have produced quite as many ritual observances as its predecessors, but they were now beginning to lose their absolute authority. The process was gradual and its pace varied not only from country to country but more significantly between classes and between subcultures. Certain regions and certain subcultures were scarcely even touched. Even those individuals and groups who were affected might well have derived intense momentary feelings from ceremonial experiences. Moreover, observances of this kind continued to be intricately interwoven into the texture of social life. What was weakening, in those places and classes where change can be traced, was the power of certain symbolic activities to determine personal and communal identity.

In view of this slow, uneven, intermittent, almost invisible decline, ceremonial play acquired new cultural implications, and not least that form of play called parody, to which I now want to turn. The medieval era had of course produced its own ceremonial parodies. It was in fact a magnificent age of parody—nothing that happened later ever surpassed the Feast of Fools. What marks the later era was the shift from inversion to displacement. The Feast of Fools was a product of the liturgy and depended on it; it was triggered by a line in the liturgy; it really testified to the dominance of the ceremonial society, and was itself a date on the ecclesiastical calendar. The improvisational parodies of later centuries bear witness to an incipient unravelling of the ceremonial fabric.

We are perhaps fortunate that one of the earliest masterpieces of the northern Renaissance, the *Praise of Folly* (1511), constitutes a mock university oration and thus set a generic precedent. Erasmus's displacement of the academic doctor by the subversive figure of Folly, gleefully stringing together her insidious paradoxes, opened a conceptual space in which Erasmus could attain an elusive and unsettling profundity he would never again approach. Erasmus's own hostility to ceremony, expressed so frequently in his writing, is never stronger or more explicit that in the *Praise,* which includes the near-heretical suggestion that the sacrament of the eucharist might actually be harmful to the Christian if it is not received in the correct spirit. This anticeremonial prejudice only renders more problematic the anticeremony that Folly herself is acting out. The reader gropes for the correct spirit in which to receive this put-on, lest he or she be damaged, as well one might, by its shattering hilarity.

Erasmus provided one model of ceremonial parody at the opening of the sixteenth century; John Skelton's "Phillip Sparrow" in England provided another. Still others can be found in the popular theaters of France and England, which produced in England such examples of bastardized ceremony as the parody of chivalric tournaments in *Fulgence and Lucrece* or the parody of a court trial in *Mankind,* and in France the subversive humor of the *soties.* In one of these we find three fools, three *sots,* and their leader Mère Sotte, performing a vigil for the dead clown Triboulet, complete with parodies of the liturgical offices for the dead. It makes no difference that Triboulet was not actually dead; he probably wrote the *sotie* himself and may in fact have been playing Mère Sotte.

Evidently Rabelais probably drew on the *sotie* as well as on Erasmus. His antihero Panurge, quintessentially rootless, lacking in ceremonial identity, is one of the supreme parodists in world literature. Panurge's highly suspect autobiography parodies a saint's life from the *Golden Legend;* his courtship of a grande dame of Paris is a parodic last tango of romantic courtship, and his debate by gesture with the English scholar Thaumaste travesties the public *disputatio,* the central ritual of the medieval university. The descriptions of Panurge's actual gestures in this public debate would be recognized by most American schoolboys. Despite Panurge's brilliance as an improviser in the early volume *Pantagruel,* the tension that tends to accompany displacement will be felt acutely only in the later, more mature *Third Book,* where improvisation takes the form it so often assumed in that century, the form of creative interpretation. Panurge's anxious indecision about whether to marry and his unpersuasive construals of the responses to his questions lead him and his friends on a great odyssey, spanning two more books, culminating in the final consultation of the oracle of the bottle. This consultation is not carried out without a certain formal preparation.

> The priestess wrapped Panurge up in a green gaberdine, tied a fair white nun's snood round his head, muffled him in a mulled wine-strainer, on the end of which . . . she tied three skewers, put two ancient codpieces on his hands for gloves, . . . bathed his face five times in the fountain, and after that threw a handful of flour in his eyes, stuck three cock's feathers on the right-hand side of his mulled-wine hood, made him turn nine times round the fountain, take three pretty little jumps, and give seven bumps with his behind on the ground. All the time she was

muttering some spells or other in the Etruscan tongue and sometimes reading from a book of ritual. . . .

To be brief, I believe that [nobody] ever invented as many ceremonies as I saw then.[5]

In the end, as we all know, the oracle's monosyllabic advice is "Trinkh!" What else would an oracle of a bottle say? But the priestess will translate this sublime reticence into counsels of wisdom that solace and release Panurge. Is his joy naive? The text will not allow us to decide. "Be yourselves interpreters of your enterprise," says the priestess, and she might well be speaking to the reader as to her visitors. Again ambiguity and creativity emerge inseparably from that playful, pseudo-ceremonial space. The relative dosage of each will depend on the individual reader, but I for one find true wisdom in the priestess's discourse, because it locates a space for creative maneuver, a space for intellectual doubt and pursuit, at the core of the human condition.

The ambiguity produced by ceremonial parody in the novel by Cervantes is deeper and darker than in Rabelais's narrative, and it reminds us that the ludic in literature can overlap on occasion with something very close to tragic. The original displacement in *Don Quixote* moves the original historical fact of knighthood to a fantasized idealization on the printed page and then to a further inscription in the mind of the hero, thus permitting the novel to explore the comedy, the need, and the risk of perpetuating withered ceremonies. The scene near the beginning of *Don Quixote* that describes the hero's supposed investiture into the order of chivalry can be regarded as a classic travesty of ceremonial faith. The hero has stopped at a seedy provincial inn in the belief that it's a castle; he has greeted two prostitutes as great ladies, and requested the innkeeper-castellan to dub him a knight after the requisite nocturnal vigil by his armor. He has placed his makeshift accoutrements by the innyard well and dealt brutally with two mule drivers who approach it to water their drove. At this juncture, the nervous innkeeper decides to proceed immediately with the investiture and his improvisation doesn't lack resourcefulness.

The castellan brought out the book in which he had jotted down the hay and barley for which the mule drivers owed him, and, accompanied by a lad bearing the butt of a candle and the two aforesaid damsels, he came up to where Don Quixote stood and commanded him kneel. Reading from the account book—as if he had been saying a prayer—he raised his hand and, with the knight's own sword, gave him a good thwack upon the neck and another lusty one upon the shoulder, muttering all the while between his teeth. He then directed one of the ladies to gird on Don Quixote's sword, which she did with much gravity and composure; although it was all they could do to keep from laughing at every point of the ceremony, but the thought of the knight's prowess which they had already witnessed was sufficient to refrain their mirth.

"May God give your Grace much good fortune," said the worthy lady as she attached the blade, "and prosper you in battle."[6]

The parodic implications of a scene such as this extend beyond the "madness" of its central figure and beyond the desuetude of a single rite. One might well make out in this scene an anticipation of the death of ceremonial symbolism. Yet the force of the scene and of the entire novel lies in the simultaneous recognition of a deep human need for this symbolism. For Cervantes's pitiless honesty shows the appeal of this chivalric ceremonial and the delight of its creative make-believe even as he shows the absurdity and the danger of its perpetuation. The women who serve as damsels are a little frightened but they are also vastly amused, as countless other characters throughout the novel will be amused, as they participate in the charade. By the end, Don Quixote is destroyed because all the others can play with this fiction only if he regards it seriously as a myth.

By displacing as far as possible the form of the investiture, however mangled, from its traditional context, Cervantes isolates and ridicules the potential equivocation of any ceremony. We are led first to see the absurdity of the serious investiture, then almost as soon the appeal and the delight of its imitation. Only slowly do we realize that this travesty has been a trap. The novel first brings us to expect the facile demystifications of a Boccaccio story, a reduction of a mystery to brutal "realism" and transparence. But in fact that process in *Don Quixote* is followed, or attended, by a process of remystification. The new emergent mystery however is secularized, anti-institutional, and tragic; it centers on the compulsive human need for myths that will always prove vulnerable. The creative improvisation of the innkeeper, the prostitutes, and all the other subsequent characters who, so to speak, play along is ambiguous because it depends on a faith that is not playful and that exacts a progressively high price—by the end, the price of life itself.

The plays of Shakespeare are rich in experimentation with ceremonial symbolism and ceremonial parody, no less painful at times and no less provocative than Cervantes's. Perhaps the grimmest instance is the scene in Shakespeare's *Henry VI, part 3,* in which the captured Duke of York has a paper crown placed upon his head by his Lancastrian enemies, who do mock-obeisance to him before he is stabbed to death. This is a scene Shakespeare found in Holinshed, who himself points to the Christological parallel. Here the twisted symbolism is less opaque than in the haunting description of Lear by Cordelia, evoking him in his madness "singing aloud, crown'd with rank fumiter and furrow weeds." In this scene we are scarcely given time to puzzle out the deranged logic of Lear's autocoronation.

The power, and the lack of power, of a coronation are of course at the center of Shakespeare's tetralogy, beginning with *Richard II*. The treacherous and even fatal ambiguity of the crown in these plays was doubtless intensified by the literal ambiguity of the coronation and anointing of the future king in Tudor England. When the boy Edward VI was crowned by Archbishop Cranmer in 1547, he heard the archbishop say that the symbols themselves had no power.

> Kings (said Cranmer) be God's Anointed, not in respect of the oil which the bishop useth, but in consideration of their power which is ordained . . . and of their persons, which are elected of God. . . . The oil, if added, is but a ceremony.[7]

We couldn't blame the boy if he secretly wondered what then all the fuss was about. Out of such puzzles are dramas made, including Shakespeare's tetralogy, which hinges directly on the blurred power of a coronation. King Richard falls through too blind a faith in symbols alone, through a kind of formalist heresy. He is trapped by the deceptive weakness of ritual power and thinks the crown renders him literally untouchable. His enemy Bolingbroke is trapped by the realist heresy, by assuming that a crown in itself has no force and no meaning. It will take many years and many insurrections before he acquires a kind of weary wisdom and recognizes the partial power of a symbol; in the closing hours of his life, he will be shocked to discover his son, so to speak, trying the symbol on. Richard, at the moment of his fall, improvises a public de-coronation, solemnly divesting himself of his royal regalia.

> Now mark me how I will undo myself.
> I give this heavy weight from off my head
> And this unwieldy sceptre from my hand,
> The pride of kingly sway from out my heart.
> With mine own tears I wash away my balm,
> With mine own hands I give away my crown. . . .
> All pomp and majesty I do forswear.
> *(Richard II. 4.1.203–8, 211)*

Richard's improvisation is performed in that space created by the literal displacement of a usurpation. His displaced status accords him the peculiar freedom together with the peculiar weight of this terrible, unbearable performance. The performance dramatizes the limits of ceremonial power, the breakdown of the continuity that a coronation is supposed to ensure. But in this improvisation there lies no seed of ulterior creativity. There is a unique ambiguity, the dual status of the king who is not a king, but beyond this symbolic undoing there is no capacity to refashion anything. There is only barrenness.

In many of the earlier plays and not only in *Richard II*, we find Shakespeare representing the tragic character of equivocal ceremonies. As the supports of a ceremonial identity grew weaker, as the power of ceremonial was felt progressively as vestigial, the indistinct sense of loss seems to have produced both nostalgia and resentment. Perhaps the true tragic protagonist in the histories is actually the dim, noble, mutable presence of the ceremonial society. Signifiers, verbal or performative, cannot in themselves cause things to happen; their effectiveness depends upon shared agreement in a society that endows a given signifier with a given result. To believe that the signifier in itself makes things happen is to believe in magic. The power and the pathos of ceremonial parody lay in a gradual repudiation of magic. It is possible to see that repudiation as right and inevitable and still to recognize the pathos it entailed. Shakespeare as always gave each response its due.

We could follow the subgenre of ceremonial parody through the brilliant and hideous malice of the fool's coronation in Dryden's "MacFlecknoe" and in Pope's *Dunciad,* which perpetuated the literary parody of coronation just as the annual pope-burning ceremonies perpetuated through performance an actual historical parody. The pope-burnings were carried out in London by derisive and fanatic anti-Catholic bigots, beginning under Charles II and finally suppressed, it appears, only under Queen Anne. *The Dunciad* is in a sense the ultimate literary parody, directing ironic gleams in all directions and reducing all the cherished ceremonies of the ages to a common jumble of burlesque. But in that great poem there is no longer any room for improvisation on the part of the personages. The older power of ceremonial action has become so weak that its displacement has lost both its destructive and constructive roles. The space for unpredictable maneuver that the Renaissance had opened up has been closed by contempt.

But I would rather not end with that neoclassic implosion; I would rather return to English poetry of an earlier generation for somewhat different instances of positive freedom. The title of Donne's poem "A nocturnal upon St. Lucy's Day" would have been understood by a Jacobean reader as a liturgical metaphor. The "Nocturn," as Dame Helen Gardner has recently reminded us, "is one of the three divisions of the office of Matins, the first of the canonical hours, which is said at midnight," the putative hour of Donne's poem. His displacement is rhetorical, the substitution of a metaphor, in this case moving the vehicle from its ecclesiastical setting to the speaker's own secular sorrow. As a younger man, Donne had played obsessively with the rites and doctrines of Christian faith in his love poetry. The main body of this poem excludes that semantic field and tells us chiefly that in response to the death of a woman he has loved, the speaker feels reduced to an absence, a quintessence of nothingness. Only in the closing lines does he revert to the liturgical imagery of his title.

> Since shee enjoyes her long nights festivall,
> Let mee prepare towards her, and let mee call
> This houre her Vigill, and her Eve, since this
> Both the yeares, and the dayes deep midnight is.[8]

This conclusion presents the poem as a secular office for the dead woman's "long nights festivall." Dame Helen informs us that "the title and the closing lines point to religious exercises: the first office of the celebration of the Feast of a Saint and the work of penitence, prayer, and fasting of the Vigil that precedes the Feast and is the preparation for it."[9] These liturgical meanings must not deceive us into thinking that the poem is essentially devotional; it remains firmly secular, and the liturgical references remain metaphoric. Nonetheless we cannot fail to note that the introduction of that metaphor breaks through the speaker's paralysis and mitigates his sense of nonbeing. In his resolve to "prepare towards her," to assume figuratively the traditional rites of mourning for a saint, the speaker overcomes his lethargy and begins actively to channel his grief. This is a parody only in the Jacobean sense, a reverent parody, which frees the individual to act by the force of its rhetorical transposition. The metaphorical clearing opened by the poem's ambiguous shift from the liturgical to the secular provides the speaker with that unique area of experience in which some minimal action is possible.

All of the various works that I have cited demonstrate implicitly a diachronic character. That is to say, we can read in each transposed ceremony an attitude toward history. Cervantes's pseudo-investiture makes a somewhat complex statement about the relationship of past to present. A benign improvisation, like Donne's, an improvisation without irony, tends to imply a hopefulness about the continuity of past and present, suggesting that the patterns and repetitions we inherit can be accommodated to transpositions, can become flexible. This accommodation is clearly at risk in ironic or blasphemous transpositions, either because the past is perceived as not worth repeating, or because the present is too degraded to repeat it, or because, as in Cervantes, we know the remote past only through romantic fictions and no authentic repetition is therefore conceivable. A ceremonial parody threatens to block a return to origins. But it need not, as we have seen in Rabelais, block a prospective opening into a nourishing future—it may retain a seed of creativity.

Each instance has to be read as a unique comment on the transitivity of history, on the possibility of a flow from past repetition to future perpetuation and modification.

One passage that makes us hopeful about that flow occurs at the close of Book I of the *Faerie Queene,* when, after the dragon is disposed of, the residents of the besieged city emerge to thank their saviors. Una is honored by a row of comely virgins, dancing toward her and playing timbrels as they dance. When they reach her, Spenser writes

> Then on her head they set a girland greene,
> And crowned her twixt ernest and twixt game;
> Who in her selfe-resemblance well beseene,
> Did seeme such, as she was, a goodly maiden Queene.
>
> (1.12.8)[10]

In that last phrase Spenser is glancing both at the royal sovereign of England and at the May queen of folk festivity. But this particular coronation lies somewhere in the middle, "twixt ernest and twixt game," open to a nourishing past but appropriating it for new symbols. This space where the ludic meets the formal productively belongs to a lost semiotics. It is scarcely thinkable for our world, but we can be grateful that during a few centuries of our past, men and women would act in that space twixt ernest and game and find it propitious for inventing meanings.

Notes

1. Author's translation. The Italian text can be found in Giovanni Boccaccio, *Il Decameron,* 2 vols. ed. C. S. Singleton (Bari: Laterza, 1955), 1:24.

2. Stephen Greenblatt, *Renaissance Self-Fashioning from More to Shakespeare* (Chicago: University of Chicago Press, 1980), 227 ff.

3. Baldassar Castiglione and Giovanni della Casa, *Opere* (Milan: Rizzoli, 1937), 579. Joachim du Bellay, *Les Regrets et autres oeuvres poetiques,* ed. J. Jolliffe and M. A. Screech (Geneva: Droz, 1966), 151. *Les Essais de Michel de Montaigne,* ed. P. Villey, reedited by V. L Saulnier (Paris: Presses Universitaires de France, 1965), 632. Montaigne continues: "La cérémonie nous emporte, et laissons la substance des choses."

4. William Shakespeare, *The Complete Works,* ed. G. L. Kittredge (Boston: Ginn, 1936).

5. François Rabelais, *The Histories of Gargantua and Pantagruel,* trans. J. M. Cohen (Baltimore: Penguin Books, 1963), 701–2.

6. Miguel de Cervantes Saavedra, *The Ingenious Gentleman Don Quixote de la Mancha,* trans. S. Putnam (New York: Viking, 1960), 40.

7. Quoted by Percy E. Schramm, *A History of the English Coronation,* trans. L. G. Wickham Legg (Oxford: Clarendon Press, 1937), 139.

8. John Donne, *The Elegies and The Songs and Sonnets,* ed. H. Gardner (Oxford: Clarendon Press, 1965), 85.

9. Helen Gardner, "A Nocturnal upon St. Lucy's Day, being the shortest day," in *Poetic Traditions of the English Renaissance,* ed. M. Mack and G. Lord (New Haven: Yale University Press, 1982), 184, 185.

10. *Spenser's Faerie Queene,* ed. J. C. Smith (Oxford: Clarendon Press, 1909), 155.

Contributors

JAMES S. ACKERMAN is Arthur Kingsley Porter Professor of fine arts at Harvard University. He has published *The Cortile del Belvedere* (1954), *The Architecture of Michelangelo* (1961, 1985), *Palladio* (1966), *Palladio's Villas* (1967), and, with Rhys Carpenter, *Art and Archaeology,* (1962). He has written and narrated the films, *Palladio the Architect and His Influence in America,* and, with Kathleen Weil-Garris, *Looking for Renaissance Rome.* His articles treat Renaissance and modern architecture, critical theory and Renaissance art and science.

NICHOLAS ADAMS is the author of *Firearms and Fortifications: Military Architecture and Siege Warfare in Sixteenth Century Siena* (1986). He is Associate Professor of fine arts in the department of art and architecture at Lehigh University.

HOWARD MAYER BROWN, Ferdinand Schevill Distinguished Service Professor of music at the University of Chicago, has published numerous books, articles, and editions on late medieval and Renaissance music. His most recent book, *A Florentine Chansonnier from the Time of Lorenzo il Magnifico,* won the Otto Kinkeldey Prize of the American Musicological Society for the best musicological book of the year. Brown is past president of the society, and currently serves as Vice-President of The International Musicological Society.

ROGER CHARTIER is Director of Studies at the Ecole des Hautes Etudes en Sciences Sociales, Paris. He has been a visiting professor at Yale University and the University of California, Berkeley. He is the author of *Livres et lecteurs dans la France d'Ancien régime* (1987), *The Cultural Uses of Print in Early Modern France* (1987), and editor of *Les usages de l'imprimé (XVe-XIXe Siècle)* (1987). *Siècle)* (1987).

BARBARA DIEFENDORF is Associate Professor of history at Boston University. She is the author of *Paris City Councillors in the Sixteenth Century: The Politics of Patrimony* (1983). She is currently working on a book-length study of the religious conflicts in sixteenth-century Paris.

THOMAS M. GREENE is Frederick Clifford Ford Professor of English and comparative literature at Yale University. His most recent book, *The Vulnerable Text: Essays on Renaissance Literature,* was published in 1986.

WERNER L. GUNDERSHEIMER is Director of the Folger Shakespeare Library and Adjunct Professor of history at Amherst College. The author of *The Life and Works of Louis LeRoy* (1966) and *Ferrara: The Style of a Renaissance Despotism* (1973), he has written and edited several other books and numerous articles on a wide variety of Renaissance and modern subjects.

RICHARD C. McCOY is Associate Professor at Queens College and the Graduate Center, CUNY, and is the author of *Sir Philip Sidney: Rebellion in Arcadia* (1979); he is currently completing a study of Elizabethan chivalry and the crisis of the aristocracy.

MYRA NAN ROSENFELD is Research Curator at the Canadian Centre for Architecture in Montreal. She is the author of *Sebastiano Serlio: On Domestic Architecture* (1978), for which she received the Alice Davis Hitchcock Book Award of the Society of Architectural Historians, and has published articles on Italian and French Renaissance architecture.

DAVID HARRIS SACKS is Assistant Professor of history and humanities at Reed College and Chairman of the Freshman Humanities Program. He is the author of *Trade, Society and Politics in Bristol, 1500–1640* (1985) and of various articles on the history of Bristol in *Past and Present* and *Social History*. He has written articles on cultural and intellectual history and on historical methodology that have appeared, or are to appear, in *The Journal of Interdisciplinary History, The Journal of British Studies, Shakespeare Quarterly,* and *The Journal of the History of Ideas*. He has just completed a book on the history of Bristol tentatively entitled *The Widening Gate: Bristol and the Atlantic Economy, 1450–1700*.

SYDEL SILVERMAN is president of the Wenner-Gren Foundation for Anthropological Research. She was formerly Professor of anthropology and Executive Officer of the Ph.D. Program in Anthropology at the City University of New York Graduate School. She is the author of *Three Bells of Civilization: The Life of an Italian Hill Town* and editor of *Totems and Teachers: Perspectives on the History of Anthropology*.

RONALD F. E. WEISSMAN is Associate Professor of Italian Renaissance history at the University of Maryland, College Park. He has published *Ritual Brotherhood in Renaissance Florence* (1982). His continuing research focuses on Florentine social history and European social theory.

ARTHUR K. WHEELOCK, JR. is Curator of Northern Baroque Painting at the National Gallery of Art and Associate Professor of art history at the University of Maryland. His publications include *Perspective, Optics and Delft Artists around 1650* (1977), *Jan Vermeer* (1981), and *Dutch Painting in the National Gallery of Art* (1984). He has helped organize a number of exhibitions, including "Gods, Saints and Heroes: Dutch Painting in the Age of Rembrandt," Washington, Detroit, and Amsterdam, 1980.

Index

Page numbers in italics refer to figures.

Abeline, Jehanne, 98 n.48
Accursi, Pietro, 76 n.25
Adams, William, 209
Albert VII (regent of Netherlands), 171
Alberti, Adovardo, 274
Alberti, Leon Battista, 27, 50, 272, 277–78
Alberti, Lionardo, 274
Albertoccio (a Pienza landholder), 76 n.27
Alfonso II (d'Este), 12, 121, 124; as "carefree ruler," 128, 129, 136; as game player, 128–29, 130–31, 136; isolation from peasantry, 122; succession of, 123–24, 137. *See also* Ferrara, Duchy of
Ampzing, Samuel, 179
Anjou, Queen Marie of, 145
Anne (queen of England and Ireland), 290
Anne of Denmark (queen of James I), 209
Arbaleste, Charlotte d', 93, 94
Arbaleste, Guy d', 85
Architecture in Italy 1400–1600 (Heydenreich), 50
Architecture of the Renaissance, The (Benevolo), 50
Aristotle, 33, 36
Aubigné, Agrippa d', 93
Augsburg: mass-housing project in, 33, 39
Authority: defined, 187–89
Averlino, Antonio di Pietro (called Filarete), 27–28, *28, 29*

Bailey, F. G., 232
Bakhtin, Mikhail, 214
Baldovini, Niccolo, 276

Bandi, Rosso, 76 n.25
Barbara of Brandenburg, 67
Barbari, Jacopo de', 33, *35*
Barisano, Antonio ("Il Greco"), 130
Bartalini, Duccio, 77 n.33
Barthe, Paul de la, 70
Becker, Marvin, 270
Becket, Thomas, 255
Bellavista, Girolamo, 70
Bellay, Joachim du, 284
Benevolo, Leonardo, 50
Benincasa family: property holdings in Pienza by, 62
Bergeron, David, 244
Bernardo, Michele di, 276
Berthrand, Jean, 99 n.58
Berthrand, Pierre, 99 n.58
Berti, Coluccio, 75 n.19
Beza, Theodore, 86–87, 89
Bible: reading aloud of, 117–18
Bindinelli, Tessa, 77 n.33
Blaeu, Joan, 175
Bleeker, Gerrit Claez., 171
Bleyswijk, Dirck van, 166
Blunt, Sir Charles (Lord Mountjoy), 125
Boccaccio, Giovanni, 281, 282
Boileau-Despréaux, Nicolas, 108
Bonime, Steven, 150
Bonner, Edmund, 240
Borgia, Cesare, 70
Boria, Nino Giovanni, 77 n.33
Bottu de Saint-Fonds, 110
Brancaccio, Giulio Cesare, 127, 130, 132, 133, 134–35, 137
Brecheux, Loys, 99 n.60
Brennus, 196
Bristol: challenges to civic authority in, 201–4; civic authority in, 13, 14, 189–90, 192, 194, 197–201, 204–9, 213–15; festival of the boy-bishop in, 198–201;

founding of, 196; government of, 190–95, 202–3; merchants in, 203–4; visits of royalty to, 195–97, 209–13

Brossette (a lawyer), 108

Brucker, Gene, 270

Budé, François, 98 n.47

Budé, Jean, 98 n.47

Budé, Marguerite, 98 n.47

Buonsignori family: property holdings in Pienza by, 62

Burgher of Delft and His Daughter, The (Steen), 182

Calderwood, James, 255

Calvin, John, 81, 85, 88, 94. *See also* Reformation

Canterbury Tales, 199

Carew, George (dean of the Chapel Royal), 241

Casa, Giovanni della, 284

Casa delle Vedove, Ferrara, 33

Castiglione, Baldassare, 124, 125, 126

Catherine de Medici, 81

Cato, Ercole, 135

Cato, Renato, 133–34, 135, 136

Celestina, La (Rojas, 1499), 104–5

Cely, George, 154

Cervantes, Miguel de, 105, 106, 113, 287–88, 291

Charles II (king of England), 290

Charles VIII (king of France), 150

Charles IX (king of France), 81

Chaucer, Geoffrey, 199, 200

Chetwin, Edward, 202

Children: conflicts with parents, 86–90

Christian III (king of Denmark), 155

Churchyard, Thomas, 210, 212

Cicero, 36

Civitates Orbis Terrarum (Braun and Hogenberg), 175, *176*

Cluny, Order of. *See* Hôtel de Cluny

Colloquy of Poissy, 87

Commentaries (Pius II), 55

Community: defined, 188

Concord of the State, The (Rembrandt), 173, *174*

Confrérie de St. Julien des Ménétriers, 144

Conrart, Valentin, 108

Convivium religiosum (Erasmus), 283

Coras, Jean de, 86

Cordier, Baude, 150, 154

Coronations: of Edward VI, 243, 258, 289; of Elizabeth I, 240, 241–43, 244, 250; in Shakespeare, 289; symbolic, 281–82, 292

Corsignano. *See* Pienza

Cortegiano, Il (Castiglione), 124, 125, 284

Council of Trent, 230

Crane, Thomas Frederick, 125, 128

Cranmer, Thomas (archbishop of Canterbury), 258, 289

Creichant, Marie, 91

Croquet, Nicolas, 90, 91

Croquet, Nicole, 90

Croquet, Pierre, 90–91

Cuchermoys, Guyonne de, 88

Cuyp, Aelbert, 175, *178, 180,* 182

Decameron (Boccaccio), 281–82, 283, 284

de la Font, M., 109–10

D'Elce, Conte Achille, 71

Delft: description of, 165–66; importance of, 165–66, 168, 180; Nieuwe Kerk in, 165, 166; paintings of, 12, 165, 166, 175, 179–83; urban iconography of, 12–13

de'Medici, Nicola di Messer Vieri, 277

de Rantigny, Mme., 84

De Republica (Quirini), 36

de'Ricci, Filippo d'Ardengo, 276

Descrittione di Tutti i Paesi Bassi (Guicciardini), 175, *176*

Dewey, John, 269

Dice playing, 199–201

Diedi, Niccolò, 77–78 n.42

Discorsi (Romei, 1585): anecdote suppressed after first edition, 126–28, 130–32; editions of, 124–25, 128; ending of, 132–36; modern view of, 125; popularity of, 124–25; topics of, 124, 125, 136–37

Disinheritance, for religious purposes, 87–90

Domestic architecture, Serlio's treatise on: and arrangement of houses, 25–27; for artisans, 22, *23;* for clergy, 25; lowest stratum of, 21–22, *22,* 46; for merchants and professionals, 22–23,

25, *25;* and social structure, 23–24, 46. *See also* Mass-housing projects
Doni, Jacopo di Lippo, 276
Donne, John, 290–91
Don Quixote (Cervantes), 105–6, 113, 287–88
Dryden, John, 290
Dufay, Guillaume, 157
Dugas, Laurent, 109–10, 116
Dunciad (Pope), 290
DuPré, Sieur, 125
Dürer, Albrecht, 28–33, *32, 34*
Dutch Courtyard, A (Hooch), 182
Duval, Valentin Jamerey, 114–15

Edict of Beaulieu (1576), 88
Edict of Nantes (1598), 88
Edit de l'Union (1588), 84
Edward III (king of England), 190
Edward VI (king of England), 243, 258, 289
Elizabeth I (queen of England and Ireland): and Accession Day Tilts, 248–50, 260; civic progress prior to coronation, 243–45, 256, 263 n.21; coronation of, 240, 241–43, 244, 250; cult of, 245, 259–60; drawings of civic progress of, 245, *247–49;* portrait of, 260, *261;* publication of civic progress of, 245, *246;* and theater, 14, 250, 251–54; visit to Bristol by, 209–13
Elyot, Sir Thomas, 199
Enoch, Loys, 99 n.48
Erasmus, Desiderius, 283, 285–86
Erondel, Anne, 99 n.57
Erondel, Louis, 99 n.57
Este, Isabella d', 155
Este, Lucrezia d', 125
Estienne, Charles, 92
Estienne, François, 92
Estienne, Henri, 92
Estienne, Robert (senior), 90, 91–92
Estienne, Robert (the younger), 92
Every Man Out of His Humor (Jonson), 254

Fabritius, Carel, 181–82, *182*
Faerie Queene (Spenser), 292
Faïl, Noël du, 111, 142
Falassi, Alessandro, 231

Family: conflict between husbands and wives in, 83–86; conflict between parents and children in, 86–90; conflict between siblings, 90–93; domination of husbands in, 83; reading aloud to, 115–18; and religious discord, 80, 82, 93–94; solidarity of, 270
Feast of Fools, 285
Femmes Savantes (Molière), 108–9
Fénélon (French ambassador to Elizabeth I), 243
Ferdinand, Cardinal-Infante, 173
Feret, Pierre, 99 n.59
Ferrara, Duchy of: conflict between scholars and soldiers in, 131–36; court behavior in, 12, 122–23, 124; decline of, 121–22; earthquake in, 123; mass housing for widows in, 33; play *(divertissements)* in, 121–22, 123, 128, 129–30, 130–32, 133–36; population of, 122, 130. *See also* Alfonso II
Filarete. *See* Averlino, Antonio di Pietro
Filocolo (Boccaccio), 282, 284
Florence: economic transactions in, 275–78; personal honor in, 273–74; plague in, 281, 282; social complexity in, 14, 270–71
Folceri, Venturelli, 76 n.25
Francesco di Giorgio Martini, 28, *30, 31*
Francis I (king of France), 21, 25
François de Lorraine, duc de Guise, 82
Frederik Hendrik (Prince of Orange), 166, 168, 171, 173–74
Fregna, Roberto, 39
Fresnel, Baude, 150
Fried, Morton, 239 n.16
Frye, Walter, 154
Fugger family: mass housing constructed by, 33
Fulgence and Lucrece, 286

Gardner, Dame Helen, 290, 291
Garin, Eugenio, 33
Geertz, Clifford, 233
Geneva: French expatriates in, 87–88, 89, 90
Geoffrey of Monmouth, 196
Ghiberti, Iacopo di Guccio, 276, 277

Gili, Francesco di Gilio, 276
Gillonne de Matignon, 125
Giovanni, Antonio di, 75 n.18
Glahn, Henrick, 155
Gobelin, Claude, 99 n.58
Gobelin, Jean, 99 n.58
Goffman, Irving, 273
Goldberg, Jonathan, 250–51
Gonzaga, Francesco, 67
Goyen, Jan van, 180
Grant monarchie de France, La (Seyssel, 1519), 25
Gratianellus (a Pienza landholder), 76 n.27
Greenblatt, Stephen, 248, 283
Gresham, Thomas, 252
Greuze, Jean-Baptiste, 118
Grilli, Grillo, 77 n.33
Guarini, Gian Battista, 130, 131
Guicciardini, Francesco, 36, 274
Guicciardini, Ludovico, 175
Guillart, André, 90
Guillart, Louis, 90
Guillaume de Machet, 143

Habert de Montmort, 108
Harcourt, comte d', 45
Heath, Nicholas, 240
Henault, Philippes, 99 n.57
Henri IV (king of France), 89, 243
Henriad (Shakespeare), 254–59
Henri de Campion, 106–7
Henry IV (king of England), 255, 256
Henry IV (Shakespeare), 255–57, 259
Henry V (Shakespeare), 257–58, 259, 285
Henry VI (Shakespeare), 288
Henry VII (king of England), 195–97, 202, 209, 212, 240
Henry VIII (king of England), 258
Henry VIII (Shakespeare), 251
Herlihy, David, 62
Het Graafschap Holland (The Countship of Holland), 174, *175*
Heydenreich, Ludwig, 50, 55
Heywood, Thomas, 251–52
Hilary, Richard, 56
Hobsbawm, Eric, 243
Hooch, Pieter de, 182
Hospital of San Giacomo degli Incurabili (Rome), 37, 39

Hôtel de Cluny, 42–45, *44–45*
Hotman, Daniel, 89
Hotman, François, 89
Hotman, Jean, 89
Houckgeest, Gerard, 181, 182
Housing. *See* Domestic architecture; Mass-housing projects
Hoyau, Germain, 42
Huizinga, Jehan, 133
Hundred Years' War, 42
Husbands: and religious conflict with wives, 83–86

If You Know Not Me, You Know Nobody (Heywood), 251–52, 256
Impruneta: distribution of property in, 62
Isabella Clara Eugenia (wife of Albert VII), 171

Jacopo, Carlo di, 76 n.27
James I (king of England), 209, 251
Joachimi, Albert, 173
Jongh, Ludolf de, 111
Jonson, Ben, 254
Jouffroy, Cardinal Jean, 70

Kepers, John, 125
Keyser, Hendrick de, 166
Kinder-Postilla (Dietrich, 1549), 117

Latimer, Hugh, 202
Laws (Plato), 33–35
Le Brun, Pierre, 98 n.48
Lee, Sir Henry, 248
Leech-Wilkinson, Daniel, 156
Le Mercier, Claude, 86
Le Nain, Mathieu, 108
Leo X (Giovanni de' Medici), 37
Leo Belgicus (Visscher), 169–71, *170, 174*
Leptis Magna, 50
Les Halles (Paris), 42, *43*
Lesure, François, 148
L'Hermite, François (Tristan), 103
L'Hospital, Michel de, 85, 93, 97 n.24
Libri della famiglia, I (Alberti), 272
Little Street, The (Vermeer), 182
London: population of, 94 n.1
Louis XI (king of France), 25, 161 n.36
Louis XIV (king of France), 145

Louvre: early scheme for, 21
Luther, Martin, 117

Macci, Antonio, 276–77
Macci, Bandecca di Giovanni, 277
"MacFlecknoe" (Dryden), 290
Machiavelli, Niccolò, 36
Maffeo, Hieronimo, 39
Maitland, F. W., 189, 215
Mander, Karel van, 179
Manetti, Giovenale di, 39
Mankind, 286
Mao Zedong, 122
Marasca, Bartolommeo, 67
Marinarezza (Venice), 33, *35*
Mass-housing projects: in Augsburg, 33, 39; in Ferrara, 33; in Venice, 33, 39
Maurits, Prince (Maurice of Nassau), 166, 168, 169, 170, 174, 180
Medici family: and control of Siena, 13–14, 235
Mémoires (Duval), 114–15
Menius, Justus, 117
Menon, Ysabeau, 87–88
Meo di Giovanni, 76 n.32, 77 n.33
Mersenne, Father Marin, 108
Meyerhoff, Barbara, 254
Minstrels, French: apprentices to, 145; classifications of, 146, 150; guilds formed for, 144, 145; history of, 144; literacy of, 153–54; repertory of, 151–56; royal, 149–50; schools for, 149, 161 n.37; specialization among, 146–47; statutes governing behavior of, 144–45; study of, 143; as urban musical phenomenon, 12, 142
Mixed-use housing: as medieval custom, 39, 46; in Paris, 45; in Rome, 39–42
Molière, Jean-Baptiste Poquelin, 108–9
Molza, Tarquinia, 130, 132
Monluc, Blaise de, 71
Montaigne, Michel Eyquem de, 103, 284
Montecatini, Antonio, 130
Monte dei Paschi bank, 231, 236
Moore, Sally, 254
Morelli, Giovanni, 272, 274–75, 277
Mornay, Jacques de, 84, 85

Mosse of Lisbon, 154
Moussy, Genevieve de, 99 n.58
Moussy, Jeanne de, 99 n.58
Music, French: in choirs, 143, 144, 148, 149; and town bands, 147–48; urban vs. courtly, 142–43, 157. *See also* Minstrels, French
Music, Italian, 158–59 n.8
Musnier, Katherine, 99 n.60
Mynier, Marie, 99 n.58

Neale, J. E., 263 n.21
Netherlands: alliance with France, 173; hostilities with Spain, 168, 169, 171–73, 174; political structure of, 168–69
Newcomb, Anthony, 121
Nicasius de Brauwere, 154
"Nocturnal upon St. Lucy's Day, A" (Donne), 290–91
Northbrooke, John, 202

Oglethorpe, Owen (bishop of Carlisle), 240, 241, 243
Oldenbarnevelt, Johan van, 169
Orange, House of, 12, 166–68, 171, 181
Orgel, Stephen, 254
Orlandi family: property holdings in Pienza by, 62
Ostran, Jehan, 152

Pacification of Ghent (1576), 168, 173
Padua, 25
Palmer, Thomas, 213
Palio (of Siena): analysis of, 232–37; continuity of, 224; description of, 224, 225–28; development of, 229–32; financing of, 228, 231, 236; as a game, 232–33, 234; medievalism of, 231, 238 n.8; regulation of, 229; as a ritual, 233–34; and Sienese identity, 13, 224, 229, 233–34, 236; traditions governing, 229
Pansier, Pierre, 147
Pantagruel (Rabelais), 286
Paolo da Certaldo, 272, 274, 275
Parents: conflicts with children, 86–90
Paris: effect of monarchy in, 80–81; governmental structure of, 25; housing practices in, 42, 45; population of, 42, 80, 94 n.1; Reformation in, 11, 81–

82, 93–94; religious conflict between husbands and wives in, 83–86; religious conflict between parents and children in, 86–90; religious conflict between siblings in, 90–93; religiously motivated violence in, 81–82; urban development of, 11, 42–46

Parody, literary, 15, 285–92

Pasquier, Thibault, 99 n.57

Passart, Marie, 91

Patrizzi da Cherso, Francesco, 130, 132–34

Peace of Bergerac (1577), 88

Peacock, James, 233

Pepys, Samuel, 110–11, 115–16

Petit, Oudin, 92

Petroni, Bartolommeo, 77 n.36

Petrucci family: property holdings in Pienza by, 62

Peverara, Laura, 130, 139–40 n.22

Phillip II (king of Spain), 168, 241

"Phillip Sparrow" (Skelton), 286

Piccolomini, Andrea, 66, 75 n.15

Piccolomini, Jacomo di Mino Battista, 64, 66, 75 n.15, 77 n.36

Piccolomini family: impact on Pienza, 52, 55–59; influence in Siena, 56; palace for, 50, *52*, 56, 70; property holdings in Pienza by, 62. *See also* Pius II

Pienza: *casa nuove* in, 69, *69;* cathedral (Church of Santa Maria) in, 50, *53;* formery Corsignano, 11, 50, 52–56; fortification of, 70–71; housing practices in, 64, 67–68; housing values in, 62–63; importance of agriculture in, 61; land values in, 66–68; location of, 50, *51;* Piazza Pio II in, 50, *54;* piazzas in, 63–64; population of, 61; problems in development of, 68–69; property ownership in 56–59, 60, 61–62, 64–66; source for information on renovations in, 59–61; urban development of, 11, 50, 52–55, 56–59, 69, 70; view of Mont' Amiata from, 50, *54*

Pietro Leopoldo (grandduke of Tuscany), 231

Pigna, Gian Battista, 130

Pius II (Enea Silvio Piccolomini): gifts to Pienza from, 69–70; influence on Sienese, 56; nepotism practiced by,

56; property owned by, 66; and renovation of Pienza, 11, 50, 55, 56–59, 64–69, 71. *See also* Piccolomini family

Piuvica: distribution of property in, 62

Plato, 33–35, 36

Platter, Felix, 117

Platter, Thomas, 117

Plutarch, 36

Poel, Egbert van der, 182

Pole, Reginald (archbishop of Canterbury), 240

Politics (Aristotle), 33

Polybius, 25, *26*

Pommeraye, Jehan de la, 99 n.57

Pope, Alexander, 290

Popham, John, 210

Porrina, Pietro Paolo, 69

Porter, Joseph, 255–56

Post, Pieter, 171

Praise of Folly (Erasmus), 285–86

Propos rustiques de Maistre Léon Ladulfi (Faïl), 111–13

Quirini, Lauro, 36

Rabelais, François, 286, 291

Ragueau, Jehan, 88

Ranucci, Guidoccio, 77 n.33

Raphael, 37

Reading aloud: depicted by Molière, 108–9; and *Don Quixote*, 105–6; within family groups, 115–18; as gift to hosts, 109–10; by Henri de Campion, 106–7; of *La Celestina*, 104–5; literate *compagnies* for, 107–8; and oral recitation, 111–14, 115; in paintings, 108, 109; among peasants, 111–14, 115; as a private act, 103–4, 118; as a public, social act, 11–12, 104, 118; and the *salon*, 107, 108–9; among travellers, 110–11

Rede, Thomas, 154

Reformation: in England, 202; in the Netherlands, 169; and religious conflict among families, 11, 80–82, 93–94. *See also* Calvin, John

Rembrandt van Rijn, 173, *174*

Renaissance: ambiguous relations in, 272–78; church hierarchy during, 36;

class distinctions during, 33–36; importance of parody in, 15, 285–92; individualism in, 269–70, 271, 279; literacy during, 11; loyalties during, 271–72; urban life during, 9–10, 15

Renaldi, Nutio, 77 n.33

Renaudot, Théophraste, 108

Repetti, Emanuele, 61

Republic (Plato), 33

Rétif de la Bretonne, 118

Ricart, Jean, 99 n.57

Ricart, Robert, 190, 191, 192, 196, 198, 202

Richard II (king of England), 260

Richard II (Shakespeare), 254–55, 256, 258, 289–90

Richard III (king of England), 240, 262 n.8

Robarts, John, 212

Rojas, Fernando de, 104

Rome: housing practices in, 36–42; plan of, *37;* property records kept in, 37, *38,* 39–41; urban development of, 10, 36–37, *40–41*

Romei, Annibale, 124

Rossellino, Bernardo, 50, 69

Rossiter, A. P., 259

Rubens, Peter Paul, 171–73

Rucellai, Giovanni, 277

Ruysdael, Salomon van, 180

Saenredam, Pieter, 179

St. Bartholomew's Day massacre, 81, 82, 86, 92

Schifanoya, Il, 240, 241

Schorske, Carl, 121

Schramm, Percy, 244

Seneca, 36

Serlio, Sebastiano: and ideal fortified city, 25, *26;* influences on, 25–28; treatise on domestic architecture by, 21–25

Ser Meo Benedicti, 76 nn. 30, 31, and 32, 77 n. 33

Severini, Niccolò, 69

Severus, Lucius Septimius, 50

Seyssel, Claude, 25

Shakespeare, William, 251, 254–59, 288–90

Shalvi, Alice, 125

Siblings: conflict between, 90–93

Sidney, Sir Philip, 252

Siena: *contrade* of, 224, 225–26, 230, 232, 234–35; housing values in, 62; influence of Piccolomini family in, 56, *57–60;* and Medici, 13–14, 235; patroness of, 224, 257, 229. *See also* Palio (of Siena)

Siffait, Mahieu, 152

Sixth Book on Roman History (Polybius), 25

Skelton, John, 286

Sleeping Mars (Terbrugghen), 171, *172*

Smits van Waesberghe, Jozef, 156

Society of Merchant Venturers, 203, 204

Solerti, Angelo, 128

Soria, Don Lope, 70

Spencer, William, 202

Spenser, Edmund, 292

Spifame, Jacques, 92

Steen, Jan, 182

Synod of Dort, 169, 171

Tapissier, Jean, 161 n.37

Tasso, Torquato, 130

Tempesta, Antonio, *37*

Temple du Goût, Le (Voltaire), 110

Terbrugghen, Hendrick, 171, *172*

Teresa de Avila, 116

Third Book (Rabelais), 286

Thompson, Thomas, 202, 204, 205

Thornborough, Bishop, 209

Treaty of Münster (1648), 173, 180

Treaty of Nemours (1585), 84

Trexler, Richard, 239 n.21

Troy, Jean-François de, 109

Truschet, Olivier, 42

Tudor kings (of England): and secular pragmatism, 250

Turini, Francesco Antoncello, 77–78 n.42

Tuscan Grand Duchy, 13

Uguccione family: property holdings in Pienza by, 62, 76 nn. 25 and 28

Union of Delft (1576), 168

Union of Utrecht (1579), 168, 173

Urban development: hierarchical, 10–11; in the Renaissance, 9–10, 15

Vaillant, Jean, 161 n.37

Varengene, Leonard de, 99 n.58
Velde, Esaias van de, 171, 175, *177*
Venice: civic roles in, 25; mass-housing project in, 33, *35*, 39
Vermeer, Johannes (Jan): paintings of Delft by, 12, 165, *166*, 175, 182–83
Vicenza, 25
View of Delft (Vermeer): description of, 165, 166, *166;* and urban iconography, 12, 175, 182–83
View of Delft with a Musical Instrument Seller's Stall (Fabritius), 181–82, *182*
Villon, François, 145
Violante Beatrice of Bavaria, 230
Visscher, Claes Jansz., 169–71, *170*, 174, *175*
Vitruvius, 35, 50
Vitry, Philippe de, 143
Vliet, Hendrick van, 181

Voltaire, 109, 110
von Martin, Alfred, 269, 270
Vosmaer, Daniel, 182
Vroom, Hendrick, 175, *177*, 179–80, 182

Wallington, Nehemiah, 117
Weber, Max, 188
Willem II (Prince William II), 166, 168, 181
William I (the Silent; of Orange): assassination of, 168; succeeded by Prince Maurits, 169; tomb of, 166–68, *167*, 180, 181
Wilson, H. A., 241
Witte, Emanuel de, 181
Wives: and religious conflict with husbands, 83–86
Wotton, Sir Henry, 251
Wright, Craig, 150, 153